GOOD HOUSEKEEPING

Complete
STEP-BY-STEP
GUIDE TO
ENTERTAINING

GOOD HOUSEKEEPING

Complete
STEP~BY~STEP
GUIDE TO
ENTERTAINING

BCA
LONDON · NEW YORK · SYDNEY · TORONTO

This edition published 1991 by BCA
by arrangement with Ebury Press
an imprint of the Random Century Group
Random Century House

CN 2830

Cookery Editor: Janet Smith
Editor: Robin Ayrdon
Design: Peartree Design Associates
Photographers: Martin Brigdale, Laurie Evans, Tim Hill,
James Murphy, Alan Newnham, Rosemary Weller,
Andrew Whittuck
Home Economists: Janet Smith, Emma-Lee Gow, Allyson Birch,
Jacqueline Clark, Janice Murfitt, Mandy Wagstaff
Stylists: Zoë Hill, Maria Jacques, Roisin Nield, Lesley
Richardson, Fiona Tillett
Recipe Writers: Janet Smith, Jeni Wright, Louise Steele,
Moyra Fraser, Maxine Clark

Typeset in New Baskerville by Textype Typesetters, Cambridge
Printed and bound in Italy by New Interlitho S.p.a., Milan

CONTENTS

HOW TO USE THIS BOOK

Recipe introductions explain the origins of each dish.

Suggested drinks to accompany the menu range from beers, non-alcoholic drinks and fruit juices to expensive wines and cheaper alternatives.

Menu variations suggest alternatives from over 200 recipes at the back of the book.

DRINKS TO SERVE

No wine is really suitable to serve with this brunch except chilled sparkling wine or champagne for a special occasion. Bucks Fizz; freshly squeezed orange juice topped with chilled champagne, or try replacing the orange juice with cranberry juice. Sparkling mineral water plus a plentiful supply of tea and coffee are always welcome.

COOK'S HINT

Other soft fruits for **these scones** are blackcurrants or blueberries (blaeberries

ATHOLL BROSE

This ancient Scottish drink, soothing but potent, is said to have been invented by one of the Dukes of Atholl. Good for a hangover and comforting on a cold winter's day.

125 g (4 oz) medium oatmeal
45 ml (3 tbsp) clear honey (preferably heather)
whisky
300 ml (½ pint) double cream

1 Put the oatmeal into a bowl and stir in 400 ml (14 fl oz) cold water to make a thick, creamy paste. Cover and leave to stand for at least 30 minutes, or overnight.
2 Strain the liquid through a sieve pressing down well with the back of a wooden spoon to extract all the moisture. Discard the oatmeal. Pour the liquid into a measuring jug and stir in the honey.
3 Add enough whisky to make up to 750ml e (1¼ pints) and stir in the cream. Chill for at least 1 hour. Pour into small wine glasses and serve.

PERFECT PORRIDGE WITH RASPBERRIES

Make this fresh on the day and serve piping hot. So brown sugar or honey may be added, but is frowne on in Scotland.

2.3 litres (4 pints) water
225 g (8 oz) medium oatmeal
salt
700 g (1½ lb) fresh Scottish raspberries
thick cream, to serve

1 Bring the water to a rolling boil in a larg saucepan and sprinkle on the oatmeal in steady stream, stirring all the time. Add th meal slowly or it will form lumps. Stir un boiling, then turn down the heat and simm gently for 30 minutes, stirring frequen until a thick *but pouring* consistency reached. Add salt at this stage – no sooner it will toughen the meal.
2 Pour into a warm bowl or tureen whe ready and serve with the raspberries a cream.

42

Colour photographs illustrate all the various dishes included in the menu.

The wide range of menus covers every occasion. Each menu is carefully balanced for flavour, texture and visual appeal.

BRAMBLE SCONES

MAKES ABOUT 16

450 g (1 lb) self-raising flour
2.5 ml (½ tsp) salt
10 ml (2 level tsp) baking powder
75 g (3 oz) butter, cubed
3 oz (75 g) caster sugar
225 g (8 oz) frozen blackberries (brambles)
about 200 ml (7fl oz) buttermilk or half-fat milk
1 egg, beaten

1 Sift the dry ingredients together in a large bowl. Rub in the butter until the mixture resembles breadcrumbs. Stir in the sugar and the still frozen blackberries.
2 Stir in enough milk to form a firm dough. Knead very lightly and roll out on a floured surface to 2.5 cm (1 inch) thick. Using a 6.5 cm (2½ inch) round cutter, stamp into rounds being careful to avoid cutting through the brambles. Knead and carefully re-roll as necessary.
3 Place the scones on a greased baking sheet and brush the tops with beaten egg. Bake in the oven at 220°C (425°F) mark 7 for about 10 minutes until well-risen and golden brown. Serve whilst still hot.
To Freeze Open freeze and store in polythene bags for up to 3 months. Thaw at room temperature and warm in the oven at 200°C (400°F) mark 6 for 5 minutes.

REAL OATCAKES

MAKES 16 GENEROUS BISCUITS

450 g (1 lb) medium oatmeal
large pinch of salt
2.5 ml (½ tsp) bicarbonate of soda
50 g (2 oz) beef dripping or lard, melted
45-75 ml (3-5 tbsp) hot water

1 In a large bowl, mix together the oatmeal, salt and bicarbonate of soda. Make a well in the centre and pour in the melted dripping. Stir in enough hot water to form a stiff, but not too dry, dough.

2 Bring the dough together with hands dipped in extra meal. Knead on a surface dusted with oatmeal until smooth.
3 Divide the dough into four and roll out each quarter into a rough 20.5 cm (8 inch) circle, about 0.5 cm (¼ inch) thick, using a plate as a guide to neaten the circle. Cut each circle into four quarters and place on greased baking sheets.
4 Bake in the oven at 170°C (325°F) mark 3 for 25–30 minutes until firm but not coloured. Cool on a wire rack. Store in an airtight container. To crisp before serving spread on a baking sheet and heat in the oven at 200°C (400°F) mark 6.

OUTRAGEOUS SALMON FISHCAKES

350 g (12 oz) cooked fresh salmon, flaked
225 g (8 oz) smoked salmon, roughly chopped
350 g (12 oz) freshly cooked mashed potato
15 ml (1 tbsp) lemon juice
freshly ground black pepper
75 g (3 oz) butter, melted
45 ml (3 tbsp) chopped fresh dill or 15 ml (1 tbsp) dried dill weed
2 eggs, beaten
about 225 g (8 oz) dried white breadcrumbs
vegetable oil for frying

1 Mix the two salmons with the mashed potato, lemon juice, pepper to taste, butter and dill. Add just enough beaten egg to bind the mixture together. It should be firm, not sloppy. Cool, then refrigerate for 1 hour until very firm.
2 Shape the mixture into 16 cakes about 2.5 cm (1 inch) thick. Brush with some of the remaining beaten egg and coat with breadcrumbs. Chill for 30 minutes to firm.
3 Coat the cakes with egg and crumbs once more. Chill again until firm.
4 Shallow fry the cakes in batches for 3–4 minutes on each side, or until golden brown. Drain on absorbent kitchen paper and keep warm in the oven.
To Freeze Open freeze the fishcakes without egg and crumbs and pack into a rigid container, interleaving with non-stick paper. Thaw overnight in the refrigerator, coat with egg and crumbs and fry as in step 4.

43

COOK'S HINTS
Bramble is the Scottish word for wild blackberries, which are small and sweet. This recipe is easier to handle if the berries are frozen when stirred into the mixture. Firmer fruit, such as blueberries can be added fresh.

MICROWAVE HINT
Make up some fluffy scrambled eggs in the microwave for guests who don't like kidneys. To serve 4 break 4 eggs into a bowl and whisk together, then whisk in 120ml (8 tbsp) milk and salt and pepper to taste. Microwave on HIGH for 2 minutes, until beginning to set around the edge. Whisk vigorously to incorporate the set egg mixture, then cook on HIGH for 2 minutes more until the eggs are just set.

COUNTDOWN
Two days before, or more: Make the oatcakes and keep in an airtight tin. Bake the bramble scones and freeze or store in an airtight tin for up to two days. Make the salmon fishcakes and freeze at stage 3.
The day before: Thaw the scones, if frozen, and the fishcakes. Prepare the kidneys and mushrooms. Soak the oatmeal for the Atholl Brose.
11.35 am: Start the porridge put the raspberries and cream into bowls and chill. Finish the Atholl Brose and chill.
12.15 pm: Fry the fishcakes and keep warm in a low oven with the door open. Put the scones into the oven to warm with the oatcakes. Thin the porridge down with a little hot water if necessary.

Cook's hints provide preparation and cookery techniques and give helpful advice on unusual ingredients, time-saving short cuts and healthy eating.

Microwave hints help to save time, oven space and washing up.

Countdown plans help you to plan ahead.

Freezer notes explain which dishes can be prepared in advance.

This special recipe file has been compiled to help you select recipes.

Here you can see at a glance all the recipes featured in the menus, so

you can 'mix and match' the various courses to suit your own tastes.

Don't forget that an additional 150 recipes are also to be found in

the Basic Recipes chapter beginning on page 242.

SOUPS AND STARTERS

Chestnut and Roasted Garlic Soup
Page 66

Maggot Soup
Page 193

Prawn Puris
Page 48

Sesame Prawn Toast
Page 59

Nonya Spring Rolls
Page 62

Spanakhopitas
Page 174

Roasted Peppers with Yogurt and Pistachio Nuts
Page 71

Aubergine Cannelloni
Page 85

Chillied Pork Dim Sum
Page 100

Smoked Salmon Roulades
Page 106

Grilled Chicory with Pears and Hazelnuts
Page 112

Steamed Mussels in Pepper Broth
Page 112

Parsleyed Linguine with Clams
and Smoked Salmon **Page 80**

Warm Salad of Mushrooms with Olive
Sourdough Bread **Page 92**

Guacamole with Vegetable and Fruit
Crudités **Page 182**

MEAT

Herbed Farmhouse Sausages
Sweet Onion Relish **Page 31**

Sausage and Bacon Oatcakes
Page 37

Spiced Kidneys with Mushrooms
Page 44

Witches Hands with Blood
Page 193

Raan
Page 49

Lamb with Olive Juices
Page 74

Roast Eye Fillet of Lamb with Candied
Lemons and Honey **Page 190**

Lamb with Three Coriander Marinade
Chicken and Prawn Skewers **Page 183**

Glazed Lamb Cutlets with Redcurrants
Page 227

Fillet of Beef with Porcini and Sweet
Peppers **Page 88**

Pork Tenderloin with Orange and Ginger
Page 123

Dijon-Glazed Pork Medallions
Page 81

POULTRY AND GAME

Chicken with Ginger
Page 102

Circassian Chicken Drumsticks
Kofta with Yogurt and Mint   **Page 174**

Fragrant Saffron Chicken   **Page 228**

Ballontine of Turkey
Page 210

Roast Turkey with Chestnut Stuffing
Pear Halves with Cranberry   **Page 108**

Crispy Duck with Mangetout
Page 101

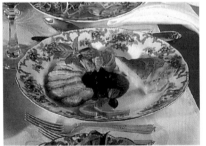

Blueberry Duck
Page 108

Venison Collops
Celeriac Straw   **Page 67**

FISH AND SHELLFISH

Outrageous Salmon Fishcakes   **Page 43**

Seafood Pilaki
Page 94

Glazed Seafood Platter
Page 56

Kettle Cooked Sea Bass
Page 62

Mullet Cooked in Vine Leaves
Page 183

Prawns with Alioli
Page 162

VEGETARIAN
AND
VEGETABLE
ACCOMPANIMENTS

Roasted Pepper and Sweet Onion Pizza
Page 112

Florentine Buckwheat Pancakes
Page 36

Filo Wrapped Brie with Mushroom
Forcemeat **Page 238**

Spinach and Garlic Tarts
Page 239

Baked Peppers with Wild Rice
Page 81

Wafer-Wrapped Apple and Gooseberry
Pouches **Page 82**

Mushrooms with Parsley
Page 32

Baked Cherry Tomatoes
Page 190

Herb-Glazed Tomatoes
Red Cabbage and Pinenut Slaw **Page 37**

Spinach and Mushroom Bhaji
Page 50

Chakchouka
Page 176

Oriental Vegetable, Fruit and Nut Stir-Fry
Page 63

Braised Mixed Vegetables
Page 102

Stir-Fried Mixed Vegetables
Page 119

Sautéed Aubergine and Courgettes
Page 74

Chestnut and Sprout Sauté
Page 211

Sweet Potatoes with Pineapple
Glazed Onions with Peas   **Page 203**

Potatoes with Roast Garlic
Page 74

Crispy Potato Galette
Page 105

Spicy Potatoes
Page 163

SALADS

Lemon Pepper Salad
Page 55

Mixed Red Leaf Salad
Page 56

Avocado, Orange and Lime Salad
Page 95

Beansprout and Sesame Salad
Page 101

Rocket, Tomato and Sugar-Snap Pea Salad
Page 114

Cherry Tomato, Bean and Mozzarella Salad
Page 228

Spiced Ratatouille Salad
Page 212

Vegetable Salamagundy
Page 239

Greek Salad
Page 176

Simple Potato Salad
Page 182

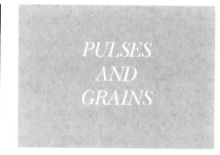
PULSES AND GRAINS

Basmati Pilaff
Page 50

Special Fried Rice
Page 102

Thai Fried Rice
Page 118

Chorizo and Chickpea Stew
Page 162

Tabbouleh
Page 176

Chole
Page 51

Smoked Trout and Lentil Salad
Page 189

DESSERTS

Fragrant Fruit Salad
Page 103

Fruits in Framboise
Page 230

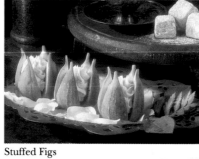

Stuffed Figs
Page 177

Spiced Fruit Wafers
Page 178

Coconut Custards with Tropical Fruit
Page 64

Autumn Pudding
Page 68

Christmas Pudding
Page 212

Trifle
Page 214

Tart of Many Fruits
Page 76

Easter Cheesecake
Page 191

Pumpkin Cheesecake
Page 204

Bruléed Lemon Tart
Page 108

Almond Cream Gâteau
Page 230

Strawberry Mousse Gâteau
Page 240

Peach and Passion Fruit Soufflé
Page 229

Tiramisu
Page 90

Cappucino Creams

Page 114

Choux Swans

Page 130

Gulab Jamun

Page 52

Jolly Lollies

Page 151

Raspberry Rose Ice Cream

Page 96

Coconut Ice Cream

Page 120

Mango Sorbet

Page 51

Apple Mint Meringues

Page 124

Rose Petal Meringues

Page 140

Pile of Bones

Page 193

Raspberry and Lavender Pavlova

Page 185

Chocolate and Chestnut Vacherin

Page 82

Blueberry Buttermilk Blinis

Page 70

SWEET BAKING

Red Nose Buns

Page 151

Harlequin Biscuits
Page 150

Pistachio Rings
Page 144

Almond Cinnamon Biscuits
Page 165

French Apple Tartlets
Page 137

Tiny Fruit Tartlets
Page 142

Spiced Pear Strudel
Page 134

Coffee House Gâteau
Cherry and Coconut Cookies **Page 136**

Chocolate, Coffee and Raspberry Eclairs
Page 141

Chocolate and Coconut Cream Roulade
Page 143

Dark and Sinful Chocolate Cake
Page 135

Clown Cake
Page 148

Creepy Cake
Page196

Christening Cake
Page 265

White Chocolate Wedding Cake
Page 232

Banana and Brazil Nut Loaf
Page 142

Pecan and Raisin Muffins

Page 38

Cinnamon Sugar Buns

Page 38

Bramble Scones

Page 43

SAVOURY BAKING

Oatcakes

Page 43

Cheese Parkerhouse Rolls

Page 31

Tomato Herb Focaccia

Page 56

Rustic Walnut Bread

Page 85

Olive Sourdough Bread   **Page 92**

Parmesan Palmiers

Page 127

Tiny Caraway Scones with Smoked Salmon
and Cream Cheese   **Page 130**

Custard Pies

Page 150

Balls of Fire

Page 149

DRINKS
AND
CANAPES

Atholl Brose

Page 42

Egg Nog
Pecan Cookies   **Page 200**

Frozen Vodka
                                Page 179

Champagne Cocktails
Pickled Vegetables   **Page 55**

Gravad Lax on Rye. Chorizo with Tomato
Fresh Figs with Prosciutto   **Page 156**

Satay of Prawn, Chicken and Beef
Baked Tiny Potatoes with Bacon   **Page 156**

Cheese and Poppyseed Bites
                                Page 158

Tortilla Espagnol
                                Page 163

Salt Cod Balls
                                Page 163

Empanadillas
                                Page 164

Prawn and Feta Purses
Smoked Salmon Samosas   **Page 168**

Five-Spice Pork with Mango Dip
                                Page 226

Blue Brie Toasts
Spiced Cashews   **Page 207**

Mushroom Tartlets
                                Page 164

Two Kinds of Marinated Olives
                                Page 158

Quick Meatballs with Mustard and Chives
Smoked Trout Canapés   **Page 227**

INTRODUCTION

This book is designed to take the stress out of entertaining. With its help there should be no more evenings spent quietly panicking in the kitchen wondering how to retrieve your latest disaster, while guests sit nervously, making polite conversation wondering how much longer they'll have to wait for their food!

It contains thirty four complete menus to suit a wide range of different occasions, all thoroughly tried and tested in the Good Housekeeping kitchens. There are suggestions for both formal and informal entertaining, indoor and outdoor meals, brunches, late night suppers and family lunches as well as coffee and tea parties, wedding and christening buffets and children's parties. Each menu comes complete with a thorough plan for each meal – from detailed recipes for each course to drink and wine suggestions, freezing and microwave hints, cook's hints and a failsafe countdown to the event. This invaluable timeplan should help you avoid any last minute panics or long waits between courses, because it provides an easy-to-follow timetable for action in the kitchen, from preparation the day before the party, right up to five minutes before your guests arrive, ensuring that everything is cooked to perfection and that you can relax. There's also a list of menu alternatives referring to the comprehensive recipe section at the back of the book. If you're vegan or someone on a diet or need to produce a dinner party in a rush, don't panic! We've even included a list of these recipes to make using the book easy (see page 279).

Whatever the occasion, this book will make entertaining your friends, family and colleagues enjoyable occasions, that cannot fail to impress.

PLANNING

What type of party do you want to have? A five-course dinner for eight with all the trimmings? A casual help-yourself supper for a few friends? Early evening drinks for twenty or so? A full-scale celebration with no expense spared? A big, informal, bring-a-bottle party with food and dancing? A Sunday lunch-time buffet in the garden, kids welcome? There are numerous possiblities to choose from depending on how many people you want to invite and how much you want to spend. Whichever type you choose, careful advance organisation will make all the difference.

Whom to ask
Having decided on the sort of party, you now have to tackle the tricky bit: how many people and whom to ask. Numbers will depend partly on space, but there are other considerations. At a dinner party, six or eight people will easily be able to talk together round the table. More than that and the conversation will break down into smaller groups.

EXTRA HELP

For large parties and buffets you will need help. Enlist family or good friends to hand round food or nibbles and keep glasses replenished. You could even consider hiring help. Students from local colleges may be glad of some pocket money. Or you may want to employ professional waiters and waitresses. Contact them through your Yellow Pages (under Caterers or Employment Agencies). For a buffet meal, one professional waitress can cope with about 25 guests, provided that the drinks, salads etc are all help-yourself. An untrained helper will find 15 people sufficient to cope with.

What will you need?
It's all very well to decide on a huge party and invite 100 people, but you must be able to cater for them. Make a list of everything you'll need, count up what you own and decide in good time if there's anything you need to buy, borrow or hire.

You'll use lots of glasses for a big party and it's as well to provide more than one per guest, as people tend to lose them as the evening wears on. A local wine merchant should be able to help out with glass hire, which will often be free if you buy your party wine at the same time. Check when you hire whether the glasses can be returned unwashed.

Depending on the formality of the occasion you can make do with paper plates and plastic cutlery (but make them good quality otherwise they won't stand up to the strain). If you must have the real thing, beg or borrow from friends or hire. Large supplies of paper napkins are essential, especially at barbecues, or if you are serving finger food. And you'll need suitable serving implements for the buffet table.

Also on your list should be ashtrays. Large candles left burning at strategic, safe points around the room help to clear smoke from the air and you can buy special 'smokers candles' for this purpose.

THE MENU

Having decided on the type of party and the number of guests, you can plan the menu. Whether catering for a large or small gathering, your plan of action should be the same: Choose the dishes you want to serve and list them, adding references to cookery books and page numbers where necessary. Highlight the dishes on your list that will freeze successfully and can therefore be cooked in advance. Read through the recipes, plan when to cook each one and start to make shopping lists.

Don't forget to add any garnishes and 'extras' like bread and butter, coffee, sugar and milk. It's a good idea to separate the list into non-perishables, which can be bought in advance, and perishables that must be bought nearer the party.

Keeping it simple

It's most important to keep the menu simple and within your capabilities. Although it's tempting to try something new and elaborate when entertaining it's a wise host or hostess who sticks to cooking dishes that have gone down well in the past and which can be relied upon to work.

Choosing the Dishes

The choice of dishes depends on a variety of factors. Are any of your guests vegetarian? (See the Special Index on page 279 for help

with this.) Do any of them dislike particular foods? It's best to avoid recipes containing ingredients that are notoriously unpopular, such as offal.

Try to achieve a balance of flavours, textures and colours in the food you serve. The 'wet and dry' rule is a good one to follow when planning actual dishes; that is a 'wet' course, such as soup or casserole, should precede a 'dry' one, such as grilled steak or an apple tart. Aim, too, for balance in 'weight' of the courses. A thick soup with dumplings, followed by steak pie and a steamed dessert may be traditional country fare, but is far too filling for all but the heartiest of appetites. Select accompaniments to compliment the main dish, taking colour, texture and flavour into consideration.

Pay attention to variety and the balance of flavours throughout the courses. If serving fish as a main course then obviously, fish is inappropriate to start. A chilled soup or a salad would be better instead. Similarly, one course based on a vegetable or fruit (such as avocado or melon), and one based on meat or fish makes a well-balanced combination. Fruit puddings go well with most menus, but avoid creamy desserts if either of the preceding courses have been served with a cream sauce. If fruit was served in either of the first courses, it is best to choose an alternative, such as a chocolate-based recipe for dessert.

Bear in mind how health-conscious most people are today, and avoid putting together a meal that consists of several rich courses. If your main dish is heavy and filling, serve it with lightly cooked fresh vegetables or a salad and keep your starter and dessert simple, light and refreshing.

The time of year will suggest the food you choose to serve and seasonal food will always be the cheapest and the freshest. In the summer, when soft fruits are plentiful, it's a shame not to make the most of them. Foods that are only available fresh for a short season, such as home-grown asparagus and new potatoes are a treat your guests will certainly enjoy.

Last but not least, plan the menu so that you leave plenty of time to be with your guests. A dish that needs careful timing, such as steak or soufflé, will not allow for the fact that guests may not be punctual or that people linger over their food longer than you had originally anticipated.

Equipment

Whilst selecting the menu, particularly for a buffet, think carefully about how you're going to cook, store or reheat the food. Do you have big enough saucepans or casseroles to feed a crowd? Do you have sufficient space in or on your cooker to reheat these recipes? There's no point in borrowing huge saucepans or preserving pans if only one will fit on your hob at a time.

A microwave cooker is useful for last-minute reheating. Decant the food into microwave-proof dishes that will fit in your cooker. Always reheat food until it is piping hot to avoid any danger of food poisoning. It is always better and safer to serve a mainly cold buffet than a selection of lukewarm dishes which could well be breeding dangerous bacteria whilst sitting in a warm room.

Your oven, too, will only have limited capacity. If you cram it full of casseroles and dishes, the heat can't circulate properly and the oven's efficiency will be greatly impaired.

The problem of fridge space must also be considered. As well as several food dishes, you may want to reserve space for wine and soft drinks. Remember, though, that white wine really only needs chilling for about an hour before serving so it need not be in the fridge for very long.

Consider, too, whether you have enough cutlery and crockery to serve all the dishes you plan to prepare. If you serve soup to start, will you have enough bowls for dessert without having to wash up halfway through the meal? If you are planning a large gathering, do you need to borrow or hire extra crockery or cutlery?

Look in your Yellow Pages under Hire Services for Catering Equipment Hire or Wedding Services. If there's no extra charge, order equipment a day ahead so you've plenty of time to unpack and check it out. Some firms will take equipment back dirty,

You may need jugs for water and fruit juice, ash trays, trestle tables and chairs and table cloths. Don't forget coffee cups and saucers and even a coffee urn if you are catering for a very large number.

Fridges, freezers and hot cupboards can be hired too, but do check that you have sufficient power points to plug them in without overloading the system - a black out on the day of the party is not helpful!

Cooking for the freezer

Dishes suitable for freezing can be cooked will in advance. Remember to make a note of how much thawing and final cooking time each dish needs, and to label frozen packages carefully. After cooking, cool food for freezing as quickly as possible, then freeze immediately, making use of the 'fast freeze' facility if your freezer has one. Before freezing a casserole, line the dish with foil so that it can be frozen and then removed and the dish can be used again. Pack foods in bags or rigid containers whenever possible so that they can be stacked neatly to save space in the freezer.

Cooking in quantity

If you are entertaining a very large number of people and want to provide a full meal, a buffet party is the ideal choice. Decide on the menu really well in advance, because it will take you a long time to finalise quantities (consult our charge on page 279 for guidance) and the logistics of the whole exercise.

This is not just a question of quadrupling your favourite recipe and then letting it simmer or bake away. Liquids will not reduce at the same speed and cooking times may vary leaving you with a watery casserole or a sunken cake. Unless an experienced caterer we do not advise you to cook recipes for more than 12 people at one time. Few casserole dishes or saucepans will take larger quantities than this and if they do it's difficult to ensure even heat right through. Just prepare food in batches and freeze for the big day.

Offer a good balance of sweet and savoury dishes and concentrate on setting the buffet table beautifully so that it will be the centre of attraction. Choose dishes that can be frozen ahead of time (most things store well in the freezer for at least three months), like quiches, flans, pâtés, tarts, pastries, sandwich fillings, cakes and gâteaux. This should leave you ample time nearer the date to deal with the perishable items like salads, fruit, vegetables and herbs.

How much to cook

The more people you're feeding the less you'll need to allow per head. For 100 people, 85 portions should be enough. Maybe this is because at buffet parties the act of balancing a glass and plate is just too much to cope with. If you're offering a selection of main courses or desserts though, you'll need to over cater a little as people like to "taste" both. And if it's a "treat" food like smoked salmon, everyone is bound to indulge so you must be generous.

Laying out the buffet

Have several serving points for the buffet food and the drinks too. This avoids bottlenecks and long delays for food. Ensure that plates, cutlery and napkins are set out at the start of the buffet table. Don't pile serving platters too high or food will spill over the table. It's better to replenish the dishes as necessary. Keep food tightly covered until it's served and if possible add garnishes at the last minute too. They'll look freshest then. Portion pies and gâteaux before the buffet starts or station one of the helpers to serve them out as guests often loathe to be the first to cut into them. Arrange the table so that guests can move easily around it, progressing naturally from plates and cutlery to the main dishes and the side dishes. If desserts are included on the same table, put them where they can be reached when other dishes are cleared away.

THE CHEESE BOARD

Which comes first, the cheese or the pudding? Many people prefer to follow the French style, and serve the cheese immediately after the main course. In that case, it makes sense to carry on drinking the same red wine that accompanied the main course. But there are those who swear by a tangy piece of cheese (and perhaps a glass of port) as the ideal way to round off a meal and clear the sweetness of the pudding from the palate. Neither is wrong, so you can decide for yourself, or ask your guests which they would prefer.

If buying cheese for a party several days in advance, take account of the degree to which it will mature before it is served, particularly if you are choosing cheeses such as Brie or Camembert which are only at their best for a short period. Store cheese wrapped in grease-proof paper in the refrigerator, unless you want it to ripen at room temperature, but always remove it from the refrigerator and unwrap it at least 1 hour before serving. As well as bringing out the flavour, this will prevent the cheese from sweating unattractively when it is served.

A good cheeseboard should contain a generous selection of different cheeses. Convention suggests that four cheeses should be provided; one soft, one hard or semi hard, one blue and one other, perhaps a goat's cheese.

To accompany the cheese, serve a selection of crackers and biscuits, plus some rolls or French bread, since many people prefer these as an accompaniment to strongly flavoured cheeses. Unsalted butter should also be offered. Sticks of crisp celery and fresh fruit, such as grapes, or figs, can either be arranged on the cheeseboard itself or served separately.

AFTER-DINNER COFFEE

If you don't have a coffee grinder, buy beans then have them ground to the required coarseness in the shop. Whatever type of coffee you choose, to ensure that it's as fresh as possible buy it from a reputable coffee merchant or other reliable outlet which has a fast turnover – good coffee merchants roast their beans on a daily basis. Unground beans will keep their freshly roasted flavour for up to two weeks in an airtight tin in the fridge. Beans will keep for 4-5 months and ground coffee for 4-5 weeks in the freezer.

Types of Coffee

These types of coffee are most suitable after dinner:

AFTER-DINNER: usually a blend of strong-flavoured, dark roasted beans.

BLUE-MOUNTAIN BLEND: a mixture of coffees, probably including some Jamaican.

BRAZILIAN: smooth and mild when at its best. A good choice for any occasion.

CHAGGA: a medium to dark roast coffee with a rich flavour, originating in Tanzania.

JAVA: an unusual, strong, dark roast coffee best served black as after dinner coffee.

KENYA: a medium roast with a distinctive aromatic quality.

MYSORE: a rich, strong coffee from India.

Making Coffee

The best coffee is made with freshly roasted and ground beans and with freshly boiled water. As a rule allow about 25 g (1 oz) coffee per 300 ml (½ pint) water. (Make strong rather than weak so that guests can dilute it to taste.) This is also about the amount you should allow per guest. However you make coffee, it should *never* be allowed to boil, since this ruins the flavour. The following are the most successful methods for smaller numbers.

Jug method: medium-ground coffee beans are placed in a warmed jug and boiling water poured over them. After 4-5 minutes' infusion, the coffee is strained straight into the cups or into a clean, warm jug. There is a more sophisticated version of the jug method marketed as *La Cafetière*. The coffee jug contains a strainer which is plunged through the coffee, forcing the grounds to the bottom of the jug, before serving.

Filter methods: in these methods, hot water passes through a filter paper containing finely ground coffee. There are many versions of this method, some incorporating electrical devices to keep the made coffee hot.

Percolator method: water is brought to the boil in the percolator and forced over coffee grounds in a basket in its top. Although electric percolators have a timing device, there is a risk of the coffee becoming 'stewed'.

Cona or syphon method: a special coffee maker in which boiling water is forced from a lower container into an upper container in which medium-ground coffee is placed. When the coffee maker is removed from the heat, the prepared coffee flows down into the lower container again, from which it is served.

Serving Coffee

Serve after-dinner coffee in small cups. If guests prefer 'white' coffee, use cold milk or thin cream, *never* boiled milk. Offer demerara sugar or special coffee sugar crystals as a sweetner. If serving warm milk (for milky breakfast and brunchtime coffee), warm it in the jug in which it is to be served in the microwave.

Liqueur Coffees

To make Irish Coffee, warm as many large wine goblets as needed, then put 1 measure of whisky and 1 teaspoon light soft brown sugar in each. Pour in piping hot coffee to come about 25cm (1 inch) from the top. Slowly pour double cream over the back of a teaspoon into the glass. The cream will float on top of the coffee.

Use other liqueurs to make the following coffees: Rum (Caribbean coffee); Kirsch (German coffee); Calvados (Normandy coffee); Tia Maria (Calypso coffee); Strega (Witch's coffee). Cointreau and Curaçao can also be used, if wished.

Petits Fours

These small sweet treats are delicious served with coffee at the end of the meal. Make your own (see the recipes on page 266) if you have time, or buy them ready made from a reputable supplier. Traditional home-made petits fours include little iced cakes, meringues and tiny crumbly biscuits. However, almost any small rich sweets are suitable; chocolate truffles, fudge and mint-flavoured chocolates are popular, as are dates stuffed with almond paste and frosted fruits.

SETTING THE SCENE

Whether the scene of your party is your own home or a hired hall, room or marquee, it is important to create a party atmosphere that will make your guests feel welcome and relaxed as soon as they walk through the front door.

Lighting

The lighting in a room can make all the difference to the atmosphere. Harsh overhead lighting is far too bright for a party mood: it's better to use side lights and table lamps that create shadow as well as light. At dinner, candles on the table, with one or two side lights in the background, may be all that is required, but remember your guests will want to be able to see what they are eating!

Flowers

It's always lovely to have flowers on the table for a formal dinner party, but practical considerations must come first. Make sure that there's room for all the table settings, serving dishes, sauces, accompaniments and glasses for each guest. Your guests should be able to see each other easily, so tall arrangements are unsuitable.

For a buffet, the flower arrangement on the table should be higher than the level of the food, and quite flamboyant. Arrangements of exotic fruits can also look eye-catching (and can be eaten later).

SEATING AT DINNER PARTIES

There are no hard and fast seating rules. Your top priority is to make sure people get a chance to enjoy the company of others, and at a small dinner party it won't matter who sits where because the conversation can range across the table without any difficulty. Couples, married or otherwise, are generally separated, on the grounds that they have plenty of opportunity to talk to each other the rest of the time. You can alternate men and women around the table if you wish, and if the party consists of even numbers of sexes. Otherwise spread out members of whichever is the minority fairly evenly.

Laying the table

When laying each place setting, arrange the knives and forks (and spoons) so that they are used from the outside inwards. Knife blades should always face inwards. The dessert spoon and fork can be placed on either side of the setting, or less formally, above it so that the handle of the dessert spoon points towards the knife blades. Arrange glasses for water and wine above the knives.

Napkins

Plain white linen napkins always look good, but napkins can be made of other fabric in a colour or pattern to complement the table setting. For less formal occasions paper napkins can be used, but make them good quality, thick ones of a generous size. Bear in mind that coloured paper napkins can stain clothes if food or drink is spilled on them.

DRINKS

What you give your guests to drink is just as important as the food. The time of day and the season will give you guidelines. Pimms and other long, cool drinks, chilled white wine and fruit wine cups are welcome for summer parties whilst in the winter, a warm glass of mulled wine or punch makes an attractive welcoming drink.

A light, fruity red and a medium-dry white with perhaps a sparkling wine for a more special occasion are good, generally acceptable choices for most parties, but you may also like to offer a choice of spirits, such as gin, whisky and vodka, with their usual accompaniments of tonics, sodas and ginger ale, dry or medium sherry and white and red vermouths. When you put out the glasses remember to put out Worcestershire sauce, a stirrer, a saucer with slices of lemon or lime, cocktail sticks and an ice bucket full of ice with tongs or a spoon. Do remember to have a good choice of nonalcoholic drinks.

Depending on the length of the party, allow about ½ – ¾ bottle of wine per person; for a dinner party, 1–2 glasses of an aperitif, 1–2 glasses of wine with the first course, 2 with the main course and another with the cheese and/or dessert. One bottle should give 6 glasses. Fill the glass about two-thirds full.

Choosing Wine

One good way to learn more about wines is to seek out a wine merchant whom you trust. It is worth keeping notes of wines, the ones which you particularly like, with what foods they were served and how well the two went together.

Pre-Dinner Drinks

An aperitif should stimulate the palate and the appetite. It is best to avoid sweet drinks such as sweet sherry and many cocktails, and those that have a high alcohol content, such as spirits, as these will deaden both the appetite and the taste buds. Good choices are fino (dry) sherry, sercial (dry) Maderia, dry vermouths and dry white wines still or sparkling. This could be the same as that being served with the first course or one that is slightly lighter in body.

MATCHING FOOD AND WINE

To gain the maximum enjoyment from both the food and the wine, as well as the occasion and to avoid wasting money or suffering a disappointment it pays to serve an appropriate wine. Follow these guidelines:

- match the quality and style of the wine to the quality and style of the food i.e. serve a light wine with light food, a full-bodied one with full-flavoured dishes

- serve white wines before red, dry before sweet, light bodied before more full-bodied, young before old, less expensive before expensive ones

- wines of a region are the best accompaniments for the foods from the region

- if a wine has been used in the making of a dish it will be the most suitable one to serve with it

- select wines that are appropriate for the occasion, i.e. lesser quality wines for informal affairs reserving the finer wines for special occasions where the guests will appreciate the qualities of the wine.

First courses

Consommés, meat and game soups – fino sherry, sercial Madeira.
Light fish soups – good quality light dry white wines.
Vegetable purées – more full-bodied white such as Graves, Pinot Grigio or mature white Rioja.
Mixed hors d'oeuvres and antipasto – fairly assertive white such as those made from the sauvignon grape or semillion if the wine is dry, or perhaps a fruity light red such as Bardolino, Valpolicella, Bando or a young Zinfandel.
Cold meats, smoked meats and sausages such as salami – strong rosé such as Tavel or a medium weight white such as Sauvignon Blanc.
Game and meat pâtés – a medium-bodied red.

Fish and Shellfish

Served as a first course or plainly cooked and simply presented – a light white wine as Soave, a Loire Chenin Blanc or Pouilly Fuissé.
Lighter fish such as sole with a creamy, not too rich, sauce – Mosel.
Firm fish such as turbot – Bulgarian, Australian or Californian Chardonnay, white Burgundy, white Rhône, Rioja, Orvieto.
Oily fish – with sardines Vinho Verde, *with trout* Alsatian Sylvaner or Riesling, *with salmon* good white Graves or Burgundy, Californian or Australian Chardonnay.
Mussels are good partnered by a dry white wine such as a good quality Muscadet or Gros Plant, *scallops* with Saviennières or Alsation or other good dry Riesling.
Shellfish need a completely dry but medium-bodied wine such as a good Burgundy and other Chardonnays or good white Rhône.
Smoked salmon – Sancerre or a Fumé Blanc or a fairly full-flavoured sparkling wine.

Poultry

Chicken plainly cooked or cold – a fairly light, dry white in any price bracket. With a creamy or full-flavoured sauce or stuffing a more full-bodied white with some acidity such as an Alsatian Riesling.
Turkey simply cooked and served - fairly full-bodied white such as white Burgundy or other Chardonnay, white Rioja, white Rhône.
Cooked in a richer or more flavoured way, try a light red such as a lesser growth Bordeaux or other light Cabernet Sauvignon, Italian or Bulgarian Merlot, Chianti Classico.
Duck – medium-quality Bordeaux or other Cabernet Sauvignon unless an acidic or fruity sauce accompanies the duck then drink a fairly assertive, not too serious wine such as an Australian Shiraz or a Zinfandel.
Goose – a full, assertive red or a full-bodied sweet white wine with some acidity such as an Alsatian Reserve Exceptionelle or a German Rheinpfalz spatlese.

Meat

Lamb plain roast lamb – a good Bordeaux or other Cabernet Sauvignon. *With chops* Bulgarian, Lebanese or Chilean Cabernet Sauvignon. *With barbecued lamb and Mediterranean-style lamb dishes* a full-bodied rosé such as Tavel, Provençal or Rioja.
Beef plain roast or fairly simply cooked steaks – red Burgundy. *Richly flavoured beef dishes* – red

Rhône, Dã, Barolo, Australian Syrah/Shiraz.
Pork and veal plainly roasted – medium quality, medium weight red or white such as Beaune, Graves, Claret or other Cabernet Sauvignon. *With grilled or fried pork chops* – a dry white with some acidity such as Alsatian Pinot Gris, Valpolicella or Penedes. *Creamy sauced or casseroled dishes* – Maçon blanc, a strong rosé or Sauvignon Blanc.
Kidneys – Pomerol, St Emilion or a Barbaresco.
Sweetbreads – a good, medium-full-bodied white wine such as a Hermitage blanc.

Game

Young feathered game plainly cooked or with a light sauce – a good claret or a medium-bodied Cabernet Sauvignon *from California or Australia.*
Venison and hare – a good Burgundy or other Pinot Noir.
Richly-flavoured game casseroles – a good Graves, full-bodied Cabernet Sauvignon, Barbaresco *or, with a really 'meaty' dish,* Portuguese Dão, a Borolo or Rioja.

Cheese

Soft, creamy fresh cheeses, including soft goats' cheese – a light-medium white wine with just a touch of acidity such as Sancerre or a Sauvignon or Pouilly Fumé.
Not too strong blue cheeses such as Bleu de Bresse – sweet white wines such as Monbazillac, Barsac and Sauternes.
Very strong blue cheeses – Marsala, Madeira or Malaga. *Stilton* – port.
Full-flavoured hard cheeses such as mature Cheddar – a mature full-bodied red wine such as a good Burgundy or Rhône.
Milder flavoured, slightly softer cheeses slightly lighter red wines eg clarets or lesser Bordeaux wines, Beaujolais, Bergerac, Californian Gamay.

Desserts

Gâteau-type, non-citrus and not too creamy desserts a sweet white wine such as Sauternes, Monbazillac, sweet Loire eg Vouvray, German Auslese or Beeren-Auslese and late-harvest Rieslings from California and Australia.
Rich-cream desserts and pastries – port, Madeira or sweet sherry.

Difficult foods

Acidity in foods makes wine taste sharp so avoid using too much dressing on a salad and use lemon juice instead of vinegar to make the dressing; avoid too much lemon with fish, citrus fruits, gherkins, chutneys and tomatoes. Eggs and egg-based dishes can cause problems and chocolate spells death to any wine as it completely coats the mouth. Really strong cheeses can overpower all but the most robust wines. Red wines do not go with desserts, with the exception of pears, peaches and strawberries.

SERVING TEMPERATURES

Wines are always more enjoyable if they are served at the temperature that shows off their particular characteristics. Coolness enhances the crisp acidity of white wines, whether sweet or dry, whilst a certain degree of warmth is needed to bring out the aroma and flavour of red ones. Generally, the cheaper or sweeter the wine, the cooler the temperature should be with a minimum of about 7°C (45°). About an hour in the refrigerator is enough for cooling good white wines, about 1½ hours for medium quality with about 2 hours for the cheaper ones. Fruity light red wines such as Beaujolais, red Loire and Valpolicella can be served cool. Serve everyday red wines at about 15–16°C (60°F) whilst more full-bodied red wines are most enjoyable if served at about 17–18°C (63–65°F).

Keeping Wine Cool

The best way to cool several bottles is to place them up to their necks in a mixture of ice cubes and water. Wine coolers are good for opened bottles.

COOKERY NOTES

1. Follow either metric or imperial measures; they are not interchangeable.
2. Size 2 or 3 eggs should be used unless otherwise stated.
3. When measuring milk the exact conversion of 568 ml (1 pint) has been used.
4. Microwave times are for a 650 watt oven.

BRUNCH PARTIES

A brunch party provides the ideal opportunity for relaxed, casual entertaining. Unless you're one of those really organized people who can find time to set the table, and gather everything together the night before, don't be tempted to invite your guests too early or you'll have to get up at the crack of dawn to get everything ready. About 11 am is ideal, since it allows time to get organized. Brunch should be a lingering affair with plenty of food and drink to feast on as the morning moves into afternoon. As well as the menus suggested here, make sure that you have a selection of croissants, rolls, bagels, toast and muffins on offer with continental-style butter, conserves and marmalades.

In winter, sliced cold meats, cheeses and smoked salmon with scrambled eggs are good filling additions. In summer, a platter of watermelon or pineapple or a bowl of ripe strawberries or cherries along with creamy Greek yogurt flavoured with honey, and muesli are light and refreshing.

To drink, alcohol is optional (although Bucks fizz made from freshly squeezed orange juice and sparkling white wine or champagne never goes amiss), but coffee and tea are essential. Offer real leaf teas served with or without milk, and in summer iced teas served with lemon are refreshing. Making large quantities of coffee can cause a problem. If you entertain a lot, it's worth investing in a couple of cafetières to make things easier. Serve with hot milk, warmed in the microwave.

QUICK AND EASY BRUNCH

M	E	N	U

EGGS BAKED WITH MUSTARD

HERBED FARMHOUSE SAUSAGES

SWEET ONION RELISH

CHEESE PARKERHOUSE ROLLS

MUSHROOMS WITH PARSLEY

BLUEBERRY AND BUTTERMILK BLINIS

RASPBERRY AND BLUEBERRY SAUCE

SERVES 8

*T*he beauty of this brunch is that the entire main course is cooked in the oven at once. No last minute scrambling, frying or boiling of eggs here! With the initial preparation done everything sits happily in the oven leaving you free for other things. A platter of fresh fruits chosen to appeal to the eye and the palate makes a good, refreshing start to the meal and helps awaken sluggish appetites. To drink, offer glasses of chilled real ale or lager and English apple juice as well as pots of freshly brewed coffee and real leaf tea.

In the time plan we've suggested that you cook the Blueberry and Buttermilk Blinis beforehand and keep them warm in the oven. However, as the brunch may well be a long, lingering affair it might be more fun to wait until your guests are ready for dessert then get them to don an apron and griddle their own.

EGGS BAKED WITH MUSTARD

*Perfectly cooked eggs served in their own
mustardy cases.*

8 thin slices of bread from a large loaf
125 g (4 oz) butter or margarine, melted
about 60 ml (4 tbsp) mild wholegrain mustard
8 eggs
salt and freshly ground pepper

*Eggs Baked with Mustard,
Herbed Farmhouse
Sausages, Sweet Onion
Relish and Mushrooms
with Parsley (below)*

1 Trim the crusts from the bread. Brush one side of each piece of bread with the melted butter or margarine.

2 Firmly press the bread, buttered-side up, into 8 greased 10 cm (4 inch) Yorkshire pudding tins.

3 Bake in the oven at 200°C (400°F) mark 6 for 15 minutes or until the bread is crisp and light golden brown.

4 Remove the tins from the oven and spread each bread case with a little wholegrain mustard. Break an egg into each case and return to the oven for 8-10 minutes or until the eggs are just set. Season to taste and serve immediately.

HERBED FARMHOUSE SAUSAGES

These rustic sausages are shaped into patties.
The recipe works equally well with minced beef.

1.4 kg (3 lb) lean minced pork
75 ml (5 tbsp) roughly chopped fresh mixed herbs such as thyme, sage, rosemary, chives
2 small garlic cloves, skinned and crushed
10 ml (2 tsp) ground mixed spice
salt and freshly ground pepper
seasoned flour

1 Mix the pork with the herbs, garlic, mixed spice and plenty of pepper and salt. Divide the mixture into 24 and shape each into a round flat cake about 1 cm (½ inch) thick.
2 Lightly coat the sausages with seasoned flour. Arrange on a rimmed baking sheet, cover and chill in the refrigerator.
3 Cook the sausages in the oven at 200°C (400°F) mark 6 for 45 minutes, turning them over once during cooking. Serve with Sweet Onion Relish.
To Freeze Open freeze at the end of step 2. Transfer to a polythene bag and store for up to 3 months. Thaw overnight in the refrigerator and cook as above.

SWEET ONION RELISH

Cooked in this way, red onions
reduce to a deliciously creamy consistency.

900 g (2 lb) red onions, skinned
30 ml (2 tbsp) olive oil
salt and freshly ground pepper
30 ml (2 tbsp) raspberry vinegar

1 Cut each onion in half then into thin crescent shaped slices. Heat the oil in a heavy-based saucepan, add the onions and fry over a high heat for 1 minute.
2 Reduce the heat, cover the pan tightly and cook gently for 40–45 minutes or until the onions are very soft and caramelised. Shake the pan occasionally during cooking, but resist lifting the lid or you will lose the steam and the onions will stick.
3 Season the onions with salt and pepper, then stir in the vinegar. Serve warm or cold with Herbed Farmhouse Sausages.
To Freeze Cool, pack into a polythene bag and freeze. Thaw at cool room temperature.

CHEESE PARKERHOUSE ROLLS

Use a good quality Farmhouse
Cheddar for the best flavour.

MAKES 24
700 g (1½ lb) strong white flour
7.5 ml (1½ tsp) salt
1 sachet fast action dried yeast
25 g (1 oz) butter
450 ml (¾ pint) tepid water
melted butter
125 g (4 oz) mature Cheddar cheese, grated

1 Put the flour, salt and yeast into a bowl. Rub in the butter until the mixture resembles fine breadcrumbs. Make a well in the centre, then pour in the water. Beat thoroughly until the dough leaves the sides of the bowl clean.
2 Turn onto a lightly floured surface and knead for about 10 minutes until smooth and elastic. Roll out the dough until it is about 1 cm (½ inch) thick. Cut out rounds using a plain 6.5 cm (2½ inch) cutter. Knead and re-roll the trimmings as necessary
3 Brush with a little melted butter. Mark a crease across each round, then fold in half along the crease.
4 Place on a baking sheet, cover with a clean tea towel and leave in a warm place for about 40 minutes or until doubled in size.
5 Brush the risen rolls with melted butter then bake in the oven at 230°C (450°F) mark 8 for 10 minutes. Reduce the temperature to 200°C (400°F) mark 6, sprinkle with cheese and bake for a further 10–15 minutes, until well risen and golden brown. Remove from the baking tray and cool on a wire rack.
To Freeze Complete as above. Cool, wrap and freeze. Re-heat from frozen at 200°C (400°F) mark 6 for 15 minutes.

COOK'S HINT
Do use a good, heavy-based saucepan or **the onions** will burn and the flavour will be ruined.

MICROWAVE HINTS
1 **To cook the onions** in the microwave, put them in a bowl with the oil, cover and cook on HIGH for 35–40 minutes until softened, shaking the bowl occasionally. Complete as step 3.

2 **Heat milk for coffee** in the jug in which it is to be served. Make sure that you use a heatproof jug and don't fill it right to the top. Don't let it boil or, as when heated in a saucepan, it will boil over. 600 ml (1 pint) will take about 2–3 minutes and 1.1 litres (2 pints) will take 4–5 minutes.

MENU SUGGESTIONS
Instead of making the sausages serve lightly smoked bacon, grilled until crisp. For vegetarians, make up more Eggs Baked with Mustard and serve with Sweet Onion Relish. Vary the Blueberry and Buttermilk Blinis and their sauce by replacing the blueberries with fresh blackcurrants.

MUSHROOMS WITH PARSLEY

Don't slice the mushrooms too thinly or they will overcook before the rest of the brunch is ready.

1.1 kg (2½ lb) large flat mushrooms
1 garlic clove, skinned and crushed
45 ml (3 tbsp) chopped fresh parsley
salt and freshly ground pepper
olive oil

1 Thickly slice the mushrooms and arrange in a greased ovenproof dish. Sprinkle with the garlic, parsley and salt and pepper to taste. Pour over enough oil to moisten the mushrooms.
2 Bake in the oven at 200°C (400°F) mark 6 for about 30 minutes. Serve hot.

BLUEBERRY AND BUTTERMILK BLINIS

These blinis are at their best served hot, straight from the griddle, but we suggest that you cook them on the morning of the party and keep them warm in a low oven.

MAKES ABOUT 24
125 g (4 oz) plain flour
125 g (4 oz) buckwheat flour
30 ml (2 tbsp) caster sugar
2.5 ml (½ tsp) salt
2.5 ml (½ level tsp) fast action dried yeast
450 ml (¾ pint) buttermilk
1 egg, separated
vegetable oil for frying
225 g (8 oz) fresh blueberries
blueberry and raspberry sauce, soured cream or maple syrup to serve

1 Put the flours, sugar, salt and yeast into a bowl and mix well. Gradually beat in the buttermilk to make a smooth batter. Cover and leave in a warm place for about 40 minutes or until doubled in size.
2 Beat in the egg yolk. Whisk the egg white until stiff, then fold into the batter with the blueberries.

3 Heat a griddle or large flat, heavy-based frying pan. Brush generously with oil and heat until the oil is hot.
4 Using a measuring jug or a ladle, drop three or four small 'pools' of batter onto the hot griddle.
5 Cook over medium heat for 2–3 minutes until bubbles rise to the surface and burst, then turn the blinis over with a palette knife. Continue cooking for a further 2–3 minutes until golden brown on the other side.
6 Keep the blinis warm, wrapped in a clean tea towel in a low oven while you cook the remainder. Re-grease the griddle or frying pan in between cooking each batch. Serve warm with Raspberry and Blueberry Sauce and soured cream or maple syrup.

RASPBERRY AND BLUEBERRY SAUCE

Use frozen fruit when fresh is unavailable. This sauce is also delicious served with ice cream (but not at breakfast time!).

450 g (1 lb) raspberries
175 g (6 oz) blueberries
45 ml (3 tbsp) icing sugar, or to taste
45 ml (3 tbsp) orange juice

1 Push the raspberries through a fine nylon sieve and mix with the orange juice and icing sugar, to taste. Stir in the blueberries. Serve cold, or warm through gently in a heavy-based saucepan.
To Freeze Cool, pack into a rigid container and freeze. Store for up to 3 months. Thaw overnight at cool room temperature.

Blueberry and Buttermilk Blinis with Raspberry and Blueberry Sauce (right)

The day before or earlier:
Prepare the Herbed Farmhouse Sausages by following steps 1 and 2. Freeze or cover and store in the refrigerator overnight. Make the Sweet Onion Relish. Freeze or cover and store in the refrigerator overnight. Make the Cheese Parkerhouse Rolls. Freeze or store in an airtight container overnight. Make the Blueberry and Raspberry Sauce. Freeze or cover and store in the refrigerator.

To serve at 11am:
10.00am: Make the batter for the blinis by following step 1. Cover and leave to stand.
10.15am: Bake the sausages. Prepare the Eggs Baked with Mustard to the end of step 2. Prepare the mushrooms by following step 1.
10.30am: Bake the cases for the eggs and complete the recipe. Bake the mushrooms in the bottom of the oven by following step 2.
10.40am: Reheat the rolls from frozen. If serving the Sweet Onion Relish warm reheat it gently over a low heat or in the microwave If serving the Raspberry and Blueberry Sauce warm, reheat gently for a few minutes.
10.50am: Cook the Blueberry and Buttermilk Blinis in batches by following steps 3–6. Wrap in a teatowel (see the recipe). Once everything else is cooked, switch the oven to low and keep the blinis warm while eating the main course.

AMERICAN BRUNCH

SERVES 8

Get this brunch off to a good start by greeting guests in true American style with a cocktail. You will need plenty of ice, as brunch-time cocktails are served 'on the rocks' in large tumblers, rather than cocktail glasses. Bloody Mary is a popular brunch-time tipple in the States, although you may prefer to serve Bucks Fizz, sparkling wine coolers or a chilled white wine. Supply jugs of iced tomato or orange juice for teetotal guests or for those who may be driving.

Other tempting and labour saving additions to the menu could include bowls of muesli, cereals and plenty of thick yogurt. A honey roast gammon, served cold for slicing, would suit guests with healthy appetites, and freshly baked hot rolls (the frozen type are excellent) are always popular.

COOK'S HINTS
1 **Buckwheat flour** is available from health food shops and larger supermarkets. You can replace it with plain white, or plain wholemeal flour, if preferred, or use a mixture of the two. Make the pancakes in the same way.

The cooked, unfilled pancakes also keep well for several days in the refrigerator. Interleave with non-stick paper and seal in a polythene bag. The tomato filling may also be made in advance and stored (tightly covered) in the refrigerator for several days.

2 Vary the dressing for **Red Cabbage** to suit personal preferences – try a soured cream or garlic mayonnaise, or use a mixture of the two. A rich herb vinaigrette or lemony dressing is also good with coleslaw.

FLORENTINE BUCKWHEAT PANCAKES

300 ml (½ pint) milk, or use a mixture of milk and water
1 egg
125 g (4 oz) buckwheat flour
salt
oil for coating
FILLING
45 ml (3 tbsp) olive oil
1 large Spanish onion, skinned and roughly chopped
2 garlic cloves, skinned and crushed
397 g (14 oz) can chopped tomatoes
45 ml (3 tbsp) tomato purée
5 ml (1 tsp) dried oregano
350 g (12 oz) frozen leaf spinach
salt and freshly ground pepper
SAUCE
25 g (1 oz) butter
25 g (1 oz) plain flour
300 ml (½ pint) milk
75 g (3 oz) Cheddar cheese, grated

1 Put the milk, egg, buckwheat flour and a pinch of salt into a blender. Blend for a few seconds until thoroughly mixed. Pour the batter into a jug.

2 Heat a little oil in an 18 cm (7 inch) frying pan, swirling it to coat the pan and pour off any excess. Pour in enough batter to thinly coat the base of the pan, tilting as you pour to spread the batter.

3 Cook over fairly high heat until the underside of the pancake is golden brown, then turn the pancake over and cook the remaining side. Remove from the pan and leave on a flat surface.

4 Cook another 7 pancakes in the same way, stirring the batter each time and greasing the pan with oil between making each pancake.

5 For the filling, heat the oil in a heavy-based saucepan over a medium heat and gently fry the onion for 5 minutes. Add the remaining ingredients for the filling and cook, uncovered, for about 25 minutes. Stir occasionally to break up the spinach and cook until the mixture is thickened.

6 Spread the pancakes with the spinach mixture and either fold into triangular shapes, or form into rolls. Arrange the filled pancakes in a greased, shallow ovenproof dish.

7 To make the sauce, melt the butter in a saucepan, add the flour and cook gently, stirring, for 1–2 minutes. Remove from the heat and gradually blend in the milk. Bring to the boil, stirring constantly, then simmer for 3 minutes until thick and smooth. Remove from the heat and stir in half the grated cheese and seasoning. Pour the sauce over the pancakes and sprinkle with the remaining grated cheese.

8 Bake at 190°C (375°F) mark 5 for 25 minutes until hot and bubbling. Serve at once. *To Freeze* Cool the pancakes and interleave with greaseproof paper. Seal in polythene bags or foil and freeze for up to 2 months. Thaw overnight in the refrigerator or for quick thawing, unwrap, spread out separately and leave at room temperature for 20 minutes. Complete as above.

RED CABBAGE AND PINE NUT SLAW

550 g (1¼ lb) red cabbage, very finely shredded
1 red onion, skinned, quartered and very finely sliced
1 large red pepper, seeded and very finely sliced
1 yellow pepper, seeded and very finely sliced
2 courgettes, coarsely grated
45 ml (3 tbsp) olive oil
45 ml (3 tbsp) corn oil
30 ml (2 tbsp) malt vinegar
15-30 ml (1–2 tbsp) clear honey, or to taste
1 garlic clove, skinned and crushed
salt and freshly ground pepper
60 ml (4 tbsp) pine kernels

1 Put the shredded cabbage into a large bowl of iced water and leave to soak for 30 minutes. Drain well and pat dry.

2 In a large bowl, combine all the prepared vegetables, cover and chill until required.

3 Thoroughly whisk together the oils, vinegar, honey, garlic and salt and pepper. Just before serving, pour over the salad and toss well together. Sprinkle with pine kernels, toss again and serve.

SAUSAGE AND BACON OATCAKES

These savoury oatcakes are also extremely good served burger-style in warm baps with a selection of relishes.

175 g (6 oz) lean back bacon, minced or very finely chopped
1 small onion, skinned and minced or very finely chopped
225 g (8 oz) pork sausagemeat
10 ml (2 tsp) wholegrain mustard
15 ml (1 tbsp) chopped fresh parsley or 10 ml (2 tsp) dried parsley
125 g (4 oz) medium oatmeal
salt and freshly ground pepper
1 egg, beaten
oil for shallow frying
8 rashers streaky bacon, rinded and thinly stretched
stuffed olives threaded onto wooden cocktail sticks, to garnish

1 Mix the minced or chopped bacon and onion with the sausagemeat, mustard, parsley, thyme, 15 ml (1 tbsp) of the oatmeal and plenty of salt and pepper.

2 Divide the mixture into 8 equal portions. On a lightly floured surface, form each portion into a 7.5–8.5 cm (3–3½ inch) round cake. Dip into the beaten egg, then coat in the remaining oatmeal, pressing on firmly with fingertips. Cover and chill in the refrigerator for at least 30 minutes (or overnight, if wished).

3 Heat the oil in a large frying pan and cook the sausage cakes, over a fairly high heat, in two batches, if necessary, for about 10 minutes, turning frequently until golden brown.

4 Wrap a streaky bacon rasher around each cake and return to the pan, join-side down. Cook for a further 2–3 minutes, turning frequently. Drain on absorbent kitchen paper.

5 Serve the oatcakes hot, garnished with stuffed olives threaded onto wooden cocktail sticks.

To Freeze Provided the sausagemeat has not already been frozen, oatcakes freeze well, without the egg and oatmeal coating. Interleave with greaseproof paper and pack in a rigid container. Freeze for up to 1 month. Thaw overnight in the refrigerator before coating. Complete as above.

HERB-GLAZED TOMATOES

4 beef tomatoes (about 550 g/1¼ lb total weight)
25 g (1 oz) butter
salt and freshly ground pepper
45 ml (3 tbsp) double cream
5 ml (1 tsp) lemon juice
25 ml (1½ tbsp) slivered fresh basil
basil sprigs, to garnish

1 Cut the tomatoes in half and trim away the cores. Melt the butter in a large frying pan and gently fry the tomatoes for 1 minute on each side. Arrange the tomatoes in a greased, shallow ovenproof dish and sprinkle with salt and pepper.

2 Off the heat, add cream, lemon juice and half the slivered basil to the buttery juices in the frying pan. Mix well and drizzle over the tomatoes. Sprinkle with more pepper.

3 Bake in the oven at 190°C (375°F) mark 5 for about 8 minutes. Sprinkle with the remaining basil and cook for a further 2–3 minutes. Serve hot, garnished with basil sprigs.

MICROWAVE HINTS
This **tomato dish** cooks successfully in the microwave. Cover the prepared dish with a plate or lid and cook on HIGH for 5-7 minutes, or until tender, rearranging halfway through cooking.

◆

COOK'S HINT
Rolled porridge oats also make a good coating for these cakes. To reduce the calories, brush oatcakes lightly with oil and bake in a moderate oven instead of frying.

◆

Herb-Glazed Tomatoes with Sausage and Bacon Oatcakes (below)

PECAN AND RAISIN MUFFINS

Serve these tasty muffins with butter and cream cheese, if wished.

MAKES 12
350 g (12 oz) plain flour
15 ml (1 level tbsp) baking powder
salt
125 g (4 oz) caster sugar
2 eggs
150 ml (¼ pint) milk
50 ml (2 fl oz) corn oil
1.25 ml (¼ tsp) vanilla flavouring
75 g (3 oz) pecan nuts, roughly chopped
75 g (3 oz) raisins

1 Line 12 deep bun or patty tins with paper cake cases, or grease 12 muffin tins.

2 Sift the flour, baking powder and a pinch of salt into a bowl. Mix in the sugar and make a well in the centre.

3 Lightly beat the eggs with the milk, oil and vanilla flavouring and pour into the centre of the dry ingredients. Mix quickly to blend the flour with the liquid. Do not over mix, the mixture should look slightly lumpy. Lightly. stir in the nuts and raisins.

4 Divide the mixture equally between the paper cake cases or muffin tins. Bake in the oven at 190°C (375°F) mark 5 for 25–27 minutes or until well risen, golden brown and cooked through. Leave in the tins to cool for a few minutes. Serve warm or cold.

To Freeze Cool cooked muffins and freeze in polythene bags for up to 2 months. To serve, reheat from frozen, on a baking sheet at 180°C (350°F) mark 4 for about 15 minutes.

CINNAMON SUGAR BUNS

A packet of bread mix means yeast buns are quickly and easily made for breakfast. Use a different spice or nuts for the filling, if wished.

MAKES 8
283 g packet white bread & pizza base mix
200 ml (7 fl oz) hand-hot water
50 g (2 oz) butter, melted
125 g (4 oz) soft light brown sugar
7.5 ml (1½ tsp) ground cinnamon
75 g (3 oz) flaked almonds
30 ml (2 tbsp) golden syrup, warmed

1 Put the bread mix into a bowl, add the hand-hot water and mix to form a dough. Knead thoroughly on a lightly floured surface for 5 minutes until smooth and elastic (or use an electric mixer fitted with a dough hook).

2 Roll out the dough on a lightly floured surface to form a rectangle measuring 35.5×23 cm (14×9 inches). Brush all over with some of the melted butter, reserving a little for later. Mix the sugar with half the cinnamon and two thirds of the nuts. Sprinkle over the dough.

3 Starting from a long side, roll up like a Swiss roll. Damp the edge with water and press down firmly to seal the roll. Cut the roll into eight equal slices. Put the slices cut-sides down and press fairly firmly with the palm of your hand to form neat pinwheels.

4 Generously butter a 23 cm (9 inch) round sandwich tin and coat with a little of the remaining sugar and cinnamon. Arrange slices of roll, cut-sides down, in the prepared cake tin. Brush all over with the remaining melted butter and sprinkle with the remaining cinnamon sugar, and flaked almonds.

5 Cover with a lightly oiled polythene bag and leave to prove in a warm place until doubled in size (the buns should fill the tin). Bake in the oven at 190°C (375°F) mark 5 for 25 minutes. Cover with foil to prevent over-browning and cook for a further 5 minutes. Drizzle, or lightly brush, with the warmed golden syrup while still hot. Serve warm.

To Freeze Freeze for up to 1 month, wrapped in a polythene bag. To serve, reheat from frozen on a baking sheet at 180°C (350°F) mark 4 for 15 minutes.

COUNTDOWN
The day before or earlier:
Bake the muffins and the Cinnamon Sugar Buns and freeze. Make the pancakes and freeze.
The day before:
Make the filling for the pancakes, cover and refrigerate. Make the Sausage and Bacon Oatcakes, cover and refrigerate.
To serve at 11.30am:
10.00am: Prepare the salad ingredients and the dressing, cover and refrigerate. Prepare the pancakes ready for baking. Prepare the tomatoes ready for baking.
11am: Fry the Sausage and Bacon Oatcakes, cover and keep warm. Bake the pancakes.
11.20am: Bake the tomatoes. Put the frozen muffins and Cinnamon Sugar Buns in the oven to warm through.
11.25am: Dress the salad, add the pine kernels and toss together.
11.30am: Serve the brunch.

Pecan and Raisin Muffins with Cinnamon Sugar Buns (left)

SCOTTISH BRUNCH

M	E	N	U

ATHOLL BROSE

PERFECT PORRIDGE WITH RASPBERRIES

BRAMBLE SCONES

REAL OATCAKES

OUTRAGEOUS SALMON FISHCAKES

SPICED KIDNEYS WITH MUSHROOMS

SERVES 8

The Scots are famous for their warm-hearted breakfasts and high teas and this rather indulgent brunch is made from old favourites. The Atholl Brose is pure nectar, and a good start to the day! Forget the porridge you hated in your youth, this is the real thing unashamedly adulterated with raspberries and cream. Warm bramble scones with butter and a large cup of steaming tea are essentials, with plainer oatcakes and honey for the less wicked. For the heartiest appetites, there are savoury fishcakes made with fresh and smoked salmon and kidneys sautéed with cream and peppery mustard.

ATHOLL BROSE

This ancient Scottish drink, soothing but potent, is said to have been invented by one of the Dukes of Atholl. Good for a hangover and comforting on a cold winter's day.

125 g (4 oz) medium oatmeal
45 ml (3 tbsp) clear honey (preferably heather)
whisky
300 ml (½ pint) double cream

1 Put the oatmeal into a bowl and stir in 400 ml (14 fl oz) cold water to make a thick, creamy paste. Cover and leave to stand for at least 30 minutes, or overnight.

2 Strain the liquid through a sieve pressing down well with the back of a wooden spoon to extract all the moisture. Discard the oatmeal. Pour the liquid into a measuring jug and stir in the honey.

3 Add enough whisky to make up to 750 ml (1¼ pints) and stir in the cream. Chill for at least 1 hour. Pour into small wine glasses and serve.

PERFECT PORRIDGE WITH RASPBERRIES

Make this fresh on the day and serve piping hot. Soft brown sugar or honey may be added, but is frowned on in Scotland.

2.3 litres (4 pints) water
225 g (8 oz) medium oatmeal
salt
700 g (1½ lb) fresh Scottish raspberries
thick cream, to serve

1 Bring the water to a rolling boil in a large saucepan and sprinkle on the oatmeal in a steady stream, stirring all the time. Add the meal slowly or it will form lumps. Stir until boiling, then turn down the heat and simmer gently for 30 minutes, stirring frequently until a thick *but pouring* consistency is reached. Add salt at this stage – no sooner or it will toughen the meal.

2 Pour into a warm bowl or tureen and serve with the raspberries and cream.

BRAMBLE SCONES

MAKES ABOUT 16
450 g (1 lb) self-raising flour
2.5 ml (½ tsp) salt
10 ml (2 level tsp) baking powder
75 g (3 oz) butter, cubed
75 g (3 oz) caster sugar
225 g (8 oz) frozen blackberries (brambles)
about 200 ml (7 fl oz) buttermilk or half-fat milk
1 egg, beaten

1 Sift the dry ingredients together in a large bowl. Rub in the butter until the mixture resembles breadcrumbs. Stir in the sugar and the still frozen blackberries.

2 Stir in enough milk to form a firm dough. Knead very lightly and roll out on a floured surface to 2.5 cm (1 inch) thick. Using a 6.5 cm (2½ inch) round cutter, stamp into rounds being careful to avoid cutting through the brambles. Knead and carefully re-roll as necessary.

3 Place the scones on a greased baking sheet and brush the tops with beaten egg. Bake in the oven at 220°C (425°F) mark 7 for about 10 minutes until well-risen and golden brown. Serve whilst still hot.

To Freeze Open freeze and store in polythene bags for up to 3 months. Thaw at room temperature and warm in the oven at 200°C (400°F) mark 6 for 5 minutes.

REAL OATCAKES

MAKES 16
450 g (1 lb) medium oatmeal
large pinch of salt
2.5 ml (½ level tsp) bicarbonate of soda
50 g (2 oz) beef dripping or lard, melted
45-75 ml (3-5 tbsp) hot water

1 In a large bowl, mix together the oatmeal, salt and bicarbonate of soda. Make a well in the centre and pour in the melted dripping. Stir in enough hot water to form a stiff, but not too dry, dough.

2 Bring the dough together with hands dipped in extra meal. Knead on a surface dusted with oatmeal until smooth.

3 Divide the dough into four and roll out each quarter into a rough 20.5 cm (8 inch) circle, about 0.5 cm (¼ inch) thick, using a plate as a guide to neaten the circle. Cut each circle into four quarters and place on greased baking sheets.

4 Bake in the oven at 170°C (325°F) mark 3 for 25–30 minutes until firm but not coloured. Cool on a wire rack. Store in an airtight container. To crisp before serving spread on a baking sheet and heat in the oven at 200°C (400°F) mark 6.

OUTRAGEOUS SALMON FISHCAKES

350 g (12 oz) cooked fresh salmon, flaked
225 g (8 oz) smoked salmon, roughly chopped
350 g (12 oz) freshly cooked mashed potato
15 ml (1 tbsp) lemon juice
freshly ground black pepper
75 g (3 oz) butter, melted
45 ml (3 tbsp) chopped fresh dill or 15 ml (1 tbsp) dried dill weed
2 eggs, beaten
about 225 g (8 oz) dried white breadcrumbs
vegetable oil for frying

1 Mix the two salmons with the mashed potato, lemon juice, pepper to taste, butter and dill. Add just enough beaten egg to bind the mixture together. It should be firm, not sloppy. Cool, then refrigerate for 1 hour until very firm.

2 Shape the mixture into 16 cakes about 2.5 cm (1 inch) thick. Brush with some of the remaining beaten egg and coat with breadcrumbs. Chill for 30 minutes to firm.

3 Coat the cakes with egg and crumbs once more. Chill again until firm.

4 Shallow fry the cakes in batches for 3–4 minutes on each side, or until golden brown. Drain on absorbent kitchen paper and keep warm in the oven.

To Freeze Open freeze the fishcakes without egg and crumbs and pack into a rigid container, interleaving with non-stick paper. Thaw overnight in the refrigerator, coat with egg and crumbs and fry as in step 4.

COOK'S HINTS

1 **Bramble** is the Scottish word for wild blackberries, which are small and sweet. This recipe is easier to handle if the berries are frozen when stirred into the mixture. Firmer fruit, such as blueberries can be added fresh.

2 Cook the potato specially for **the fishcakes**; leftovers will be too stodgy. Invest in a gadget called a potato ricer which looks like a giant garlic press. It makes mashing potatoes easy – and no lumps!

3 If **dried white breadcrumbs** are difficult to find, try using medium matzo meal.

MICROWAVE HINT

Make up some fluffy **scrambled eggs** in the microwave for guests who don't like kidneys. To serve 4 break 4 eggs into a bowl and whisk together, then whisk in 120 ml (8 tbsp) milk and salt and pepper to taste. Microwave on HIGH for 2 minutes, until beginning to set around the edge. Whisk vigorously to incorporate the set egg mixture, then cook on HIGH for 2 minutes more until the eggs are just set.

Atholl Brose and Perfect Porridge with Raspberries (opposite)

COUNTDOWN
Two days before, or more:
Make the oatcakes and keep in an airtight tin. Bake the Bramble Scones and freeze or store in an airtight tin for up to two days. Make the salmon fishcakes and freeze.
The day before:
Thaw the scones, if frozen, and the fishcakes. Prepare the kidneys and mushrooms. Soak the oatmeal for the Atholl Brose.
To serve at 1pm:
11.35am: Start the porridge, put the raspberries and cream into bowls and chill. Finish the Atholl Brose and chill.
12.15pm: Fry the fishcakes and keep warm in a low oven with the door slightly ajar. Warm the scones in the oven with the oatcakes. Thin the porridge down with a little hot water if necessary.
12.45pm: Finish the kidneys and serve immediately.

MENU SUGGESTIONS
Make a parsley sauce for the fishcakes by placing the following in a saucepan: 15 g (½ oz) butter, 15 g (½ oz) plain flour, 300 ml (½ pint) milk and seasoning. Bring to the boil, whisking all the time until the sauce thickens. Stir in 15-30 ml (1-2 tbsp) chopped fresh parsley. Parsley can also replace dill in the fishcakes.

SPICED KIDNEYS WITH MUSHROOMS

These kidneys are delicious with chanterelle mushrooms but brown cap or oyster mushrooms are good, too.

700 g (1½ lb) lamb's kidneys, skinned
50 g (2 oz) unsalted butter
225 g (8 oz) mushrooms, thickly sliced
30 ml (2 tbsp) green peppercorn mustard (Maille)
15 ml (1 tbsp) wholegrain mustard
dash of Worcestershire sauce
5 ml (1 tsp) anchovy paste or essence
300 ml (½ pint) double cream
salt and freshly ground pepper
plenty of roughly chopped fresh parsley, to garnish

1 Halve the kidneys and using scissors, snip out the white cores. Heat the butter in a frying pan until foaming. Add the kidneys in batches and cook briskly until brown. Remove from the pan with a slotted spoon and transfer to a sieve to drain out the bitter juices.
2 Fry the mushrooms in the same pan, stirring occasionally just until tender, and remove to the sieve.
3 Add the mustards, Worcestershire sauce and anchovy paste to the pan. Cook over moderate heat, stirring for 1–2 minutes. Stir in the cream and bring to the boil. Return the kidneys and mushrooms to the pan with any juices. Stir to coat with the sauce and simmer for 5 minutes. Season to taste and transfer to a warm serving dish. Sprinkle with plenty of chopped parsley.

Spiced Kidneys with Mushrooms (right)

LUNCH PARTIES

Introduction

Lunch, particularly weekend lunch, has assumed a new significance these days; in many families it is perhaps the one time in the week when everyone gathers and sits down together to eat. At weekends, lunch can be the main event of the day, with time to prepare for it, linger over it – and to recover after it! Even if not a family occasion, lunchtime is the ideal time for relaxed entertaining. Cooking can often be a solitary affair. At weekends there are usually people around who can be coerced into helping – or indeed to taking responsibility for the whole event, so it's the ideal time to prepare a splendid feast.

Lunch has none of the tension implicit in that anxious phrase 'dinner party'. but there should still be some sense of occasion and celebration. Though some people may have fixed ideas about the essential ingredients of a good lunch, particularly Sunday lunch, there are no absolutes. This section contains a range of menus with something for everyone. To cater for the ever-present dieter or pudding hater, offer a selection of fruit for dessert as an alternative to the pudding.

Pre-dinner drinks at lunchtime are best kept simple. Arrange aperitifs and glasses on a tray well in advance just in case any guests arrive unfashionably early. The basic minimum you can offer is gin (with tonic or bitter lemon), whisky (with soda or water) and sherry (dry, medium and sweet). A good sparkling wine or champagne are also possibilities. You will also need a selection of soft drinks such as mineral water (fizzy and still) and orange juice, and don't forget to make sure that there's plenty of ice ready and waiting in the freezer.

INDIAN SUMMER LUNCH

M E N U

PRAWN PURIS

RAAN

SPINACH AND MUSHROOM BHAJI

BASMATI PILAFF

CHOLE

MANGO SORBET

GULAB JAMUN

SERVES 8

When the heat is on, keep cool with this fabulous Indian Lunch. Virtually everything can be prepared ahead, leaving you plenty of time during the morning of the party for last minute touches. Guests can help themselves to the food buffet-style, which can be served in the garden if the weather is fine. When serving pre-lunch drinks, offer your guests snacks such as poppadoms, Bombay mix and mini puris. With the main course, serve bowls of mango chutney, lime pickle and natural yogurt, together with other Indian accompaniments like chapati and naan bread, all of which can be bought at supermarkets and Indian specialist shops.

Prawn Puris with Lassi (above right)

PRAWN PURIS

30 ml (2 tbsp) vegetable oil
1 medium onion, skinned and finely chopped
2 garlic cloves, skinned and crushed
450 g (1 lb) peeled cooked prawns, drained and thoroughly dried if frozen
5–10 ml (1–2 tsp) chilli powder, to taste
8 ripe tomatoes, skinned, seeded and roughly chopped
150 ml (¼ pint) coconut milk (see page 64)
10 ml (2 tsp) lime or lemon juice
salt and freshly ground pepper
chopped fresh coriander, to garnish
PURIS
225 g (8 oz) plain wholemeal flour
pinch of salt
10 ml (2 tsp) vegetable oil
vegetable oil for deepfrying

1 Heat the oil in a heavy flameproof casserole, add the onion and cook gently, stirring frequently, for 5–7 minutes until softened. Add the garlic, prawns and chilli powder, increase the heat to moderate and stir fry for just 2–3 minutes. Remove with a slotted spoon and set aside.

2 Add the tomatoes and coconut milk to the casserole and bring to the boil, stirring. Simmer until the tomatoes are broken up and the sauce is thickened, stirring frequently, then return the prawn mixture and its juices to the pan and stir well to mix. Add the lime or lemon juice and salt and pepper to taste, then remove from the heat.

3 To make the puris, put the flour, salt and oil in a bowl and mix together. Gradually stir in 100–150 ml (3½–5 fl oz) tepid water to make a fairly stiff dough. Knead on a floured surface for at least 5 minutes, until smooth and elastic, then return to the bowl, cover with a damp cloth and leave to rest for 15 minutes.

4 Divide the dough into 8 equal pieces and

roll each one out to a round about 12.5 cm (5 inches) in diameter. Cover each one as you finish rolling, to prevent drying out.

5 Heat about 5 cm (2 inches) oil in a deep, heavy frying pan until hot. Add the puris one at a time and deepfry for about 10–15 seconds on each side until puffed and golden. Remove with a slotted spoon, drain on absorbent kitchen paper and keep warm.

6 Return the prawn mixture to the heat and bring quickly to the boil, stirring. Place a puri on each of 8 plates and top with the prawn mixture. Sprinkle with chopped fresh coriander and serve immediately.

To Freeze Cool at the end of step 2, pack into a rigid container and freeze for up to 1 month. Thaw in the refrigerator overnight. Reheat quickly.

RAAN

The secret of this fragrant festival dish lies in the long marinating. Coated in a rich mixture of yogurt and spices, the lamb becomes meltingly tender after roasting.

2.7 kg (6 lb) leg of lamb
5 cm (2 inch) stick cinnamon, broken into small pieces
6 cardamom pods, split
6 whole cloves
15 ml (1 tbsp) cumin seeds
450 ml (¾ pint) natural yogurt
5 cm (2 inch) piece of fresh root ginger, peeled and roughly chopped
4–6 garlic cloves, skinned and roughly chopped
2 fresh green chillies, roughly chopped (see Cook's Hint)
thinly pared rind of ½ lemon
30 ml (2 tbsp) lemon juice
10 ml (2 tsp) ground turmeric
10 ml (2 tsp) salt
slivered almonds, sultanas, fresh coriander sprigs, to garnish

1 Remove and discard the membrane and any fat from around the lamb. With a sharp pointed knife, make deep slashes in the lamb, especially near the bone.

2 Put the cinnamon, cardamom, cloves and cumin seeds in a heavy frying pan and dry fry over moderate heat for 2–3 minutes, stirring

constantly. Remove from the pan and crush in a mortar and pestle.

3 Transfer the crushed spices to a blender or food processor, add all the remaining ingredients and work together.

4 Place the lamb, meaty side uppermost, in a roasting pan. Pour the marinade over the lamb, spreading it so that it seeps down into the cuts. Cover and marinate in the refrigerator for at least 48 hours, turning the meat over after 24 hours and spooning over the marinade.

5 When ready to cook, uncover the lamb, turn the meat the right way up and spoon over the marinade. Allow the lamb to come to room temperature. Meanwhile, preheat the oven to 220°C (425°F) mark 7.

6 Roast the lamb in the oven for 20 minutes. Remove from the oven, spread with the marinade in the pan, then lower the oven temperature to 180°C (350°F) mark 4 and return the lamb to the oven. Roast for a further 30 minutes.

7 Remove the lamb from the oven. Lower the oven temperature to 150°C (300°F) mark 2. Cover the lamb with foil, return to the oven and roast for a further 2 hours, or until very tender.

8 Remove the lamb from the oven and transfer to a warmed serving dish. Leave to rest, covered, for 10 minutes. Meanwhile, place the roasting pan on the hob and gradually pour in 450 ml (¾ pint) boiling water, stirring vigorously with a metal spoon to scrape up as much of the sediment from the meat and marinade as possible. Boil the liquid rapidly for about 5 minutes, stirring constantly, until reduced slightly, then strain into a warmed jug or gravy boat.

9 Arrange the almonds and sultanas in a floral pattern over the lamb and garnish with coriander. Serve hot or warm, with the gravy handed separately.

COOK'S HINTS
1 Dry-frying is an essential technique in oriental cooking. Whole spices are cooked in a dry pan for 2–3 minutes without any oil or fat until they begin to pop and burst and their aroma is released. Use a heavy-based pan and take care not to overheat the spices or they will burn and taste bitter. Stir constantly and remove the pan from the heat as soon as you smell the spices cooking. After frying, spices are easier to crush in a mortar and pestle.

2 Chillies differ in hotness according to variety, but generally the green ones are less hot than the fiery reds. The seeds are the hottest part, so it is up to you whether you include some or not. Handle chillies with caution, preferably wearing rubber gloves, as the juices are very powerful and pungent. Take care to wash your hands thoroughly after preparing chillies and don't get your fingers near your eyes as this can be extremely painful.

MENU SUGGESTIONS
For a vegetarian lunch start the meal with Spinach Puris, replacing the prawns with 225 g (8 oz) fresh spinach simmered in the sauce for 2–3 minutes at step 2. Serve Mixed Vegetable Curry (page 259) in place of Raan, and offer Naan bread to soak up the juices. Finish with the puddings suggested or serve Coconut Ice Cream (page 120) with sliced fresh mango or pineapple.

SPINACH AND MUSHROOM BHAJI

Fresh spinach is used in this recipe, although frozen spinach can be used. You will need 450 g (1 lb) frozen leaf spinach, thawed and well drained.

15 ml (1 tbsp) black mustard seeds
10 ml (2 tsp) coriander seeds
5 ml (1 tsp) cumin seeds
2 garlic cloves, skinned and roughly chopped
2.5 cm (1 inch) piece of fresh root ginger, peeled and roughly chopped
45 ml (3 tbsp) vegetable oil
2 large onions, skinned and thinly sliced
10 ml (2 tsp) ground turmeric
5–10 ml (1–2 tsp) chilli powder, to taste
450 g (1 lb) button mushrooms, wiped and thickly sliced
397 g (14 oz) can chopped tomatoes
900 g (2 lb) fresh spinach, washed and roughly shredded
salt and freshly ground pepper
about 60 ml (4 tbsp) shredded or desiccated coconut, to garnish

1 Put the mustard, coriander and cumin seeds in a large, heavy flameproof casserole and dry fry over moderate heat for 2–3 minutes, stirring all the time. Remove from the pan and crush in a mortar and pestle with the garlic and ginger.

2 Heat the oil in the casserole, add the onions and cook gently, stirring frequently, for about 10 minutes until softened and golden. Add the spice paste, turmeric and chilli powder and cook gently, stirring all the time, for 5 minutes.

3 Add the mushrooms and mix with the spiced onions, then add the tomatoes and bring to the boil, stirring all the time. Simmer for 10 minutes, stirring occasionally.

4 Add the spinach and stir well, then add salt and pepper to taste. Lower the heat, cover and simmer for 15 minutes, stirring frequently to blend in the spinach as it cooks down.

5 Taste, adjust the seasoning, and turn the mixture into a warmed serving dish. Sprinkle with the coconut just before serving. *To Freeze* Cool, pack into a rigid container and freeze for up to 1 month. Thaw in the refrigerator overnight. Reheat gently.

BASMATI PILAFF

For a luxurious touch, you can fork a good-sized knob of ghee or butter into the pilaf at the same time as the pistachios.

450 g (1 lb) easy-cook basmati rice, washed
8 cardamom pods, split
8 black peppercorns
6 whole cloves
2.5 cm (1 inch) stick cinnamon
15 ml (1 tbsp) cumin seeds
45 ml (3 tbsp) vegetable oil
1 large onion, skinned and finely chopped
10 ml (2 tsp) turmeric
3 curry leaves or bay leaves, torn in pieces
salt and freshly ground pepper
75 g (3 oz) shelled pistachio nuts, roughly chopped
50 g (2 oz) raisins (optional)

1 Put the rice in a bowl, cover with cold water and leave to soak for 30 minutes. Drain off the water, transfer the rice to a sieve and rinse under cold running water until the water runs clear.

2 Put the cardamom pods, peppercorns, cloves, cinnamon stick and cumin seeds in a large, heavy flameproof casserole and dry fry over moderate heat for 2–3 minutes, stirring all the time until they pop and release their flavour. Add the oil and stir until hot, then add the onion and turmeric and cook gently, stirring frequently, for 10 minutes until the onion is softened.

3 Add the rice and stir until coated in the spiced onion mixture, then slowly pour in 1.1 litres (2 pints) boiling water. (Take care as the water may sizzle and splash.) Add the curry or bay leaves and salt and pepper to taste, bring to the boil and stir well. Lower the heat, cover and cook very gently for 15 minutes, without lifting the lid. Remove from the heat and leave to stand for 15 minutes for the flavours to develop.

4 Uncover the rice, add half the pistachio nuts and the raisins, if using, and gently fork through, to fluff up the grains. Taste and adjust seasoning. Spoon the pilaff on to a warmed serving platter, mounding it up in the centre, then sprinkle over the remaining pistachios. Serve hot.

CHOLE

Like all curried dal dishes, Chole tastes best if cooked the day before required. When reheating, you will need to add water as the dal will be dry after standing.

275 g (10 oz) channa dal, stones removed
45 ml (3 tbsp) vegetable oil
2 medium onions, skinned and finely chopped
15 ml (1 tbsp) ground coriander
15 ml (1 tbsp) ground cumin
5–10 ml (1–2 tsp) chilli powder, to taste
450 g (1 lb) potatoes, peeled and cut into small dice
4 tomatoes, skinned, seeded and chopped
15 ml (1 tbsp) garam masala
salt and freshly ground pepper
a few spoonfuls natural yogurt (optional), 4 tomatoes, skinned and sliced, coriander sprigs, to serve

1 Put the channa dal in a large bowl, pour over 1.1 litres (2 pints) cold water and leave to soak for at least 8 hours, or preferably overnight.

2 Place the channa dal and soaking liquid in a saucepan and bring to the boil. Skim off the scum, half cover the saucepan with a lid and simmer for 20 minutes or until soft and almost dry. Remove from the heat and leave to cool.

3 Heat 30 ml (2 tbsp) of the oil in a heavy flameproof casserole over a medium heat, add the onions and cook gently, stirring frequently, for about 10 minutes until softened. Add the remaining oil and when hot, add the coriander, cumin and chilli powder. Stir for 2–3 minutes. Add the channa dal and stir well to mix.

4 Add the potato, tomatoes and garam masala. Pour in 450 ml (¾ pint) cold water and bring to the boil, stirring all the time. Add 5 ml (1 tsp) salt, and pepper to taste, then lower the heat, cover and simmer for 30 minutes or until the potato is very soft. Stir occasionally during the cooking time and add more water if necessary, to prevent the dal sticking to the bottom of the pan.

5 Transfer the Chole to a warmed serving dish. Drizzle over a little yogurt, if using, and garnish with tomatoes and coriander. Serve immediately.

MANGO SORBET

To make serving easier, scoop the sorbet into balls the night before and place on a chilled tray; return to the freezer until ready to serve.

175 g (6 oz) granulated sugar
3 cardamom pods, split
2 ripe mangoes
3 egg whites

1 Put the sugar and cardamom pods in heavy metal saucepan, pour in 600 ml (1 pint) cold water and heat gently, stirring occasionally, until the sugar has dissolved. Increase the heat and bring to the boil, then boil for 7 minutes without stirring. Remove from the heat and leave to cool.

2 Meanwhile, peel the mangoes and remove as much flesh as possible from the stones. Put the flesh in a blender or food processor and work to a purée, then pour into a shallow freezerproof container.

3 Strain the cooled sugar syrup into the mango purée and stir well to mix. Freeze uncovered for about 3 hours or until slushy and beginning to form ice crystals around the edges.

4 Whisk the egg whites until stiff. Turn the mango mixture into a bowl and beat with a fork until broken up. Fold in the egg whites until evenly incorporated, then return the mixture to the freezer container. Cover and freeze overnight until firm.

5 Transfer the sorbet in its container to the refrigerator for 20 minutes to soften slightly, then scoop the sorbet into balls. Serve immediately.

To Freeze Freeze for up to 1 month.

COOK'S HINTS

1 **Channa dal** is the husked, split black chick pea, popular with vegetarian Indians because of its high-protein content. It is available in Indian specialist stores and some health food shops.

2 **Basmati** is prized for its long, slender grains and fine flavour. Indian and Pakistani shops often sell Basmati rice in its natural, unwashed state that is sometimes difficult to cook. Easy-cook basmati rice, sold in large supermarkets, gets round this problem and always gives a good result. Rinsing and soaking the rice before cooking is essential, even with easy-cook basmati.

3 **Curry leaves** come from an attractive perennial herb that is widely available at garden centres. Although not used in authentic curries, these leaves have a strong curry-like odour and flavour, and taste good in pilaffs, soups, stews and stuffings.

4 **Silver Leaf**: This unusual ingredient is unique to Indian cooking. It is made by beating tiny pellets of silver into paper thin sheets.

Silver leaf is spread on desserts and on festive meat and rice dishes. Silver leaf is not only decorative but, as it is edible, can provide essential minerals in the diet. It can be obtained from specialist shops.

COUNTDOWN
Up to 1 month
before:
Make and freeze the
Mango Sorbet.
2 days before:
Marinate the lamb.
The day before:
Make the Gulab
Jamun; chill in the
refrigerator overnight.
Make the Chole; cover
and refrigerate. Make
the Spinach and
Mushroom Bhaji up to
the end of step 4; cool,
and refrigerate. Make
the prawn mixture for
the prawn puris; keep
in a covered container
in the refrigerator.
Scoop the Mango
Sorbet on to a freezer
tray; return to the
freezer.
To serve at 1 pm:
10am: Bring the lamb
to room temperature
and continue from step
5 of the recipe.
12 noon: Soak the
rice and prepare the
other ingredients for
the Basmati Pilaff.
Make the puris but do
not deep-fry; keep
covered.
12.30pm: Cook the
Pilaff. Complete the
Spinach and
Mushroom Bhaji.
12.45pm: Reheat the
topping for the Prawn
Puris and deep-fry
puris. Reheat Chole.

GULAB JAMUN

Scented with rose water, these Indian sweetmeats
should be steeped in the warm sugar syrup while they
are still hot after deep frying.

175 g (6 oz) self-raising flour
1.25 ml (¼ tsp) salt
175 g (6 oz) ground almonds
75 g (3 oz) unsalted butter
about 150 ml (¼ pint) natural yogurt
flour for dusting
225 g (8 oz) granulated sugar
few drops of rose water
vegetable oil for deep frying
rose petals, to decorate

1 Sift the flour and salt into a bowl, then stir in the ground almonds. Cut in the butter, then rub in with the fingertips. Stir in enough yogurt to make a firm dough.

2 Roll the dough into 32 small balls, dust lightly with flour and place in a single layer on a tray. Chill in the refrigerator for at least 30 minutes.

3 Meanwhile, put the sugar in a heavy metal saucepan, pour in 600 ml (1 pint) cold water and heat gently until the sugar has dissolved. Increase the heat and bring to the boil. Lower the heat to moderate and simmer for 7–10 minutes until the mixture is syrupy. Remove from the heat, pour into a large, shallow serving bowl and stir in the rose water.

4 Heat the oil in a deep-fat fryer to 190°C (375°F) or until a cube of stale bread turns golden in 30 seconds. With a slotted spoon, lower the balls one at a time into the hot oil and deep fry in batches for 2–3 minutes until light golden all over. Remove with a slotted spoon and drain on absorbent kitchen paper while deep frying the remainder.

5 When all the balls have been deep fried, gently lower them into the warm sugar syrup. Leave until lukewarm, shaking the bowl occasionally and spooning over the syrup so that all the balls become impregnated with syrup. Serve lukewarm or chill in the refrigerator overnight and serve chilled. Sprinkle with rose petals just before serving.

Gulab Jamun (above right)

CELEBRATION LUNCH

This menu is ideal for a celebration as most of it is prepared well in advance with very little last minute attention required. Get the party off to a sparkling start by serving Champagne Cocktails and hand round some colourful and tangy Pickled Vegetables to sharpen appetites for the pleasures to come. The seafood platter is a light and attractive main dish to offer – and endlessly versatile. We've used a mixture of white fish with shellfish but you could use salmon instead of the haddock and halibut. If time is short and you don't want to make your own bread, buy 1 or 2 of the continental breads now available. Drizzle them with olive oil, sprinkle with chopped herbs, then wrap in foil and warm through in a hot oven. The dessert is ready and waiting in the fridge – a light mix of fine biscuits and poached, spiced fruits.

CHAMPAGNE COCKTAILS

Serve these luxurious cocktails in tulip or flute-shaped glasses to preserve the champagne bubbles for as long as possible.
The wine should be chilled, but not iced.

8 sugar lumps
Angostura bitters
40 ml (8 tsp) brandy
about 1 bottle Champagne or good quality dry, sparkling white wine

1 Place a lump of sugar in the bottom of each glass and soak with two or three dashes of Angostura bitters.
2 Add a teaspoon of brandy to each glass and top up with champagne or sparkling white wine just before serving.

Champagne Cocktails (above)

PICKLED VEGETABLES

The marinade can also be used for other lightly cooked vegetables, smoked oysters, and wild mushrooms.

400 g (14 oz) can artichoke hearts, drained
125 g (4 oz) black olives
2 medium courgettes, sliced
150 ml (¼ pint) oil
10 ml (2 tsp) dry mustard powder
30 ml (2 tbsp) white wine vinegar
grated rind of 1 orange and 45 ml (3 tbsp) juice
30 ml (2 tbsp) chopped fresh parsley
salt and freshly ground pepper

1 Quarter the artichoke hearts and place in a bowl with the olives and courgettes. Whisk together the remaining ingredients and stir in well.
2 Cover and marinate in the refrigerator for at least 12 hours. Serve with wooden cocktail sticks.

LEMON PEPPER SALAD

It's worth taking the time to shred the onions and peppers finely; use a very sharp knife to make it easier.

350 g (12 oz) mange tout, trimmed or fine asparagus tips
2 bunches spring onions, finely shredded
4 medium green peppers, cored, seeded and finely shredded
grated rind and juice of 1 lemon
pinch of caster sugar
125 ml (4 fl oz) olive oil
salt and coarsely ground pepper

1 Cook the mange tout or asparagus in boiling, salted water for 2–3 minutes or until just tender. Drain and refresh under cold water. Toss with the onions and peppers in a bowl.
2 Whisk together the grated rind and strained lemon juice, the sugar, olive oil and seasoning. Stir into the salad before serving.

DRINKS TO SERVE
Champagne is the obvious choice of wine for a celebration but it's expensive to serve throughout the meal. Offer your guests a champagne cocktail when they first arrive and perhaps serve champagne with dessert but move onto white wine with the rest of the meal.

GLAZED SEAFOOD PLATTER

Choose large heatproof platters for this dish.

450 g (1 lb) haddock fillet, skinned
900 g (2 lb) halibut fillet, skinned
175 g (6 oz) Florence fennel
600 ml (1 pint) dry white wine
300 ml (½ pint) fish stock
1 bay leaf
450 g (1 lb) queen scallops, cleaned
225 g (8 oz) shelled fresh mussels
225 g (8 oz) cooked peeled prawns
75 g (3 oz) butter
75 g (3 oz) plain flour
2 egg yolks
300 ml (½ pint) double cream
salt and freshly ground pepper
125 g (4 oz) Emmenthal cheese, coarsely grated

1 Cut the fish fillets into bite-sized pieces. Remove the feathery tops from the fennel, finely chop and reserve. Cut the fennel into wafer thin slices.

2 Place the fish and fennel in a large shallow pan and pour on the wine, stock and bay leaf. Bring to the boil, cover and simmer for 7–8 minutes or until the fish is just cooked.

3 With a slotted spoon remove the fish and fennel from the cooking liquor and arrange in a single layer on two large heatproof platters. Add the scallops and mussels to the cooking liquid, return to the boil and immediately remove with a slotted spoon. Scatter over the fish with the prawns.

4 Cover the platters with foil and keep warm in the oven at 170°C (325°F) mark 3. Melt the butter in a medium saucepan. Stir in the flour and cook, stirring, for 1–2 minutes. Strain in the poaching liquor, bring to the boil, stirring all the time, then simmer for 2–3 minutes until thickened.

5 Heat the grill. Beat the egg yolks and cream into the sauce. Season. Spoon evenly over the seafood and sprinkle with cheese. Place the platters under the grill until golden brown. Serve immediately garnished with the reserved fennel tops.

TOMATO HERB FOCACCIA

50 g (2 oz) sun dried tomatoes in oil, drained and chopped
450 g (1 lb) strong white flour
2.5 ml (½ tsp) salt
50 g (2 oz) butter
1 × 7 g sachet fast action dried yeast
15 ml (1 tbsp) chopped fresh thyme or rosemary
45 ml (3 tbsp) olive oil
1 egg
coarse salt
chopped fresh thyme or rosemary, to serve

1 Place the tomatoes in a small bowl and pour over 200 ml (7 fl oz) boiling water. Leave to soak for 15 minutes.

2 Place the flour and salt in a medium bowl and rub in the butter. Stir in the yeast.

3 Drain the tomatoes, reserving the liquid. Stir into the dry ingredients with the thyme.

4 Beat together the reserved liquid, olive oil and egg. Make a well in the centre of the flour mixture and pour in the egg mixture. Mix to a dough.

5 Turn the dough out onto a floured surface and knead for 5 minutes or until smooth.

6 On a greased baking sheet, press the dough into a rough 25.5 cm (10 inch) square. Cover with a clean tea towel and leave in a warm place for about 30 minutes until doubled in size. Brush with salt water, slash the top with a sharp knife and sprinkle with a little coarse salt.

7 Bake at 220°C (425°F) mark 7 for 15-20 minutes until golden brown. Sprinkle with chopped fresh thyme before serving.

To Freeze Overwrap and freeze for up to 1 month. Reheat from frozen at 200°C (400°F) mark 6 for about 10 minutes.

MIXED RED LEAF SALAD

Mix together a colourful combination of red salad leaves e.g. radicchio, oak leaf, lollo rosso, etc. Break into fork-sized pieces. Add a few sliced radishes. Toss in vinaigrette before serving.

Vanilla Wafers (left)

BUTTERED NEW POTATOES

1.4 kg (3 lb) small new potatoes, washed
salt
40 g (1½ oz) butter
45 ml (3 tbsp) chopped fresh mixed herbs such as parsley, chives, dill, tarragon

1 Put the potatoes in a saucepan of cold, salted water. Bring to the boil and boil for 10-20 minutes until tender.

2 Drain thoroughly, return to the pan with the butter and herbs and toss together.

SPICED FRUIT WAFERS

175 g (6 oz) caster sugar
pared rind and juice of 1 orange
1 cinnamon stick
6 fresh peaches
225 g (8 oz) redcurrants
225 g (8 oz) strawberries
300 ml (½ pint) double cream
142 ml (5 fl oz) soured cream or Greek-style yogurt
24 vanilla wafers
icing sugar for dusting
sprigs of redcurrants, strawberries and leaves, to decorate

1 Place the caster sugar in a medium saucepan with 300 ml (½ pint) water. Add the pared orange rind and cinnamon stick. Stir over a low heat until the sugar has completely dissolved. Bring to the boil, bubble for 2 minutes then remove from the heat.

2 Thickly slice the peaches into the hot liquid and add the redcurrants. Return to the heat and simmer for 2–3 minutes or until just tender. With a slotted spoon, remove the fruit to a bowl. Stir in the sliced strawberries, cover and set aside.

3 Return the liquid to the heat, bring to the boil and bubble for 4–5 minutes or until reduced and syrupy. Add the strained orange juice and cool.

4 Whip the double cream until it just holds its shape. Fold in the soured cream. Layer up the Vanilla Wafers with the cream and spiced fruits (allowing three wafers per person). Dust the top with icing sugar, decorate with redcurrants, or strawberries and leaves.

VANILLA WAFERS

MAKES 24
75 g (3 oz) butter, softened
75 g (3 oz) caster sugar
few drops vanilla flavouring
pinch of grated nutmeg
2 egg whites
75 g (3 oz) plain flour

1 Grease two baking sheets. Cream together the butter and sugar until very soft and light. Add the vanilla flavouring and nutmeg.

2 Lightly whisk the egg whites and gradually beat into the creamed mixture with a little of the flour. Fold in the remaining flour.

3 Drop heaped teaspoons of the mixture onto the baking sheets allowing plenty of space to spread. Bake at 200°C (400°F) mark 6 for 6–7 minutes or until set and pale golden around the edges. Remove from the baking sheet and leave to cool on a wire rack. Continue until all the mixture is used. Store in an airtight tin.

COUNTDOWN
One week ahead or more:
Make the Vanilla Wafers and freeze. Make the Tomato Herb Focaccia and freeze.
The day before:
Make the sauce for the Glazed Seafood Platter to the end of step 4. Cool, cover and refrigerate. Coarsely grate the cheese and refrigerate in a polythene bag. Prepare the Lemon Pepper Salad to the end of step 2. Cover and refrigerate. Whisk together the dressing ingredients. Cover and refrigerate. Prepare the fruit for the Spiced Fruit Wafers to the end of step 3. Cover and refrigerate the fruit and syrup separately.
To serve at 1pm:
11.00am: Prepare the mixed red salad leaves, cover and refrigerate. Make a vinaigrette dressing.
11.30am: Assemble the Spiced Fruit Wafers and refrigerate. Cook the fish and keep warm, covered, in a low oven.
12.30pm: Turn up the oven to 220°C (425°F) mark 7. Bring the sauce for the Glazed Seafood Platter to the boil. Off the heat beat in the egg yolks and cream. Season. Pour off any liquid from the fish platters back into the sauce. Spoon the sauce over the fish, sprinkle with cheese.
12.45pm: Reduce the oven temperature to 200°C (400°F) mark 6 and place the Tomato Herb Focaccia in the oven to reheat. Brown the seafood platters under the grill. Boil the new potatoes. Toss together the Lemon Pepper Salad and Mixed Red Leaf Salad and serve.

SINGAPORE LUNCH

SERVES 8

Go oriental and surprise your friends with your culinary skills. This informal lunch menu is perfect for easy entertaining, because everything apart from the dessert can be eaten buffet-style with fingers or chopsticks. Your guests will have great fun 'rolling their own' spring rolls and dunking them into a spicy hot dipping sauce, while the main course of whole sea bass can be spooned easily into bowls, with rice and stir fried vegetables, fruit and nuts making the perfect accompaniments. The delicately flavoured dessert, with its colourful decoration of coconut and tropical fruits, makes a splendid finale to a sumptuous meal.

SESAME PRAWN TOASTS

These crunchy fingers have a strong fishy flavour and make excellent nibbles for tempting guests' appetites when they arrive. Hand them round on a tray at the same time as the Singapore Slings.

175 g (6 oz) peeled prawns, thawed and thoroughly dried if frozen
2 spring onions, trimmed and roughly chopped
2.5 cm (1 inch) piece of fresh root ginger, peeled and roughly chopped
2 garlic cloves, skinned and roughly chopped
30 ml (2 level tbsp) cornflour
10 ml (2 tsp) soy sauce
10 ml (2 tsp) anchovy essence
12 slices stale white bread from a small loaf, crusts removed
25–40 g (1–1½ oz) sesame seeds
about 600 ml (1 pint) vegetable oil for deep frying
soy sauce for dipping
spring onion tassels to garnish (optional)

1 Put the prawns, spring onions, ginger and garlic in a food processor. Add the cornflour, soy sauce and anchovy essence and work to a thick paste.

2 Spread the bread slices evenly with the paste, then cut each slice lengthways into 3 rectangles. Sprinkle with sesame seeds and press down with your fingers so that they adhere to the paste. Chill in the refrigerator for at least 30 minutes.

3 Heat the oil in a wok to 190°C (375°F) or until a cube of stale bread turns golden in 30 seconds. With a slotted spoon, lower a batch of the bread slices, paste side down, into the hot oil. Deep fry for 2–3 minutes, turning for the last minute. Lift out with the slotted spoon, shake off the excess oil, then drain on absorbent kitchen paper and keep warm while deep frying the remainder.

4 Place a bowl of soy sauce in the centre of a large tray or platter. Arrange the toasts around the bowl like the spokes of a wheel. Garnish with spring onion tassels, if using. Serve immediately.

To Freeze Open freeze at the end of step 2. Pack into rigid containers, interleaving with greaseproof paper. Thaw in the refrigerator overnight, and continue from step 3.

SINGAPORE SLING

This heady aperitif was originally concocted at the famous Raffles Hotel in Singapore. It is the perfect cocktail to serve before an oriental meal.

225 ml (8 fl oz) gin
120 ml (8 tbsp) cherry brandy
120 ml (8 tbsp) lime or lemon juice
ice cubes
1.1 litres (2 pints) soda water
lime or lemon slices, cherries and fresh mint leaves (optional), to garnish

1 In a jug, mix together the gin, cherry brandy and lime or lemon juice.

2 Fill the bottoms of 8 glass tumblers with ice cubes. Pour over the gin mixture.

3 Top up the glasses with soda water, then quickly garnish with lime or lemon slices, cherries, and mint if using. Serve immediately.

Sesame Prawn Toasts, Singapore Sling and Nonya Spring Rolls (below)

DRINKS TO SERVE
Choose Singapore Slings as a cocktail to set the scene, then offer refreshing drinks for the rest of the meal. Chilled Tiger beer or lager; champagne or sparkling dry white wine; and plenty of mineral water or iced water.

COOK'S HINT
Spring onion tassels make an attractive garnish. Trim, then make several lengthways cuts in the onions, keeping the root end intact. Drop into a bowl of iced water and chill for at least 30 minutes until the cut ends curl and open out.

NONYA SPRING ROLLS

1 bunch spring onions, trimmed
2 fresh green chillies
125 g (4 oz) pork fillet
20 g (¾ oz) dried shiitake mushrooms, soaked in warm water for 20 minutes
30 ml (2 tbsp) vegetable oil
2 garlic cloves, skinned and finely chopped
175 g (6 oz) peeled prawns, thawed and thoroughly dried if frozen
125 g (4 oz) beansprouts
45 ml (3 tbsp) soy sauce
salt and freshly ground pepper
16 rice paper wrappers (see Cook's Hint)
about 120 ml (8 tbsp) hoisin (barbecue) sauce
16 small crisp Cos or iceberg lettuce leaves
fresh mint or basil leaves
DIPPING SAUCE
125 ml (4 fl oz) dry sherry
125 ml (4 fl oz) soy sauce
2 garlic cloves, skinned and crushed
5 ml (1 tsp) caster sugar
5 ml (1 tsp) lemon juice

1 Cut the spring onions, on the diagonal, into 2.5 cm (1 inch) lengths. Cut the chillies lengthways, then open out and rinse under cold running water to remove the seeds. Chop the flesh finely, discarding the ends. Finely chop the pork. Drain the shiitake mushrooms and slice thinly.

2 To make the sauce, mix all the ingredients together in a small serving bowl.

3 Heat a wok until hot. Add the oil and heat until hot but not smoking. Add the spring onions, chillies and garlic and stir fry over moderate heat for 5 minutes. Remove from the pan with a slotted spoon and set aside to drain on absorbent kitchen paper.

4 Meanwhile, add the pork to the pan and stir fry for 2–3 minutes or until it changes colour. Add the prawns, mushrooms and beansprouts and stir fry over high heat for 3–5 minutes, then return the spring onion mixture to the pan and add the soy sauce. Stir until all the ingredients are evenly blended, then add salt and pepper to taste. Remove from the heat and keep warm.

5 One at a time, dip the rice paper wrappers in a bowl of lukewarm water, to make them pliable, then drain them.

6 Let each guest take a rice paper wrapper, spread it with about 7.5 ml (1½ tsp) hoisin sauce, then place 1 lettuce leaf on top, a few basil or mint leaves and a spoonful of pork and prawn filling. The ends of the wrapper and lettuce should then be tucked in, and the wrapper and lettuce rolled up together around the filling. Hand the sauce separately so that guests can dip their spring rolls into it before eating.

KETTLE-COOKED SEA BASS

Nothing is quite so impressive for a dinner party as a whole fish carried to the table on a large fish platter, and yet nothing could be more quick and easy to prepare and cook.

1.6–1.8 kg (3½–4 lb) sea bass, gutted with head and tail left on
1 large bunch spring onions, trimmed
2 celery stalks, trimmed
5 cm (2 inch) piece of fresh root ginger
vegetable oil for brushing
60 ml (4 tbsp) soy sauce
60 ml (4 tbsp) dry sherry
salt and freshly ground pepper
30 ml (2 tbsp) vegetable oil, 15 ml (1 tbsp) sesame oil, 30 ml (2 tbsp) soy sauce, 5 ml (1 tsp) caster sugar, 8 spring onions, trimmed and finely shredded, celery leaves to serve

1 Wash the fish inside and out, then dry thoroughly, With kitchen shears or scissors, cut the tail into a 'V' shape. With a sharp knife, make several deep diagonal slashes on both sides of the fish.

2 Finely shred the spring onions and slice the celery and root ginger into very thin matchsticks.

3 Pour water under the rack of a fish kettle and place half of the spring onion, celery and ginger on the rack. Brush the outside of the fish lightly with oil, then place over the flavourings on the rack. Sprinkle the remaining spring onions, celery and ginger over the fish, then the soy sauce, sherry, and salt and pepper to taste.

4 Cover the kettle with its lid, bring the

water slowly to the boil, then simmer for 20 minutes or until the flesh of the fish is opaque when tested near the bone.

5 To serve, heat the oils in a wok or heavy frying pan, add the soy sauce and sugar and stir well to mix. Add the shredded spring onions and stir to coat.

6 Discard the flavourings from on top and transfer the fish to a warmed large serving plate. Arrange the freshly cooked spring onion over the fish in a criss-cross pattern and drizzle with the cooking liquid. Serve immediately, garnished with celery leaves.

ORIENTAL VEGETABLE, FRUIT AND NUT STIR FRY

SAUCE
1–2 fresh green chillies, halved, seeded and chopped
15 ml (1 tbsp) sambal rojak (see cook's hint)
15 ml (1 tbsp) dark soft brown sugar
juice of 1 lime or lemon
10 ml (2 level tsp) cornflour
30 ml (2 tbsp) crunchy peanut butter
60 ml (4 tbsp) soy sauce
STIR FRY
45 ml (3 tbsp) vegetable oil
1 bunch spring onions, trimmed and cut diagonally into 2.5 cm (1 inch) lengths
5 cm (2 inch) piece of fresh root ginger, peeled and cut into matchsticks
2 garlic cloves, skinned and cut into slivers
6 medium carrots, cut into matchsticks
3 medium red peppers, cored, seeded and sliced lengthways
225 g (8 oz) fine green beans, topped and tailed, and cut in half, crossways
225 g (8 oz) mange tout, topped and tailed and cut in half, crossways
1 small pineapple, peeled, cored and cut in chunks
75 g (3 oz) dry roasted peanuts, coarsely chopped
125 g (4 oz) bean sprouts
salt and freshly ground pepper

1 To make the sauce, pound the chilli flesh in a mortar and pestle with the sambal rojak, sugar and lime or lemon juice. Dissolve the cornflour in a jug with a few teaspoonfuls of cold water. Add the chilli mixture, the peanut butter and soy sauce and stir well to mix, then stir in 150 ml (¼ pint) cold water.

2 Heat a wok until hot. Add 30 ml (2 tbsp) oil and heat until hot but not smoking. Add the spring onions, ginger and garlic and stir fry for about 5 minutes to flavour the oil. Remove from the pan with a slotted spoon and set aside to drain on absorbent kitchen paper.

3 Heat the remaining oil in the wok, add the carrots to the wok and stir fry for 3 minutes, then add the peppers and stir fry for 2–3 minutes. Next add the beans and mange-touts and stir fry for 2–3 minutes until evenly mixed with the carrots and peppers but still very crisp. Remove all the vegetables from the wok and set aside with the spring onion mixture.

4 Stir the sauce ingredients in the jug, then pour into the wok. Stir over high heat until thickened and dark, then return all the vegetables to the wok. Add the pineapple, beansprouts and two-thirds of the peanuts and stir fry for a few minutes until heated through and evenly mixed with the vegetables. Add salt and pepper to taste, then turn into a warmed large serving bowl. Sprinkle with the remaining peanuts and serve hot.

STEAMED OR BOILED RICE

Allow about 50 g (2 oz) long grain or glutinous rice per person. Boil in salted water or steam until al dente (following the packet instructions for timings).

Rice may be cooked in advance and reheated in a steamer, in a tightly covered greased dish in the oven, or in the microwave.

COOK'S HINT
To make 600 ml (1 pint) thin **coconut milk**, put half of a 200 g (7 oz) packet creamed coconut in a heatproof measuring jug and pour in boiling water to come up to the 600 ml (1 pint) mark. Stir until dissolved. For thick milk, use the whole packet.

◆

COUNTDOWN
The day before:
Make Coconut Custards to end of step 3. Prepare Sesame Prawn Toasts to end of step 2; chill in the refrigerator overnight.
On the day:
Prepare sea bass and leave in fish kettle in a cold place. Prepare ingredients for the stir fry; cover and refrigerate. Prepare coconut and fruits for dessert; keep covered in refrigerator. Prepare dipping sauce, lettuce and ingredients for filling for spring rolls; cover and refrigerate. Make spring onion tassels, if using, and prepare serving tray and bowl of soy sauce for Sesame Prawn Toasts. Measure ingredients and get garnishes ready for Singapore Slings.
To serve at 1pm:
12.15pm: Turn out Coconut Custards; keep in refrigerator.
12.30pm: Deep fry Sesame Prawn Toasts; keep warm, uncovered, in moderate oven.
12.45pm: Cook filling and moisten rice-paper wrappers for Nonya Spring Rolls; keep filling warm.
1pm: Make Singapore Slings and serve Sesame Prawn Toasts. Put rice and sea bass on to cook while starter is being served. Cook vegetable stir fry in between courses. Arrange tropical fruit around dessert and top with coconut just before serving.

◆

COCONUT CUSTARDS WITH TROPICAL FRUITS

These little custards are an oriental version of crème caramel. The coconut milk used in the making of the custard separates out and forms a coconut-flavoured layer, with smooth creamy custard underneath.

225 g (8 oz) granulated sugar
3 eggs
2 egg yolks
30 ml (2 tbsp) caster sugar
600 ml (1 pint) thin coconut milk (see Cook's Hint)
300 ml (½ pint) evaporated milk
150 ml (¼ pint) fresh milk
60 ml (4 tbsp) shredded or desiccated coconut, 2 mangoes, peeled, 1 large pawpaw (papaya), peeled, juice of 1–2 limes, pulp from 2 passion fruit, to serve

1 Have ready 8 warmed 150 ml (¼ pint) ramekin dishes. Put the granulated sugar in a heavy metal saucepan, pour in 150 ml (¼ pint) cold water and heat gently, stirring occasionally, until the sugar has dissolved. Increase the heat and boil, without stirring, until dark caramel in colour. Immediately pour into the ramekins, swirling the caramel around the sides as quickly as possible. Set aside.

2 Put the eggs, egg yolks and caster sugar in a bowl and beat to mix. Pour the coconut and evaporated milks into a saucepan and heat to scalding point. Pour over the egg mixture, stirring all the time.

3 Strain the custard into the ramekins. Place the ramekins in a roasting pan and pour in enough hot water to come halfway up the sides. Cover with lightly oiled foil, then bake in the oven at 170°C (325°F) mark 3 for 50 minutes or until set, but still wobbly around the edges. Remove from the oven and leave to cool in the pan of hot water. Chill in the refrigerator overnight.

4 Meanwhile, put the coconut in a wok or heavy frying pan and dry fry over low heat for 5–6 minutes, stirring all the time until an even golden colour. Cut the mangoes and pawpaw lengthways into neat thin slices.

5 To serve, run a knife around the edge of each custard, then carefully invert onto dessert plates, allowing the caramel to run down the sides. Arrange a few slices of mango and pawpaw to the side of each custard, then sprinkle with lime juice and squeeze the passion fruit pulp over the top. Sprinkle toasted coconut on top of each custard.

Coconut Custards with Tropical Fruits (below)

VENISON LUNCH

M	E	N	U

CHESTNUT AND ROASTED GARLIC SOUP

CELERIAC 'STRAW'

VENISON COLLOPS WITH ORANGES

AUTUMN PUDDING

SERVES 8

This autumnal meal makes the most of seasonal ingredients. Roasting the garlic and chestnuts for the soup gives it a sweet and smoky flavour, so that the garlic loses its sting! Young venison is best cooked quickly and served pink or rare as in this dish; don't be tempted to overcook or it will become tough. Cutting the celeriac into straw is well worth the effort – it looks pretty and tastes marvellous with the venison. Serve with your favourite vegetables in season.

Finish with the prettiest Autumn Pudding made with fruits such as blackberries or loganberries and a little apple or pear. Served with lashings of cream, there's nothing more tempting.

CHESTNUT AND ROASTED GARLIC SOUP

225 g (8 oz) dried chestnuts, soaked overnight
4 large garlic cloves, unpeeled
three 425 g (15 oz) cans game or beef consommé
pinch freshly grated nutmeg
salt and freshly ground pepper
120 ml (8 tbsp) Greek-style yogurt
5 ml (1 tsp) curry paste
fresh coriander leaves, to garnish

1 Drain the chestnuts and place in a medium saucepan. Cover with cold water, bring to the boil and simmer for about 20 minutes until tender. Drain.

Chestnut and Roasted Garlic Soup (page 65)

2 Place the garlic cloves with the chestnuts on a baking tray and roast in the oven at 200°C (400°F) mark 6 for 15-20 minutes or until the garlic is soft to the touch and the chestnuts are browning. Cool slightly then pop the garlic cloves out of their skins.

3 Place the garlic, chestnuts and consommé in a blender or food processor and process until smooth. Pour into a saucepan, bring almost to the boil and season to taste with nutmeg, salt and pepper. Simmer very gently for 5 minutes to allow the flavours to blend. If necessary, add a little water to thin.

4 Mix the yogurt with the curry paste. Serve the soup in warmed bowls with a dollop of yogurt, garnished with coriander leaves.

To Freeze Cool, then chill the soup in the refrigerator. Pour into rigid containers and seal. Freeze for up to three months. Thaw overnight and reheat gently. Do not freeze the yogurt mixture.

CELERIAC 'STRAW'

| 450 g (1 lb) celeriac, washed and peeled |
| lemon juice |
| salt |
| vegetable oil for deep frying |

1 Halve the celeriac bulbs and lay cut sides down. Slice *very* thinly and cut these slices into thin strips by stacking and slicing them with a very sharp knife. Drop into a bowl of cold water with a little lemon juice added.
2 Heat the vegetable oil in a deep fat fryer to 180°C (350°F). Drain and dry the celeriac. Fry in small batches for 1–2 minutes or until crisp and golden. Drain on absorbent kitchen paper, sprinkle with salt and keep warm while frying the remainder. Serve hot.

VENISON COLLOPS WITH ORANGES

Oranges go well with the rich flavour of venison. High protein, low fat venison is ideal cooked quickly in this way. Fillet steak is an alternative if venison is unavailable.

| 900 g (2 lb) venison fillet or eight 125–175 g (4–6 oz) venison steaks |
| 15–30 ml (1–2 tbsp) vegetable oil |
| 600 ml (1 pint) good venison or beef stock |
| 15–30 ml (2–3 tbsp) orange marmalade |
| 3 juniper berries, crushed |
| 3 oranges |
| salt and freshly ground pepper |

1 Cut the venison into eight steaks, if necessary. Heat the oil in a heavy frying pan, until smoking. Add the steaks and fry for 1–2 minutes on each side until well browned. Transfer to a shallow ovenproof dish, cover with foil and set aside.
2 Add half of the stock to the frying pan, scraping the bottom to dislodge any sediment. Add the remaining stock, marmalade and juniper berries and bring to the boil. Meanwhile, grate the rind from one of the oranges and add to the pan. Boil until reduced by half, then season with salt and pepper.
3 Cut the rind and pith from the oranges. Cut down in between each membrane to remove the segments. Cover and set aside.
4 Bake the steaks in the oven at 200°C (400°F) mark 6 for 10 minutes only. Uncover and pour any juices into the sauce.
5 While the meat is cooking, reheat the sauce with the orange segments over low heat.
6 Serve the steaks on individual heated plates surrounded with orange segments and a little of the sauce.

DRINKS TO SERVE
Serve a chilled dry sherry with the soup and a hearty red Burgundy or Bordeaux with the venison. A small glass of Marsala or Madeira with the dessert would be sheer indulgence!

COOK'S HINTS
1 Good **meat or game stock** is essential for this dish – save and freeze meat bones until you have enough for a big pot of stock.

2 **Dried chestnuts** are available in good health food stores or Italian and continental delicatessens. If using fresh chestnuts, slit the shells with a sharp knife to prevent them exploding, place in a pan of cold water and slowly bring to the boil. Turn off the heat and remove the shells and the inner brown skins while still hot. Keep them in hot water while you shell them, then cook as above. If really pressed for time, use two 425 g cans peeled whole chestnuts in water, drained, or one 425 g can unsweetened chestnut purée, but the flavour will not be as good.

MICROWAVE HINT
To roast **fresh chestnuts** in the microwave, slit the skins with a sharp knife, spread the chestnuts out on a plate and cook on HIGH for 3 minutes per 225 g (8 oz). Stir once during cooking.

AUTUMN PUDDING

Exactly the same as summer pudding, but with a juicy mixture of the finest fruits of autumn. Keep any left-over juice to 'top up' any dry patches of bread.

MAKES 2 PUDDINGS

1.4 kg (3 lb) mixed autumn fruit, such as apples, loganberries, blackberries, plums, prepared

about 50 g (2 oz) light soft brown sugar

16-20 thin slices of day old bread, crusts removed

---

1 Stew the fruit gently with 60-90 ml (4-6 tbsp) water and the sugar until soft but still retaining their shape. The exact amount of water and sugar depend on the ripeness and sweetness of the fruit.

2 Meanwhile cut two rounds from two slices of bread to neatly fit the bottom of two 1.1 litre (2 pint) pudding basins and cut 12-16 slices of bread into fingers about 5 cm (2 inches) wide. Put the rounds at the bottom of the basins and arrange the fingers around the sides, overlapping them so there are no spaces.

3 When the fruit is cooked, and still hot, pour it gently into the basins, dividing it equally between the two. Be careful not to disturb the bread framework. Reserve about 90 ml (6 tbsp) of the juice. When the basins are full, cut the remaining bread and use to cover the fruit so that lids are formed.

4 Put a basin or saucer which just fits inside the basin, on top of each, and put weights on top. Leave the puddings until cold, then put into the refrigerator and chill overnight.

5 To serve, run a knife carefully around the edge to loosen, then invert each pudding onto a serving plate. Pour the reserved juice on top. Serve cold with cream.

To Freeze Pack and freeze at the end of step 5. Freeze any extra juices seperately. Thaw overnight at cool room temperature and chill before turning out to serve. (The pudding will be quite soft after freezing.)

Autumn Pudding (right)

DINNER PARTIES

Dinner parties, whether formal or informal, need to be planned and prepared in advance if you are to enjoy them. Formal dinner parties need rather more in the way of advanced preparation. Start by making a list of the food you intend to give your guests at each course, bearing in mind how busy you will be around the day of the dinner party, and choosing dishes that will fit into your schedule. Start your menu with one or two items to offer your friends to eat with drinks before dinner – a bowl of cashews, almonds or pecan nuts, which have been toasted and sprinkled with salt and a little cayenne pepper, or a plate of marinated black or green olives, or a dish of vegetable crudités served on a large platter with a bowl of dip in the middle.

If you wish, offer more elaborate eats with the pre-dinner drinks and dispense with a first course at dinner. Eats such as small savoury profiteroles, triangles of wholemeal toast spread liberally with smoked fish pâté, smoked salmon rolled in brown bread rolls with walnut butter – there are numerous delicious things to be eaten with the fingers with drinks before dinner.

If you don't have much time available on the day, plan at least one cold course, if not two – ideally, the first course and the dessert – making maximum use of the freezer. If you can, set the first course out on plates and garnish shortly before your friends arrive. A cold pudding means that, once the main course is served, the cook can relax at last, knowing that the evening's cooking is complete.

MEDITERRANEAN DINNER PARTY

SERVES 8

This robust menu marries the special flavours from the Mediterranean. Bright, sun-ripened peppers; sweet, pink-skinned garlic; fruity olive oil and creamy yogurt – all tastes and colours that evoke memories of leisurely meals enjoyed in a hot, sunny climate. To establish the theme as soon as guests arrive, serve plump green or black olives with aperitifs. Alternatively, pistachio nuts, salted almonds, toasted hazelnuts or sunflower seeds are all appropriate and good for nibbling.

The starter is a mouthwatering mixture of marinated peppers and creamy Greek yogurt. It should be served at room temperature with warm bread (olive or sesame is good), or sliced, toasted baguettes, spread with Tapenade (see page 245). Lamb is popular throughout the Mediterranean; roasted whole, barbecued over charcoal on a spit or in chunks on skewers for kebabs. Here it's cooked with a heady mixture of rosemary, garlic and anchovies.

For dessert, a tart straight from the Pâtisserie of France, a crisp sweet pastry crust full to bursting with crème pâtissière and glistening fruits.

ROASTED PEPPERS WITH YOGURT AND PISTACHIO NUTS

For maximum visual impact, choose a colourful mixture of peppers for this simple starter.

8 large sweet peppers
60 ml (4 tbsp) virgin olive oil
salt and freshly ground pepper
60 ml (4 tbsp) chopped fresh marjoram or oregano
few salad leaves
450 ml (¾ pint) Greek-style yogurt
125 g (4 oz) shelled pistachio nuts, roughly chopped
fresh herb sprigs, to garnish

1 Place the peppers in a grill pan and cook under a hot grill until the skin is blackened. Turn the peppers over and cook until the other side is blackened. This will take at least 10–15 minutes.

2 Cover with a damp cloth and leave until cool enough to handle. Carefully peel off the skins. Cut into chunky strips and place in a shallow dish. Pour over the olive oil and season generously with salt and pepper. Sprinkle with the marjoram. Leave to marinate until ready to serve.

3 To serve, arrange the peppers on eight plates with a few salad leaves. Place a large spoonful of yogurt on each plate and sprinkle with the pistachio nuts. Generously grind black pepper over the top and garnish with herb sprigs.

DRINKS TO SERVE
Richly flavoured foods call for robust wines and a Spanish Rioja would be ideal with Mediterranean flavours. Offer a choice of red or white to suit all tastes.

COOK'S HINTS
1 If making the **pepper and yogurt** starter a long time in advance, keep it covered in the refrigerator. Remove from the refrigerator at least 1 hour before serving. It should be served at room temperature, not chilled.

2 If you can, buy **marinated olives** from a good Greek or Italian delicatessen, or make your own by storing the olives in jars with garlic, thyme and lemon slices. If kept covered with olive oil, the olives will keep indefinitely.

MENU SUGGESTIONS
Alternative starters for this meal: Tomatoes with Goat's Cheese and Basil (page 245) or Fennel and Orange Soup (page 243). For a quick alternative pudding slice sweet seedless oranges, sprinkle with a little orange flower water and dust generously with icing sugar.

Roasted Peppers with Yogurt and Pistachio Nuts (left)

LAMB WITH OLIVE JUICES

50 g (2 oz) can anchovy fillets in oil
1 garlic clove, skinned and crushed
15 ml (1 tbsp) chopped fresh rosemary
2 kg (4½ lb) leg lamb
60 ml (4 tbsp) virgin olive oil
150 ml (¼ pint) meat stock
45 ml (3 tbsp) white wine vinegar
300 ml (½ pint) dry white wine
salt and freshly ground pepper
fresh rosemary and thyme, to garnish

1 Crush the anchovies with their oil, and the garlic and rosemary in a pestle and mortar. Put a roasting rack in a roasting tin, large enough to hold the lamb. Place the lamb on the rack and spread with the anchovy paste. Pour in the oil.

2 Roast the lamb in the oven at 180°C (350°F) mark 4 for 20 minutes per 450 g (1 lb), basting occasionally with the olive oil. Transfer the lamb to a warmed serving platter and keep warm for about 15 minutes before carving. To make the gravy, skim off the fat from the roasting tin.

3 Pour the stock, wine vinegar and the wine into the tin and stir to dislodge the sediment. Bring to the boil, and simmer for a couple of minutes then season to taste with salt and pepper. Pour the gravy into a gravy boat. Serve the meat garnished with herbs.

POTATOES WITH ROAST GARLIC

1.8 kg (4 lb) potatoes, peeled
2 whole bulbs of garlic
lard, dripping or olive oil
salt and freshly ground pepper
chopped fresh parsley, to garnish

1 Cut the potatoes into large even sized pieces, place them in cold salted water and bring to the boil. Boil for 2 minutes then drain thoroughly.

2 Heat the fat in a roasting tin in the oven. Add the potatoes and baste with the fat until all sides are coated. (Meanwhile separate the garlic into cloves, and remove the loose papery skins leaving the inner skin attached). Scatter the garlic over the potatoes. Cook at 180°C (350°F) mark 4 for the same amount of time as the lamb, turning occasionally.

3 When the meat is cooked, continue roasting the potatoes at 220°C (425°F) mark 7 for 15 minutes until crisp and golden brown. Season with salt and pepper and sprinkle with parsley.

SAUTÉED AUBERGINES AND COURGETTES

Choose small aubergines, in preference to the larger plump variety, as they are less bitter.

4 small aubergines
salt and freshly ground pepper
450 g (1 lb) courgettes
45 ml (3 tbsp) olive oil
30 ml (2 tbsp) chopped fresh oregano or marjoram
15 ml (1 tbsp) toasted sesame seeds

1 Cut the aubergines lengthways into 2.5 cm (1 inch) slices. Cut the slices across into 1 cm (½ inch) wide fingers. Put the aubergines in a colander and sprinkle generously with salt. Leave to dégorge for at least 30 minutes.

2 Rinse the aubergines and dry thoroughly. Trim the courgettes and cut into pieces about the same size as the aubergine.

3 Heat the oil in a large heavy-based frying pan and sauté the aubergines for 3 minutes. Add the courgettes and continue cooking for 3–4 minutes or until just tender but not soggy. Season with salt and pepper. Serve garnished with oregano or marjoram and sprinkle with the sesame seeds.

Tart of Many Fruits, page 76 (shown right)

MIXED LEAF SALAD

Include a good mixture of crisp green leaves choosing several from the wonderful varieties now available. Mâche, watercress, oak leaf lettuce, rocket and curly endive are good perhaps with chicory and radicchio for bitterness. Dress in a sharp vinaigrette made in the usual way with virgin olive oil and white wine vinegar, flavoured simply with a little French mustard and salt and pepper.

GOAT'S CHEESE AND BREAD

Offer several different goat's cheeses at the peak of ripeness. Look out for different varieties in your local cheese shop or delicatessen. Serve arranged on a wicker tray or platter, decorated with vine leaves and perhaps a few fresh dates, figs or grapes. Serve with good, fresh bread and unsalted butter.

> **COOK'S HINT**
> **Aubergines** can contain bitter juices, especially when mature. Salting and draining before cooking helps to remove these juices and also reduces the aubergine's tendency to absorb large quantities of oil during cooking. This process is known by the French name – dégorger. Courgettes and cucumber may also be treated in this way.

MICROWAVE HINT
To make the **apricot glaze** in the microwave, put all the ingredients in a small heatproof bowl and cook on HIGH for 30 seconds–1 minute or until just melted.

COUNTDOWN
The Day Before:
Prepare the peppers by following step 1. Cover and refrigerate. Make and bake the pastry for the tart. Store in an airtight container. Make the crème pâtissière and refrigerate.
On the Day:
Prepare the paste for the lamb. Cover and refrigerate. Peel the potatoes and leave in salted cold water.
To serve at 8pm:
6.00pm: Cook the potatoes as in step 1. Spread the paste over the lamb and roast following step 2. Put the potatoes for roasting in at the same time following step 2. Fill the pastry case with the crème pâtissière and decorate with the fresh fruit. Make the glaze and brush the tart. Leave in the refrigerator until ready to serve. Wash the salad ingredients, dry well, cover and refrigerate. Make the dressing but don't add yet.
7.00pm: Arrange the starters, cover and leave in a cool place. Prepare the aubergines and leave to dégorge. Prepare the courgettes. Arrange the goat's cheeses on a plate and decorate.
7.45pm: Cook the Sautéed Aubergines and Courgettes. Cover and keep warm in a low oven.
Remove the lamb from the oven and keep warm. Make the gravy. Continue cooking the potatoes by following step 3.

TART OF MANY FRUITS

Choose a colourful mixture of fruits to top this tart. Be generous with the fruit so that the Crème Pâtissière is well covered. It can also be served without the glaze and decorated simply with a dusting of icing sugar.

CRÈME PÂTISSIÈRE
568 ml (1 pint) milk
1 vanilla pod
4 eggs
75 g (3 oz) caster sugar
60 ml (4 level tbsp) plain flour
75 ml (5 level tbsp) cornflour
300 ml (½ pint) double cream
PASTRY
175 g (6 oz) plain flour
pinch of salt
75 g (3 oz) caster sugar
125 g (4 oz) butter, chilled
1 egg, beaten
FILLING AND GLAZE
selection of fresh fruit in season, prepared as necessary
135 ml (9 tbsp) apricot conserve
45 ml (3 tbsp) orange flavour liqueur
15 ml (1 tbsp) orange flower water

1 Put the milk and the vanilla pod in a heavy-based saucepan and heat gently until just boiling. Remove from the heat and leave to infuse for 30 minutes.

2 To make the pastry, sift the flour and salt together on a clean surface. Make a well in the centre of the mixture and add the sugar, butter and egg. Using the fingertips of one hand, pinch and work the sugar, butter and egg together until well blended.

3 Gradually work in all the flour, adding a little water if necessary to bind together. Knead lightly until the dough is smooth, then wrap and leave to rest in the refrigerator for about 1 hour.

4 Roll out the pastry on a lightly floured surface and use to line a greased 28 cm (11 inch) fluted, round, loose-bottomed flan tin. Cover and chill in the refrigerator for at least 30 minutes.

5 When the milk has infused for at least 30 minutes, make the crème pâtissière. Cream the eggs and sugar together until really pale and thick.

6 Sift the flour and cornflour into a bowl, then gradually add a little of the milk to make a smooth paste. Gradually beat the flour mixture into the egg mixture.

7 Remove the vanilla pod from the milk, then reheat until just boiling. Pour onto the egg mixture, in a steady stream, stirring all the time.

8 Strain the mixture back into the saucepan. Reheat gently, stirring all the time until the custard coats the back of a spoon. Pour the custard into a clean bowl, cover the top with a piece of damp greaseproof paper and leave to cool.

9 Bake the pastry case blind in the oven at 190°C (375°F) mark 5 for about 15–20 minutes. Remove the baking beans and greaseproof paper and cook for a further 10 minutes or until the base is cooked through. Cool on a wire rack.

10 When both the pastry and the crème pâtissière are cool, remove the pastry case from the tin and place on a large flat serving plate or platter. Lightly whip the cream and fold into the crème pâtissière. Fill the pastry case with the mixture. Arrange the fruit on top, allowing some of it to tumble over the edge.

11 To make the glaze, gently heat the apricot conserve with the liqueur and orange flower water. Do not boil. Brush the tart generously with the glaze. Serve on a large platter surrounded by fresh flowers, leaves and fruits.

To Freeze The baked pastry case can be frozen. Bake as directed, cool, overwrap and freeze for up to 3 months. Thaw at room temperature for 3–4 hours. If liked, re-crisp in a warm oven for a few minutes, cool and use as directed.

WINTER DINNER PARTY

M	E	N	U

PARSLEYED LINGUINE WITH CLAMS AND SMOKED SALMON

DIJON-GLAZED PORK MEDALLIONS

BAKED PEPPERS WITH WILD RICE

JULIENNE OF ROOT VEGETABLES

WAFER-WRAPPED APPLE AND GOOSEBERRY POUCHES

CHOCOLATE AND CHESTNUT CREAM VACHERIN

SERVES 8

Here is a menu rich in flavours to perk up jaded winter palates. A simple, yet impressive linguine dish starts the meal. Then versatile pork tenderloin is sliced and glazed with a rich sauce of mustard, Madeira and crème fraîche. Vegetable accompaniments are kept simple to complement the richness of the pork. A julienne of winter roots makes the most of vegetables in season and a dish of green and red peppers filled with wild rice risotto adds a touch of extravagance. If guests are potato fans, include some jacket baked potatoes, too, to keep everyone happy. Pretty little filo pouches of apple and gooseberry sauce can be made in advance, ready to reheat before serving with the pork.

For those with a sweet tooth, the dessert should fit the bill splendidly. Layers of hazelnut meringue are sandwiched together with a luscious mixture of sweetened chestnut purée, chocolate and cream. Alternatively, for a simpler dessert, serve a bowl of fresh strawberries, a luxury during winter.

Parsleyed Linguine with Clams and Smoked Salmon (above)

PARSLEYED LINGUINE WITH CLAMS AND SMOKED SALMON

If available, use a mixture of spinach and egg linguine.

15 ml (1 tbsp) vegetable oil
550 g (1¼ lb) fresh or 450 g (1 lb) dried linguine
75 g (3 oz) unsalted butter
1 garlic clove, skinned and crushed
45–60 ml (3–4 tbsp) chopped fresh parsley or use 30 ml (2 tbsp) dried parsley
30 ml (2 tbsp) lemon juice
freshly ground black pepper
290 g (10 oz) can baby clams in brine, drained and rinsed
225 g (8 oz) thinly sliced smoked salmon, cut in thin strips
15–30 ml (1–2 tbsp) grated Parmesan cheese

1 Bring a large saucepan of salted water to the boil. Add the oil and linguine. Return to the boil and cook until just tender (about 3–4 minutes for fresh; 10–12 minutes for dried or according to the packet instructions). Drain well.

2 Melt the butter in a large frying pan, add the garlic, parsley and drained pasta and toss together for 1 minute. Add the lemon juice and pepper (do not add any salt), then stir in the clams and smoked salmon and toss over a medium heat for 1–2 minutes or until heated through.

3 Sprinkle with the Parmesan cheese and serve at once.

DIJON-GLAZED PORK MEDALLIONS

Fillet of pork is a lean and tender choice for a special meal. In this dish it is cut into medallions and beaten out to form thin rounds (which cook quickly). Veal escalopes could be used instead of pork, if wished.

1.4 kg (3 lb) pork tenderloins
salt and freshly ground pepper
15 ml (1 tbsp) vegetable oil
1 onion, skinned and finely chopped
1 garlic clove, skinned and crushed
65 g (2½ oz) butter
45 ml (3 tbsp) Madeira or Marsala
450 ml (¾ pint) chicken stock
15 ml (1 tbsp) Dijon mustard
175 g (6 oz) crème fraîche
25 ml (1½ level tbsp) plain flour
fresh sage leaves, shredded, to garnish

1 Using a sharp knife at a slightly diagonal angle, slice each tenderloin into 1 cm (½ inch) thick slices. Put the slices between two sheets of greaseproof paper and, using a meat mallet or rolling pin, pound the slices firmly until they are thin. Sprinkle with salt and pepper.

2 Heat the oil in a large frying pan and gently fry the onion and garlic for about 5 minutes, then remove from pan. Add 50 g (2 oz) butter to the pan and fry the medallions, a few at a time, for 2-3 minutes until the pork is just cooked on each side. Remove from the pan and keep warm while cooking the remainder in the same way. Remove from pan and keep warm.

3 Add the Madeira to the pan and stir in the onion mixture, stock, mustard and crème fraîche. Bring to the boil and boil rapidly for about 4 minutes until partially reduced. Meanwhile, mix together the remaining butter and flour to form a paste. Gradually add to the sauce, stirring all the time. Boil for 2 minutes, stirring until the sauce is thickened.

4 Return pork to the pan and heat through for 2 minutes, spooning the sauce over during heating. Serve garnished with sage.

BAKED PEPPERS WITH WILD RICE FILLING

Despite its name, wild rice is an aquatic grass native to Canada and North America. It has a fragrant, nutty flavour and a crunchy texture. Prepare the rice mixture and the peppers well in advance to save time later on.

175 g (6 oz) mixed long grain and wild rice
salt and freshly ground pepper
2 small red peppers
2 small green peppers
a little oil, for brushing
50 g (2 oz) butter
1 onion, skinned and chopped
175 g (6 oz) button mushrooms, sliced
good pinch of cayenne pepper

1 Cook the rice in a large saucepan of boiling water for about 15 minutes or until tender. Drain well and rinse with boiling water, then drain well again.

2 Cut the peppers in half lengthways. Leave the stalks in place but discard the seeds and pith. Blanch the peppers in boiling water for 5 minutes; drain, then plunge into cold water and leave until cold. Drain and pat dry, then brush with oil.

3 Melt the butter in a saucepan and fry the onion and mushrooms until lightly golden. Stir in the rice, salt and pepper and cayenne. Remove from heat and spoon the mixture into the prepared peppers and arrange in a greased, shallow ovenproof dish. Cover with lightly greased foil.

4 Bake at 190°C (375°F) mark 5 for 30-35 minutes or until the peppers are tender and the filling is heated through. Uncover, then fluff up the rice with a fork. Serve hot.

DRINKS TO SERVE

With the Linguine choose an Italian dry white wine such as Soave Classico, Orvieta or Verdicchio.

A good French white wine such as Pouilly-Fumé, or Montrachet would be ideal with the Pork. Followed by a Vouvray with dessert.

COOK'S HINTS

1 The sauce may be made less rich and lower in calories by using natural yogurt instead of crème fraîche. However, to prevent the sauce separating, the Madeira, stock and mustard should first be boiled rapidly to reduce before adding natural yogurt and heating through gently, without boiling.

2 Peppers for stuffing are usually first blanched in boiling water to make them pliable and reduce the baking time. If wished, peppers may also be skinned which makes them more digestible – grill or bake peppers whole until the skin blisters and blackens, then peel off the thin skin and discard.

MENU SUGGESTIONS

Wintry days call for hearty, comforting food. Chicken and Spiced Apricot Casserole (page 251) would be perfect in this menu (but omit the Wafer-wrapped Apple and Gooseberry Pouches).

JULIENNE OF ROOT VEGETABLES

Matchsticks of carrot, celeriac and young turnips make an attractive and delicious accompaniment. Place the prepared vegetables in separate bowls and cover with cold water until ready to cook. Add a few drops of lemon juice to the celeriac water to stop discoloration.

450 g (1 lb) carrots, peeled and cut into matchsticks
450 g (1 lb) celeriac, peeled and cut into matchsticks
450 g (1 lb) turnips, peeled and cut into matchsticks
50 g (2 oz) butter
10 ml (2 tsp) caster sugar
salt and freshly ground pepper
10 ml (2 tsp) lemon juice
5 ml (1 tsp) chopped fresh thyme

1 Using a tiered steamer, steam the vegetables at the same time, but in separate portions, for about 6 minutes or until just tender. Remove from the heat.

2 Melt the butter in a large pan, add the sugar, salt and pepper, lemon juice and thyme. Add the steamed vegetables and heat through for 2–3 minutes, tossing gently to coat in the butter juices.

3 Turn the vegetables into a warm serving dish and spoon over the juices from the pan.

WAFER-WRAPPED APPLE AND GOOSEBERRY POUCHES

An unusual and attractive way to serve apple sauce.

2 cooking apples, peeled, cored and roughly chopped
15 ml (1 tbsp) granulated sugar
salt and freshly ground pepper
forty 12.5 cm (5 inch) squares of filo pastry (see Cook's Hint)
75 g (3 oz) butter, melted
40 ml (8 level tsp) gooseberry conserve
8 long chives, to garnish

1 Mix the apples with the sugar and salt and pepper.

2 Lay 8 squares of filo pastry on a work surface, brush each one lightly with melted butter, then cover each one with another square of filo pastry. Cover each with a third square of filo pastry, place at an angle of 45°; brush lightly with melted butter and top each with a fourth square of filo. Place one more filo square, set at an angle of 45° on top of each pile and brush lightly with melted butter.

3 Divide the apple mixture evenly between each filo pile and top with 5 ml (1 tsp) gooseberry conserve. Gather the edges of the pastry into a bundle, pressing firmly together, to form neat pouches.

4 Transfer to a lightly greased baking sheet (with raised edges). Brush with melted butter. Bake at 190°C (375°F) mark 5 for 15–30 minutes or until golden brown and cooked through, brushing halfway through cooking with butter from the baking sheet.

5 Tie a long chive around the neck of each pouch, to garnish. Serve hot.

CHOCOLATE AND CHESTNUT CREAM VACHERIN

Layers of hazelnut meringue are sandwiched together with a delicious mixture of chestnut purée, melted chocolate and cream.

6 egg whites
350 g (12 oz) caster sugar
75 g (3 oz) hazelnuts, skinned, toasted and finely chopped
175 g (6 oz) plain chocolate, broken into pieces
500 g (1.1 lb) can sweetened chestnut purée
300 ml (½ pint) double cream
a little icing sugar for dusting
whipped cream and cocoa powder, to decorate

1 Line 3 baking sheets with non-stick baking parchment and draw a 20 cm (8 inch) circle on each.

2 Stiffly whisk the egg whites, then gradually whisk in the sugar a little at a time, whisking well until the meringue is smooth and shiny. Very lightly fold in the hazelnuts.

3 Either spread the mixture over the

Chocolate and Chestnut Cream Vacherin (left)

COUNTDOWN
The day before:
Make the meringue layers for the vacherin; cool, wrap and store in an airtight tin.
On the morning:
Slice and beat out the pork; cover and refrigerate. Chop onion; crush garlic and shred the sage for the garnish. Cook and prepare the wild rice filling. Prepare peppers, spoon in the filling and arrange in a dish. Cover with greased foil ready for baking.
In the late afternoon:
Cut vegetables into matchsticks. Place in separate bowls; cover with cold water adding a few drops of lemon juice to the celeriac. Make but don't bake the Apple and Gooseberry Pouches; cover and refrigerate.
To serve at 8pm:
6pm: Make the filling for the vacherin.
7.30pm: Turn on the oven at 190°C (375°F) mark 5.
7.40pm: Put a large pan of salted water on to boil for the linguine if using dried; cook fresh at 7.50 pm.
7.45pm: Place the rice-stuffed peppers in the oven to cook. Assemble the vacherin; decorate and keep in a cool place.
7.50pm: Start cooking the pork; keep warm while making the sauce. Prepare a steamer ready for the root vegetables.
8pm: Serve the linguine. Place the Apple and Gooseberry Pouches in the oven to bake. Drain and start cooking julienne vegetables.

marked circles, or transfer to a piping bag fitted with a plain 1 cm (½ inch) nozzle and pipe the meringue in a spiral over the marked circles, starting from the centre.

4 Bake at 140°C (275°F) mark 1 for 1-1½ hours or until dried out. Change the positions of the baking sheets during cooking so that the meringues dry out evenly. Remove from the oven and leave to cool, then carefully remove the lining papers.

5 Melt the chocolate in a heatproof bowl set over a pan of hot water. Soften the chestnut purée in a bowl and stir in the melted chocolate. Lightly whip the cream until soft peaks form and fold into the chestnut mixture.

6 To assemble the vacherin, sandwich the meringues together with a little of the chestnut cream. Cover the top and sides with the remainder and decorate with whipped cream and cocoa powder.

ITALIAN DINNER PARTY

M	E	N	U

RUSTIC WALNUT BREAD

AUBERGINE CANNELLONI

BEEF WITH PORCINI AND SWEET PEPPERS

NEW POTATOES WITH BUTTER AND FRESH
HERBS

SALAD OF MIXED LEAVES

TIRAMISU

SERVES 8

*I*talian food is always a favourite with guests, no matter what the occasion. This dinner party menu takes inspiration from the Italian philosophy of life – it's relaxed, informal and fun. Most of the work is done beforehand, leaving you plenty of time to sit down with your guests and enjoy their company. It doesn't rely heavily on fresh seasonal foods and, with new potatoes coming into the shops from all over the world, you can even make New Potatoes with Butter and Fresh Herbs (see page 57) at any time of the year.

To end the meal in true Italian style, serve tiny cups of strong, syrupy espresso coffee and hand round some deliciously crunchy Amaretti. These pretty, individually wrapped almond biscuits are a great favourite with Italians, and are available from most large supermarkets and food halls.

*The Italian Dinner Party is
illustrated on pages 84 and 85*

RUSTIC WALNUT BREAD

*Fast action dried yeast, available
at supermarkets, is an absolute boon to the busy
cook. Only one kneading, rising and proving is
necessary, and there is no messy mixing, as the dried
yeast is stirred straight into the flour; the water is
added afterwards.*

600 g (1 lb 5 oz) strong white flour
5 ml (1 tsp) salt
25 g (1 oz) butter or margarine
1 sachet fast action dried yeast
125 g (4 oz) shelled walnuts, roughly chopped
about 350 ml (12 fl oz) tepid water

1 Sift the flour and salt into a warmed large mixing bowl. Rub in the margarine or butter with your fingertips, then stir in the yeast and chopped walnuts.

2 Pour in enough tepid water to make a smooth dough, mixing with a wooden spoon, then form the mixture into a ball of dough with your hands.

3 Turn the dough out onto a floured surface and knead for 10 minutes until smooth and elastic, adding a little more flour if the dough becomes too sticky.

4 Divide the dough in half and shape each piece into a roll. Place on oiled baking sheets, cover with oiled polythene and leave to rise in a warm place for about 1 hour, or until doubled in size.

5 Uncover the loaves and slash the tops with a knife. Bake in the oven at 220°C (425°F) mark 7 for 10 minutes. Reduce the oven temperature to 190°C (375°F) mark 5 and bake for a further 25 minutes or until the loaves are crusty on top and feel hollow when tapped on the bottom, swapping over oven shelves halfway through to ensure even cooking. If the loaves become too brown during baking, cover them with greaseproof paper or foil.

6 Leave the loaves to cool on a wire rack before serving.

To Freeze Cool, overwrap with foil and freeze for up to 1 week. No more, or the crust will lift off. Thaw at room temperature, then refresh in the oven at 190°C (375°F) mark 5.

AUBERGINE CANNELLONI

4 aubergines, each weighing about 250 g (9 oz)
about 150 ml (¼ pint) extra-virgin olive oil
450 g (1 lb) ricotta cheese
125 g (4 oz) Parmesan cheese, freshly grated
30 ml (2 tbsp) finely shredded fresh basil leaves
salt and freshly ground pepper
S A U C E
900 g (2 lb) ripe fresh tomatoes, skinned, seeded and chopped
30 ml (2 tbsp) extra-virgin olive oil
2 shallots or ¼ large Spanish onion, skinned and finely chopped
2 garlic cloves, skinned and crushed
about 300 ml (½ pint) vegetable stock or water
15 ml (1 tbsp) tomato purée
2.5 ml (½ tsp) caster sugar, or to taste
30 ml (2 tbsp) dry white wine
freshly grated Parmesan cheese and fresh basil sprigs, to serve

1 Heat the olive oil in a heavy saucepan, add the shallots or onion and cook gently, stirring frequently, for 5–7 minutes until softened. Add the tomatoes and garlic, cover with a lid and sweat over gentle heat, stirring occasionally, for 10 minutes. Add the stock, tomato purée, sugar and salt and pepper to taste, half cover the pan and simmer for 30 minutes, stirring frequently.

2 Remove the pan from the heat, then work the tomato mixture through a fine sieve into a clean saucepan. Bring to the boil, stirring, then add the white wine and set aside while preparing the cannelloni.

3 Cut the aubergines lengthways into thin slices, discarding the ends and rounded pieces from the sides. Heat 30–45 ml (2–3 tbsp) olive oil in a large non-stick frying pan. Add a single layer of aubergine slices and fry over moderate heat until light golden on both sides. Remove from the pan, drain, then place on absorbent kitchen paper. Repeat with more oil and the remaining aubergine slices.

4 Put the ricotta and Parmesan cheeses in a bowl with the shredded basil and salt and pepper to taste. Beat well to mix.

DRINKS TO SERVE
Red or white Cinzano is the perfect aperitif to enjoy before an Italian dinner. Follow it with a soft, elegant white wine such as Pinot Grigio (Bianco) and serve a full bodied red, such as San Lorenzo Conero with the beef. If serving liqueurs, choose the Italian almond flavoured Amaretto, or a coffee liqueur such as Kahlua.

COOK'S HINTS
1 When making fresh **tomato sauce**, use only juicy ripe tomatoes in season, preferably Italian plum tomatoes, which are now available in large supermarkets, specialist greengrocers and street markets.

In winter it is better to use canned tomatoes. For this recipe you will need an 800 g (1¾ lb) can. If necessary, add an extra pinch or two of sugar.

2 Skinning and seeding tomatoes gives a smooth sauce with a sweet flavour. Immerse tomatoes, one at a time, in boiling water for 15 seconds then plunge into ice cold water. Remove, peel off the skins and cut the tomatoes into halves or quarters. Discard the cores and seeds and chop the flesh.

5 Place the aubergine slices on a surface; if the slices are small or broken, overlap 2 slices so that they will roll up as one (you will need 24 cannelloni altogether). Spoon the cheese mixture along the length of the aubergines, then roll the slices up around it.
6 Place the rolls, seam-side down, in a single layer in an ovenproof dish. Bake in the oven at 190°C (375°F) mark 5 for 10–15 minutes until hot. Meanwhile, reheat the tomato sauce until bubbling, taste and adjust seasoning, and add more stock or water if necessary.
7 To serve, arrange 3 cannelloni on each warmed plate. Drizzle over the tomato sauce, then sprinkle lightly with Parmesan and garnish with fresh basil sprigs. Serve hot, with extra Parmesan handed separately for those who like it.

To Freeze Cool the tomato sauce at step 3. Pack into a rigid container and freeze for up to 1 month. Thaw at room temperature.

BEEF WITH PORCINI AND SWEET PEPPERS

A whole fillet of beef is the perfect cut of meat for a dinner party. It looks impressive and generous, and guests will appreciate it as a real treat. Fillet of beef slices beautifully, so is very easy to serve, and there is absolutely no waste.

1.4 kg (3 lb) trimmed fillet of beef
25 g (1 oz) porcini, soaked and drained
285 g (9½ oz) jar pepperoni (sliced red and yellow peppers in sunflower oil), drained
375 g (12 oz) pancetta slices
30 ml (2 tbsp) extra-virgin olive oil
10 ml (2 tsp) plain flour
150 ml (¼ pint) full-bodied Italian red wine
300 ml (½ pint) beef stock
30 ml (2 tbsp) Marsala wine or redcurrant jelly
10 ml (2 tsp) dried mixed herbs
salt and freshly ground pepper
chopped fresh parsley, to garnish

Beef with Porcini and Sweet Peppers (above right)

1 Cut a slit along the side of the fillet, keeping both ends attached. Open it out with your fingers a little, to make a pocket.

2 Roughly chop the porcini; reserve half for the sauce. Mix the remainder with half of the pepperoni and use to fill the pocket. Grind black pepper over the meat, then wrap the pancetta around the fillet to enclose it completely. Tie with string at regular intervals.

3 Heat the oil in a large non-stick frying pan, add the meat and sear on all sides. Lift the fillet out of the oil, drain over the pan, then place on absorbent kitchen paper. Reserve the juices in the pan for making the sauce later.

4 Roast the fillet in the oven at 190°C (375°F) mark 5 for 45 minutes. Remove from the oven, cover with foil and leave to rest in a warm place for 10–15 minutes.

5 Meanwhile, reheat the reserved juices in the frying pan, sprinkle in the flour and cook, stirring, over moderate heat for 2–3 minutes. Gradually stir in the red wine and the stock, then bring to the boil, stirring. Lower the heat, add the Marsala or redcur-

rant jelly, the herbs and salt and pepper to taste. Simmer until thickened, stirring all the time. Add the remaining pepperoni and mushrooms and heat through.

6 Remove the string and carve the meat into neat slices and arrange them on a warmed serving platter. Remove the pepperoni and mushrooms from the sauce with a slotted spoon and use to garnish the meat. Spoon over a little sauce to glaze, then garnish with parsley. Serve immediately, with the remaining sauce handed separately in a sauceboat.

SALAD OF MIXED LEAVES

There is such an enormous variety of salad leaves available today that we are spoilt for choice. This combination is merely a suggestion; change the number and type of leaves to suit your fancy or the season, so long as you choose different shapes, flavours and colours to keep the overall effect interesting.

150 g (5 oz) fresh spinach leaves
150 g (5 oz) lollo rosso
1 small head radicchio, leaves separated
3 sprigs of fresh basil
120 ml (8 tbsp) extra-virgin olive oil
30 ml (2 tbsp) balsamic vinegar
50 g (2 oz) sun dried tomatoes, drained if packed in oil
1–2 garlic cloves, skinned and crushed (optional)
salt and freshly ground pepper

1 Wash the spinach well and remove any coarse stems and ribs; tear the leaves into bite-sized pieces. Wash the lollo rosso and radicchio leaves and tear into bite-sized pieces also. Tear the basil leaves.

2 Put the olive oil and vinegar in the bottom of a large bowl and whisk vigorously with a fork until thickened. Thinly slice the sun-dried tomatoes and add to the bowl with the garlic, if using. Whisk again, then add salt and pepper to taste.

3 Add the prepared salad leaves and basil to the dressing and toss well to coat. Taste and adjust seasoning. Transfer to a salad bowl and serve immediately.

COOK'S HINTS

1 **Salad leaves** quickly become limp and soggy if left coated in dressing. To avoid this happening when entertaining, mix the dressing in the bottom of the bowl, then place the salad servers in the bowl, crossing them over one another to form an X shape. Gently place the salad leaves on top of the servers, then leave until ready to toss and serve. The salad servers will keep the leaves out of the dressing so that they remain fresh and crisp.

2 **Balsamic vinegar**, called 'aceto balsamico' in Italian, comes from Modena, where it was originally believed to have had medicinal qualities. It has a syrupy consistency and a sweet and sour flavour and is quite strong, so should be used sparingly. It is often used in salad dressings as here, also in sauces and gravies, and sprinkled over meat and fish.

MENU SUGGESTIONS

If you are short of time serve Garlic Bread (page 221) with wafer thin slices of Parma ham and ripe, juicy figs as a starter. Italian Braised Beef (page 246) or Italian-style Braised Pork (page 249) are good alternatives to the Beef with Porcini.

COUNTDOWN
The day before:
Make Rustic Walnut
Bread; cool and wrap
well, then store in
airtight container.
Make Tiramisù.Make
tomato sauce; cool,
cover and refrigerate.
Fill aubergines with
ricotta mixture, place
in dish , cover and
refrigerate. Prepare
beef up to the end of
step 2.
On the day:
Wash salad ingredients,
place in polythene bag
and refrigerate.Prepare
salad dressing; keep in
covered container in
refrigerator.Scrub
potatoes (see page 57).
Chop fresh herbs; keep
in airtight container in
refrigerator.
To serve at 8pm:
6.30pm: Sear meat;
place in roasting tin.
7.05pm: Put fillet of
beef in oven to roast.
7.30pm: Put potatoes
on to cook.
7.45pm: Put
Aubergine Cannelloni
in the oven to heat
through; reheat tomato
sauce on top of stove.
Place salad dressing
and leaves in serving
bowl but do not toss.
7.50pm: Take meat
from the oven; cover
and leave to rest in
warm place. Drain the
potatoes and toss with
butter and herbs; keep
hot, covered in the
oven. Make sauce for
the meat; remove from
heat and keep warm.
Put bread into the oven
to heat through.
8pm: Between the
first and main courses,
carve meat and reheat
sauce; toss salad with
dressing.

Tiramisu (above right)

TIRAMISU

*Tiramisù in Italian means 'pick me up', describing
the heady nature of this wickedly rich Venetian
dessert. It is a dessert that nobody can resist, so the
quantity given here is on the generous side, to allow
for second helpings. Tiramisù is incredibly quick and
easy to make, but be sure to make it the day before
required as Tiramisù needs time for the layers to
merge into one another and the flavours to mature.*

four 250 g (9 oz) cartons mascarpone cheese
40 g (1½ oz) caster sugar
3 eggs, separated
250 ml (8 fl oz) Kahlúa or other coffee-flavoured liqueur
425 ml (14 fl oz) very strong cold black coffee
about 30 savoiardi (Italian sponge fingers)
cocoa powder, for sprinkling

1 Put the mascarpone cheese, sugar and egg
yolks in a bowl and beat with an electric
mixer until evenly blended and creamy.

2 Beat the egg whites in a separate bowl
until standing in stiff peaks. Fold into the
mascarpone mixture until evenly incorporated. Spoon about one quarter of the mixture into the bottom of the glass serving
bowl.

3 Mix the liqueur and coffee together in a
shallow dish. One at a time, dip one third of
the savoiardi in this mixture for 10–15 seconds, turning once so they become soaked
through but do not lose their shape. After
each one has been dipped, place it on top of
the mascarpone in the bowl, making a single
layer of savoiardi that covers the mascarpone
completely.

4 Cover the savoiardi with one third of the
remaining mascarpone, then dip another
third of the savoiardi in the liqueur and coffee mixture and layer them in the bowl as
before.

5 Repeat with another layer of mascarpone
and savoiardi, then spread the remaining
mascarpone over the top and swirl with a
palette knife. Sift cocoa powder liberally all
over the top. Cover the bowl and refrigerate
for 24 hours. Serve chilled.

SEAFOOD DINNER PARTY

SERVES 8

This cosmopolitan menu takes on flavours from many cuisines. A warm salad with homemade bread never fails to impress and is guaranteed to get the taste buds tingling. The salad must be cooked just before serving and consumed immediately for maximum impact, so it's essential to get everything ready and have your guests seated before starting to cook the mushroom mixture. It takes a mere 5–10 minutes, so you won't be tied to the kitchen for long. The Olive Sourdough Bread is moist and rich enough to be eaten plain, but serve some good continental style unsalted or slightly salted butter for those who must.

The main course is a delicious, easy to make mixture of monkfish, squid and mussels served with a subtly fragrant pilaff and a tangy Avocado and Orange Salad, dressed with a hint of chilli. For dessert an unusual raspberry ice cream, with a hint of rose makes a stunning finale.

COOK'S HINTS

1 If you make bread regularly a **sourdough starter** is a convenient way of leavening bread. Providing it is replenished as it is used, it will keep indefinitely.

After making the olive sourdough bread, blend about 75 g (3 oz) strong flour with about 150 ml (¼ pint) water to make a runny paste. Stir it into the remaining starter, recover as before and leave for at least 24 hours before using.

Providing it is nourished every 4 days with a paste made from at least 25 g (1 oz) strong flour and water, the starter will always be ready to use. If you do not use it for a few days store it in the refrigerator.

2 If you are serving this salad in mid or late autumn, look out for **wild mushrooms** in the shops, or if you have time and live in an area where they are likely to grow wild, set out on a mushroom hunt. Always check your booty against a reliable guide book before eating.

Seafood Pilaki with Mixed Rice Pilaff and Avocado and Orange Salad (opposite)

OLIVE SOURDOUGH BREAD

One taste of this rich moist bread, and guests will ask for more! So allow plenty.

SOURDOUGH STARTER
15 g (½ oz) fresh yeast or 7.5 ml (1½ level tsp) dried and a pinch of sugar
450 ml (¾ pint) tepid water
225 g (8 oz) strong white flour
BREAD
400 g (14 oz) strong white flour
75 g (3 oz) rye flour
75 g (3 oz) strong wholemeal flour
5 ml (1 tsp) salt
45 ml (3 tbsp) chopped fresh mixed herbs
45 ml (3 tbsp) virgin olive oil
225 g (8 oz) mixed pitted black and green olives, roughly chopped

1 To make the sourdough starter, in a large bowl, blend the fresh yeast with 150 ml (¼ pint) of the tepid water. If using dried yeast sprinkle it onto 150 ml (¼ pint) of the water with the pinch of sugar and leave in a warm place until frothy.

2 Mix in the remaining water and enough of the flour to form a thick, pourable mixture. Don't worry if it's not perfectly smooth, the yeast will break down lumps. Tightly cover the bowl with a damp cloth. Leave at warm room temperature for 3 days to ferment and develop the sourdough flavour. (Ring out the cloth in cold water if it dries out.)

3 To make the bread, put the flours, salt and herbs in a bowl and mix together. Add 200 ml (7 fl oz) of the starter and the olive oil and 225 ml (8 fl oz) tepid water or enough to make a soft dough.

4 On a lightly floured surface, knead the dough for about 10 minutes until smooth and elastic. Put the dough in a large oiled bowl, cover with a clean tea towel and leave in a warm place for about 1 hour or until doubled in size.

5 Knock back the dough on a lightly floured surface, then carefully knead in the olives. Shape into a long sausage then curl it round to form a coil. Wrap one end of the dough over the other and pinch with your fingers to mould them together.

6 Transfer the coil to a greased baking sheet and cover loosely with a clean tea towel. Leave in a warm place for about 20 minutes or until doubled in size.

7 Remove the tea towel and with a sharp pair of scissors, snip around the top of the loaf to make a zig-zig pattern. Brush with water and bake in the oven at 230°C (450°F) mark 8 for 15 minutes. Reduce the temperature to 190°C (375°F) mark 5 and bake for a further 20–25 minutes or until the loaf sounds hollow when tapped. Cool on a wire rack.

To Freeze Cool, overwrap and freeze. Reheat from frozen, wrapped in foil, at 200°C (400°F) mark 6 for 35 minutes. Remove the foil for the last 5 minutes to crisp the crust.

WARM SALAD OF MUSHROOMS

Failing a supply of wild mushrooms this salad works well with cultivated oyster or shiitake mushrooms or cup mushrooms.

selection of mixed salad leaves, cleaned and trimmed
175 g (6 oz) young spinach leaves, cleaned and trimmed weight
175 g (6 oz) smoked streaky bacon
700 g (1½ lb) mushrooms (see introduction), cleaned
90 ml (6 tbsp) olive oil
1 garlic clove, skinned and crushed (optional)
salt and freshly ground pepper
25 ml (1½ tbsp) tarragon vinegar

1 Arrange the salad leaves and the spinach on eight plates. Remove the rind from the bacon and discard. Cut into thin strips. Cut the mushrooms into thick slices.

2 Heat a heavy-based frying pan and fry the bacon until the fat runs. Increase the heat and fry for a couple of minutes until crisp. Add the oil and mushrooms and cook over a high heat for 3–4 minutes until the mushrooms are just tender. Add the garlic, if using and pepper and cook for a minute longer.

3 Using a slotted spoon, remove the mushrooms from the pan and scatter over the salad leaves. Quickly add the vinegar to the juices remaining in the pan and boil rapidly for 2 minutes. Season with salt and pepper. Pour over the salads and serve immediately.

Seafood Pilaki (above)

SEAFOOD PILAKI

MENU SUGGESTIONS
Vichysoisse (page 243) or Pâté de Foie de Volaille (page 244) served with the sourdough bread or Melba toast would make an equally good start to this dinner. Instead of ice cream for dessert, try Baked Cheesecake (page 275) or Chocolate Milles Feuilles (page 263).

30 ml (2 tbsp) olive oil
2 garlic cloves, skinned and crushed
1 large onion, skinned and chopped
2 celery sticks, trimmed and chopped
3 large carrots, sliced
finely grated rind and juice of 1 lemon
397 g (14 oz) can chopped tomatoes
700 g (1½ lb) monkfish fillet, trimmed and cut into chunks.
450 g (1 lb) cleaned squid, cut into rings
900 g (2 lb) mussels, cleaned
chopped fresh parsley
salt and freshly ground pepper

1 Heat the oil in a large heavy-based pan. Add the garlic, onion, celery, carrots and lemon rind and cook for about 5 minutes, stirring all the time.

2 Add the lemon juice and the tomatoes with their juice, cover and cook on a low heat for about 25 minutes or until the vegetables are very tender. Stir occasionally and add a little water if the liquid is evaporating too rapidly.

3 Add the fish and squid and a little water. Re-cover and cook for 3–5 minutes or until the fish is just tender. Arrange the mussels on the top, recover the pan and cook for about 5 minutes, stirring occasionally. The mussels should have opened; discard any that remain shut. Stir in plenty of parsley and season to taste with salt and pepper. Serve hot or cold.

1 Crush the aniseed in a mortar and pestle. Heat the oil in a large heavy-based saucepan and fry the crushed aniseed with the nuts for a few minutes.

2 Add the rice and 1.1 litres (2 pints) water. Bring to the boil, stir and then cover and simmer for 15 minutes or until the water has been absorbed. Season to taste with salt and pepper. Sprinkle with the sesame seeds.

To Freeze Cool, pack in polythene bags and freeze for up to 3 months. To use, transfer the rice to a greased ovenproof dish. Cover and cook in the oven at 180°C (350°F) mark 4 for 15–20 minutes or until piping hot. Stir before serving.

AVOCADO AND ORANGE SALAD WITH LIME AND CHILLI

If available, the best avocados for this salad are the small brown, knobbly skinned Hass avocados. Pickled chillies are relatively mild and are sold in jars in supermarkets.

7 small juicy blood oranges
3 ripe avocados
finely grated rind and juice of 1 lime
60 ml (4 tbsp) virgin olive oil
salt and freshly ground pepper
2 pickled chillies (or to taste)

1 Squeeze the juice from one orange. Halve the avocados, remove the stone then carefully peel off the skin. Thinly slice the avocado. Sprinkle generously with the juice from the orange.

2 Peel the remaining oranges, removing as much of the bitter white pith as you can. Using a very sharp knife, thinly slice the oranges and arrange on the plate with the avocado.

3 Mix the lime rind and juice with the oil and season to taste with salt and pepper. Pour over the salad.

4 Chop the chillies and sprinkle over the salad.

To Freeze Cool the sauce at the end of step 2. Pack in a rigid container, leaving headspace and freeze for up to 3 months. Gently reheat the sauce from frozen, stirring occasionally until boiling. Complete the recipe from step 3, adding a little water if necessary.

MIXED RICE PILAFF

10 ml (2 tsp) aniseed
30 ml (2 tbsp) vegetable oil
125 g (4 oz) mixed nuts, roughly chopped
450 g (1 lb) mixed long grain and wild rice
salt and freshly ground pepper
30 ml (2 tbsp) toasted sesame seeds

COUNTDOWN
4 days before:
Make the sourdough starter for the Olive Sourdough Bread.
The day before:
Make the Olive Sourdough Bread. Make the Raspberry Rose Ice cream.
On the Day:
Prepare the sauce for the Seafood Pilaki. Cover and refrigerate. Prepare the oranges and the chillies for the salad. Cover and refrigerate. Make the dressing for the salad and store in the refrigerator. Clean the mushrooms for the Warm Salad of Mushrooms. Remove the rind and cut the bacon into thin strips. Cover and refrigerate.
To serve at 8pm:
7.00pm: Arrange the salad and spinach leaves on plates. Cover and refrigerate. Prepare the avocados for the salad by following step 1 and complete the recipe.
7.30pm: Make the Mixed Rice Pilaff. Cover and keep warm in the bottom of the oven.
7.45pm: Warm the Olive Sourdough Bread at 200°C (400°F) mark 6 for 10-15 minutes. Reheat the Pilaki sauce and continue step 3. Complete the Warm Salad of Mushrooms by following steps 2 and 3.
8.00pm: Serve the starter. Turn the oven to its lowest setting to keep the Pilaff and Pilaki warm.

MICROWAVE HINT

To cook the custard for the **ice cream** in the microwave, in step 1 put the ingredients in a large bowl and microwave on HIGH for 3 minutes or until almost boiling. In step 2 microwave on LOW for 12–15 minutes or until slightly thickened, stirring frequently.

COOK'S HINTS

1 To make a lower calorie **ice cream**, make the custard with 600 ml (1 pint) skimmed milk, 30 ml (2 tbsp) skimmed milk powder, 30 ml (2 tbsp) custard powder and 15–30 ml (1–2 tbsp) sugar in the usual way, infusing the milk with the rose petals as before. Omit the cream. Flavour and freeze as recipe.

2 The use of **flowers in cookery** dates back for centuries. Not only are they useful for decorative purposes, but they lend a subtle aroma and flavour to a wide range of dishes.
    Common garden flowers such as roses, lavender, violets, primroses and elderflowers are all delicious infused in sugar syrups to flavour drinks, sorbets, ice creams, sauces and cakes. Others such as nasturtiums are delicious in salads and in the height of summer, they may be found in boxes in the salad compartment of large supermarkets.

RASPBERRY ROSE ICE CREAM

To show this vivid pink ice cream at its best, serve it in plain white or glass dishes.

300 ml (½ pint) milk
2 large handfuls of fragrant pink rose petals
3 egg yolks
75 g (3 oz) caster sugar
450 g (1 lb) raspberries
15 ml (1 tbsp) rose water
300 ml (½ pint) double cream
rose petals or mint sprigs, to decorate

1 Put the milk and rose petals in a heavy-based saucepan and bring almost to the boil. Remove from the heat and leave to infuse for at least 30 minutes.

2 Beat the egg yolks and sugar together until well blended. Stir in the milk and rose petals, then strain back into the pan, discarding the rose petals. Cook over a gentle heat, stirring all the time until it thickens very slightly. Do not let the custard boil or it will curdle. Pour into a bowl and leave to cool.

3 While the custard is cooling, mash the raspberries then push through a nylon sieve to make a purée. Stir in the rosewater.

4 Whisk the cream into the cold custard mixture, then stir in the raspberry purée. Pour into a shallow non-metallic, freezer container. Cover and freeze on fast freeze for about 3 hours or until just frozen.

5 Spoon into a bowl and mash with a fork to break down the ice crystals. Work quickly so that the ice cream does not melt completely.

6 Return the mixture to the container and freeze again for about 2 hours until mushy.

7 Mash again as step 4, then return to the freezer for a further 3 hours or until firm.

8 Remove from the freezer and leave at room temperature for about 20–30 minutes to soften. Serve with the figs, cut into quarters, sprinkled with a few raspberries and rose petals. (Do not forget to return the freezer setting to normal.)

To Freeze Ice cream can be stored in the freezer for up to 3 months

Raspberry Rose Ice Cream (above)

CHINESE DINNER PARTY

M	E	N	U

CHILLIED PORK DIM SUM

BEANSPROUT AND SESAME SALAD

CRISPY DUCK WITH MANGE TOUT

BRAISED MIXED VEGETABLES

CHICKEN WITH GINGER

SPECIAL FRIED RICE

FRAGRANT FRUIT SALAD

SERVES 8

A Chinese dinner is a fun way to entertain and, provided you are well prepared, the cooking is quick and simple. This menu consists of several dishes with contrasting textures and flavours. Steamed pork dim sum start the meal in splendid fashion, followed by tangy Chicken with Ginger and rich-glazed duckling with mange tout. Colourful fried rice and a dish of braised vegetables complete the main meal in fine style.

Serve the meal in traditional Chinese fashion, with the dishes placed in the centre of the table for guests to help themselves. Chinese plates and rice bowls are pretty and help make the table stunning and authentic, but are not essential. Re-useable chopsticks are attractive and fun to use, but provide spoons and forks as a standby. Finger bowls of warm water with slices of lemon or rose petals are an elegant touch and sure to be appreciated by guests.

Fragrant Fruit Salad makes a tempting finale and, although not authentic, when flavoured with lychees and ginger is bound to please. Or if preferred, finish with a refreshing fruit sorbet, or simply a bowl of fresh lychees.

CHILLIED PORK DIM SUM

15 ml (1 tbsp) vegetable oil
125 g (4 oz) lean pork, minced
1 garlic clove, skinned and crushed
½ onion, skinned and very finely chopped
15 ml (1 tbsp) finely chopped bamboo shoots
2 whole dried red chillies, finely chopped
10 ml (2 tsp) dark soy sauce
15 ml (1 tbsp) oyster sauce
10 ml (2 tsp) tomato purée
5 ml (1 tsp) sesame oil
125 g (4 oz) self-raising flour
several good pinches of salt
20 g (¾ oz) lard
15 ml (1 tbsp) caster sugar
10 ml (2 tsp) sesame seeds

1 Heat the oil in a frying pan, add the pork, garlic, onion, bamboo shoots and chillies and stir fry for 5 minutes. Add the soy sauce, oyster sauce and tomato purée and cook for 5 minutes, stirring occasionally. Stir in sesame oil and leave to cool.

2 Sift the flour and salt into a bowl and rub in the lard finely. Stir in the sugar and sesame seeds. Add about 60 ml (4 tbsp) water and mix to form a soft dough. Divide into 24 portions. Form each into a ball and roll out on a lightly floured surface to an 8.5 cm (3½ inch) round.

3 Put a teaspoonful of pork mixture into the centre of each round. Dampen the edges and gather together, sealing well. Form each into a little 'pouche' by twisting the tops together sealing the edges well.

4 Cook in a bamboo steamer (or conventional steamer) over simmering water for about 15 minutes until cooked through. Serve hot accompanied by a dipping sauce (see Cook's Hint).

Chillied Pork Dim Sum (right)

BEANSPROUT AND SESAME SALAD

A crisp and refreshing combination of vegetables for guests to enjoy between courses while you stir fry the duckling. Also provide a bowl of prawn crackers and crispy noodles for guests to nibble, if wished.

175 g (6 oz) fresh beansprouts, soaked in cold water for 10 minutes and drained before using
125 g (4 oz) mooli (daikon), cut into matchsticks
½ onion, skinned, thinly sliced lengthways and separated into strands
6 spring onions, cut into thin slivers
1 red or green pepper, seeded and thinly sliced
4 sticks celery, cut into thin matchsticks
125 g (4 oz) button mushrooms, sliced
2 bamboo shoots, cut into matchsticks
DRESSING
90 ml (6 tbsp) vegetable oil
1 large garlic clove, skinned and crushed
15 ml (1 tbsp) finely chopped fresh ginger
30 ml (2 tbsp) dry white wine
30 ml (2 tbsp) malt vinegar
5 ml (1 tsp) caster sugar
5 ml (1 tsp) hot mustard
2.5 ml (½ tsp) sesame oil
30 ml (2 tbsp) toasted sesame seeds

1 Pat the beansprouts dry on absorbent kitchen paper and put into a large bowl. Add the remaining prepared vegetables and mix together. Cover and chill for at least 1 hour before serving.

2 To prepare the dressing, place all the ingredients in a bowl or screw-topped jar and whisk or shake together until well blended. The dressing improves in flavour if made several hours in advance.

3 Whisk or shake the dressing ingredients together once again until well blended and pour over the prepared vegetables. Toss the ingredients together lightly until coated in dressing. Turn the salad into a serving dish and sprinkle with the toasted sesame seeds. Serve immediately.

CRISPY DUCK WITH MANGE TOUT

Crispy-skinned, duckling makes a splendid main course. It is pre-cooked and sliced ready to stir fry just before serving. You could substitute 4 duck breast fillets (roasted on a rack for about 30 minutes) or, if your guests are hearty meat eaters, use 700–900 g (1½–2 lb) thinly sliced rump steak instead.

2.3 kg (5 lb) duckling
salt
25 ml (1½ tbsp) clear honey
45 ml (3 tbsp) vegetable oil
1 bunch spring onions, trimmed and cut into 2.5 cm (1 inch) lengths
1 large green pepper, seeded and cut into thin strips
225 g (8 oz) mange tout, topped and tailed
2 garlic cloves, skinned and crushed
2–3 good pinches five spice powder
45 ml (3 tbsp) caster sugar
45 ml (3 tbsp) dark soy sauce
45 ml (3 tbsp) malt vinegar
16 water chestnuts, sliced
40 g (1½ oz) toasted cashew nuts, chopped

1 Pat the duckling dry inside and out with absorbent kitchen paper (damp duckling will not crisp easily). Put breast side up, on a rack or trivet in a roasting tin. Prick the skin all over with a skewer or fork and rub well with salt to help crisp the skin.

2 Bake in the oven at 180°C (350°F) mark 4 for 2¾ hours. Brush the skin with the honey and cook for a further 15 minutes or until cooked through. Remove from the oven and leave to cool. When cold, remove the skin and flesh from the carcass and cut into thin strips.

3 In a wok or large frying pan, heat the oil. Add the onion, green pepper, mange tout, garlic and five spice powder and stir fry for 2 minutes. Add the sugar, soy sauce, vinegar and duckling flesh and skin and toss in the sauce to heat through and glaze. Add the water chestnuts and toss through lightly. Serve at once, sprinkled with toasted cashews.

CHINESE INGREDIENTS

Fortunately the less exotic **Chinese ingredients** like fresh root ginger, sesame oil, soy sauces, canned bamboo shoots and water chestnuts, oyster sauce, hoisin sauce, five spice powder and so on are available in most large supermarkets. You will also find bean curd (tofu) in most health food shops whilst the more exotic items, such as dried mushrooms, dried shrimps, dried seaweed and lotus leaves can be found in Chinese supermarkets.

However, this dinner party menu has been designed to use mainly the more widely available ingredients for your convenience.

MICROWAVE HINT

It is possible to cook a **duckling** in the microwave but the skin will not be brown or crisp. Cook the duck for 7–9 minutes per 450 g (1 lb) on HIGH, spooning off the fat during cooking to prevent spattering, and cover with a split roasting bag. To achieve a brown and crisp skin, simply cook under a hot grill for a few minutes.

COOK'S HINTS

1 A little **hoisin sauce** or finely chopped fresh ginger may be added to the dish during the final stages, if wished. A few drops of sesame oil added to the finished dish add aromatic flavour and sheen.

2 **Five spice powder** is a mixture of cloves, cinnamon, fennel seeds, star anise and Szechuan peppercorns. It should be used very sparingly.

BRAISED MIXED VEGETABLES

A pleasing mixture of flavours and textures gives a vegetable dish that complements the two main courses. Vary the vegetables according to personal preference.

10 dried Chinese mushrooms, such as shiitake
45 ml (3 tbsp) peanut oil
1 garlic clove, skinned and crushed
1 Chinese cabbage, cut crossways into 2.5 cm (1 inch) strips
2 onions, skinned and cut into eighths and separated into layers
2 carrots, peeled and thinly sliced
16 baby sweetcorns
225 g (8 oz) broccoli, cut into very small florets
2.5 cm (1 inch) piece of fresh root ginger, peeled and grated
175 ml (6 fl oz) chicken stock
15 ml (1 level tbsp) cornflour
30 ml (2 tbsp) light soy sauce
5–10 ml (1–2 tsp) caster sugar

1 Soak the mushrooms in hot water for 20 minutes. Squeeze out as much water as possible. Discard the stalks and thinly slice the caps.
2 Heat the oil in a wok or large frying pan. Add the garlic, cabbage, carrots, onions, baby sweetcorn, broccoli and ginger and stir-fry for 2 minutes. Stir in the stock, cover with foil and cook for 2–3 minutes.
3 Blend the cornflour with the soy sauce to a smooth paste. Remove vegetables from the wok or pan, using a slotted spoon and keep on one side. Stir the cornflour mixture into the wok and bring to the boil, stirring all the time. Boil for 1 minute. Add the sugar.
4 Return the vegetables to the pan and toss lightly to heat through. Serve at once.

CHICKEN WITH GINGER

Do not overcook the chicken or it will become dry.

4 chicken breast fillets, skinned
4 cm (1½ inch) piece of fresh root ginger, peeled and grated
1 garlic clove, skinned and crushed
60 ml (4 tbsp) soy sauce
45 ml (3 tbsp) dry sherry
30 ml (2 tbsp) dark soft brown sugar
30 ml (2 tbsp) bland vegetable oil such as corn or sunflower
3 spring onions, trimmed and shredded, to garnish

1 Cut each chicken breast in half lengthways to make two thinner fillets. Arrange in a single layer in a shallow dish.
2 Mix the remaining ingredients together stirring until the sugar dissolves and pour over the chicken. Cover and leave in a cool place to marinate for at least 30 minutes.
3 Cook the chicken under a very hot grill for about 6–8 minutes, turning once and basting with the marinade. Do not overcook or the chicken will be dry. To serve, arrange the chicken on a platter, pour over any juices collected in the pan and any remaining marinade, then sprinkle with the spring onions.

SPECIAL FRIED RICE

Cook the rice several hours in advance and leave it to cool before it is stir fried with the vegetables.

450 g (1 lb) long-grain white rice
salt and freshly ground pepper
45–60 ml (3–4 tbsp) vegetable oil
3 carrots, coarsely grated
2 garlic cloves, skinned and crushed
125 g (4 oz) frozen peeled prawns, thawed
175 g (6 oz) frozen peas, thawed
175 g (6 oz) fresh beansprouts, soaked in cold water for 10 minutes and drained before using
45 ml (3 tbsp) light soy sauce
1 bunch spring onions, thinly sliced diagonally
5–10 ml (1–2 tsp) sesame oil

1 Cook the rice, following the packet instructions, until almost tender. Drain then rinse with boiling water. Spread out on a large tray and leave to cool.

2 Just before serving, heat the oil in a wok or large frying pan (you may need to do this in two batches). Add the carrots and garlic and stir fry for 2 minutes. Add the prawns, peas and beansprouts and stir fry for 1 minute. Stir in the rice and stir fry for 3 minutes. Stir in the soy sauce and seasoning, to taste and the spring onions; remove from heat and turn into a serving dish. Sprinkle with the sesame oil and serve at once.

FRAGRANT FRUIT SALAD

50 g (2 oz) caster sugar
grated rind and juice of 1 lemon
2 stem ginger (from a jar of ginger in syrup), finely chopped
60 ml (4 tbsp) ginger wine
700 g (1½ lb) lychees
3 ripe mangoes, peeled
450 g (1 lb) fresh or canned pineapple in natural juice
4 ripe kiwi fruit, peeled
50 g (2 oz) Cape gooseberries, to decorate (optional)

1 Put the sugar in a pan with 150 ml (¼ pint) water and the lemon rind and juice. Heat gently until the sugar dissolves. Bring to the boil and simmer for 1 minute. Remove from the heat and stir in the chopped ginger and wine. Leave to cool.

2 Peel the lychees, cut in half and remove the shiny stones. Cut the mango flesh away from the stones. Cut the flesh into cubes.

3 If using fresh pineapple, peel, slice and remove the tough centre from each slice. Cut the pineapple slices into cubes. Thinly slice the kiwi fruit and halve the slices.

4 Mix together the fruit and syrup. Cover and refrigerate for several hours to allow the flavours to develop. If using Cape gooseberries, peel back each calyx to form a 'flower', clean the orange berry by wiping with a damp cloth. Arrange on top of the fruit salad to serve.

Fragrant Fruit Salad (above)

COUNTDOWN

The day before:
Cook the pork mixture and make the dough for the Dim Sum. Wrap and refrigerate. Prepare the rice to the end of step 2. Prepare the Chicken with Ginger to the end of step 2. Cover and marinate overnight. Roast the duckling.

On the day:
Make the fruit salad, cover and refrigerate. Complete the Dim Sum to the end of step 3, cover and refrigerate. Make the Dipping Sauce, cover and refrigerate. Prepare the Braised Mixed Vegetables and soak the dried mushrooms. Cover and refrigerate. Prepare the vegetables for the Special Fried Rice, cover and refrigerate. Prepare the vegetables for the Crispy Duck, chill until required. Strip the duckling carcass and cut the skin and flesh into strips, refrigerate until required.

To Serve at 8.00pm:
7.15pm: Cook the Special Fried Rice, transfer to a serving dish, cover and keep warm in a very low oven. Toss together the salad, dressing and add sesame seeds. Stir fry the braised vegetables. Transfer to a warm serving dishes, cover and keep warm.

7.30pm: Stir fry the Crispy Duck. Transfer to a warm serving dish, cover and keep warm. Grill the Chicken with Ginger. Transfer to warm serving dishes, cover and keep warm.

7.45pm: Steam the Dim Sum.

8.00pm: Serve the Dim Sum and dipping sauce. Garnish the dishes before serving.

CELEBRATION DINNER PARTY

M E N U

SMOKED SALMON ROULADES

CRISPY POTATO GALETTE

BLUEBERRY DUCK

TOSSED GREEN SALAD

BRULÉED LEMON TART

SERVES 8

For a special occasion such as a birthday or anniversary, here's a trouble-free menu that will allow you to relax and enjoy having guests. Only the main course needs a little last minute attention, everything else can be prepared in advance. Presentation is all important with a special meal of this kind, so allow yourself plenty of time during the morning or afternoon of the party to lay the table beautifully with your best china, silverware and glass, plus fresh cut flowers and prettily folded napkins. If you have time, you could also make decorative menu cards, together with matching place names for each setting.

SMOKED SALMON ROULADES

These pretty smoked salmon and cream cheese rolls can be prepared well ahead of time. Serve them with warm crusty granary or wholemeal rolls.

275 g (10 oz) cream cheese, at room temperature
30 ml (2 tbsp) mayonnaise
finely grated rind of 1 lime or lemon
225 g (8 oz) peeled cooked prawns, thawed, drained and thoroughly dried if frozen
15 ml (1 level tbsp) powdered gelatine
30 ml (2 tbsp) lime or lemon juice
8 large thin slices smoked salmon
60–75 ml (4–5 tbsp) finely chopped fresh dill
freshly ground pepper
lime or lemon twists and fresh dill sprigs, to garnish

1 Beat the cream cheese in a bowl with the mayonnaise and lime or lemon rind. Chop the prawns finely.

2 Sprinkle the gelatine over 60 ml (4 tbsp) cold water in a small heatproof bowl. Leave for about 5 minutes until spongy, then stand the bowl in a saucepan of gently simmering water and heat until the gelatine has dissolved. Remove from the water and leave to cool for a few minutes.

3 Stir the dissolved gelatine into the cream cheese mixture until evenly blended, then stir in the lime or lemon juice. Cover the bowl and chill in the refrigerator for about 30 minutes, or until the mixture is just firm enough to hold its shape.

4 Spread about 22.5 ml (1½ tbsp) cream cheese mixture over each salmon slice, then sprinkle evenly with chopped dill.

5 Sprinkle the chopped prawns over the dill and press down gently with your fingertips. Grind black pepper over the top. Carefully roll up the salmon slices from 1 short end, then place seam side down on a plate. Cover and chill in the refrigerator for at least 2 hours, until firm.

6 To serve, cut each salmon roll on the diagonal into 8 neat slices, then arrange the slices, slightly overlapping, on individual plates. Garnish with the lime or lemon twists and the dill sprigs. Serve at room temperature.

CRISPY POTATO GALETTE

In French cookery, a galette is a kind of flat round cake made from flaky pastry. This version is made of very thinly sliced potatoes arranged in an attractive circular pattern. It's incredibly more-ish, so we suggest that you make two. Make the first following the recipe, then turn it out into a greased 20.5 cm (8 inch) sandwich tin, at end of step 3 and cook the second in the frying pan. Serve one divided into wedges on the plates with the duck. Serve the other whole and place on the table, to allow for second helpings.

1 kg (2 lb) old potatoes, peeled
50 g (2 oz) butter
15 ml (1 tbsp) olive oil
salt and freshly ground black pepper

1 Cut the potatoes into very thin rings and dry thoroughly on a clean tea towel.

2 Melt the butter with the oil in a 20 cm (8 inch) non-stick frying pan or skillet with a lid. Heat until foaming, then remove the pan from the heat and add the potato rings, overlapping them in a circular pattern. Season well with salt and pepper, then press the potatoes down firmly with a metal spatula.

3 Cover the potatoes with a sheet of buttered greaseproof paper, then with the pan lid. Cook over moderate heat for 10–15 minutes until the potatoes are golden brown on the underside.

4 Transfer the covered pan to the oven. Bake at 200°C (400°F) mark 6 for 30 minutes, or until the potatoes feel tender when pierced with a skewer. Remove from the oven and leave to rest, covered, for 10 minutes.

5 Uncover the potatoes and place a warmed flat serving plate on top. Invert the potato galette on to the plate. Serve hot, cut into 8 equal wedges.

Note You will need a frying pan or skillet with an ovenproof handle and lid to make this galette – the French cast iron type is ideal. If your pan handle and lid knob are not ovenproof, cover them with several thicknesses of foil for protection, or bake the galette in a sandwich tin. Any leftover galette can be reheated at 200°C (400°F) mark 6 for about 15 minutes. Wrap in foil and brush with a little extra butter, unwrap for the last 5 minutes.

DRINKS TO SERVE
A fruity dry white wine is ideal to serve as an aperitif and with the smoked salmon. Choose a Chardonnay, Chablis or a Sauvignon Blanc and then follow with a full-bodied red wine such as a vintage Rioja to serve with the duck.

COOK'S HINTS
1 The best **smoked salmon** for making roulades is sold in supermarkets in packets labelled 'complete slices' or 'perfect slices'. With these you are guaranteed to have the correct number of large whole slices you need. There will be no waste and no ragged or torn pieces that are difficult to roll up around the filling.

To cut the salmon into even slices, use a very sharp knife and a sawing action. Dip the knife into lukewarm water between each slice so that it cuts cleanly and neatly.

2 Starch is essential to help the **potatoes** stick together as a 'cake'. If you want to get ahead with preparation, you can peel the potatoes and leave them to soak in a bowl of cold water, but do not slice them into rings as this will cause the starch to leach out into the water.

The potatoes should be sliced very thinly for them to cook evenly. The fine cutting blade of a food processor is ideal for this, or you can use a mandoline.

Smoked Salmon Roulade (opposite)

MENU SUGGESTIONS
Any of the classics such as Beef Wellington (page 246) or Coq au Vin (page 250) fit splendidly into this menu. For pudding, try Hazelnut Brûlée or Ginger Meringues with Rhubarb Sauce (both on page 263).

BLUEBERRY DUCK

8 boneless duckling breast fillets, each weighing about 175 g (6 oz)
salt and freshly ground pepper
BLUEBERRY SAUCE
300 g (11 oz) blueberries
150 ml (¼ pint) dry white wine
10 ml (2 tsp) caster sugar, or to taste
90 ml (6 tbsp) freshly squeezed orange juice
60 ml (4 tbsp) crème de cassis
30 ml (2 tbsp) wine vinegar, preferably blackcurrant
25 g (1 oz) unsalted butter, at room temperature
30 ml (2 tbsp) chopped fresh mint
orange slices and mint sprigs, to garnish

1 Lay the duckling fillets, skin side down, on a board. Cover with greaseproof paper and pound with a meat mallet or rolling pin to flatten the fillets slightly. Turn the fillets skin side up and score the skin on the diagonal with a sharp knife. Sprinkle with salt and pepper.

2 Place the duckling fillets, skin side up, in a single layer on a rack in a large roasting pan. Cook in the hottest part of the oven at 200°C (400°F) mark 6 for 20–30 minutes, according to how well done you like duck cooked.

3 Make the blueberry sauce, reserve about one quarter of the blueberries to garnish. Put the remainder in a heavy saucepan with the white wine and 10 ml (2 tsp) sugar. Bring to the boil, stirring, then cover and simmer for 10 minutes until the blueberries are soft, stirring occasionally. Remove from the heat and work through a sieve into a jug.

4 Return the puréed blueberries to the pan and add the orange juice, cassis, wine vinegar and salt and pepper to taste. Bring to the boil, then whisk in the butter a little at a time until melted. Simmer until the sauce is reduced and thickened, stirring constantly, then taste and adjust seasoning, adding more sugar if the sauce seems too tart. Keep the sauce hot, on the lowest possible heat, stirring occasionally.

5 Remove the duckling from the oven and cut into neat, thin slices, diagonally across the grain. Remove and discard the skin, if you prefer. Transfer the duckling fillets to warmed dinner plates, fanning out the slices attractively.

6 Remove the blueberry sauce from the heat and stir in the reserved whole blueberries and the chopped mint. Spoon a little blueberry sauce next to the duckling slices, then garnish with orange slices and mint sprigs. Serve hot, with any remaining blueberry sauce handed separately in a sauceboat.

To Freeze Cool the blueberry sauce at the end of step 4. Pack into a rigid container and freeze for up to 3 months. Thaw at room temperature for at least 4 hours, then continue.

BRULÉED LEMON TART

The unusual topping of sweet bruléed sugar contrasts well with the tangy lemon filling in this luscious tart.

PASTRY
175 g (6 oz) plain flour
pinch of salt
75 g (3 oz) caster sugar
75 g (3 oz) unsalted butter, chilled
3 egg yolks
FILLING AND TOPPING
4 eggs
4 egg yolks
125 g (4 oz) caster sugar
finely grated rind of 1 lemon
175 ml (6 fl oz) lemon juice
50 g (2 oz) unsalted butter, at room temperature
300 ml (½ pint) double cream
50 g (2 oz) icing sugar

1 Make the pastry, sift the flour, and salt on to a cold surface. Sprinkle with the sugar. Make a well in the centre. Cut the butter in small pieces into the well, then add the egg yolks. With your fingertips, work the ingredients until they draw together to form a soft dough, gradually bringing the flour in from around the edge. Form the dough roughly into a ball and knead lightly until smooth.

2 Lightly flour the surface. Flatten the dough with a floured rolling pin, then roll out thinly and use to line a 28 cm (11 inch) loose-bottomed fluted flan tin. Prick all over with a fork, then chill in the refrigerator for 30 minutes.

3 Line the dough with foil and fill with bak-

Bruléed Lemon Tart (left)

ing beans. Bake blind on a preheated baking sheet at 190°C (375°F) mark 5 for 10 minutes. Remove the foil and beans, return the pastry case to the oven and bake for a further 10 minutes. Preheat the grill to hot.

4 Make the filling, beat the eggs and egg yolks lightly together, then pour into a heavy-based saucepan. Add the sugar and lemon rind and juice. Cook over a low heat, stirring all the time, until the mixture thickens and looks like lemon curd. Do not let the mixture boil or the eggs may scramble.

5 Remove the pan from the heat and whisk in the butter until melted.

6 Leave the filling to cool slightly. Lightly whip the cream then fold into the lemon filling. Remove the pastry case from the oven, pour in the filling and spread level. Sift the icing sugar evenly over the lemon filling. Carefully cover the pastry edge with a strip of foil then place the tart under the hot grill, as close to the source of heat as possible. Grill for 2–3 minutes, or until the sugar has melted and is beginning to caramelise. Remove the foil.

7 Remove the tart from the grill and leave to cool. Chill in the refrigerator for 1–2 hours then carefully remove the side of the tin and slide the tart on to a flat serving plate. Serve the tart chilled with chilled pouring cream if you like.

COUNTDOWN
The day before:
Make the Smoked Salmon Roulades to the end of step 5; cover and refrigerate. Make the pastry case for the Bruléed Lemon Tart to the end of step 2; cover and refrigerate.

On the day:
Wash the green salad; place in a polythene bag and refrigerate. Prepare a vinaigrette dressing for the salad, using lemon juice and a little mustard to make it sharp and tangy; keep in a covered container in the refrigerator. Pound the duckling fillets and score the skin as in step 1; place on the rack in the roasting pan and keep covered in a cool place. Make the blueberry sauce to serve with the duckling; keep covered in a cool place. Peel the potatoes for the galettes, but leave whole; keep in a bowl of cold water in a cool place.

To serve at 8pm:
6.00pm: Bake and grill the lemon tart. Chill in the refrigerator.
6.30pm: Slice the salmon rolls and arrange on plates with the garnish; keep covered in the refrigerator. Place the salad dressing and green leaves in a serving bowl but do not toss; keep covered in the refrigerator.
7.10pm: Continue with the potato galettes.
7.45pm: Allow the roulades and salad to come to room temperature. Cook the duckling as in step 2 of the recipe. In between courses, reheat the blueberry sauce and enlist help to slice the duckling; continue with step 5 of the recipe. Serve the green salad on side plates.

SUPPER PARTIES

A supper party should be a cosy, informal affair. The perfect host, at the end of a hard day, has a welcoming drink ready and a relaxed no-fuss evening planned. Create a calming atmosphere by decorating the room with fresh flowers and lighting it with candles or table or spot lights. If the whole room is flooded with centre lighting it tends to look business-like and harsh. If your lights have dimmer switches, make use of them.

To make sure that you are in a relaxed frame of mind, don't leave obvious chores, like cleaning, until the last minute. Get as much as possible ready the evening or morning before. If planning a supper party after work, opt for quick starters that guests can eat while you're preparing the rest of the meal. This saves worry if buses run late, or trains are delayed. Favoured delicatessen standbys are Parma ham served with fresh figs or melon, hummus, taramasalata and tzatziki served with pitta bread, or sliced goat's cheese on ciabatta flashed under the grill, or perhaps Bruschetta – thickly sliced bread, rubbed with garlic, toasted and topped with chopped tomato and basil.

If you don't have time to make dessert, buy a special gâteau or fruit tart from a reputable pâtisserie or offer fresh fruit instead. Follow this with one or two cheeses served with biscuits, then offer chocolates with the coffee to make a splendid end to the meal.

VEGETARIAN SUPPER

SERVES 8

This Italian-influenced supper is easy to prepare in advance, or it could be prepared from scratch in a couple of hours on the day. If you decide not to have the starter, the pizza recipe should be multiplied by one and a half. Individual pizzas look good, but might be difficult to fit into your oven, so we suggest that you make two huge pizzas and divide each one into four. The rocket salad is deliciously fresh, cutting the richness of the pizza. Follow with bitter-sweet coffee and chocolate Cappuccino Creams to complete the Italian mood of the meal.

GRILLED CHICORY WITH PEARS AND HAZELNUTS

Grilling the chicory transforms it by caramelising the juices. Pears brushed with hazelnut oil cut any bitterness associated with the vegetable.

4 large or 8 small heads of chicory, halved and cored

olive oil, for basting

2 ripe pears, halved, cored and sliced

45 ml (3 tbsp) hazelnut oil

15 ml (1 tbsp) chopped fresh thyme or 5 ml (1 tsp) dried thyme

freshly ground pepper

50 g (2 oz) hazelnuts, toasted and chopped

sprigs of fresh thyme, to garnish

1 Brush the chicory all over with olive oil. Place in a grill pan cut side up, and cook under a really hot grill (as near to the heat as possible) for about 3–4 minutes (2–3 minutes for smaller heads) or until just beginning to char and soften. Turn, baste with more oil and cook for a further 2–3 minutes (1–2 minutes for smaller heads).

2 Carefully turn the chicory again and top with slices of pear. Brush with hazelnut oil, sprinkle on the thyme, season with pepper and grill for 5-6 minutes (4-5 minutes for smaller heads). The chicory will be very soft, so carefully transfer it to warmed plates, scatter with the hazelnuts, garnish with extra sprigs of thyme and drizzle with remaining hazelnut oil. Serve with crusty Italian bread.

ROASTED PEPPER AND SWEET ONION PIZZA

This pretty pizza is easy to make and the topping ingredients can be prepared in advance, but don't use ordinary small onions – they will linger on the breath!

4 large yellow or red peppers

4 large white or red onions, skinned and sliced

olive oil

three 283 g (10 oz) packets white bread and pizza mix

two 200 g (7 oz) mozzarella cheeses, sliced

two 397 g (14 oz) cans chopped tomatoes, well drained

6 garlic cloves, skinned and thinly sliced

salt and freshly ground pepper

60 ml (4 tbsp) fresh oregano or basil leaves or 15 ml (1 tbsp) dried

1 Preheat the oven to 200°C (400°F) mark 6 or the grill to the hottest temperature. Bake or grill the peppers until blackening all over. Cover with a damp cloth and leave until cool enough to handle. Carefully peel off the skins. Remove and discard the stalks and seeds. Cut the flesh into thick strips.

2 Heat 60 ml (4 tbsp) olive oil in a frying pan, and fry the onions gently for 5 minutes until softened but not coloured. Set aside.

3 Make up the pizza dough following manufacturer's instructions substituting 60 ml (4 tbsp) oil for a similar amount of the liquid measurement. Divide in two and roll out into thin 30.5 cm (12 inch) rounds on a floured surface. Place each on a baking sheet.

4 Cover the pizza bases with the mozzarella. Scatter over the tomatoes, onions and peppers, then the slivers of garlic. Season with salt and pepper, drizzle with olive oil and brush the edges of the pizza with oil. Leave in a warm place for 20-30 minutes or until doubled in size. Bake in the oven for 15–20 minutes until golden and bubbling. Scatter with the herbs 5 minutes before the pizzas are cooked. Serve immediately whilst still hot.

To Freeze Make up the pizza dough, roll out and open freeze the bases until solid. Overwrap and freeze. Thaw 1–2 hours at cool room temperature.

Grilled Chicory with Pears and Hazelnuts (extreme right)

Cappuccino Creams (right)

COUNTDOWN
The day before:
Make the Cappuccino Creams, cover and refrigerate. Prepare pizza toppings. Roast, skin and slice the peppers, cover and chill. Prepare the onions, soften, cool, cover and chill. Skin and slice the garlic, cover and chill. Skin and chop the tomatoes, cover and chill. Slice the mozzarella, cover and chill. Cook the sugar snap peas, cool, cover and chill. Make the dressing in a screw-top jar. Wash and trim the rocket or watercress and store in a plastic bag in the fridge.
On the day:
Make up the pizza dough, put in a bowl and cover with a plastic bag. Refrigerate until 1 hour before.
To serve at 8pm:
6.45pm: Roll out the dough, slide onto baking sheets and scatter over the toppings. Leave in a warm place to prove. Grill the chicory, top with pears, cover and set aside. Place the rocket, tomatoes and sugar-snaps in salad bowl.
7.30pm: Take the Cappuccino Creams and Pizzas out of the fridge. Unwrap Creams and decorate with grated chocolate.
7.45pm: Put chicory in the oven to reheat for 10 minutes. Drizzle pizzas with oil. Tear herbs for the pizza garnish. Dress and toss salad.
7.55pm: Put the pizzas in the oven whilst you eat your first course. If you forget to scatter the herbs whilst cooking, do it just as the pizzas come out of the oven.

ROCKET, TOMATO AND SUGAR SNAP PEA SALAD

A crisp and colourful salad to freshen the palate! If you can't find rocket, (a peppery salad leaf much loved in Italy) use watercress for a similar flavour.

350 g (12 oz) sugar snap peas, topped and tailed
225 g (8 oz) rocket (roquette)
450 g (1 lb) cherry tomatoes
DRESSING
60 ml (4 tbsp) olive and sunflower oil, mixed
15 ml (1 tbsp) cider vinegar or lemon juice
5 ml (1 tsp) wholegrain mustard
salt and freshly ground pepper
pinch of sugar

1 Bring a pan of salted water to the boil and add the peas. Boil for 4 minutes then drain and refresh in cold water to stop the cooking process and keep the colour. Pat dry on absorbent kitchen paper.
2 Mix all the vegetables together, halving the cherry tomatoes, if liked.
3 Whisk all the dressing ingredients together and pour over the vegetables, mixing well to coat. Serve immediately.

CAPPUCCINO CREAMS

These little desserts are light but creamy and can be made with low-fat fromage frais if preferred. Use a good dark chocolate – the flavour is so much better.

550 g (1¼ lb) fromage frais
15–30 ml (1–2 tbsp) finely ground espresso coffee
15–30 ml (1–2 tbsp) icing sugar (optional)
175 g (6 oz) dark or bitter chocolate
chocolate curls, to decorate

1 Mix the fromage frais with the coffee and icing sugar, if liked.
2 Pulverise the chocolate in an electric blender or liquidiser until very fine. Alternatively grate finely.
3 Spoon half the fromage frais into eight individual ramekins or glass dishes. Sprinkle over most of the chocolate mixture. Top with the remaining fromage frais and sprinkle with the remaining chocolate mixture to give a speckled appearance like a cappuccino. Decorate with chocolate curls.

THAI INSPIRED SUPPER

SERVES 8

The ultimate in seafood suppers, Thai Prawn Curry is a deliciously fragrant, spicy dish that is remarkably quick to cook. In Thailand large, raw prawns are plentiful and inexpensive, here they are a luxury but are well worth the money, as they have much more flavour and texture than the small pre-cooked variety. Look out for them in good fishmongers, where they may be sold loose, or in the freezer cabinet. Served with a dish of Thai Fried Rice this makes a stunning main course.

Authentic Thai desserts are sweet concoctions, not always suited to Western tastes; so we've opted for a homemade Coconut Ice Cream that is cooling after the fiery main course, yet rich, creamy and flavoursome. A bowl of exotic fruits such as rambutans, mangosteens, custard apples, guavas or lychees, on the table would look good and guests can help themselves after the ice cream.

In Thailand the meal is likely to be served in brightly coloured plastic bowls. Use colourful china at home, if you have a choice, or invest in bright napkins. Light the room with candles and decorate it with exotic flowers such as orchids, to capture a little of the essence of Thailand.

THAI PRAWN CURRY

2 large onions, skinned and chopped
4 garlic cloves, skinned
7.5 cm (3 inch) piece of fresh root ginger, peeled and chopped
1 stalk of lemon grass, trimmed and roughly chopped
1–2 small chillies, or to taste
15 ml (1 tbsp) ground coriander
5 ml (1 tsp) ground cumin
1.25 ml (¼ level tsp) ground nutmeg
15 ml (1 tbsp) nam pla fish sauce
60 ml (4 tbsp) chopped fresh coriander
finely grated rind and juice of 2 limes
30 ml (2 tbsp) oil
1.8 kg (4 lb) medium or large, raw prawns in the shell
600 ml (1 pint) thick coconut milk (see page 64)
300 ml (½ pint) fish or vegetable stock
salt and freshly ground pepper
very finely shredded spring onions and chopped fresh coriander, to garnish

1 Put one onion, the garlic, ginger and lemon grass into a blender and process until finely chopped. Add the chillies, ground coriander, cumin, nutmeg, fish sauce, fresh coriander, lime rind and half of the oil and continue processing to make a paste.

2 Prepare the prawns, remove most of the shell, leaving the tail piece attached. Using a small, sharp knife, cut each prawn along the outer curve, stopping at the tail shell, to expose the dark vein (take care not to split the prawn completely in half).

3 Open each prawn and remove the dark vein. Rinse the prawns and drain thoroughly.

4 Heat the remaining oil in a large, shallow flameproof casserole dish. Add the remaining onion and cook for 5 minutes until golden brown, stirring all the time.

5 Add the spice paste and cook over a high heat for about 5 minutes until browned, stirring all the time. Add the milk and stock. Bring to the boil and simmer for 2 minutes.

6 Add the prawns and cook for a further 2–3 minutes or until the prawns are just pink. Turn off the heat and stir in the lime juice and salt and pepper to taste. Transfer to a serving dish and sprinkle with the coriander.

To Freeze Freeze the sauce at step 5. Open freeze previously unfrozen, prepared prawns

and pack into a polythene bag. Freeze the sauce and prawns for up to one month. To use, gently reheat the frozen sauce in a heavy-based saucepan, bring to the boil and add the frozen prawns. Complete as above.

THAI FRIED RICE

450 g (1 lb) basmati rice
salt
75 ml (3 fl oz) bland vegetable oil, such as corn or sunflower
15 ml (1 tbsp) nam pla fish sauce
2 hot chillies, chopped
4 spring onions, chopped
3 eggs, beaten (optional)
30 ml (2 tbsp) soy sauce
10 ml (2 tsp) brown sugar

MENU SUGGESTIONS
Satay of Prawn, Chicken and Beef would be an appropriate start to this meal. Halve the quantities and serve with chunks of cucumber, spring onions and prawn crackers. Raspberry Rose Ice Cream (page 96) or Coconut Custards with Tropical Fruits (page 64) are suitable alternatives to end the meal.

A selection of exotic fruit juices (above left)

1 Cook the rice, following the packet instructions, until almost tender. Drain, then rinse with boiling water. Spread out on a tray and leave to cool.

2 Heat the oil in a wok, then add the fish sauce, chillies and onions and stir fry for 1–2 minutes to flavour the oil.

3 Add the eggs, if using and stir fry until the egg scrambles, stirring all the time so that the egg sets in small pieces rather than one large lump.

4 Stir the rice with a fork to separate the grains, then tip into the hot oil. Stir fry with the eggs for 5–8 minutes until really hot (the time will depend on whether the rice was cold or warm before stir frying). Mix the soy sauce with the sugar, then stir into the rice. Serve immediately.

STIR FRIED MIXED VEGETABLES

4 large, fat carrots, peeled and trimmed
1 bunch of spring onions, trimmed
half a head of Chinese leaves, trimmed
30 ml (2 tbsp) vegetable oil
225 g (8 oz) French beans, trimmed
225 g (8 oz) mange tout, trimmed

1 Run a sharp potato peeler along the length of each carrot to peel off long, thin, ribbon-like strips. Cut the onions into long strips and the cabbage into large chunks.

2 Heat the oil in a large wok, add the beans and fry for 3–4 minutes, stirring all the time. Add the cabbage and carrots and stir fry for a further 2 minutes, then add the mange tout and cook for 1 minute. Pile onto a hot serving dish and serve immediately.

Coconut Ice Cream (right)

COUNTDOWN
The day before:
Make the prawn crackers and store in an airtight container. Make the Coconut Ice Cream.
On the day:
Prepare the paste and sauce for Thai Prawn Curry following steps 1, 4 and 5. Cover and store in a cool place. Prepare the prawns following steps 2 and 3. Cover and store in the refrigerator.
To serve at 8pm:
7.00pm: Prepare the vegetables for the Stir Fried Mixed Vegetables by following steps 1 and 2. Cover and store in the refrigerator.
7.30pm: Cook the rice. Cover and keep warm in a heatproof serving dish in the oven until ready to serve. Reheat the sauce for the Thai Prawn Curry.
7.55pm: Stir fry the mixed vegetables and when they are almost ready, add the prawns to the curry sauce. Remove the ice cream from the freezer and leave at room temperature for 20–30 minutes to soften before serving.

COCONUT ICE CREAM

This is not a true ice cream since it doesn't contain fresh cream. Strictly speaking it is a sorbet, but the coconut milk gives a creamy texture and flavour. It's extremely moreish!

275 g (10 oz) granulated sugar
600 ml (1 pint) water
four 450 ml (¾ pint) cans coconut milk

1 To make the syrup, place the sugar and water in a medium saucepan. Heat gently until the sugar dissolves, then boil gently for 10 minutes without stirring. Leave to cool.

2 Mix the cold syrup with the coconut milk and pour into a shallow freezer container. Cover and freeze on fast freeze for about 3 hours or until just frozen all over. The mixture will have a mushy consistency.

3 Spoon into a bowl and mash with a fork to break down the ice crystals. Work quickly so that the ice cream does not melt completely.

4 Return the mixture to the container and freeze for about 2 hours, or until mushy. Mash as step 4. Return to the freezer and freeze for about 3 hours or until firm.

5 Remove from the freezer and leave at room temperature for 20–30 minutes to soften before serving (do not forget to return the freezer setting to normal).

LOW CALORIE SUPPER

*D*ieting and dinner parties are not usually synonymous. Yet, with a little imagination, it is possible to entertain and count calories without putting your guests through an endurance test of dull food. By choosing ingredients carefully and making use of low fat and low sugar products available, we show you how to entertain in grand style on about 720 calories (or 900 with two glasses of wine) and your non-dieting guests need never know.

Mussels make an excellent starter – rich in protein and vitamins, yet low in fat and calories. Cooked in this way, they need no accompaniment, but some guests may want bread to dip into their delicious broth. Serve it without butter, and remember that it will add about 65 calories per slice to the meal. Lean white meat or white fish is always the best choice for a main dish when counting the calories. We've opted for pork tenderloins in a citrus sauce spiked with ginger.

To finish there are splendid Apple Mint Meringues. Light meringue bases topped with dollops of Greek-style yogurt and apple purée, dusted lightly with icing sugar (a little of this superfine sugar goes a long way!). Meringues are surprisingly low in calories since they contain no fat.

COOK'S HINT

Soaking **mussels** helps to purge them of any impurities. Adding a handful of oatmeal, flour or bran can help plump them up before cooking. Don't soak in the same water for longer than 2 hours or they will die. If time is short this soaking process can be omitted.

MICROWAVE HINT

Reheat the Pepper Broth in a large bowl on HIGH for about 8–10 minutes, stirring occasionally. To reheat the Creamed Garlic Potatoes in the microwave, add 30 ml (2 tbsp) skimmed milk, cover and cook on HIGH for 6–10 minutes, stirring occasionally.

Steamed Mussels in Pepper Broth (above)

STEAMED MUSSELS IN PEPPER BROTH

2.7 kg (6 lb) fresh mussels
salt and freshly ground pepper
a little oatmeal
15 ml (1 tbsp) olive oil
2 medium onions, skinned and finely chopped
275 g (10 oz) red peppers, seeded and finely chopped
2 bay leaves
1 garlic clove, skinned and crushed
450 g (1 lb) tomatoes, skinned, seeded and chopped
30 ml (2 tbsp) chopped fresh dill
diced red pepper, to garnish

1 Discard any cracked mussels and any that remain open when tapped smartly on the shell. Scrub the mussels, pull off the coarse threads (the beard) from the side of the shells and soak in cold water with a little salt and oatmeal for at least 30 minutes or a couple of hours.

2 Heat the oil in a medium saucepan. Sauté the onion with the red pepper, 1 bay leaf and the garlic until it begins to soften. Add the tomatoes and cook, stirring, for 1–2 minutes before adding 900 ml (1½ pints) of water. Bring to the boil, cover and simmer for about 15 minutes. Purée the mixture in a blender or food processor then sieve into a clean saucepan. Season.

3 Drain and rinse the mussels. Place in a large saucepan. Add 150 ml (¼ pint) of water and the remaining bay leaf. Cover the pan tightly and place over a high heat. Steam the mussels, shaking the pan occasionally, for about 3–5 minutes. Discard any mussels that have not opened.

4 Strain the cooking liquid from the mussels into the pepper broth. Stir in the chopped dill and bring to the boil. Adjust the seasoning. Divide the mussels between 8 serving bowls and pour over the pepper broth. Garnish with the diced red pepper.

5 To eat, use an empty shell like a pair of tweezers to pinch the mussels from their shells. Set a plate beside each guest for the 'empties'. You will also need spoons for the delicious pepper broth left in the bowls.

To Freeze Freeze the pepper broth only, in a rigid container. Thaw overnight at cool room temperature.

PORK TENDERLOIN WITH ORANGE AND GINGER

Pork tenderloin is very lean, but trim off all visible fat before cooking.

grated rind and juice of 1 orange
grated rind and juice of 1 lemon
50 g (2 oz) piece fresh root ginger, peeled and finely grated
30 ml (2 tbsp) Hoisin sauce
15 ml (1 tbsp) granulated artificial sweetener
1 garlic clove, skinned and crushed
900 g (2 lb) pork tenderloins
275 g (10 oz) carrots
vegetable oil
350 g (12 oz) chicken stock
50 g (2 oz) half-fat butter spread
salt and freshly ground pepper
chopped fresh parsley and orange segments, to garnish

1 Stir together the grated orange and lemon rind and 50 ml (2 fl oz) each of orange and lemon juice. Add the ginger, Hoisin sauce, artificial sweetener and the garlic.

2 Trim the tenderloins of any excess fat. Place in a large, shallow dish. Pour over the ginger mixture and roll the tenderloins to coat completely. Cover and marinate in the refrigerator for at least 3–4 hours, preferably overnight.

3 Cut the carrots into 5 cm (2 inch) matchstick lengths. Drain the pork from the marinade. Lightly grease a large non-stick frying pan with a little oil. Brown the pork tenderloins on all sides. Pour over the ginger marinade and the chicken stock. Add the carrots. Cover and simmer very gently for 25–30 minutes or until the pork and carrots are cooked.

4 Remove the tenderloin with a slotted spoon and slice thickly. Boil the pan juices to reduce until slightly thickened and syrupy – about 2–3 minutes. Off the heat, gradually whisk the half-fat butter spread into the sauce. Adjust the seasoning.

5 Return the tenderloin to the pan, cover and simmer very gently for 1–2 minutes, until heated through. Sprinkle generously with chopped parsley and garnish with the orange segments to serve.

Pork Tenderloin with Orange and Ginger (above)

MENU SUGGESTIONS
Other suitable main courses are Pheasant Breasts with Vermouth (page 254) or for vegetarians, Stir Fry Salad with Paneer (page 258). Autumn Pudding (page 68) with artificial sweetener is a splendid alternative to the meringues.

Apple Mint Meringues (right)

COUNTDOWN
The day before:
Make the Pepper Broth by following stages 2 and 3. Cool, cover and refrigerate. Marinate the pork. Cover and refrigerate. Prepare the carrots and shred the cabbage. Refrigerate in polythene bags. Make the meringues. Cool and store in an airtight container. Cook the apple, cool, cover and refrigerate.
On the day:
Prepare the mussels and garnishes for the mussels and the pork . Cook, drain and sieve the potatoes. Cool, cover and refrigerate.
To serve at 8pm:
7.00pm: Assemble the Apple Mint Meringues and refrigerate. Drain the mussels, then put into a large saucepan with the water and a bay leaf.
7.20pm: Brown and cook the tenderloins. Remove to a board but don't slice yet. Cover loosely with foil. Boil and reduce the pan juices, then set to one side.
7.30pm: Put the broth in a saucepan ready to reheat. Place the potatoes in a saucepan with the yogurt or cream and seasoning, ready to reheat. Put a pan of water on to boil for the cabbage.
7.40pm: Cook the cabbage and toss with the half-fat spread. Reheat the potatoes. Keep both warm, covered, in ovenproof dishes in a low oven.
7.50pm: Steam the mussels and reheat the broth. Strain the cooking liquid from the mussels into the broth and add the dill. Slice the pork and add to the ginger sauce with the half-fat spread. Bring the pork and sauce to the boil, cover and simmer very gently while serving the mussels.

SHREDDED CABBAGE

900 g (2 lb) savoy cabbage, trimmed and finely shredded
salt and freshly ground pepper
25 g (1 oz) half-fat butter spread

1 Cook the cabbage in boiling salted water for a few minutes only, until just tender. Drain well. Toss with the half-fat butter spread. Adjust seasoning.

CREAMED GARLIC POTATOES

1.8 kg (4 lb) old potatoes
salt and freshly ground pepper
1 large garlic clove, skinned and crushed
60 ml (4 tbsp) Greek-style yogurt or single cream
grated nutmeg

1 Peel and roughly chop the potatoes. Cook in boiling salted water for about 15–20 minutes or until very tender. Drain well. Sieve, or press through a potato ricer until very smooth.
2 Beat in the crushed garlic and the yogurt or cream. Adjust the seasoning and reheat gently before serving sprinkled with the grated nutmeg.

APPLE MINT MERINGUES

2 egg whites
125 g (4 oz) caster sugar
450 g (1 lb) sweet eating apples, peeled, cored and thinly sliced
15 ml (1 tbsp) granulated artificial sweetener
4 fresh mint sprigs
150 g (5 oz) Greek-style yogurt, or fromage frais
15 ml (1 level tbsp) icing sugar, sprigs of fresh mint and apples slices, to decorate

1 Whisk the egg whites until stiff but not dry. Add half of the sugar and whisk until stiff and shiny. Fold in the remaining sugar.
2 Mark sixteen 7.5 cm (3 inch) rounds on a sheet of non-stick baking parchment. Place on a baking sheet, pencil side down. Divide the meringue mixture between the rounds and spread with a round bladed knife to fill. Alternatively, using a 5 mm (¼ inch) plain nozzle, pipe the mixture into the rounds. Bake at 140°C (275°F) mark 1 for about 1 hour or until completely dried out and crisp. Leave to cool on a wire rack.
3 Place the apple in a saucepan with the sweetener,the mint and 30 ml (2 tbsp) water. Cover and cook very gently for about 10 minutes or until the apple has softened. Cool, cover and chill for at least 1 hour.
4 To serve, spoon a little apple onto 8 meringue rounds. Top with the yogurt and the remaining meringues. Dust lightly with icing sugar and decorate with the sprigs of fresh mint and apple slices to serve.

TEA AND COFFEE PARTIES

This type of party may be a purely social occasion for a sizeable number of friends, neighbours and family, such as a Christening or birthday, or it may arise because there is a committee meeting or some other activity taking place in your home. Whatever the reason, it's a good way of entertaining a number of people without going to all the expense and effort of a dinner or cocktail party.

Hand round food on trays or platters lined with napkins (enlist a friend to help with the serving), and provide plenty of extra napkins for your guests to use. Serve dainty sandwiches for tea, with the crusts cut off. Cut them into different shapes, using pastry cutters to add interest, and garnish with mustard and cress, watercress, parsley or cherry tomatoes. In winter, a few hot savoury pastries would be welcome, or some hot buttered scones, crumpets or muffins.

Provide both China and Indian tea, with milk and sugar, and also thinly cut slices of lemon for those who prefer it. If serving coffee, offer both cream and milk and coffee sugar.

A tea party provides the perfect excuse for bringing out your prettiest china; there's no doubt that tea tastes infinitely better from a fine bone china cup. Pastry knives and forks are useful on these occasions, and don't forget your most beautiful tablecloths and a vase of flowers. The exception to all this is, of course, a children's party, when disposable cups, plates and tablecloths are most suitable, even essential!

CHRISTENING TEA

MENU

OPEN SANDWICHES

PARMESAN PALMIERS

TINY CARAWAY SCONES WITH SMOKED
SALMON AND CREAM CHEESE

CHOUX SWANS

CHRISTENING CAKE

SERVES 20

A Christening is a once-in-a-lifetime event that is remembered forever, by the parents of the child and the invited friends and relations. The menu suggested here is ideal for just such an occasion. Our party is for 20, but the recipes are all easy to double up if yours is a larger affair. To welcome the guests on their arrival from church there are delicious appetisers to be eaten with drinks. The main spread is a colourful array of open sandwiches. They can all be assembled before you go to church, and can be as elaborate or simple as you like depending on the time available. The choux swans, filled with Grand Marnier flavoured cream and strawberries, look very pretty and are easier to make than you think. Then, there is the Christening Cake which makes an eye-catching centrepiece. Instructions for making the cake can be found on page 267. If you have kept the top tier of your wedding cake especially for this day, simply remove the original icing and the marzipan and re-ice the cake following the instructions given here. It is customary to offer a glass of champagne with the cake, and to drink a toast to the new arrival.

OPEN SANDWICHES

Each makes one sandwich
(allow at least two per person).

Prawns with Lemon and Coriander
Mix 15 ml (1 tbsp) mayonnaise with a little chopped fresh coriander and spread it on crustless toast or dark rye bread. Cover with 50 g (2 oz) juicy prawns. Season to taste. Garnish with a twist of lemon and coriander.

Lumpfish Roe with Eggs
Lightly spread oblong wheat crackers or brown bread with butter and arrange a small bundle of fresh watercress or mustard cress at one end. Cover the remainder with 5 ml (1 tsp) lumpfish roe topped with slices of hard-boiled egg.

Blue Brie, Bacon and Lamb's Lettuce
Lightly spread pumpernickel bread with butter. Arrange lamb's lettuce leaves along one long edge. Cover the bread with very thin slices of blue Brie cheese, overlapping them on to the lettuce. Top the cheese with 1 slice of crisp, grilled back bacon.

Poached Salmon on Pumpernickel
Spread pumpernickel bread with 25 g (1 oz) soft cheese mixed with horseradish sauce to taste. Cover with flakes of poached salmon, fresh dill sprigs or celery leaves and lemon wedges.

Roast Beef and Mustard Mayonnaise
Spread lightly toasted, crustless bread with Dijon mustard and mayonnaise. Top with slices of rare roast beef and garnish with fine onion rings and bows of fresh chives.

Hummus with Sesame
Spread crunchy crispbreads with hummus. Sprinkle liberally with toasted sesame seeds and garnish with olives and parsley.

Smoked Chicken and Orange
Stamp out rounds of light rye bread. Mix together equal quantities of Greek yogurt and soft cheese with herbs; spread on the bread rounds. Top with thin slices of smoked chicken, orange segments and shreds of spring onion.

Salami and Tomato
Spread lightly toasted, crustless Granary bread with mayonnaise. Top with slices of salami and halved cherry tomatoes. Garnish with basil leaves.

Emmenthal and Watercress on Rye
Spread dark rye bread with mild mustard blended with butter. Top with sprigs of watercress and thin slices of Emmenthal cheese.

Ham and Mango
Spread lightly toasted, crustless Granary bread with butter and thin slices of juicy mango and thin slices of ham. Garnish with parsley.

PARMESAN PALMIERS

Delicate little cheese flavoured biscuits.

MAKES 48
two 368 g (13 oz) packets frozen puff pastry, thawed
50 g (2 oz) freshly grated Parmesan cheese
mild paprika, for sprinkling
sesame seeds

1 Roll out each packet of pastry on a lightly floured surface to a rectangle measuring 30 × 25 cm (12 × 10 inches).
2 Sprinkle with a little of the Parmesan cheese and the paprika. Fold the long sides of the puff pastry halfway towards the centre.
3 Dredge with cheese and paprika and fold again, taking the sides right to the centre.
4 Dredge with paprika and fold in half lengthways, hiding the first folds and pressing down lightly.
5 Cut across each length into 24 equal sized slices. Dampen 2 baking sheets and place the palmiers on, cut-side down. Flatten them slightly with a palette knife or the palm of your hand. Sprinkle with sesame seeds.
6 Bake in the oven at 220°C (425°F) mark 7 for 8 minutes until golden brown. Turn each over and bake for a further 6–8 minutes. Transfer to wire racks and leave to cool.
To Freeze Pack in rigid containers and freeze for up to 1 month. Thaw overnight at cool room temperature.

COOK'S HINTS
1 Private Christenings, which do not form part of another service, usually take place in the afternoon, in which case it's customary to follow them with a tea. All those who attend the service, including the priest or vicar, should be invited. A small lunch or drinks party would be just as appropriate if the Christening forms part of the morning or early evening service.

2 Presentation is most important when preparing **open sandwiches.** Serve them on large flat platters. Pay particular attention to arrangement of the food and garnishing. If you are expecting lots of children at the party, make some plainer sandwiches for them. Keep the sandwiches in a cool place until ready to serve.

MENU SUGGESTIONS
If you wish to serve a Christening lunch instead of tea, a buffet is simplest. Welcome guests with the savouries given here, and offer a buffet spread of Spiced Chicken Terrines with herbed mayonnaise (page 270), Seafood Filo Bundles (page 273) with a selection of yopur favourite salads. For dessert try Strawberry Flans with Praline Cream or Chocolate and Grand Marnier Meringues (both on page 274).

TINY CARAWAY SCONES WITH SMOKED SALMON AND CREAM CHEESE

MAKES ABOUT 44
450 g (1 lb) self-raising flour
5 ml (1 level tsp) salt
5 ml (1 level tsp) baking powder
15 ml (1 tbsp) caraway seeds
75 g (3 oz) butter
2 eggs, beaten
about 150 ml (¼ pint) milk
beaten egg, to glaze
poppy seeds
125 g (4 oz) cream cheese
125 g (4 oz) thinly sliced smoked salmon
dill sprigs, to garnish

1 Preheat 2 large baking sheets in the oven set at 230°C (450°F) mark 8. To make the scones, sift the flour, salt and baking powder into a bowl. Crush the caraway seeds in a pestle and mortar and stir into the dry ingredients. Rub in the butter.

2 Make a well in the centre of the dry ingredients. Beat the eggs and milk together then pour into the well. Mix with a knife to give a fairly stiff dough. Add the remaining milk mixture if necessary.

3 Turn onto a floured surface, knead very lightly then roll out to 2 cm (¾ inch) thick.

4 Cut out 4 cm (1½ inch) round, heart or oval shapes. Carefully gather up the trimmings, re-roll and cut out more scones. Place on the hot baking sheets. Brush the tops with egg and sprinkle with a few poppy seeds.

5 Bake near the top of the oven for 10–12 minutes, until well risen and golden brown. Transfer to wire racks to cool.

6 To serve, split the scones, spread with a little cream cheese and top with a piece of smoked salmon. Place a dill sprig on each so that it pokes out from the middle. Pile up the scones on serving platters decorated with more dill sprigs.

To Freeze Cool the scones, pack in polythene bags, and freeze for up to 3 months. To thaw, place frozen scones on a baking sheet, cover with foil and cook in the oven at 200°C (400°F) mark 6 for 10 minutes.

CHOUX SWANS

These little swans are prepared the day before, ready to cook from frozen on the day. Don't assemble them too far ahead as they will become soggy.

MAKES 20
CHOUX PASTRY
250 g (9 oz) unsalted butter
350 g (12 oz) plain flour
9 eggs, beaten
FILLING AND DECORATION
75 g (3 oz) cornflour
75 g (3 oz) caster sugar
900 ml (1½ pints) full cream milk
5 ml (1 tsp) vanilla flavouring
900 ml (1½ pints) double cream
75 ml (5 tbsp) Grand Marnier
450 g (1 lb) fresh strawberries, hulled and sliced if large
icing sugar
2 large fully blown roses (pink ones for a girl, white ones for a boy) or blue borage flowers for a boy, depending on the time of year

1 To make the choux pastry, put 675 ml (23 fl oz) of water and the butter into a large saucepan and heat gently until the butter melts. Bring to the boil. Stir in the flour, all at once, and beat thoroughly. Cook over a moderate heat until the mixture forms a ball. Remove the paste from the heat and allow to cool a little, then put into the bowl of an electric mixer. Gradually beat in the eggs, a little at a time, beating well between each addition, to make a very shiny paste.

2 Line several large baking sheets with foil. Put some of the choux pastry into a large piping bag fitted with a 5 mm (¼ inch) plain nozzle and pipe 20 long 'S' shapes about

Choux Swans (top right)
Christening Cake (opposite)

10 cm (4 inches) long, on one baking sheet, spacing them apart to allow for rising. Any unpiped mixture in the piping bag can be returned to the bowl. These 'S' shapes will form the heads and necks of the swans.

3 To form the 'bodies', take well rounded tablespoonfuls of the choux paste and place them on baking sheets, easing the paste off the tablespoon with another tablespoon so as to keep the oval shape, spacing them well apart. Open freeze the choux shapes.

4 To prepare the filling, blend the cornflour and caster sugar with a little of the milk to form a smooth paste. Bring the remaining milk to the boil, then pour it on the cornflour mixture, stirring all the time. Return the mixture to a clean saucepan and bring back to the boil, stirring all the time. Take care that the custard does not burn. Reduce the heat and simmer for 2–3 minutes, stirring continuously. Beat in the vanilla flavouring. Pour the custard into a large bowl and cover the surface closely with damp greaseproof paper to prevent a skin forming. Cool, then refrigerate overnight.

5 Bake the choux shapes from frozen at 220°C (425°F) mark 7, until well risen, golden brown and firm. The 'bodies' will take about 35 minutes, and the 'S' shapes 20 minutes. Remove the 'bodies' from the oven and make a slit along the top of each one to

allow the steam to escape, then return to the oven for 5–10 minutes to dry out completely. Remove the 'S' shapes from the oven and make a small hole in the end of each one, then return to the oven for 5 minutes to dry. Cool on wire racks.

6 To complete the swans, whisk the chilled custard until it is very smooth. Whip 600 ml (1 pint) of the double cream with 60 ml (4 tbsp) of the Grand Marnier until it is thick, but not buttery. Fold the cream into the custard.

7 Cut each 'body' almost in half from the top to the bottom, just enough so that they can be pulled apart for filling. Three-quarters fill each one with the custard mixture, then insert an 'S' shape in the end of each one to resemble the head of a swan. Fill the swans with the strawberries.

8 Whisk the remaining cream with the remaining Grand Marnier until thick, but not buttery. Put the cream into a piping bag fitted with a star nozzle and use to decorate each swan. Sift icing sugar all over the swans.

9 Arrange the swans on large flat serving platters, and scatter with rose petals or borage flowers. Refrigerate until ready to serve.

To Freeze If you want to make Choux Swans well ahead of time, remove the frozen shapes from the baking sheets and pack into rigid containers. Freeze for up to 3 months.

COUNTDOWN
2 months before or more:
Make the cake, wrap and leave to mature. See page 266.
2 weeks before or more:
Marzipan and ice the cake. Make the icing swans and store in a safe place.
The week before or more:
Make the Parmesan Palmiers and the Caraway Scones and freeze. Make the choux paste for the Swans and freeze.
The day before:
Make the filling for the Choux Swans and refrigerate. Bake the choux cases, cool and store in an airtight container. Remove the Parmesan Palmiers and Caraway Scones from the freezer.
On the morning:
Assemble the cake. Prepare the open sandwiches, cover and refrigerate. Fill the Choux Swans and refrigerate. Fill the scones and refrigerate.

MORNING COFFEE PARTY

MENU

SPICED PEAR STRUDEL

DARK AND SINFUL CHOCOLATE CAKE

COFFEE HOUSE GATEAU

FRENCH APPLE TARTS

CHERRY AND COCONUT COOKIES

SERVES 8

A morning coffee party should be a friendly and relaxed affair; simply a good excuse for a get-together with friends, or perhaps an ideal opportunity to welcome a new neighbour. Either way, it is a perfect time to indulge in something deliciously wicked with a cup of lovely fresh coffee.

Goodies that can be prepared ahead of time and served with the minimum fuss are perfect for the occasion. Essential to the proceedings, and the ideal partner to coffee, is a rich and delicious chocolate cake or luscious gâteau (you could serve both if you are feeling particularly indulgent!). Prepare them in advance ready to add the finishing touches on the morning of the party.

A choice of mouthwatering pastries, such as Spiced Pear Strudel or tangy, refreshing French Apple Tarts served with lashings of whipped cream should appeal to everyone. And for those guests who still have room, provide a plate of cookies for them to sample. Finally, remember to keep making fresh brews of good, hot coffee throughout the party.

SPICED PEAR STRUDEL

For convenience, make the strudel in advance ready to reheat just before serving.

75 g (3 oz) fresh white breadcrumbs
150 g (5 oz) unsalted butter
50 g (2 oz) light soft brown sugar
50 g (2 oz) sultanas
2.5 ml (½ tsp) mixed spice
2.5 ml (½ tsp) ground cinnamon
450 g (1 lb) pears, peeled, cored and sliced
4 large sheets of filo pastry (see Cook's Hint on page 82)
50 g (2 oz) blanched almonds, toasted and chopped
15 ml (1 tbsp) redcurrant jelly (optional)
icing sugar, for dusting

1 Fry the breadcrumbs in 50 g (2 oz) of the butter, stirring frequently until crisp and golden. Mix together the brown sugar, sultanas, mixed spice, cinnamon and pear slices.

2 Melt the remaining butter. Brush one sheet of filo pastry with a little of the melted butter. Cover with a second sheet of pastry and brush with a little more melted butter.

3 Cover the pastry with half of the fried crumbs, leaving a 5 cm (2 inch) border on all sides. Arrange half the pear mixture over the crumbs and sprinkle with half of the chopped almonds. Dot with half of the redcurrant jelly, if using.

4 Fold the edges over the filling and brush with a little melted butter. Roll up, like a Swiss roll, starting from a long side. Place the strudel on a lightly greased baking sheet (with raised edges) and brush with melted butter.

5 Make a second strudel in the same way using the remaining ingredients.

6 Bake at 190°C (375°F) mark 5 for 35 minutes until crisp and golden, covering with foil during cooking if necessary, to prevent overbrowning. Brush halfway through cooking, with butter from the baking sheet.

7 Allow the strudels to cool slightly, then sprinkle liberally with sifted icing sugar. Serve warm or cold, cut into chunky slices.

To Freeze Cool, wrap and freeze at the end of step 6. Reheat from frozen at 180°C (350°F) mark 4 for 20 minutes. Finish as above.

DARK AND SINFUL CHOCOLATE CAKE

Especially for chocoholics! A tempting confection of moist chocolate cake, rich icing, chocolate caraque and cream. Make it in advance and add the finishing touches just before serving.

CAKE
200 g (7 oz) plain chocolate, broken into pieces
125 g (4 oz) unsalted butter
3 eggs, separated
125 g (4 oz) dark soft brown sugar
50 ml (2 fl oz) brandy
2.5 ml (½ tsp) vanilla flavouring
75 g (3 oz) plain flour
50 g (2 oz) ground almonds

ICING
175 g (6 oz) plain chocolate, broken into pieces
25 g (1 oz) unsalted butter
175 g (6 oz) icing sugar, sifted
45 ml (3 tbsp) warm water
300 ml (½ pint) double cream, stiffly whipped
plain and white chocolate caraque , to decorate

1 Grease and flour a deep 20 cm (8 inch) round cake tin and line the base with greaseproof paper.

2 To make the cake, put the chocolate and butter into a heatproof bowl and set over a pan of hot water until melted.

3 Meanwhile, put the egg yolks and sugar in a large bowl, place over a pan of hot water and whisk with an electric whisk until very pale and creamy and thick enough to leave a trail on the surface when the whisk is lifted. Remove from the heat and whisk until cool. Add the brandy and vanilla flavouring and whisk in the melted chocolate and butter mixture.

4 Add the sifted flour and the ground almonds and fold in gently using a metal spoon. Whisk the egg whites until stiff then very lightly fold into the mixture, a little at a time.

5 Pour the mixture into the prepared tin and bake at 180°C (350°F) mark 4 for 45–50 minutes or until firm to the touch. Cool in the tin for 10 minutes, then turn out and cool completely on a wire rack.

6 To make the icing, melt the chocolate and butter in a bowl set over a pan of hot water. Remove from the heat and gradually stir in the icing sugar and warm water to make a thick icing. Keep warm over the pan of hot water until ready to use.

7 Cut the cake in half and spread one-third of the icing over one half; cool, then top with one-third of the whipped cream. Put the remaining cake on top. Spoon the rest of the icing over the cake at once and swirl quickly with a knife to completely coat the top and sides of the cake. Leave to set.

8 Decorate the cake with the remaining whipped cream and chocolate caraque.

<u>*To Freeze*</u> Open-freeze the iced cake until icing is solid. Overwrap, seal and pack in a rigid container. Freeze for up to 2 months. Unwrap before thawing at room temperature for 6 hours, or overnight in the refrigerator. Chocolate caraque freezes quite well so it is worth keeping some for special occasions. Store caraque in a rigid container for up to 6 weeks.

Dark and Sinful Chocolate Cake (above)

Coffee House Gâteau
(above)

COFFEE HOUSE GATEAU

This delicious gâteau of whisked sponge, layered and decorated with smooth coffee crème au beurre and praline, can be made the day before it's needed. Refrigerate overnight and remove to room temperature at least 2 hours before serving.

SPONGE
75 g (3 oz) caster sugar
3 eggs
100 g (3½ oz) plain flour
CRÈME AU BEURRE
140 g (4½ oz) caster sugar
90 ml (6 tbsp) water
3 egg yolks
250 g (9 oz) unsalted butter
25 ml (1½ tbsp) coffee granules, dissolved in 15 ml (1 tbsp) boiling water
PRALINE
50 g (2 oz) unblanched almonds
50 g (2 oz) caster sugar

1 Grease a 33×23 cm (13×9 inch) Swiss roll tin and line the base and sides with greaseproof paper.

2 To make the sponge, put the sugar and eggs in a bowl, place over a pan of hot water and whisk with an electric whisk until very-pale and creamy and thick enough to leave a trail on the surface when the whisk is lifted.

Remove the mixture from the heat and whisk until cool.

3 Sift the flour, a little at a time, over the mixture and fold in lightly using a metal spoon, do not overmix. Turn the mixture into the prepared tin and very gently level the surface.

4 Bake at 190°C (375°F) mark 5 for 10–12 minutes until well risen and golden brown. Have ready a large sheet of greaseproof paper, sprinkled with a little caster sugar. Turn the sponge out onto the paper, remove the lining paper and leave to cool.

5 To make the Crème au Beurre, put the sugar and water into a small heavy saucepan and dissolve over a low heat. Once dissolved, boil steadily for 2-3 minutes until the syrup reaches a temperature of 107°C (225°F) on a sugar thermometer.

6 Beat the egg yolks in a bowl and pour over the hot syrup in a thin, steady stream, whisking all the time. Continue whisking until the mixture is thick and cool. In another bowl, cream the butter until soft, then gradually beat in the egg syrup, a little at a time, until thoroughly combined. Beat in the cold coffee mixture.

7 To make the praline, put the almonds and sugar in a non-stick frying pan. Heat very gently until the sugar melts and turns a rich dark golden brown. Meanwhile, well butter a baking sheet. Pour the almond caramel onto the baking sheet (take care as the mixture is very hot). Quickly coat and separate 8 almonds and leave to one side to set individually; leave rest of the praline to cool and set.

8 Roughly crush the praline in a blender or place between two sheets of greaseproof paper and crush with a rolling pin or meat mallet.

9 Cut the sponge crossways into 3 equal strips. Spread half the quantity of crème au beurre over 2 strips of sponge, then sandwich all three together. Spread the remaining crème au beurre over the top and sides of the gâteau. Cover the sides of the gâteau with the crushed praline. Put the remaining crème au beurre into a piping bag fitted with a small star nozzle and pipe along the top edge of the gateau. Decorate with caramel coated almonds.

To Freeze Open freeze without the praline coating until solid. Wrap, seal and freeze. Unwrap and thaw at room temperature for 2–3 hours. Coat and decorate.

FRENCH APPLE TARTS

Crisp golden pastry cases filled with tangy apple purée and topped with glazed apple slices can be prepared two days ahead of the party and stored in the refrigerator or at cool room temperature.

PASTRY
225 g (8 oz) plain flour
150 g (5 oz) unsalted butter
25 g (1 oz) caster sugar
1 egg yolk
15 ml (1 tbsp) cold water

FILLING
900 g (2 lb) cooking apples, peeled, cored and sliced
50 g (2 oz) caster or light soft brown sugar
15 g (½ oz) butter or margarine
finely grated rind of ½ lemon
15 ml (1 tbsp) lemon juice

TOPPING
2-3 small green dessert apples, peeled, cored and thinly sliced
15 ml (1 tbsp) lemon juice
25 g (1 oz) granulated sugar
icing sugar for dusting

1 Sift the flour into a bowl and rub in the butter until the mixture resembles fine breadcrumbs. Stir in the sugar, egg yolk and water and mix to form a dough. Knead lightly until smooth. Divide into 8 portions.

2 Roll out each portion on a lightly floured surface and use to line 8 greased 10 cm (4½ inch) diameter, loose based, fluted, flan tins. Press pastry firmly into the flutes, trim the top edges and prick the bases well with a fork. Chill for 30 minutes.

3 To make the filling, put the cooking apples in a saucepan with the sugar, butter, lemon rind and juice. Cover and cook gently for 10 minutes until tender. Beat to form a smooth purée. Leave to cool.

4 Bake the pastry case blind in the oven at 190°C (375°F) mark 5 for about 10-15 minutes. Remove the baking beans and greaseproof paper and cook for a further 5-10 minutes or until cooked through. Cool on a wire rack. (Leave in the tins.)

5 Spoon the cold apple purée into the pastry cases. Cover with the sliced dessert apples, then brush with lemon juice and sprinkle with the granulated sugar.

6 Put the tartlets on a baking sheet and bake at 190°C (375°F) mark 5 for 20-25 minutes until the apple is golden brown. Leave to cool before removing from the tins and serving dusted with icing sugar.

To Freeze Cool and open freeze the pastry cases until solid. Wrap in greaseproof and pack in rigid containers. Unwrap and thaw at room temperature for 1–2 hours. Complete as above.

CHERRY AND COCONUT COOKIES

MAKES 16
125 g (4 oz) butter or margarine
75 g (3 oz) caster sugar
50 g (2 oz) light soft brown sugar
2.5 ml (½ tsp) vanilla flavouring
1 egg
175 g (6 oz) plain flour
2.5 m l (½ level tsp) bicarbonate of soda
50 g (2 oz) desiccated coconut
15 ml (1 tbsp) milk
12 glacé cherries, quartered

1 Cream together the butter, sugars and vanilla flavouring until soft. Beat in the egg, beating until light and fluffy. Sift the flour and bicarbonate of soda into the mixture and stir lightly to combine.

2 Add 60 ml (4 tbsp) of the coconut and the milk. Divide into 16 portions and roll in the remaining coconut to coat.

3 Place the cookies, about 5 cm (2 inches) apart, on lightly greased baking sheets and press to form 6.5 cm (2½ inch) rounds. Arrange 3 quarters of cherry on top of each cookie.

4 Bake at 180°C (350°F) mark 4 for about 12 minutes until lightly golden and cooked through. Transfer to a wire rack to cool.

To Freeze Cool the cookies and then seal in polythene bags. Freeze for up to 3 months. Thaw cookies for about 1 hour at room temperature.

MICROWAVE HINT
Put the sliced **cooking apples** for the filling in a dish with the butter, lemon rind and juice. Cover and cook on HIGH for 4–5 minutes or until tender, stirring halfway through cooking. Stir in the sugar and leave to cool. If necessary boil to reduce and thicken the mixture before using.

COUNTDOWN
Two days before:
Make French Apple Tarts; fill, decorate and glaze. Cool, cover and refrigerate. Make the strudel; cool, cover and refrigerate. Make the cookies; cool and store in polythene bags. Make the chocolate caraque and store in a rigid container in the refrigerator.
The day before:
Make the chocolate cake; cool. Make the icing; fill and ice the cake. Refrigerate or keep at cool room temperature. Make the Coffee House Gâteau; cool. Meanwhile make crème au beurre; make and crush the praline. Assemble the gâteau; decorate and refrigerate overnight.
To serve at 11am:
8.00am: Remove Coffee House Gâteau from the refrigerator to allow crème au beurre to soften. Remove French Apple Tarts from refrigerator, if necessary, and leave at room temperature. Arrange cookies on a serving plate.
9.00am: Decorate the chocolate cake with whipped cream and chocolate caraque and keep at cool room temperature.
10.35am: Turn on the oven at 170°C (325°F) mark 3.
10.50am: Warm the Spiced Pear Strudel and dust with icing sugar before serving.
11.00am: Serve coffee, cakes, pastries and cookies.

AFTERNOON TEA

SERVES 8

Even in today's fast moving world afternoon tea remains a popular and elegant way to entertain. It also provides a marvellous opportunity to show off one's baking skills! Dainty sandwiches, plus a mouthwatering selection of goodies like tiny fruit tartlets; éclairs; meringues; plus biscuits and cake are usual tea-time fare. Bear in mind that a good balance of flavours, colours and textures ensures a tempting spread. And remember, too, that you don't have to cook it all on the day. Choosing recipes wisely means a good many items can be prepared in advance.

Sandwiches are nicest when freshly made and you can add interest by cutting them into pretty shapes with biscuit cutters, or by rolling and filling the bread before slicing. Meringues, éclairs, tartlet cases and biscuits can all be prepared beforehand and stored in airtight tins ready to fill and ice before serving. The banana loaf actually improves in flavour and slices better if wrapped and stored for 2–3 days before serving

SANDWICH PLATTER

A tempting selection of bite sized sandwiches .

AVOCADO AND MASCARPONE BITES
1 large avocado
5ml (1 tsp) lemon juice
125 g (4 oz) mascarpone (see Cook's Hint page 99)
salt
2 pinches of cayenne pepper
a little butter for spreading
4 slices light rye bread or pumpernickel
16 peeled prawns
16 tiny sprigs of dill

CHICKEN AND HAM PINWHEELS
125 g (4 oz) cooked chicken, minced or very finely chopped
30 ml (2 tbsp) mayonnaise
15 ml (1 tbsp) snipped chives
salt and freshly ground pepper
two 0.5 cm (¼ inch) thick lengthways slices of bread, cut from a large unsliced white sandwich loaf
a little butter for spreading
4 thin slices cooked ham

ROQUEFORT AND GRAPE SQUARES
50 g (2 oz) butter
few drops of lemon juice
⅓ bunch watercress, trimmed and very finely chopped
4 slices pumpernickel
50–75 g (2–3 oz) Roquefort cheese, crumbled
small black or green grapes, or use a mixture of each, halved and seeded

1 To make the Avocado and Mascarpone Bites, peel and mash the avocado until smooth. Add the lemon juice and mascarpone and mix well. Add salt and cayenne.

2 Transfer the mixture to a piping bag fitted with a large star nozzle. Spread slices of rye bread or pumpernickel with butter and cut out sixteen 4.5 cm (1¾ inch) rounds, using a fluted or plain cutter

3 Pipe the avocado mixture in swirls on the pumpernickel rounds. Garnish each one with a prawn and a sprig of dill.

4 To make the Chicken and Ham Pinwheels, mix together the chicken, mayonnaise, chives, and salt and pepper. Cut off crusts from the bread. Using a rolling pin, firmly roll each slice to flatten.

5 Spread each slice of bread with butter and cover with the ham. Spread the chicken mixture over the ham.

6 Roll up each slice, like a Swiss roll. Wrap individually in greaseproof paper and chill for at least 2 hours.

7 Unwrap and cut each roll into 1 cm (½ inch) thick slices.

8 To make the Roquefort and Grape Squares, blend the butter with the lemon juice and finely chopped watercress. Spread the butter mixture over slices of pumpernickel.

9 Cut the slices of pumpernickel into 4 cm (1½ inch) squares. Sprinkle a little cheese over each and top with a grape half. Arrange the sandwich selection on a platter.

ROSE PETAL MERINGUES

Unfilled meringue nests keep well in an airtight container for several weeks. To prevent meringues softening, serve the cream separately in a bowl and allow guests to help themselves. Once filled, meringues should be eaten right away.

3 egg whites
175 g (6 oz) caster sugar
FILLING
225 g (8 oz) clotted cream, or 300 ml (½ pint) double or whipping cream, whipped
a few drops rose water (optional)
crystallised rose petals (see Cook's Hint)

1 Mark eight 6.5 cm (2½ inch) circles on a sheet of non-stick baking parchment. Place on a baking sheet, pencil side down.

2 Whisk the egg whites until stiff but not dry. Add half of the sugar, and whisk until thick and glossy. Fold in the remaining sugar.

3 Transfer the meringue to a piping bag fitted with a 1 cm (½ inch) plain or star-shaped nozzle. Starting at the centre of each circle, pipe the meringue in a spiral out to the edge of the marked circles. Pipe another ring around the edge of each round to form small nest shapes.

4 Bake at 140°C (275°F) mark 1 (or at your oven's lowest setting) for about 1-1½ hours or until firm and dried out. Leave to cool on the baking sheet. Store in airtight containers until required.

5 Flavour the cream with a few drops of rose water, if wished and use to fill the meringues. Sprinkle with crystallised rose petals.

To Freeze Pack unfilled meringues into rigid containers and freeze for up to 3 months. To use, thaw meringues for about 1 hour at room temperature.

CHOCOLATE, COFFEE AND RASPBERRY ÉCLAIRS

A mouthwatering selection of dainty éclairs filled and iced in three different ways.

CHOUX PASTRY
65 g (2½ oz) plain flour
pinch of salt
150 ml (¼ pint) water
50 g (2 oz) butter, cut into pieces
2 eggs, beaten
FILLINGS
300 ml (½ pint) double cream
2 pieces stem ginger, chopped
15 ml (1 tbsp) seedless raspberry jam
10 ml (2 tsp) icing sugar
1.25 ml (¼ tsp) ground cinnamon
CHOCOLATE GINGER ICING
25 g (1 oz) plain chocolate, broken into pieces
7 g (¼ oz) butter
15 ml (1 tbsp) warm water
75 g (3 oz) icing sugar
5 ml (1 tsp) stem ginger syrup
RASPBERRY ICING
75 g (3 oz) icing sugar
15 ml (1 tbsp) seedless raspberry jam
10–15 ml (2–3 tsp) water
COFFEE ICING
5 ml (1 tsp) coffee granules
15 ml (1 tbsp) hot water
75 g (3 oz) icing sugar

1 To make the choux pastry, sift the flour and salt on to a piece of greaseproof paper. Put the water and butter in a saucepan and heat gently until the butter melts. (Do not allow the water to boil before the butter has melted.) Quickly bring to the boil, remove from the heat and immediately add the flour all at once. Stir quickly, using a wooden spoon, until the dough is smooth.

2 Return the pan to a medium heat and beat the dough with a wooden spoon until it forms a ball and leaves the sides of the pan clean.

3 Remove from the heat and cool slightly. Gradually add the beaten egg, a spoonful at a time, beating well after each addition. Continue beating to form a shiny dough which holds its shape, but is not stiff.

4 Transfer the choux pastry to a piping bag fitted with a large star nozzle. Pipe twenty four 5 cm (2 inch) lengths, about 5 cm (2 inches) apart on lightly greased baking sheets, cutting off at the ends with a wet knife.

5 Bake at 200°C (400°F) mark 6 for 12–15 minutes until well risen and lightly golden. Reduce oven temperature to 180°C (350°F) mark 4 and continue cooking for a further 10–15 minutes until crisp and golden brown. Slit along the side of each éclair to allow the steam to escape and return to the oven for 5 minutes. Leave to cool on a wire rack.

6 Whip the cream until thick, then divide into 3 portions. To one portion add the chopped ginger; stir the raspberry jam into another portion and the icing sugar and cinnamon into the remaining portion. Pipe or spoon each mixture into 8 éclairs.

7 To make the Chocolate and Ginger Icing, melt the chocolate and butter in a small heatproof bowl set over a pan of hot water. Stir in the warm water and icing sugar and mix well. Add the ginger syrup and stir to combine. (Stir icing occasionally to keep it smooth.) Dip the tops of the ginger-filled éclairs in chocolate icing and leave to set.

8 To make the Raspberry Icing, mix the icing sugar with the raspberry jam and water to form a smooth icing. Dip the raspberry cream-filled éclairs in icing and leave to set.

9 To make the Coffee Icing, dissolve the coffee in the hot water and mix with the icing sugar to form a smooth icing. Dip the cinnamon cream filled éclairs into the coffee icing and leave to set before serving.

To Freeze Open-freeze cooked (unfilled) éclairs until firm, then pack in layers in rigid containers. To use, place frozen éclairs on a greased baking sheet and refresh at 190°C (375°F) mark 5 for 5 minutes. Cool, then complete as above.

COOK'S HINT
To make the fillings lower in calories, use half quantity of cream mixed with fromage frais or natural yogurt.

A mixture of crème pâtissière and whipped cream makes an extremely good filling for **sweet éclairs**.

If preferred, the choux pastry may be piped into small balls instead of short lengths. Cook, fill and ice in the same way as éclairs.

MENU SUGGESTIONS
Toasted muffins or crumpets (bought from local bakers) and fruit scones are quick and easy alternatives or additions to this menu. To make fruit scones, follow the recipe on page 130 for Caraway Scones, making half the quantity and omitting the caraway. Add 50 g (2 oz) dried mixed fruit and 15-30 ml (1-2 tbsp) caster sugar to the dry ingredients.

TINY FRUIT TARTLETS

PÂTE SUCRÉE
65 g (2½ oz) plain flour
25 g (2 oz) caster sugar
40 g (1½ oz) butter, at room temperature, cut into small pieces
1 egg yolk
CRÈME PÂTISSIÈRE
1 egg yolk
25 g (2 oz) caster sugar
15 g (½ oz) plain flour
150 ml (¼ pint) milk
15 g (½ oz) butter
a few drops vanilla flavouring
a selection of fresh fruits, such as small whole strawberries, raspberries and black and green grapes

1 To make the pastry, sift the flour onto a clean surface. Make a well in the centre and add the sugar, butter and egg yolk. Using the fingertips of one hand pinch and work the sugar, butter and egg together until well blended. Gradually work in the flour, adding a little water if necessary to bind together. Knead lightly, then wrap and chill for about 1 hour.

2 Meanwhile to make the crème pâtissière, put the egg yolk and sugar in a bowl and beat until smooth and creamy. Stir in the flour and mix well. Heat the milk until hot, but not boiling, and gradually stir into the egg mixture. Return the mixture to the pan and bring to the boil over a low heat, stirring all the time. Remove from heat and beat in the butter and vanilla flavouring. Cover with damp greaseproof and leave to cool.

3 Roll out the pastry fairly thinly on a lightly floured surface and use to line about twenty four 4–5 cm (1½–2 inch) small fluted or plain tartlet tins. Prick the bases with a fork and chill for 15 minutes before baking.

4 Bake at 190°C (375°F) mark 5 for 6–8 minutes until golden brown and cooked through. Remove from tins and leave to cool.

5 Fill each tartlet with a little crème pâtissière and top each with an individual fruit.

To Freeze Freeze un-filled pastry cases in a rigid container. Thaw overnight at cool room temperature. Complete as above.

BANANA AND BRAZIL NUT LOAF

Ripe bananas give the best flavour to this cake. Choose fruit with yellow skins that are flecked with brown.

75 g (3 oz) soft margarine
175 g (6 oz) caster sugar
3 eggs
450 g (1 lb) ripe bananas
50 g (2 oz) whole shelled Brazil nuts, roughly chopped
225 g (8 oz) self-raising flour
Brazil nuts and icing sugar, to decorate

1 Grease a 900 g (2 lb) 1.4 litre (2 pint) loaf tin and line the base with greaseproof paper.

2 Cream together the margarine and sugar until light and fluffy. Gradually add the eggs, beating well after each addition.

3 Peel and mash the bananas with a fork, then stir into the creamed mixture. Add the chopped nuts. Sift the flour over the mixture and fold in lightly. Turn the mixture into the prepared tin and smooth the surface. Decorate with a few Brazil nuts.

4 Bake at 180°C (350°F) mark 4 for about 1½ hours until golden brown, firm to the touch and cooked through. Cover with foil if the loaf becomes too brown. Leave to cool in the tin. Sift icing sugar over the loaf to decorate just before serving.

To Freeze Wrap and freeze cake, without its topping, for up to 1 month. Thaw at room temperature overnight. Complete as above.

CHOCOLATE AND COCONUT CREAM ROULADE

The roulade needs to stand overnight before filling.

165 g (5½ oz) plain chocolate, broken into pieces
5 eggs, separated
175 g (6 oz) caster sugar
15 ml (1 tbsp) water
15 g (½ oz) cocoa powder, sifted
caster sugar, for dusting
300 ml (½ pint) double cream
50 g (2 oz) creamed coconut, grated or finely chopped
25 g (1 oz) flaked or shredded coconut, toasted

1 Grease a 33×23 cm (13×9 inch) Swiss roll tin and line with greased greaseproof paper.

2 Melt 125 g (4 oz) chocolate in a heatproof bowl set over a saucepan of hot water. Leave the chocolate to cool.

3 Whisk the egg yolks with the sugar until pale and fluffy. Add the water, melted chocolate and cocoa and whisk well to combine

4 Stiffly whisk the egg whites and lightly fold into the mixture. Turn the mixture into the prepared tin and level the surface.

5 Bake at 180°C (350°F) mark 4 for 20 minutes until well risen and firm to the touch. Remove from the oven, but do not turn out of the tin. Cover with a sheet of greaseproof paper and a damp tea towel and leave at room temperature overnight.

6 The next day, have ready a large sheet of greaseproof paper dusted with caster sugar. Turn the cake out on to the paper and remove the lining paper.

7 Stiffly whip the cream and fold in the creamed coconut. Spread half of the cream over the chocolate mixture and roll up, like a Swiss roll. (Don't worry when it cracks during rolling, as this won't show once the roll is complete).

8 Cover the roll with the remaining coconut cream and arrange the toasted coconut down the centre. Melt the remaining chocolate and, drizzle over the roll. Leave to set before serving.

To Freeze Open freeze, without the coconut and chocolate, until solid, then pack in a rigid container and freeze for up to 2 months. Thaw overnight in the refrigerator. Complete as above.

COOK'S HINT
Fresh coconut flakes
are easily made: first remove the tough dark skin from shelled coconut, then, using a potato peeler, 'shave' pieces of coconut into thin flakes. These flakes can then be shredded, if wished. Use strand or desiccated coconut for the decoration when fresh is unavailable.

MICROWAVE HINT
To melt the **chocolate**, break into small pieces into a bowl and melt on LOW for 4 minutes, stirring occasionally.

Chocolate and Coconut Cream Roulade (below)

143

COUNTDOWN
Two to three days before:
Make meringues. Cool, wrap and store in an airtight tin. Bake the éclairs. Cool and wrap in a polythene bag; store at room temperature. Bake the Banana and Brazil Nut Loaf, but do not add icing sugar. Cool, wrap and store at cool room temperature.
The day before:
Make and bake the tartlet cases. Cool and store in a rigid container. Make the Crème Pâtissière; cool, cover with damp greaseproof and refrigerate. Bake the chocolate mixture for the Chocolate and Coconut Cream Roulade; cover with greaseproof and a damp teatowel and leave at room temperature overnight. Make the Pistachio Rings.
The morning:
Fill and decorate the chocolate roulade., Leave to set. Sift icing sugar over the top of the Banana and Brazil Nut Loaf.
To serve at 4pm:
1.00pm: Prepare the Chicken and Ham Pinwheels; wrap and refrigerate.
2.00pm: Refresh the éclair cases; cool. Make the éclair fillings and use to fill éclairs; then prepare icings and finish éclairs. Leave to set.
2.30pm: Fill pastry cases with crème pâtissière and fruit; glaze and leave at room temperature to set.
3.00pm: Make the Avocado Mascarpone Bites; cover and refrigerate. Make the Roquefort and Grape Squares; cover and refrigerate.
3.45pm: Slice Chicken and Ham Pinwheel rolls. Arrange all three types of sandwich on a serving platter.
4.00pm: Serve afternoon tea.

Pistachio Rings (right)

PISTACHIO RINGS

These pretty biscuits are glazed while still warm with a thin glacé icing and chopped pistachios.

MAKES ABOUT 20
175 g (6 oz) butter
50 g (2 oz) caster sugar
225 g (8 oz) plain flour, sifted
15 ml (1 tbsp) milk
ICING
125 g (4 oz) icing sugar, sifted
30 ml (2 tbsp) fresh lime juice
40 g (1½ oz) shelled pistachio nuts, skinned and chopped

1 Cream the butter and sugar together until light and creamy. Stir in the flour and milk and mix to form a fairly soft dough.

2 Put the mixture into a piping bag fitted with a 1 cm (½ inch) star nozzle. Pipe the mixture into 5.5 cm (2¼ inch) diameter rings, spaced well apart, on greased baking sheets.

3 Bake at 180°C (350°F) mark 4 for 8–10 minutes until lightly golden and cooked through. Transfer to wire racks to cool slightly.

4 To make the icing, blend the icing sugar with the lime juice to make a thin consistency. Brush over the rings while still warm to glaze and sprinkle at once with chopped nuts. Leave to set before serving.

ALL THE FUN OF THE CIRCUS

M	E	N	U

CLOWN CAKE

BALLS OF FIRE

POPCORN

CUSTARD PIES

HARLEQUIN BISCUITS

JOLLY LOLLIES

RED NOSE BUNS

SERVES 12

A circus party calls for bright colours, silly games and lots of fun. To establish the circus theme, send out written invitations beforehand. Get your children to help design the invitations and decorate them with glitter or gummed shapes. Children are always delighted to receive a letter addressed personally to them. Make sure that the invitations ask guests to dress for the part (and that includes the adults!).

Cover the table with a brightly coloured paper tablecloth and tie a helium balloon to the back of each chair. Using an indelible marker write each guest's name onto a balloon, everyone will know where to sit and the balloons can be taken home after the party. Choose paper plates, cups and napkins with a circus feel – anything with a star, spot, stripe or harlequin pattern is ideal.

All the food in this menu can be prepared well in advance leaving plenty of time on the day for organising the decorations, music, games and goodie bags for the children to take home.

CLOWN CAKE

Make a podium for the clown to stand on by covering a deep upturned cake tin with foil or coloured paper and ribbons. Small helium-filled balloons are best for him to hold, because they remain airborn. If you can't find helium balloons, use the ordinary variety and attach to a coloured pipe cleaner so that the balloon stays up.

LARGE CAKE
45 ml (3 level tbsp) cocoa powder
350 g (12 oz) self-raising flour
10 ml (2 level tsp) baking powder
350 g (12 oz) caster sugar
350 g (12 oz) soft margarine
6 eggs

SMALL CAKE
30 ml (2 level tbsp) cocoa powder
175 g (6 oz) self-raising flour
2.5 ml (½ level tsp) baking powder
175 g (6 oz) caster sugar
175 g (6 oz) soft margarine
3 eggs

ICING AND DECORATION
five 227 g (8 oz) packets ready-to-roll icing
red and yellow edible food colouring
coloured paper
liquorice catherine wheels and bootlaces
assorted sweets, such as Smarties
cocktail sticks, satay sticks, coloured pipe cleaners
2 chocolate mini rolls

1 Grease a 1.6 litre (2¾ pint) pudding basin, and a 2.8 litre (5 pint) pudding basin. Line the bases with greaseproof paper.

2 To make the cakes (it's easiest to make one at a time unless you have a large capacity food processor), put all the ingredients in a food processor and process until smooth. Do not over process. Pour into the prepared basin and bake in the oven at 180°C (350°F) mark 4 for about 1 hour for the small cake and 1½ hours for the large cake, covering the tops of the cakes if they become too brown. Cool on wire racks.

3 To assemble the cake, trim the base of the large cake, if necessary, so that it stands level. Sit the larger cake, with the flat side down, on a board.

4 Hold the small cake upright in the palm of your hand. Using a sharp knife, trim around the wide top edge so that the cake curves inwards rather than outwards.

5 Colour one and a half packets of icing red, and one and a half packets yellow (or colours of your choice). Roll out the red icing and drape it over the large cake so that it covers half of it. Trim the icing around the base of the cake. Wrap the trimmings in greaseproof paper and set aside. Repeat with the yellow icing, covering the other half of the large cake. Neaten the join in the middle and press lightly together.

6 Cut a ruff for the clown's neck from the coloured paper. Moisten the top of the large cake with a little water and arrange the ruffle on top, pressing it in lightly, so that it sticks in position.

7 Roll out the remaining packets of icing and use to cover the small cake. Trim the icing so that it is neat around the base. Reserve the trimmings as before. Smooth out any creases with your fingers using firm rubbing movements. If the icing seems dry, moisten it with a little water.

8 Roll out the yellow icing trimmings and cut out star shapes with a small cutter. Stick onto the red icing. Unwind a liquorice catherine wheel and use to make stripes or checks on the yellow icing. Stick a Smartie onto the middle of each star. Stick the sweets from the centre of the catherine wheels or other large sweets of your choice, down the centre of the clown to represent buttons.

9 Roll a piece of the remaining red icing into a ball for the clown's nose. Rub it with your fingers until it shines. Stick it into position using a cocktail stick to secure it if necessary (it will depend how big you make the nose!) Cut two short pieces of catherine wheel to make crosses for the eyes. Stick onto the cake with water. Make the mouth from a piece of yellow icing and a piece of liquorice.

10 Mould two oval shapes from the icing trimmings to represent hands. Push a satay stick into the sides of the cake where one arm should be. Push a chocolate mini roll onto the satay stick so that it goes all the way through the roll and sticks out just enough at the end to spear the clown's hand. Push the hand into position. Repeat, to make another arm, pushing the satay stick in at an angle so that this arm is raised. Cut two small ruffles from the coloured paper and attach one to each arm between the hand and the mini roll.

11 Cut lengths of liquorice boot laces and stick onto his head to make his hair (moisten the icing with a little water if necessary to make it stick.)

12 Cover an upturned cake tin with coloured paper or kitchen foil and decorate with ribbon. Carefully transfer the clown onto the cake tin. Tie the balloons onto his raised arm.

13 Cut a 23 cm (9 inch) circle from a piece of coloured paper. Make a cut from one edge of the circle to the centre. Curve the paper round to make a hat. Secure with staples. Decorate the top with a pompom of shredded paper.

To Freeze Freeze the un-iced cakes until solid, overwrap and freeze for up to 3 months. Thaw overnight at cool room temperature.

BALLS OF FIRE

*Pizzas in different sizes cope
with large and small appetites;
add flavourings that children will like.*

MAKES 24
two 283 g (10 oz) packets of white bread and pizza mix
half a 440 g (1 lb) jar tomato sauce
chopped ham or chicken, crispy bacon, sausage, mushrooms, a few olives, sweetcorn
grated Cheddar cheese

1 Make up the bread mix according to the packet instructions. Divide it into small balls, some the size of walnuts others the size of ping pong balls and some slightly larger. You should make about 24 balls.

2 Flatten each ball with the palm of your hand, or a rolling pin. Using scissors, snip all the way around the piece to give the fire ball effect. Place on greased baking sheets, cover with a clean teatowel and leave in a warm place to prove until doubled in size.

3 When the dough has doubled in size, spread with the tomato sauce and topping of your choice. Sprinkle with the grated cheese. Bake in the oven at 230°C (450°F) mark 8 for 10–15 minutes (depending on their size).

To Freeze Open freeze the cooked pizzas. Overwrap and freeze for up to 3 months. To use bake as above, covered in foil adding an extra 5–10 minutes to cooking time.

Clown Cake, Jolly Lollies, Custard Pies, and Milkshakes (above)

POPCORN

*Serve popcorn in small paper cups or make cones
from semi-circular pieces of brightly coloured card,
curved round and secured with sticky tape.*

30 ml (2 tbsp) vegetable oil
150 g (5 oz) popping corn
about 30 ml (2 tbsp) caster sugar, or salt

1 Heat the oil in a large saucepan. Add the corn and cover with a tight-fitting lid. Keep the heat fairly high until the corn starts to pop.

2 Lower the heat slightly and continue to cook, shaking the pan occasionally for 2–3 minutes or until the popping stops. Season with caster sugar or a little salt.

> **COOK'S HINT**
> **Homemade popcorn**
> is lower in fat and salt than the shop bought equivalent. Once 'popped', corn will keep in an airtight container for up to 3 days.

CUSTARD PIES

*Custard Pies are universally favoured by clowns as
objects to throw at unsuspecting victims. This version
is not a foam and cardboard concoction, but a
delicious child size savoury. Vary the fillings to suit
the preferences and ages of the children. Chopped
cooked chicken, peas, mushrooms, crisp bacon, cooked
vegetables and smoked mackerel all work well.*

MAKES 24
225 g (8 oz) plain flour
salt and freshly ground pepper
225 ml (8 fl oz) semi-skimmed milk
2 spring onions, chopped
100 g (3½ oz) can tuna in brine, drained and flaked
2 small tomatoes, chopped
25 g (1 oz) Cheddar cheese, finely grated
2 slices lean cooked ham, chopped

1 To make the pastry, put the flour and a
pinch of salt in a bowl. Rub in the fat until
the mixture resembles fine breadcrumbs.
Add enough water to bind the mixture
together. Knead lightly then roll out on a
floured surface.

2 Thoroughly grease two 12 hole bun trays.
Cut out 7 cm (2¾ inch) rounds with a fluted
cutter. Press a round of pastry into each hole
in the bun tin.

3 Mix the eggs with the milk in a jug. Put a
few spring onions and flakes of tuna in eight
of the pastry cases. Arrange slices of tomato
and sprinkle with cheese in another eight
cases. Divide the chopped ham amongst the
remaining cases. Carefully pour the custard
into the pastry cases. Bake in the oven at
200°C (400°F) mark 6 for 35 minutes or
until the filling is just set and the pastry
lightly browned. Serve warm, or cold.

To Freeze When cold, pack in a rigid container, interleaving layers with greaseproof
paper and freeze for up to 3 months. Reheat
from frozen at 180°C (350°F) mark 4 for
10–15 minutes or until warmed through.

HARLEQUIN BISCUITS

MAKES 30
75 g (3 oz) plain flour
1.25 ml (¼ level tsp) bicarbonate of soda
2.5 ml (½ tsp) ground ginger
25 g (1 oz) butter or block margarine
40 g (1½ oz) light soft brown sugar
15 ml (1 tbsp) golden syrup
1 egg, size 6, beaten
227 g (8 oz) packet ready-to-roll icing
liquid food colourings
juice of ½ small orange
edible silver balls, to decorate

1 Grease two large baking sheets. Sift the
flour, bicarbonate of soda and ginger into a
bowl. Rub the fat into the flour and stir in
the sugar. Add the syrup with enough egg to
form a soft dough, then turn onto a lightly
floured surface and knead until smooth.

2 Using a floured rolling pin, roll out the
dough to a 25.5 cm (10 inch) square. Cut
into 5 cm (1 inch) wide strips. Separate the
strips then, cutting at an angle, cut off pieces
to make diamond shapes.

3 Place the biscuits on the prepared baking
sheets and bake in the oven at 190°C (375°F)
mark 5 for 8–10 minutes until golden brown.
Cool slightly then transfer to a wire rack.

4 When the biscuits are completely cold,
roll out the icing on a surface dusted with
icing saugar. Cut the icing into strips (as
when making the biscuits) Paint each strip a
different colour using a little food colouring. Wash and dry your brush between each
colour. Cut off diamond shapes. Moisten the
surface of each biscuit with a little orange
juice and top each biscuit with a piece of
icing and three edible silver balls. Leave to
set.

5 Serve the biscuits on a platter, arranged in
a harlequin pattern.

To Freeze Cool, pack and freeze the un-iced
biscuits at the end of step 4. Store for up to 6
months. Thaw at cool room temperature for
1–2 hours. Complete the recipe as above.

Place on a baking sheet. Repeat until all the bananas are covered. While the chocolate is still soft, sprinkle the bananas with hundreds and thousands, desiccated coconut or decorate with a few Smarties or sugar flowers.

4 Once the chocolate has set, open freeze the lollies (still on the baking sheets) then, transfer to rigid containers, interleaved with greaseproof paper.

5 To serve, remove from the freezer about 10–15 minutes before the party. Cut a slice off the grapefruit and oranges so that they will stand flat and place each, cut side down, on a plate. Using a sharp knife, make small cuts in the fruit skins. Push the lolly sticks into the cuts, so that the lollies stand up. Dot around the table.

RED NOSE BUNS

MAKES ABOUT 36
50 g (2 oz) soft margarine
50 g (2 oz) caster sugar
1 egg beaten
50 g (2 oz) self-raising flour
1.25 ml (¼ level tsp) baking powder
1 ripe banana, peeled and mashed
125 g (4 oz) icing sugar, sifted
about 15 ml (1 tbsp) orange juice
red glacé cherries or red spherical sweets

1 Put the margarine, sugar, egg, flour and baking powder in a food processor and process until smooth and well mixed. Add the banana and process for 1 minute.

2 Put a teaspoonful of the mixture into about 36 small petits fours cases. Arrange the filled cases on a baking sheet and bake in the oven at 190°C (375°F) mark 5 for about 12–15 minutes or until golden brown. Cool on a wire rack.

3 When the buns are cold, make the glacé icing by mixing the icing sugar with the orange juice until smooth and just thick enough to coat the back of a spoon. Top each bun with a small blob of icing and stick half a cherry or a sweet onto each. Leave to set.

To Freeze Cool, pack and freeze the un-iced buns at the end of step 2. Store for up to 6 months. Thaw at cool room temperature for 1–2 hours. Complete the recipe from step 3.

JOLLY LOLLIES

These jolly lollies are easy to make, relatively healthy to eat and fun to look at. Almost any sweet can be stuck onto the chocolate to decorate, but don't use nuts, small children can choke on them. Bananas will go black if frozen for any length of time, so make these lollies the evening before the party, no earlier.

450 g (1 lb) plain dessert chocolate
10 large bananas
20 lolly sticks
hundreds and thousands
toasted desiccated coconut
Smarties or sugar flowers
grapefruit and oranges to serve

1 Melt the chocolate in a bowl over a saucepan of simmering water.

2 Cut a banana in half widthways. Push a lolly stick into each of the cut ends to make two lollies from each banana.

3 Dip the banana halves into the chocolate. Use a pastry brush, if necessary to brush the chocolate along the banana. It must be completely coated (don't forget the cut end).

COUNTDOWN
One month before or more:
Make the sponge for the Clown Cake, the Balls of Fire, the Custard Pies, the un-iced Harlequin Biscuits, the un-iced Red Nose Buns.
The day before:
Assemble the cake. Ice the Harlequin biscuits and the Red Nose Buns. Make the Jolly Lollies and freeze.
On the morning:
Decorate the table and make any extras, like sausage rolls or sandwiches.
Just before teatime:
Bake the Balls of Fire, then reheat the custard pies.

COOK'S HINT
To **decorate the table**, cut out large stars, circles or diamonds from coloured paper. Tiny cherry tomatoes are pretty and edible to decorate the Custard Pies.

MICROWAVE HINT
Melt the chocolate for **the lollies** in a bowl on LOW for about 8 minutes, stirring occasionally.

DRINKS PARTIES

Introduction

Small-space living or lack of time needn't curb would-be party givers, for one of the easiest ways to entertain is to serve food with drinks. It has to be more than nuts, olives and crisps, but needn't be really complicated – just manageable with fingers and thumbs, interesting, plentiful and attractive.

What you give your guests to drink is just as important as the canapés. Your budget and the season, to some extent, will give you guidelines. Champagne-based cocktails such as Kir Royale are always popular but are expensive for large lengthy parties. Pimms and other long, cool drinks, chilled white wine and fruit wine cups are welcome for summer parties, whilst in the winter a warm glass of mulled wine or punch makes a welcoming drink.

For real cocktails you'll need lots of ice. Crushed ice is more efficient at cooling than large blocks, so make your ice in a tray with fairly small sections and crush it either with a special ice crusher or wrapped in a tea towel with a kitchen mallet or rolling pin. The ice should not melt in the drink, but remain in the base to cool it, so do not get it out of the freezer until it is needed. Measuring is also critical – there's no need to buy a cocktail measure, as long as you use a consistent measure for each ingredient – a small glass or an egg cup is ideal. If giving a party single-handed, ask one or two people to lend you a hand serving drinks or you'll have no time to enjoy yourself.

QUICK AND EASY COCKTAIL PARTY

M	E	N	U

GRAVAD LAX ON RYE

CHORIZO WITH TOMATO

SATAY OF PRAWN, CHICKEN AND BEEF

BAKED TINY POTATOES WITH CRISP
BACON, ROQUEFORT AND SOURED CREAM
DIP

FIGS WITH PROSCIUTTO

TWO KINDS OF MARINATED OLIVES

'HIDDEN' CHEESES AND GRAPES

CHEESE AND POPPYSEED BITES

SERVES 20

*C*ocktail parties invariably involve lots of fiddly, time consuming preparation of mini tartlet cases, croûtes or bite-size choux buns. So it's not surprising that many people offer shop-bought snacks such as peanuts and crisps with drinks. This menu offers all the style and taste sensations of a cocktail party, but doesn't require hours of hard labour in the kitchen.

If you want to expand on this menu, buy frozen mini bouchée cases and fill with a well-flavoured herb mayonnaise mixed with prawns, chicken or avocado. Button mushrooms, upturned with the stalk removed, make good containers for soured cream or lumpfish roe. Spread crisp crescents of apple with good pâté and garnish with a sprinkling of paprika. Toast thin slices of French bread, rub with garlic and top with carpaccio or creamy goat's cheese, or spread good taramasalata or hummous on thick cucumber slices.

DRINKS TO SERVE
One of the easiest and most popular cocktails is Kir Royale. Simply pour a splash of crème de cassis into champagne flutes and top with chilled champagne or good quality sparkling white wine. Alternatively, a light-hearted cocktail such as a Harvey Wallbanger is ideal to serve with this carefree food. Allow two parts vodka to 6 parts orange juice and pour over crushed ice packed into tall glasses. Float one part Galliano on top and serve at once.

COOK'S HINT
Instead of marinating the meat and prawn Satay overnight, it may be prepared in advance and frozen in the marinade. Using previously unfrozen meat and prawns, follow step 1, putting everything in a large, shallow freezer container. Freeze for up to 6 months. Defrost in the refrigerator overnight then continue from the beginning of step 2 – nothing could be simpler!

MENU SUGGESTIONS
One of the easiest cocktail party foods is a dip served with ready-cut crudités (from the chilled cabinet in large supermarkets), or crisps or strips of toasted pitta bread. Mayonnaise, with crème fraîche or Greek-style yogurt makes the ideal base for flavourings such as chopped herbs, garlic, curry paste, crumbled blue cheese or freshly grated ginger.

GRAVAD LAX ON RYE

This Swedish speciality makes an impressive but simple cocktail snack. You can buy packs of Gravad Lax from most large supermarkets, which come with a separate sachet of sauce.

MAKES 72
three 150 g (5 oz) packets Gravad Lax
75–125 g (3–4 oz) unsalted butter, softened
6 large slices of rye bread
sprigs of fresh dill, to garnish

1 Lightly spread each slice of rye bread with butter. Cover the bread with pieces of smoked salmon and spread a little of the sauce over each piece

2 Cut the rye bread into neat fingers and then halve each finger diagonally to make small triangles. Arrange on a platter and decorate with dill sprigs. Cover with damp greaseproof paper and chill in the refrigerator until ready to serve.

CHORIZO WITH TOMATO

Chorizo is a spicy pork and pimiento sausage, sold like salami on the delicatessan counter.

MAKES 60
30 cherry tomatoes
60 thin slices of Chorizo sausage (about 175 g/6 oz)
freshly ground black pepper
60 small basil leaves

1 Cut each tomato in half and season well with freshly ground black pepper. Fold each piece of Chorizo sausage in half. Push a cocktail stick through one side of a slice of Chorizo, then holding a tomato half, cut side uppermost, push the stick through one side of the tomato and out the other.

2 Wind the Chorizo over the tomato and spear the cocktail stick through the other side to secure it. Push a basil leaf on to the longer end of each stick, so the basil leaf is eaten last. Cover with damp greaseproof paper and chill until ready to serve.

SATAY OF PRAWN, CHICKEN AND BEEF WITH SATAY SAUCE

MARINADE
3 garlic cloves, skinned and crushed
4 cm (1½ inch) piece fresh root ginger, peeled and finely grated
150 ml (¼ pint) soy sauce
125 ml (4 fl oz) vegetable oil
30 ml (2 tbsp) dark brown sugar
450 g (1 lb) chicken breast fillets, skinned
450 g (1 lb) beef fillet or rump steak
450 g (1 lb) medium raw prawns, peeled and deveined

SAUCE
4 small onions, skinned
45 ml (3 tbsp) vegetable oil
200g (7 oz) creamed coconut, chopped
10 ml (2 level tsp) chilli powder
2 stems of lemon grass, trimmed and chopped
2 garlic cloves, skinned and crushed
75 ml (3 fl oz) soy sauce
200 g (7 oz) crunchy peanut butter (half a large jar)
chopped fresh coriander, to garnish

1 Mix together all the marinade ingredients in a large shallow dish. Cut the chicken and beef into bite-size pieces. Stir into the marinade with the prawns. Cover and leave for 2–3 hours or overnight, stirring occasionally.

2 To make the sauce, halve the onions and slice very thinly into crescents. Fry the onion in the oil in a heavy-based frying pan until well browned, stirring all the time. Remove and drain on absorbent kitchen paper.

3 Put the remaining sauce ingredients in a saucepan. Add 450 ml (¾ pint) boiling water and mix well. Heat gently until boiling, then cook for a couple of minutes, stirring all the time. Add half of the onions to the sauce.

4 Thread the prawns, chicken and beef onto cocktail sticks or small bamboo skewers.

5 Bake the satay on lightly greased baking sheets at 180°C (350°F) mark 4 for 10–15 minutes. Turn over halfway through cooking. Leave to cool.

6 To serve, pour the sauce into small bowls and sprinkle with the remaining fried onions. Arrange the satay on platters and sprinkle with coriander.

Gravad Lax and Figs with Prosciutto di Parma (top right), and Satay of Prawn, Chicken and Beef with Satay Sauce and Tiny New Potatoes with Crisp Bacon, Roquefort and Soured Cream Dip (bottom left)

BAKED TINY NEW POTATOES WITH CRISP BACON, ROQUEFORT AND SOURED CREAM DIP

1.4 kg (3 lb) small, blemish-free new potatoes
salt and freshly ground pepper
50 g (2 oz) butter, melted
125 g (4 oz) smoked streaky bacon, rinded
50 g (2 oz) Roquefort cheese
300 ml (½ pint) soured cream
200 g (7 oz) low fat soft cheese
fresh parsley or chives, to garnish

1 Wash the potatoes well, but do not peel. Cook in boiling salted water for 5 minutes. Drain well. Place on one or two shallow roasting tins. Drizzle over the melted butter.
2 Bake in the oven at 200°C (400°F) mark 6 for about 45 minutes hours or until tender.
3 Meanwhile, make the dip. Grill the bacon until very crisp. Drain on absorbent kitchen paper, leave to cool then chop very finely.

4 Mash together the Roquefort and soft cheese then blend in the soured cream. Stir in most of the bacon. Season with pepper. Sprinkle with the remaining bacon, to garnish.
5 To serve pile the potatoes in a large dish and garnish with chives. Serve with the dip.

FRESH FIGS WITH PROSCIUTTO DI PARMA

MAKES 60
10 firm ripe figs
225 g (8 oz) very thinly sliced Prosciutto di Parma
vine leaves, to decorate

1 Cut each fig in half. Then cut each half into three wedges.
2 Wrap a slice of Prosciutto around each piece of fig and arrange on a platter. Cover with damp greaseproof paper while preparing, to prevent the Parma ham from drying out. Cover with damp greaseproof and clingfilm and chill until ready to serve.

MARINATED OLIVES

HOT AND SPICY
450 g (1 lb) stoned green olives
2 hot chillies, seeded and chopped
45 ml (3 tbsp) finely chopped fresh coriander
45 ml (3 tbsp) virgin olive oil
GARLIC AND LEMON
450 g (1 lb) stoned black olives
3 garlic cloves, skinned and crushed
finely grated rind of 1 large lemon
45 ml (3 tbsp) chopped fresh parsley
45 ml (3 tbsp) virgin olive oil

1 Mix all the ingredients together. Cover and leave to marinate for at least 24 hours.

'HIDDEN' CHEESES AND GRAPES

a selection of hard and soft cheeses
green and white seedless grapes
a selection of leaves, such as vine, good cabbage leaves, salad leaves

1 Cut the cheeses into bite size pieces and spear each piece with a cocktail stick. Using scissors, snip the grapes into small bunches.
2 Line a large flat serving platter, wicker basket or wooden board with leaves. Arrange the cheese and grapes on top. Cover with more leaves.

CHEESE AND POPPYSEED BITES

MAKES 40
225 g (8 oz) plain flour
pinch of salt
10 ml (2 tsp) dry mustard
125 g (4 oz) butter
125 g (4 oz) Farmhouse Cheddar, finely grated
25 g (1 oz) poppyseeds
milk
ground paprika, cayenne or poppyseeds
freshly grated Parmesan cheese

1 Put the flour, salt and mustard in a bowl and mix thoroughly, rub in the butter until the mixture resembles fine breadcrumbs.
2 Stir in the poppyseeds and cheese and enough water to make a firm dough. Knead lightly together.
3 Roll out the pastry on a lightly floured surface. Using cutters measuring about 5 cm (2 inches) in diameter, cut out different shapes. Brush with milk and sprinkle some with poppyseeds, some with paprika or cayenne and some with Parmesan.
4 Transfer to baking sheets and bake at 220°C (425°F) mark 7 for 10–15 minutes until golden brown. Cool on wire racks. Once cold, store in airtight containers until ready to serve.
To Freeze Cool, pack and freeze. Store for up to 3 months. Thaw at cool room temperature. Refresh in a warm oven, if liked.

TAPAS PARTY

*T*apas are deliciously varied, tasty little appetisers served with pre-dinner drinks in bars throughout Spain. For entertaining at home, tapas are perfect for a relaxed, leisurely drinks party. They are more substantial than canapés and usually less time consuming and fiddly to make. This menu is a hearty combination of dishes, designed as a meal in itself rather than a prelude to something else.

Serve the tapas in small dishes so that they can be dotted around the room or table. Provide plates and napkins and lots of crusty bread cut into manageable chunks. Tapas such as the salt cod balls and the tortilla are bite-sized and should be picked up with cocktail sticks or the fingers. For large parties this type of tapas is most appropriate.

This menu is easily expanded to cater for larger numbers by adding extra dishes such as olives or anchovies, good ham or spicy chorizo sausage arranged on two-bite sized slivers of bread, chunks of salty Spanish Manchego cheese, or even tiny, well-flavoured meatballs or grilled sardines.

*Gambas al Ajillo and
Garbanzos en Salsa con
Chorizo (right)*

DRINKS TO SERVE
In Spain, a chilled fino or amontillado sherry is sipped as an aperitif with tapas. Offer your guests a glass as they arrive but then move on to something less potent. A well chilled bottled Spanish beer such as San Miguel or a Spanish wine such as Rioja are good choices, while in summer, Sangria (see p. 164) is refreshing. At the end of the evening, offer strong, fresh coffee and a glass of brandy with the Cinnamon Biscuits.

COOK'S HINTS
We've used canned **chickpeas** in this recipe for convenience. If you prefer to cook your own, you will need 225 g (8 oz). Soak them overnight in enough water to cover. Drain, then cover with fresh water, bring to the boil and simmer for about 1½ hours (the time will depend on how fresh the peas are). Add salt towards the end of cooking. Alternatively, soak the peas and then pressure cook at high (15 lb) pressure for 40 minutes until tender.

GAMBAS AL AJILLO
(Prawns with Garlic and Oil)

*This sauce can be made by hand using a pestle and
mortar. It has a very potent garlicky flavour. Use 2
cloves for a less powerful flavour.*

about 900 g (2 lb) freshly cooked prawns in the shell
5 large juicy garlic cloves, skinned
salt
75 ml (5 tbsp) chopped fresh parsley
40 g (1½ oz) ground almonds
5 ml (1 tsp) paprika
about 300 ml (½ pint) fruity olive oil
juice of half a lemon

1 Pile the prawns on a serving platter and chill until ready to serve.

2 To make the sauce, put the garlic, ground almonds, salt, parsley and paprika in a blender or food processor and blend for about one minute. With the motor running, carefully add all the oil, in a gentle stream. When all the oil has been incorporated, gradually pour in the lemon juice. Blend the sauce for about 30 seconds, until smooth, thick and well combined. Adjust the seasoning to taste. Serve with the prawns.

GARBANZOS EN SALSA CON CHORIZO
(Chorizo and Chickpea Stew)

*This really easy tapas is equally good served as a
supper dish with boiled rice.*

15 ml (1 tbsp) olive oil
1 large onion, skinned and chopped
1 red pepper, seeded and chopped
2 garlic cloves, skinned and crushed
397 g (14 oz) can chopped tomatoes
two 400 g (14 oz) cans chickpeas, drained and rinsed
350 g (12 oz) piece of chorizo sausage
salt and freshly ground pepper
chopped fresh parsley, to garnish

1 Heat the oil in a heavy based saucepan. Add the onion, pepper and the garlic and cook over a high heat for a couple of minutes. Add the tomatoes and simmer for 5 minutes.

2 Cut the sausage into chunks and add to the tomato sauce with the chickpeas. Cover and simmer for about 10 minutes, stirring occasionally. Season to taste with salt and pepper and garnish with parsley. Serve warm.

TORTILLA ESPANOLA

(Spanish Potato Omelette)

about 60 ml (4 tbsp) olive oil
450 g (1 lb) waxy potatoes, peeled and diced
2 medium onions, skinned and sliced
6 large eggs
salt and freshly ground pepper

1 Heat half the oil in a heavy based, non-stick frying pan until it is very hot. Add the potatoes and the onions and cook over a high heat for a couple of minutes, stirring all the time, so that the potatoes are coated with oil and sealed on all sides.

2 Reduce the heat and cook for about 5–10 minutes or until the potatoes are soft. Loosen any sediment at the bottom of the pan with a wooden spatula. Add a little extra oil, if necessary and heat for a minute until really hot. Beat the eggs with a fork and season to taste with salt and pepper. Stir into the hot oil.

3 Cook over a high heat for a couple of minutes then reduce the heat and cool until the omelette looks set. Loosen the tortilla from the sides of the pan then turn it out onto a serving plate.

4 Add the remaining oil to the pan, then add the tortilla, browned side up and cook for a further minute or so. Serve cold cut in squares. Spear each square with a cocktail stick for serving.

PATATAS BRAVAS

(Spicy Potatoes)

700 g (1½ lb) waxy potatoes, scrubbed
salt and freshly ground pepper
30 ml (2 tbsp) olive oil
2 garlic cloves, skinned and crushed
1 green chilli, seeded and chopped
10 ml (2 tsp) mild paprika
397 g (14 oz) can chopped tomatoes
chopped fresh parsley, to garnish

1 Cook the potatoes in boiling salted water until just tender. Drain and leave to cool.

2 Meanwhile, heat the oil in a deep frying pan, add the garlic, chilli and paprika and cook for a couple of minutes, stirring all the time. Add the tomatoes, increase the heat and cook for about 10 minutes until the sauce is reduced and very thick.

3 Carefully peel the potatoes, and cut into large chunks. Add to the tomato sauce and cook for about 10 minutes, stirring occasionally, until the sauce is reduced further and just clings to the potato. Season to taste with salt and pepper. Serve warm or cold, sprinkled generously with parsley.

FIAMBRE DE BACALAO

(Salt Cod Balls)

225 g (8 oz) dried salt cod
700 g (1½ lb) floury potatoes
1 garlic clove, skinned and crushed
45 ml (3 tbsp) chopped fresh parsley
1 egg yolk, beaten
freshly ground pepper
flour
oil, for frying
lemon wedges, to serve

1 Soak the cod in cold water for at least 24 hours. Change the water frequently.

2 Drain the cod and break up into small pieces, removing any skin or bones.

3 Cook the potatoes in boiling salted water until tender. Drain and mash with the garlic, parsley and egg yolk. Fold in the cod. Season generously with pepper.

4 Using lightly floured hands, shape the mixture into about 20 walnut sized balls.

5 Heat the oil in a deep fat fryer to 180°C (350°F) or until a cube of stale bread turns brown in 40 seconds. Fry in batches until golden brown. Drain on absorbent paper and keep warm while frying the remainder. Serve with wedges of lemon.

To Freeze When cold, open freeze the cod balls, then transfer to polythene bags. Arrange on a baking tray and reheat from frozen at 190°C (375°F) mark 5 for 15–20 minutes.

COOK'S HINTS

1 Most **salt cod** sold in Britain is imported from Spain where it is known as bacalao. Look for thick fillets with creamy white flesh; when past its best it starts to look yellow. Don't be put off by the strong smell, when cooked the flavour is surprisingly mild. Extra salt for seasoning is not necessary.

2 When buying **potatoes**, it's important to choose the variety best suited to the dish being made. For Tortilla and Patata Bravas a waxy potato with firm, creamy flesh, that won't disintegrate during cooking is best. Look out for potatoes such as Diana, Morag, Asperge (La Ratte, Cornichon), Wilja, Spinta or Civa. These are good for sautéing or salads. For bacala choose floury fleshed potatoes such as King Edward, Maris Piper or Desirée. For baking choose creamy fleshed Marfona, Cara or Vanessa.

3 The **Spanish tortilla** should be much thicker than an omelette. Use a good heavy-based frying pan about 25.5 cm (10 inches) in diameter to get the right depth with this number of eggs. Cook it until firm on the outside and light and soft in the middle.

MICROWAVE HINT

Patatas Bravas reheat well in the microwave. Put small portions into heatproof serving dishes, cover and microwave on HIGH for about 3–4 minutes or until piping hot. Stir or shake once during cooking.

EMPANADILLAS DE CARNE

(Spicy Meat Turnovers)

MAKES ABOUT 30
PASTRY
5 ml (1 level tsp) salt
50 g (2 oz) butter
30 ml (2 tbsp) olive oil
300 g (11 oz) plain flour
2 egg yolks
FILLING
1 rasher streaky bacon, rinded and chopped
1 small onion, skinned and chopped
1 garlic clove, skinned and crushed
175 g (6 oz) lean minced beef, lamb or veal
10 ml (2 tsp) tomato purée
1 hot chilli, seeded and finely chopped (optional)
75 ml (3 fl oz) dry red wine
salt and freshly ground pepper
chopped fresh parsley
beaten egg
oil for frying

1 To make the pastry, heat 175 ml (6 fl oz) water with the salt, butter and oil until the butter has melted and the water is just boiling. Remove from heat, then quickly add the flour all at once. Beat vigorously with a wooden spoon then beat in the egg yolks.

2 Turn the dough onto a lightly floured surface and knead until smooth and elastic. Cover with a damp tea towel and leave in a warm place for 20–30 minutes to rest.

3 Make the filling, cook the bacon in a heavy-based saucepan until the fat starts to run. Add the onion and garlic and cook over a high heat for a couple of minutes. Add the meat and cook, stirring all the time until the meat is thoroughly browned. Add the tomato purée and chilli and fry for a minute.

4 Stir in the wine, bring to the boil then cover and simmer gently for 30 minutes, stirring occasionally. Add a little water, if the mixture starts to stick. Season generously with salt and pepper. Stir in the parsley. The mixture should be thick but moist.

5 Roll out the pastry on a lightly floured surface and cut out 7.5 cm (3 inch) rounds using a plain cutter. Place a teaspoonful of the meat mixture onto each circle of pastry. Brush the edges with beaten egg. Fold in half. Twist the edges together to seal.

6 Heat the oil in a deep fat fryer to 190°C (375°F) or until a cube of stale bread turns brown in 30 seconds. Fry the empanadillas in batches for 2–3 minutes until golden brown. Drain on absorbent kitchen paper while frying the remainder. Keep warm in a low oven until ready to serve, or serve cold.

To Freeze Cool, open freeze then store in a polythene bag. Reheat from frozen at 190°C (375°F) mark 5 for 15–20 minutes.

TARTALETAS DE CHAMPINONES

(Mushroom Tartlets)

MAKES 24
225 g (8 oz) plain flour
salt and freshly ground pepper
125 g (4 oz) butter or margarine
275 g (10 oz) mushrooms, wiped and chopped
1 garlic clove, skinned and crushed
120 ml (8 tbsp) mayonnaise
60 ml (4 tbsp) chopped fresh parsley
lemon juice
canned pimientos and parsley, to garnish

1 To make the pastry, put the flour and a large pinch of salt in a bowl. Rub in the fat until the mixture resembles fine breadcrumbs. Stir in enough water to make a stiff dough. Roll out on a lightly floured surface and cut out 7 cm (2¾ inch) rounds using a fluted cutter. Place the rounds in a greased bun tin. Prick well with a fork.

2 Bake in the oven at 200°C (400°F) mark 6 for about 10–12 minutes or until slightly browned around the edges. Leave to cool in the tins for a couple of minutes, then remove from the tins and cool on a wire rack.

3 About an hour before serving mix the mushrooms with the garlic, mayonnaise, parsley and lemon juice and salt and pepper to taste. Pile into the tartlet cases. Garnish with pimento and parsley.

To Freeze Pack and freeze the unfilled pastry cases in a rigid container. Thaw at cool room temperature and complete step 3.

GALLETAS DE CANELA

(Cinnamon Biscuits)

Serve these at the end of the evening with coffee.

MAKES ABOUT 24
275 g (10 oz) plain flour
90 ml (6 level tbsp) ground almonds
10 ml (2 level tsp) ground cinnamon
125 g (4 oz) caster sugar
225 g (8 oz) butter
egg yolk, to glaze
flaked almonds
icing sugar and drinking chocolate, for dredging

1 Sift the flour into a bowl. Add the almonds, cinnamon and sugar and mix together. Work in the butter with your fingertips. Knead well.

2 Roll out on a surface dusted with icing sugar until about 2.5 cm (½ inch) thick. Cut out heart or flower shapes with small pastry cutters. Brush with egg yolk and sprinkle with a few almonds. Bake in the oven at 170°C (325°F) mark 3 for about 40 minutes, until firm and pale golden brown. Cool on a wire rack. Dredge a few biscuits with sifted icing sugar and a few with drinking chocolate powder.

To Freeze Pack in a rigid container and store for up to 6 months. Thaw at room temperature for about 1–2 hours.

COUNTDOWN
The week before or more:
Make the Salt Cod Balls, Mushroom Tartlet cases, Empanadillas and the Cinnamon Biscuits and freeze.
The day before:
Soak the Salt cod. Make the Ajillo, cover and refrigerate.
On the day:
In the morning:
Remove the biscuits and tartlet cases from the freezer. Make the Spicy Potatoes, cool, cover and refrigerate. Make the Chorizo and Chick-Pea Stew. Cool, cover and refrigerate.
To serve at 8pm:
6.00pm: Make the Tortilla and leave to cool. Pile the prawns on a platter and chill.
7.00pm: Complete the Mushroom Tartlets.
7.40pm: Reheat the Empanadillas and the Salt Cod Balls from frozen on baking sheets at 190°C (375°F) mark 5 for about 15–20 minutes. Gently reheat the Chorizo and Chickpea Stew and the Spicy Potatoes (add a little water if necessary to prevent sticking).
8.00pm: Serve.

Galletas de Canela (left)

ELEGANT DRINKS PARTY

SERVES 8

A special occasion calls for special food and these canapés are easy to make, take little time to prepare, taste delicious and look stunning. If this is to be pre-dinner drinks, allow about 5 canapés per person. If it is a real cocktail party and your guests will be eating later, allow about 10 servings per person. However, if the party is to be the 'meal' allow about 14 canapés for each guest. Decide which recipes to cook more of depending on the occasion, trying to mix colours, flavours and textures to their best advantage. Be sure to supply extra nibbles such as nuts, olives, Chinese rice crackers and Indian bombay mix.

Whizz up a quick dip using fromage frais, mayonnaise or full fat soft cheese with herbs and garlic or something more exotic. Serve this with freshly cut vegetables, or tortilla chips, pitta bread or prawn crackers.

SMOKED SALMON SAMOSAS

MAKES 64
225 g (8 oz) smoked salmon (or salmon trimmings)
225 g (8 oz) full fat soft cheese or curd cheese
45 ml (3 tbsp) chopped fresh dill
30 ml (2 tbsp) lemon or lime juice
freshly ground black pepper
8 long slices from a side of smoked salmon, halved lengthways
sprigs of fresh dill, to garnish
lime or lemon wedges, to serve

1 Chop the 225 g (8 oz) smoked salmon into tiny pieces and mix with the cheese. Stir in the dill and season with lots of black pepper and lemon juice to taste.

2 Cut the long slices in half widthways to give 32 pieces. Place a teaspoonful of the cheese on one end of each slice of smoked salmon. Fold over to form the beginning of a triangle. Keep folding in this manner, forming a triangle each time until the filling is completely enclosed. Cut each samosa in half.

3 Arrange on a flat serving dish, cover and chill until ready to serve. Garnish with sprigs of dill and serve with lime or lemon wedges.

TOMATO PARMESAN TWISTS

Try using anchovy paste or olive paste instead of tomato purée for a change.

MAKES ABOUT 80
two 370 g (13 oz) packets puff pastry, thawed if frozen
90 ml (6 tbsp) tomato purée
freshly ground black pepper
60 ml (4 tbsp) milk
90 ml (6 tbsp) freshly grated Parmesan cheese

1 Roll out one packet of pastry to measure approximately 35 × 40 cm (14 × 16 inches). Spread over half the tomato purée and season well with black pepper. Trim the edges.

2 Fold the pastry in half widthways. Brush with a little milk and sprinkle over half the Parmesan cheese. Use a sharp knife to cut the pastry into thin strips, approximately 1 cm (½ inch) wide. Cool on wire racks.

3 Take a strip and attach one end to a baking sheet, using a little milk to help it stick. Then, still gently pressing down this end, twist the strip like barley sugar and stick down the other end. Repeat with the other strips.

4 Bake at 200°C (400°F) mark 6 for 8–12 minutes or until risen and golden brown. Repeat with the remaining ingredients. Cool the twists on a wire rack and then cut each one in half. Arrange in a basket and serve.

To Freeze Pack the finished twists in a rigid container and freeze for up to 3 months. Reheat from frozen in a warm oven and serve.

PRAWN AND FETA PURSES

MAKES 25
125 g (4 oz) cooked prawns, thawed and well drained if frozen
225 g (8 oz) feta cheese, crumbled
1.25 cm (½ inch) fresh ginger, peeled and grated
salt and freshly ground pepper
30 ml (2 tbsp) chopped fresh chives or dill
pinch ground nutmeg
75 10 cm (4 inch) squares of filo pastry, (see Cook's Hint)
melted butter
chives, to garnish

1 Roughly chop the prawns and mix with the feta cheese, ginger, seasoning, chives and nutmeg.

2 Brush each square of pastry with butter and lay 3 on top of each other to make 25 piles. Place a teaspoonful of filling in the middle of each square. Draw the pastry up around the filling, pinching the middle to form a money bag shape. Pull out and arrange frilly tops.

3 Place on greased baking sheets and brush lightly with melted butter. Bake at 200°C (400°F) mark 6 for 10–15 minutes until golden brown.

4 Cool slightly and serve while still warm or when completely cold garnished with chives.

A selection of cocktails
(above)

OLIVE AND QUAIL'S EGG TARTLETS

If you can't find olive paste, then buy stoned black olives, drain and dry them and chop finely.

MAKES ABOUT 24
PASTRY
225 g (8 oz) plain flour
75 g (3 oz) butter, cubed
45 ml (3 tbsp) black olive paste
salt and freshly ground pepper
FILLING
175 g (6 oz) stoned black olives, finely chopped
50 g (1.76 oz) can anchovies, drained and finely chopped
15 ml (1 tbsp) olive oil
12 fresh quail's eggs
olive strips and parsley leaves, to garnish

1 Rub the fat into the flour and stir in the olive paste. Season with salt and pepper and add enough chilled water to bind. Knead lightly on a floured surface, then wrap and chill in the refrigerator for 30 minutes.

2 Meanwhile mix together all the filling ingredients. Cover and chill in the refrigerator until needed. Place the quail's eggs into a pan of cold water and slowly bring to the boil. Boil for 1 minute then drain and rinse with cold water. Leave to cool slightly, then peel very carefully under cold running water.

3 Roll the pastry out on a floured surface as thinly as you can and cut out about 24×4 cm (1½ inches) diameter small rounds , to fit the smallest tart tins you can find. Line the tins with the pastry, prick the bases and bake in the oven at 180°C (350°F) mark 4 for 10–15 minutes. Cool on a wire rack.

4 To assemble, put a small spoonful of filling in each case. Cut each quail's egg in half and place a half on each tartlet. Garnish each tartlet with strips of olive and a parsley leaf. Serve immediately.

Smoked Salmon Samosas, Prawn and Feta Purses, Teeny Blinis, Tomato and Parmesan Twists, and Olive and Quail's Egg Tartlets (clockwise, from top right)

COUNTDOWN
Up to a day before:
Make the blinis and freeze. Make the cheese twists. Make the olive pastry cases, the filling and boil the quail eggs. Keep the eggs under cold water. Make the salmon samosas, cover and chill until needed.
On the day:
Make the prawn purses, chill. Arrange the samosas, cheese twists in bowls or platters. At the last moment, assemble the olive and quail's egg canapés and blinis. Bake the purses.

MENU SUGGESTIONS
Teeny Blinis are also delicious served topped with peeled prawns and chopped dill, or mix a little creamed horseradish with the soured cream and top with tiny flakes of smoked trout. For vegetarians, crumbled feta cheese, fresh coriander and a little chopped olive is delicious.

TEENY BLINIS

125 g (4 oz) buckwheat flour or wholemeal flour
1 sachet fast action dried yeast
5 ml (1 tsp) sugar
350 ml (12 fl oz) milk, heated to blood temperature
125g (4 oz) plain flour
salt
15 ml (1 tbsp) melted butter
2 eggs
oil or lard, for frying
150 ml (¼ pint) soured cream
50 g (2 oz) jar each red and black lumpfish roe
chervil sprigs, to garnish

1 Mix the buckwheat flour with the yeast, sugar and half of the warm milk. Beat well.
2 Sift the plain flour and salt into another

bowl. Make a well in the centre and add the remaining milk, the melted butter and one whole egg and one yolk, reserving one white. Beat well to form a batter. Beat into the yeast mixture, cover and leave in a warm place to rise for 1–2 hours.

3 Whisk the reserved egg white until it just forms soft peaks and fold into the batter. Heat a heavy pan or griddle and grease with oil or lard. Pour dessertspoons of batter onto the griddle or pan. Turn over when bubbles appear on the surface. Cook until just turning brown.

4 Transfer to a wire rack. Cool. Top with a teaspoonful of soured cream and a little lumpfish roe and arrange on flat platters. Garnish with chervil sprigs. The pancakes can be stored in an airtight container for up to two days.

To Freeze Layer the pancakes with greaseproof paper, pack into a rigid container and freeze. Thaw for 2–3 hours before serving.

BARBECUE PARTIES

Introduction

Barbecues have a unique atmosphere of informality, so they are an ideal way to entertain children and guests of all ages. The most important thing to bear in mind is that the fire needs to be lit early, and the cooking of the food started in good time as it has to be cooked and served in relays. It's advisable to limit your guests to twenty (or less if your barbecue is small), otherwise you'll have to barbecue the first batch of food early and keep it warm in an oven indoors, or keep half of the guests waiting while the others tuck in. To stave off hunger pangs while the first batch is cooking, it's a good idea to serve a first course. A dip such as Guacamole is ideal, or hot garlic bread, or a chilled soup that can be portioned out in advance.

Eating outdoors tends to increase appetites, so make sure that there is plenty of non-barbecue food on the table. Baked potatoes, potato salad, or rice and pasta salads are all good filling accompaniments. As well as these, offer one or two crisp, refreshing salads to offset any greasiness.

For informal barbecue parties, disposable plates, cups and napkins ensure no breakages and are convenient when it comes to clearing up afterwards. For more elegant barbecues, use paper napkins with proper plates.

For an evening barbecue, ensure that the garden is well lit. Even if the party starts off in daylight, it may well be very dark by the end of the evening. Light from the house or a few spot lights may be enough. Candles, flares or nightlights stuck in jam jars can be dotted round the garden.

MIDDLE EASTERN BARBECUE PARTY

SERVES 8

*C*elebrate summer with this barbecue menu from the Middle East. Cooking in the open air is lots of fun, and somehow everything tastes much better, especially when everyone joins in and gives a hand with the cooking.

On a practical note, prepare your barbecue well in advance of your guests' arrival (it's a good idea to have a dummy run first), and allow time for the coals to turn grey before starting to cook. Sprigs of fresh herbs laid on the barbecue grid will give your garden a Mediterranean aroma, tempting guests' tastebuds as soon as they arrive. And don't forget to light the barbecue area adequately if you're planning an evening affair, or you'll be cooking in the dark!

COOK'S HINTS

1 **Spanakhopitas** makes a very tasty and nutritious meal for vegetarians; this quantity would serve 4–6 people as a main course, with a mixed side salad.

For vegans, substitute tofu for the two cheeses, and either cut it into small dice or mash it into the spinach. Tofu is soya bean curd, a complete vegetable protein used by vegetarians and vegans; it is also used in the orient as a low fat alternative to meat. You will find tofu at health food shops and oriental specialist stores.

2 **Drumsticks** are the perfect cut of chicken for barbecue parties because they are easy to eat with your hands (don't forget to provide plenty of paper napkins for sticky fingers), and they are very meaty. Large packs of economically priced drumsticks are available at most supermarkets; they are excellent value for money.

The skin of chicken drumsticks chars and crisps beautifully on the barbecue, and helps protect the tender flesh from the direct heat, keeping it moist and succulent, but if you prefer to keep the fat content down, you can remove the skin before marinating.

SPANAKHOPITAS

Originally from Greece, this spinach and cheese pie can now be found all over the Middle East.

about 150 ml (¼ pint) olive oil
1 medium onion, skinned and very finely chopped
10 ml (2 tsp) ground cumin
2 garlic cloves, skinned and crushed
450 g (1 lb) frozen chopped spinach, thawed and well drained
125 g (4 oz) feta cheese, crumbled
125 g (4 oz) full fat soft cheese or curd cheese
salt and freshly ground pepper
400 g (14 oz) packet filo pastry, (see Cook's Hint on page 82)

1 Heat 30 ml (2 tbsp) olive oil in a frying pan, add the onion and cook gently, stirring frequently, for about 10 minutes until softened. Sprinkle in the cumin and stir for 2 minutes, then stir in the garlic and spinach. Remove the pan from the heat and stir in the two cheeses until evenly mixed. Add salt and pepper to taste.

2 Brush the inside of a 30.5 × 23 cm (12 × 9 inch) baking dish with olive oil. Place 1 sheet of filo in the dish, bringing it up the sides and letting the short edges hang over at either end. Brush the pastry in the dish with oil, then continue in this way until half of the filo sheets are used.

3 Spread the spinach and cheese mixture over the top sheet of filo, then cover with the remaining sheets, brushing olive oil between them as before. Trim the overhanging edges of filo, then tuck the edges in to seal. brush all over the top layer with oil. With a sharp knife, cut through the layers right to the base of the dish to make 16 squares.

4 Bake at 190°C (375°F) mark 5 for 30 minutes. Leave to cool for about 10 minutes, then cut into the marked squares and remove from the dish. Serve hot or warm.

To Freeze Overwrap at the end of step 3. Freeze for up to 3 months. Bake from frozen allowing extra time.

CIRCASSIAN CHICKEN DRUMSTICKS

Circassian dishes invariably have nuts amongst their ingredients. Walnuts are used here, but they could be almonds or hazelnuts, or a mixture of two or three different kinds of nuts

16 chicken drumsticks
125 g (4 oz) shelled walnuts, roughly chopped
150 ml (¼ pint) tomato ketchup
60 ml (4 tbsp) soft brown sugar
60 ml (4 tbsp) wine vinegar
10 ml (2 tsp) chilli powder
10 ml (2 tsp) celery salt
freshly ground black pepper
300 ml (½ pint) chicken stock

1 With a sharp knife, score the skin of the drumsticks right through to the flesh. Place in a single layer in a shallow dish.

2 Mix together all the remaining ingredients, except the stock. Pour over the drumsticks, cover and leave to marinate in the refrigerator for 24 hours, turning the drumsticks over and coating with the marinade occasionally.

3 Place the drumsticks on the grid of a preheated barbecue. Cook for 15–20 minutes, turning occasionally.

4 Meanwhile, transfer the marinade to a heavy saucepan, pour in the stock and bring to the boil, stirring. Lower the heat and simmer until reduced slightly, stirring occasionally.

5 Serve the drumsticks warm, with the marinade handed separately in a jug.

To Freeze Freeze the previously unfrozen drumsticks in the marinade for up to 1 month. Thaw in the refrigerator overnight.

Kofta with Yogurt and Mint Dip (left)

KOFTA WITH YOGURT AND MINT DIP

Kofta are Middle Eastern meatballs which come in many different shapes, sizes and flavours. These are unusual in that barbecued aubergine is combined with the meat and spices.

1 large aubergine
750 g (1½ lb) minced lamb
1 medium onion, skinned and roughly chopped
2 garlic cloves, skinned and roughly chopped
1 egg, beaten
15 ml (1 tbsp) ground coriander
15 ml (1 tbsp) ground cumin
salt and freshly ground pepper
olive oil, for brushing
DIP
225 ml (8 fl oz) Greek-style yogurt
60 ml (4 tbsp) chopped fresh mint
10 ml (2 tsp) mint jelly
fresh mint sprigs, to garnish

1 Put the aubergine on the grid of a pre-heated barbecue and cook for 10–15 minutes until the skin is blistered and charred, turning frequently. Leave until cool enough to handle, then remove the skin and chop the flesh roughly.

2 Put the aubergine flesh in a food processor with the lamb, onion, garlic, egg, spices, and salt and pepper to taste. Work until the mixture is smooth, with a paste-like consistency.

3 With dampened hands, shape the mixture into 32 balls. Spear 4 balls on each of 8 oiled skewers. Chill in the refrigerator for 30 minutes.

4 Make the dip, put all the ingredients, except the garnish, in a blender or food processor. Add salt and pepper to taste and work until evenly blended. Transfer to a serving bowl and float mint sprigs on top.

5 Brush the kofta with olive oil. Put the skewers on the grid of a preheated barbecue and cook for 5–6 minutes, turning frequently and brushing with more oil if necessary. Slide the kofta off the skewers with a fork, then spear each one with a cocktail stick. Serve hot, with the dip handed separately.

To Freeze Cool, pack into a polythene bag and freeze. Thaw in the refrigerator overnight.

TABBOULEH

This Middle Eastern salad relies on lots of mint and parsley for flavour. The amount of lemon juice you use is a matter of taste.

225 g (8 oz) burghul
90 ml (6 tbsp) olive oil
90 ml (6 tbsp) lemon juice, or more to taste
about 4 garlic cloves, skinned and finely chopped
25 g (1 oz) fresh parsley, finely chopped
25 g (1 oz) fresh mint, finely chopped
salt and freshly ground pepper
4 ripe tomatoes, skinned, seeded and chopped
1 bunch spring onions, trimmed and finely chopped

1 Soak the burghul in 600 ml (1 pint) lukewarm water for 30 minutes.

2 Drain the burghul in a sieve, squeezing it with your hands to extract the water. Tip out on to a clean teatowel, gather the corners together and wring out the water so that the burghul is as dry as possible.

3 Whisk the oil and 90 ml (6 tbsp) lemon juice together in a bowl with the garlic, herbs and salt and pepper to taste. Add the burghul and toss to coat in the dressing.

4 Add the tomatoes and spring onions and fork through until evenly distributed. Taste and adjust seasoning, adding more lemon juice if you like. Serve at room temperature.

GREEK SALAD

4 large beefsteak tomatoes (about 700 g/1½ lb)
1 large cucumber
2 medium red onions, skinned
1 head of crisp Cos lettuce
125 g (4 oz) black olives, pitted
225 g (8 oz) feta cheese
DRESSING
135 ml (9 tbsp) olive oil
45 ml (3 tbsp) lemon juice
45 ml (3 tbsp) chopped fresh coriander
good pinch of sugar
salt and freshly ground pepper

1 Cut the tomatoes into bite-sized chunks, discarding the cores. Cut the cucumber in half crossways, then cut a cross in the end of each piece and cut down into quarters. Cut the quarters crossways into bite-sized pieces. Cut the onions into thin wedges. Shred the lettuce.

2 Whisk the dressing ingredients together in a jug (go easy on the salt because of the saltiness of olives and feta cheese). Put all the salad vegetables in a large bowl, add the olives and toss the ingredients together with your hands. Pour over the dressing and toss gently to mix, then crumble over the feta cheese. Serve as soon as possible.

CHAKCHOUKA

Cut the aubergine, peppers and courgettes more or less the same size, so they will be easy to eat.

1 large aubergine
salt and freshly ground pepper
60 ml (4 tbsp) olive oil
1 large onion, skinned and finely chopped
2 garlic cloves, skinned and crushed
1 red pepper, cored, seeded and diced
4 medium courgettes, diced
450 g (1 lb) ripe tomatoes, skinned, seeded and chopped
30 ml (2 tbsp) tomato purée
5–10 ml (1–2 tsp) chilli powder, according to taste
good pinch of sugar

1 Top and tail the aubergine, and cut into small dice. Place in a colander, sprinkle liberally with salt and cover with a plate or saucer. Place heavy weights on top of the plate or saucer, then leave to dégorge for 30 minutes.

2 Rinse the aubergine under cold running water, then drain thoroughly. Heat the oil in a large, heavy flameproof casserole, add the aubergine and onion and cook gently, stirring frequently, for 10 minutes until softened.

3 Add the garlic, peppers, courgettes and tomatoes, Stir well to mix, then pour in 300 ml (½ pint) water and bring to the boil, stirring. Lower the heat, add the tomato purée,

Stuffed Figs (left)

COUNTDOWN
The day before:
Prepare the chicken drumsticks up to the end of step 2.
Prepare the kofta up to the end of step 3; keep covered in the refrigerator.
Prepare the dip, without the garnish; keep in a covered bowl in the refrigerator.
Prepare the chakchouka; keep in a covered bowl in the refrigerator.
Prepare the Tabbouleh up to the end of step 3; keep covered in the refrigerator.
On the day:
Prepare the Spanakhopitas up to the end of step 3; keep covered in a cool place.
Prepare the ingredients and dressing for the Greek Salad, but do not mix; keep in separate containers or bags in the refrigerator.
Prepare the Stuffed Figs; keep in the refrigerator.
To serve at 8pm:
7.30pm:
Light the barbecue; allow the chicken drumsticks and meatballs to come to room temperature in time to cook on the barbecue.
Put the Spanakhopitas in the oven to bake.
Continue with the Tabbouleh from the beginning of step 4.
Allow the ingredients for the Greek Salad to come to room temperature, then mix together.
Reheat the Chakchouka, adding water if necessary.

chilli powder, sugar and salt and pepper to taste, then cover and simmer gently for 30 minutes, stirring occasionally and adding more water if the chakchouka becomes dry (this will depend on the ripeness and juiciness of the tomatoes). Taste and adjust seasoning before serving.

To Freeze Cool, pack into a rigid container and freeze for up to 2 months. Thaw at room temperature.

STUFFED FIGS

---
225 g (8 oz) ricotta cheese, at room temperature
---
150 ml (¼ pint) double or whipping cream
---
few drops of almond extract or rose water
---
16 ripe fresh figs
---
fig or vine leaves and rose petals, to serve
---

1 Beat the ricotta cheese in a bowl until softened. Whip the cream in another bowl until just standing in soft peaks, then fold into the ricotta, with almond extract or rose water according to taste.

2 With a sharp knife, cut a cross in each fig at the top (stem end). Continue cutting down almost to the base of the fig, but keeping the fruit whole. With your fingers, gently prise the four 'petals' of each fig apart, to allow room for the filling.

3 Spoon the ricotta mixture into a piping bag fitted with a large rosette nozzle and pipe into the centre of each fig. Chill in the refrigerator until serving time.

4 To serve, arrange fig or vine leaves decoratively over a flat serving platter, place the stuffed figs on top and scatter rose petals around. Serve chilled.

FRESH AIR FEAST

M	E	N	U

FROZEN VODKA

GUACAMOLE DIP WITH VEGETABLE AND FRUIT CRUDITÉS

SUMMER HERB SALAD

SIMPLE POTATO SALAD

CHARRED COURGETTE RIBBONS WITH HERB VINAIGRETTE

MULLET COOKED IN VINE LEAVES

LAMB WITH THREE CORIANDER MARINADE

PRAWN AND CHICKEN WITH CHILLI AND GINGER

ZAHTER BREAD

RASPBERRY AND LAVENDER PAVLOVA

SERVES 8

*T*here's nothing like the smell of a barbecue to get the taste buds tingling, and nothing worse than waiting for food to cook while stomachs rumble! Keep guests happy while waiting for the main event by offering them Guacamole with a selection of fruit and vegetable crudités. To drink with the dip there's a potent frozen vodka served encased in a flower filled ice bucket.

The main courses are marinated so that they're meltingly tender and flavoursome. Add a few sausages or burgers if you have children coming. There's also a potato salad and a stunning Summer Herb Salad, but a rice or a pasta salad would be equally delicious. You can never have too much food at a barbecue, so a dessert is a must; pavlova is ideal since it can be prepared in advance. For those with never ending appetites buy a bunch of bananas to barbecue as the fire dies down. Allow to blacken, then split and serve with a splash of rum and a dollop of ice cream. Pure bliss! . . .

FROZEN VODKA

Frozen Vodka is a deliciously intoxicating, but refreshing drink perfect for serving as an aperitif with the Guacamole dip. You will need to dilute the vodka, with a mixer of your choice as neat alcohol won't freeze. When diluted in this way it becomes 'slushy' rather like a very potent sorbet! Try diluted lime cordial, an exotic fruit juice such as mango or guava or tonic water or lemonade.

You will need a container that is large enough to hold a vodka bottle and leave a 7.5 cm (3 inch) space around the sides of the bottle. A plastic freezer container is ideal. Dilute the vodka as required, but don't fill the bottle right to the top (to allow for expansion as the liquid freezes). Stand the bottle upright in the container and fill it with water. Push flowers, herbs or greenery of your choice down the sides of the bottle into the water.

Carefully transfer the entire thing to the freezer (stand upright, you may need to rearrange your freezer shelves) and freeze for 24 hours.

To serve, dip briefly in hot water to loosen the plastic container. Remove the container. Stand on a tray with a lip, to catch any drips and decorate the tray with flowers and leaves. Stand the vodka well away from the barbecue or it will melt quickly! To pour the vodka, wrap the entire thing in a cloth and pour carefully.

Frozen Vodka and Guacamole Dip with Vegetable and Fruit Crudités (above)

179

GUACAMOLE DIP WITH VEGETABLE AND FRUIT CRUDITÉS

If you don't own a food processor, finely chop the onion, garlic, ginger and tomato then mash the avocado before mixing with the chopped vegetables and the remaining ingredients.

1 small onion, skinned
2–3 garlic cloves, skinned
2.5 cm (1 inch) piece of fresh root ginger, peeled
4 large ripe avocados
finely grated rind and juice of 2 small limes
60 ml (4 tbsp) chopped fresh coriander
10 ml (2 tsp) ground coriander
10 ml (2 tsp) ground cumin
5 ml (1 tsp) chilli powder
2 ripe tomatoes, seeded and roughly chopped
salt and freshly ground pepper
paprika and coriander, to garnish

1 Using a food processor and with the machine running, drop the onion, garlic and ginger through the funnel. Process until finely chopped.

2 Peel and stone the avocados, then put in the blender with all the remaining ingredients except the tomato. Process until almost smooth. Stir in the tomato, taste and adjust seasoning as necessary. Transfer to a serving bowl and chill for 30 minutes to let the flavours develop. Serve with crudités.

Crudités to serve with Guacamole

Serve an assortment of crudités chosen and prepared to appeal to the eye as well as the taste buds. Baby vegetables such as carrots, baby corn, cherry tomatoes and button mushrooms can be served whole. Traditionally, crudités are cut into neat strips, all about the same size and arranged in tidy rows of colour. You may prefer the wild approach where vegetables are cleaned and trimmed to a manageable size retaining their original shape. Arrange these in a more chaotic fashion on plain white china or a bed of crushed ice.

Sliced fresh fruit such as apples, pears, nectarines, grapes, mangoes, star fruit and fresh dates, as well as dried figs, dates and apricots all make good crudités.

SUMMER HERB SALAD

This refreshing salad uses some of the more unusual herbs.

Selection of herb leaves – Good King Henry, rocket, sorrel, lamb's lettuce, dandelion, alecost, salad burnet
handful of fresh chervil sprigs
handful of fresh parsley sprigs
a few herb flowers – sweet violet, marigold, if available
15 ml (1 tbsp) dry mustard
10 ml (2 tsp) clear honey
60 ml (4 tbsp) lemon juice
2.5 ml (½ tsp) paprika
60 ml (4 tbsp) sunflower oil
30 ml (2 tbsp) walnut oil
salt and freshly ground pepper

1 Wash and dry the leaves carefully. Shred them roughly with the hands and place them in a bowl with the chervil and parsley sprigs. Sprinkle the herb flowers over the top.

2 Blend the mustard powder with the honey until smooth. Add the lemon juice, paprika, sunflower and walnut oils and seasoning and mix well.

3 Dress the salad about 10 minutes before serving.

SIMPLE POTATO SALAD

1.4 kg (3 lb) small new potatoes, preferably Jersey Royals
300 ml (½ pint) mayonnaise
150 ml (¼ pint) soured cream
salt and freshly ground pepper
chopped fresh herbs

1 Clean the potatoes, but do not peel. Cut any large potatoes in half. Cook them gently in lightly salted boiling water until just tender. Drain and cool.

2 Mix the mayonnaise and cream together and season to taste with salt and pepper. Toss the potatoes in the dressing. Sprinkle with fresh herbs to serve.

CHARRED COURGETTE RIBBONS WITH HERB VINAIGRETTE

Wafer thin courgette slices take on a deliciously smoky flavour if allowed to char slightly on the barbecue.

8 large courgettes (about 1.1 kg/2 ½ lb)
60 ml (4 tbsp) olive oil
15 ml (1 tbsp) garlic vinegar
45 ml (3 tbsp) chopped fresh herbs
salt and freshly ground pepper

1 Run a sharp potato peeler along the length of each courgette to peel off long thin ribbon-like strips. Put two strips of courgettes together and 'sew' them onto bamboo skewers. Thread several pairs of courgette ribbons onto each skewer.

2 To make the vinaigrette, whisk together the remaining ingredients. Generously brush the courgettes with vinaigrette.

3 Cook the courgettes on the barbecue for about 10–15 minutes, until they are slightly blackened and soft, keep turning and basting them with the vinaigrette as they cook. Serve with the remaining dressing poured over.

MULLET COOKED IN VINE LEAVES

90 ml (6 tbsp) olive oil
30 ml (2 tbsp) white wine vinegar or lemon or lime juice
salt and freshly ground pepper
8 red mullet, each weighing about 275 g (10 oz) cleaned and scaled
8–10 vine leaves (depending on size)
lime or lemon wedges and a few grapes, to garnish

1 Whisk the oil, vinegar or lemon or lime juice together and season to taste with salt and pepper.

2 Put the fish into a shallow dish and pour over the oil and vinegar. Leave in a cool place for at least 30 minutes to marinate.

3 Remove the fish from the marinade and wrap each in one or two of the vine leaves. Secure the leaves with string.

4 Place the fish in a greased barbecue rack and cook over a barbecue for about 12–15 minutes or until the fish is cooked, turning occasionally and brushing with the marinade. Serve on a platter lined with vine leaves, decorated with lemon or lime wedges and a few grapes.

LAMB WITH THREE CORIANDER MARINADE

1.1 kg (2½ lb) lamb fillet
30 ml (2 tbsp) coriander seeds
1–2 garlic cloves, skinned and crushed
1 hot chilli, seeded and chopped
45 ml (3 tbsp) chopped fresh coriander
2.5 cm (1 inch) piece of fresh ginger, peeled and chopped
10 ml (2 tsp) ground cumin
15 ml (1 tbsp) ground coriander
10 ml (2 tsp) ground turmeric
600 ml (1 pint) Greek-style yogurt
salt and freshly ground pepper
30 ml (2 tbsp) lemon juice
30 ml (2 tbsp) lemon juice
fresh coriander, to garnish

1 Trim the lamb of all excess fat and cut into neat cubes.

2 Crush the coriander seeds in a pestle and mortar then add the garlic, chilli, fresh coriander and ginger and work to a paste. Add the cumin, ground coriander and turmeric and mix thoroughly together.

3 Stir the paste into the yogurt and season generously with salt and pepper. Stir in the lemon juice. Pour the yogurt marinade into a large glass bowl, then add the lamb. Mix until all the lamb is coated with the marinade. Cover and leave in a cool place to marinate for at least 1 hour or overnight.

4 Thread the meat onto skewers. Barbecue until the meat is brown on the outside and just pink and tender on the inside, about 20 minutes. Serve on a platter garnished with fresh coriander.

COOK'S HINTS
1 Use **fresh vine leaves** when in season, or use vine leaves packed in brine sold in vacuum packs in supermarkets and delicatessens. Canned vine leaves don't work as they tend to disintegrate.

2 After lighting the **barbecue**, allow the fire to burn for about 30 minutes until the coals turn to a greyish ash with a red glow. At this point the fire is ready for cooking to begin. Extra fuel should be placed around the edge of the fire and gradually drawn into the centre as it ignites.
   Food can be placed directly on a greased grid placed several inches above the coals, or it can be put on kitchen foil.

MENU SUGGESTIONS
Homemade burgers are far superior to the shop bought variety. To make 8 burgers, mince 900 g (2 lb) lean beef and mix it with a finely grated onion, chopped mixed herbs and plenty of salt and pepper. Add a little crushed garlic, chopped chilli, or prepared mustard, if liked. Thoroughly mix everything together and shape into 8 burgers. Brush with a little oil, then barbecue until cooked as desired. Serve in buns or warm pitta bread.

PRAWN AND CHICKEN WITH CHILLI AND GINGER

If you have non-meat eaters coming to the party, use a few extra prawns and thread them onto skewers on their own.

16 medium raw prawns
700 g (1½ lb) chicken breast fillets, skinned
16 mild chillies
MARINADE
5 cm (2 inch) piece of fresh ginger, peeled and finely chopped
finely grated rind and juice of 1 lime
120 ml (8 tbsp) vegetable oil
10 ml (2 tsp) soft brown sugar
45 ml (3 tbsp) soy sauce
1–2 chillies, seeded and chopped
4 spring onions, chopped
shredded spring onions, to garnish

1 To prepare the prawns, remove most of the shell, leaving the tail piece attached. Using a small, sharp knife, cut each prawn along the inner curve, stopping at the tail shell, to expose the dark vein. (Take care not to split the prawn completely in half).

2 Spread each prawn open and remove the dark vein. Rinse the prawns and drain thoroughly. Cut the chicken into large chunks.

3 Mix together all the marinade ingredients in a large shallow dish. Place the prawns and chicken in the marinade. Stir so that everything is coated in the marinade. Cover and leave to marinate for 2–3 hours or overnight, stirring occasionally.

4 When ready to cook, thread one prawn, one piece of chicken, one chilli and another piece of chicken onto bamboo or metal skewers.

5 Barbecue until the chicken is cooked through and the prawns turn pink, about 15–20 minutes. Serve sprinkled with spring onion shreds.

ZAHTER BREAD

Herby zahter seasoning can be made in large quantities and stored in a screw topped jar ready for flavouring soups, stews, pilaffs and vegetable dishes.

MAKES 4 BREADS
two 283 g packets white bread and pizza mix
125 g (4 oz) butter
finely grated rind of 1 lemon
45 ml (3 tbsp) sesame seeds
45 ml (3 tbsp) dried marjoram
15 ml (1 tbsp) dried thyme
salt and freshly ground pepper

1 Make up the bread mix according to the packet instructions. Divide the mixture into four and roll each out on a lightly floured surface to a oval about 25.5 cm (10 inches) long.

2 Place the breads on two large baking sheets. Using a sharp knife, slash the dough in a criss cross pattern. Cover and leave to prove in a warm place until doubled in size.

3 Meanwhile, beat the butter with the remaining ingredients and salt and pepper to taste.

4 Bake the bread in the oven at 230°C (450°F) mark 8 for 5 minutes. Remove from the oven and spread with the Zahter mixture. Return to the oven for about 10 minutes until golden. Serve the bread warm cut into generous chunks.

To Freeze Cool, wrap and freeze for up to 1 month. Reheat from frozen at 200°C (400°F) mark 6 for about 10 minutes.

Raspberry and Lavender Pavlova (opposite)

RASPBERRY AND LAVENDER PAVLOVA

To make the lavender sugar, put a few sprigs of fresh or dried lavender in a screw topped jar filled with caster sugar. Leave for at least two weeks. Shake well then discard the lavender and use as required.

3 egg whites
190 g (6½ oz) lavender sugar
5 ml (1 level tsp) cornflour
5 ml (1 tsp) raspberry vinegar
300 ml (½ pint) Greek-style yogurt
450 g (1 lb) fresh raspberries
150 ml (¼ pint) double cream
a few lavender flowers, to decorate

1 Draw a 23 cm (9 inch) oval on a piece of non-stick baking paper and place on a baking sheet.

2 To make the meringue, whisk the egg whites in a large bowl until very stiff. Add 50 g (2 oz) of the sugar and whisk until stiff.

Add another 50 g (2 oz) of the sugar and whisk again. Add a further 50 g (2 oz) of the sugar (save the remaining 15 g (½ oz) for the topping) and continue whisking until the meringue forms soft peaks. Fold in the cornflour and vinegar.

3 Pile or pipe the meringue into the oval marked on the baking sheet. Make a dip in the middle to hold the filling.

4 Bake in the oven 180°C (350°F) mark 4 for 5 minutes then at 130°C (250°F) mark ½ for a further 45–50 minutes or until set but still soft in the middle.

5 Leave to cool slightly, then carefully peel off the paper. Don't worry if the meringue cracks at this stage.

6 When completely cold, whip the cream with the remaining sugar until it just holds its shape, then fold in the yogurt. Roughly crush half of the raspberries and fold into the cream mixture. Pile on top of the Pavlova.

7 Push the remaining raspberries through a sieve to make a raspberry sauce. Drizzle the sauce over the Pavlova. Decorate with lavender flowers. Serve on a plate lined with leaves and flowers.

COUNTDOWN

At least two weeks before:
Make the lavender sugar for the Pavlova.

The day before:
Make the Pavlova to the end of step 6. Cool, wrap in greaseproof and store in an airtight container. Make and cool the Zahter Bread. Store in an airtight container. Make the frozen vodka.

The night before:
Prepare the Lamb with Three Coriander Marinade by following steps 1, 2 and 3. Prepare the Prawn and Chicken with Chilli and Ginger by following steps 1 and 2. Cover both and refrigerate.

On the day:
Prepare the crudités. Refrigerate in polythene bags. Prepare the Potato Salad and the vinaigrette for the Charred Courgette Ribbons. Cover both and leave in a cool place. Make the dressing for the Herb Salad. Store in a screw top jar in a cool place.

To serve at 8pm:
5.45pm: Finish the Pavlova. Chill in the refrigerator.

6.00pm: Thread the Lamb and Prawn and Chicken onto skewers, cover and refrigerate.

6.30pm: Marinate the mullet following steps 1 and 2. Prepare the courgette ribbons following step 1. Prepare the Summer Herb Salad by following step 1. Cover both and refrigerate.

7.00pm: Make the Guacamole Dip by following steps 1 and 2. Wrap the mullet in the vine leaves. Cover both and refrigerate.

7.30pm: Arrange the Guacamole Dip on a serving platter with the crudités. Place the marinated lamb on the barbecue by following step 3. Five minutes later, start cooking the Prawn and Chicken, followed 5 minutes later by the mullet.

7.45pm: Put the courgette ribbons on the barbecue by following step 3. Shake the dressing and dress the salad.

8pm: Serve.

ANNUAL CELEBRATIONS

Introduction

Annual celebrations, such as Christmas, Easter and Thanksgiving, are usually family times, when everyone from both near and far gathers in one home for the festivities. The best celebrations last a few days – that means having a house packed with people and lots of entertaining. To make things run smoothly, get organized early.

After noting what you have in store, the first step is to make a shopping list – try to shop for the entire holiday period in one or two trips. Don't be too rigid about your list – an impulse-buy may be a bargain, provided it doesn't mean having to juggle the entire meal plan. Don't count on finding a certain ingredient – have an alternative cut of meat or a different vegetable in mind in case what you originally planned turns out to be unavailable or exorbitantly priced.

A freezer will help with holiday meals, but don't fall into the trap of living totally on frozen foods. A casserole that can be made ahead and frozen can be served on Boxing Day with a crisp green salad, to save effort in the kitchen after the intensive cooking of Christmas Day. Use our time plans and the Special Index on page 279 as a guide to pick out recipes suitable for advance preparation or freezing.

Along with the food, pay attention to practical and logistical considerations like seating, table linen, flowers, fresh towels in the bathroom and sleeping arrangements.

EASTER LUNCH

M E N U

SMOKED TROUT AND LENTIL SALAD

ROAST EYE FILLET OF LAMB WITH
CANDIED LEMONS AND HONEY

ROAST NEW POTATOES

BAKED CHERRY TOMATOES

STEAMED BROCCOLI, BROAD BEANS
AND SUGAR SNAP PEAS

EASTER CHEESECAKE

SERVES 8

*H*oliday weekend lunches provide an excellent opportunity to get together with friends and family. It's the best time to enjoy a meal which is unhurried and light hearted, with none of the pressures of evening meals.

Whatever the numbers, this menu based around a tender roast of new season's lamb fillet, is easily doubled up to cope with more guests and easily prepared, too. The timing of the meal should also be flexible, especially if some guests are travelling a distance. The starter salad of smoked trout and lentils holds happily in the fridge until you're ready to eat. The roast lamb with its accompanying vegetables takes less than 30 minutes so you can start this cooking after guests arrive.

Once the pudding's been served children will probably disappear into the garden or to watch T.V. Now's the time to produce an interesting cheeseboard to enjoy at leisure with coffee. It needn't be lavish – perhaps a selection of locally produced goat's cheese or a wedge of mature Farmhouse Cheddar with a bowl of fresh fruit.

Smoked Trout and Lentil Salad (left)

SMOKED TROUT AND LENTIL SALAD

DRESSING:
150 ml (¼ pint) olive oil
90 ml (6 tbsp) white wine vinegar
5 ml (1 tsp) ground coriander
2.5 ml (½ tsp) caster sugar
10 ml (2 tsp) Dijon mustard
salt and freshly ground pepper
SALAD
2 medium onions, skinned
350 g (12 oz) green lentils
700 g (1½ lb) smoked trout fillets
1 bunch watercress, trimmed

1 Whisk together all the dressing ingredients and set aside. Cut the onions into wafer thin rings.

2 Pick over the lentils and rinse well. Place in a saucepan, cover with cold water and add 5 ml (1 tsp) salt. Bring to the boil, cover and simmer for 15–20 minutes or until the lentils are tender but still *al dente*. Drain well, turn into a non-metallic bowl and stir in the dressing and onion rings. Cover and leave in a cool place overnight.

3 To serve, roughly flake the smoked trout. Spoon a small mound of lentils onto eight individual serving plates. Top with pieces of smoked trout. Roughly chop the watercress and sprinkle over the top to serve.

MENU SUGGESTIONS
Offer Toasted Seed and Nut Mix (page 246) with drinks as guests arrive. Suitable alternatives to the Smoked Trout and Lentil Salad are Fennel and Orange Soup (page 243) or Seafood Roulade (page 244). Ginger Meringues with Rhubarb Sauce (page 263) make a splendid Easter pudding.

ROAST EYE FILLET OF LAMB WITH CANDIED LEMONS AND HONEY

This cut of lamb is expensive but is so lean and tender there's no wastage. The same marinade could also be used with grilled lamb cutlets. Allow 2 per person.

4 small, thin-skinned lemons
3 fillets of lamb, about 1.4 kg (3 lb) total weight
MARINADE
30 ml (2 tbsp) chopped fresh rosemary
2 bay leaves
2 garlic cloves, skinned and crushed
2.5 cm (1 inch) piece fresh root ginger, peeled and thinly sliced
150 ml (5 fl oz) clear honey
75 ml (5 tbsp) vegetable oil
salt and freshly ground pepper
sprigs of fresh thyme, rosemary and bay leaves, to garnish

1 Mix together all the marinade ingredients. Add the strained juice of 2 of the lemons. Place the remaining 2 lemons in a small saucepan and cover with cold water. Bring to the boil, cover and simmer for 7–10 minutes or until just beginning to soften. Cool and cut into thickish slices discarding any pips.
2 Place the lamb fillets in a shallow, non-metallic dish, add the lemon slices and the marinade, cover and leave in the refrigerator overnight.
3 Remove the lamb from the marinade and place in a shallow roasting tin and roast at 220°C (425°F) mark 7 for 20–25 minutes. This produces a medium rare roast.
4 About 5 minutes before the end of cooking time, bring the marinade and lemon slices to the boil in a small saucepan. Simmer, stirring occasionally for about 5 minutes or until syrupy. Carefully add any pan juices from the lamb. Adjust the seasoning.
5 Serve the lamb thickly sliced with the candied lemon slices. Pour over the remaining honey sauce and garnish with sprigs of fresh thyme, rosemary and bay leaves.

ROAST NEW POTATOES

1.4 kg (3 lb) small new potatoes
salt and freshly ground pepper
45 ml (3 tbsp) vegetable oil

1 Scrub the potatoes but do not peel. Halve any large ones.
2 Place in a saucepan and cover with cold salted water. Bring to the boil and boil for about 7 minutes or until almost tender. Drain well.
3 Heat the oil in a large roasting tin and add the hot potatoes. Bake in the oven at 220°C (425°F) mark 7 for 20–25 minutes until golden and tender. Adjust seasoning before serving.

BAKED CHERRY TOMATOES

It's not essential to peel the tomatoes but it does give a better finish.

32 cherry tomatoes, about 700 g (1½ lb) total weight
50 g (2 oz) butter
30 ml (2 tbsp) chopped fresh parsley
salt and freshly ground pepper

1 Make a small slash in the skin of each tomato. Place in a large bowl and pour over enough boiling water to cover. Leave for 1 minute, drain and refresh under cold running water.
2 Peel each tomato and place in a large ovenproof dish.
3 Melt the butter and stir in the parsley. Brush over the tomatoes and season well.
4 Bake at 220°C (425°F) mark 7 for about 10 minutes or until hot and just beginning to soften.

Easter Cheesecake (opposite)

EASTER CHEESECAKE

125 g (4 oz) butter
225 g (8 oz) plain flour
caster sugar
400 g (14 oz) full fat soft cheese
2 eggs, separated
2.5 ml (½ tsp) vanilla flavouring
200 ml (7 fl oz) double cream
150 ml (5 fl oz) soured cream
1 ripe pear, optional
icing sugar, for dusting
crystallized primroses, to decorate

1 Rub the butter into the flour with 45 ml (3 tbsp) caster sugar. Bind to a dough with about 60 ml (4 tbsp) water. Roll out on a lightly floured surface and use to line a 21.5 cm (8½ inch) deep, fluted loose bottomed flan tin. Chill for 15 minutes then bake blind at 200°C (400°F) mark 6 for 20–25 minutes or until pale golden brown and cooked through.

2 Beat together the soft cheese, egg yolks and vanilla flavouring. Gradually beat in the creams until thoroughly combined.

3 Whisk the egg whites until they just hold their shape. Fold in 25 g (1 oz) caster sugar and continue whisking until stiff. Whisk in a further 25 g (1 oz) sugar. Fold into the cheese mixture.

4 Peel, core and thinly slice the pear into the prepared flan case if using. Spoon over the cheese mixture. Place the tin on a baking sheet and bake at 220°C (425°F) mark 7 for 20 minutes. Reduce the oven temperature to 180°C (350°F) mark 4 for a further 35–40 minutes or until the cheesecake is golden brown and just set. Cool in the tin.

5 Serve the cheesecake warm dusted with icing sugar and decorated with crystallized primroses.

COOK'S HINT
To **crystallize primroses** pick about a dozen clean primrose heads. Lightly beat 1 egg white. Place about 25 g (1 oz) caster sugar on a flat plate. Brush each bloom all over with the egg white and dip in the caster sugar. Spoon the sugar over the blooms to coat completely.

Place the flowers on a baking sheet lined with non-stick baking parchment. Leave to dry at cool, room temperature for 4–5 hours. Store in an airtight container.

COUNTDOWN
The day before:
Prepare the Smoked Trout & Lentil Salad to the end of stage 2. Prepare the lamb to the end of stage 2. Prepare the Baked Cherry Tomatoes to the end of stage 2. Prepare the Easter Cheesecake to the end of stage 2. Make the crystallized primroses, if using.
To serve at 1pm:
11.30am: Heat the oven to 220°C (425°F) mark 7. Prepare the green vegetables.
12.25pm: Boil the new potatoes. Heat the oil.
12.30pm: Put the new potatoes in the oven to bake. Put the lamb in the oven to cook.
12.40pm: Place the cheesecake in the oven to cook. Assemble the Smoked Trout and Lentil Salad.
12.50pm: Put the cherry tomatoes in the oven to cook.
1pm: Serve the starter. Start steaming the green vegetables. Cover the lamb loosely with foil. Turn the temperature down to 180°C (350°F) mark 4 and continue to cook the cheesecake as directed for a further 40 minutes.

TRICK OR TREAT
HALLOWE'EN SUPPER

Hallowe'en is the night when all souls wander the earth. It is a time to dress up as ghouls and ghosts, witches and wizards, duck for apples and go around disguised and performing for a reward of sweets or a small coin (this is called 'Trick or Treat' in America). The meal should be creepy and fun. The soup is full of make-believe maggots and this is followed by a macabre version of Toad-in-the-Hole. Excited children and adults can nibble on twiglet broomsticks, crunch on meringue bones and gorge on moist Creepy Cake. Decorate the table with garlic and onions, as they are said to ward off evil! Serve warming mulled wine (see page 278) and hot malted drinks if the weather is particularly cold.

MAGGOT SOUP

1.4 litres (2½ pints) milk
1.4 kg (3 lb) fresh pumpkin, peeled, seeds removed and cubed
finely grated rind and juice of 2 oranges
125 g (4 oz) small maggot-like pasta shapes!
50 g (2 oz) butter
45 ml (3 tbsp) light soft brown sugar
salt and freshly ground pepper
pinch ground cinnamon
freshly grated nutmeg
fresh coriander sprigs, to garnish (optional)

1 Scald the milk in a large saucepan; add the cubed pumpkin, orange juice and rind. Bring to the boil, turn down the heat, cover and simmer gently for about 20 minutes or until the pumpkin is very tender.

2 Meanwhile, cook the pasta in plenty of boiling salted water until tender, according to the manufacturer's instructions. Drain and reserve.

3 Pour the pumpkin mixture into a blender or food processor and process until smooth. Return to the pan and add the butter, sugar, salt, pepper, cinnamon and nutmeg to taste. Reheat without boiling and stir in the pasta, to serve. Garnish with coriander leaves, if liked. Serve with crusty rye bread.

WITCHES' HANDS WITH BLOOD

250 g (9 oz) plain flour
pinch of salt
4 eggs
568 ml (1 pint) half-fat milk
60 ml (4 tbsp) melted dripping or vegetable oil
700 g (1½ lb) long thin chipolata sausages
tomato sauce, to serve

1 Make the batter, place the first four ingredients in a blender or liquidiser and blend until smooth, cover and leave to stand for at least 30 minutes. This will swell the starch grains and give a lighter batter.

2 Heat the dripping or oil in a large roast-ing tin and add the sausages. Bake in the oven at 220°C (425°F) mark 7 for 5 minutes or until browning and the fat is very hot. If the fat is not sizzling hot, place the tin on the top of the cooker and heat until it is. (The pudding will not rise if the fat isn't hot enough.) Remove the sausages with kitchen tongs.

3 Stir the batter and pour into the tin. The batter should sizzle as soon as it hits the fat. Quickly arrange the sausages in fives to look like hands in the batter.

4 Immediately return to the oven and bake for 40–45 minutes until the pudding is risen and golden brown. Serve drizzled with tomato blood.

PILE OF MERINGUE BONES

MAKES ABOUT 16
two egg whites, at room temperature
125 g (4 oz) caster sugar
cocoa powder, for dusting

1 With an electric hand beater whisk the egg whites until stiff but not dry. Add the sugar one teaspoon at a time, whisking until very stiff between each addition. The meringue should be very stiff and shiny.

2 Spoon into a piping bag fitted with a 1 cm (½ inch) plain nozzle. Pipe onto non-stick baking parchment in rows. First pipe a finger about 7.5 cm (3 inches) long. At each end, pipe two small blobs touching each other to form the nubs of the bones.

3 Bake in the oven at 140°C (275°F) mark 1 for about 1½ hours or until hard and dry. Remove from the baking parchment and cool on a wire rack. Pile on a plate and dust with cocoa.

COOK'S HINTS

1 If using canned **pumpkin**, use two 400 g cans and a pinch of saffron to brighten the colour.

2 If syrup oozes from the **meringue**, the oven is too hot. To release the meringue from the paper, turn upside down and moisten the underside – the paper should peel off easily.

3 To make **Twiglet Broomsticks**, break 4 Grissini breadsticks in half and squeeze a ring of Primula cheese (from a tube) around the broken end of each breadstick broom-handle. Press twiglets into the cheese to form the bristles of the broom. Carefully tie coloured string around the twiglets at the base of the breadstick.

MENU SUGGESTIONS

For a more conventional Hallowe'en serve Italian Braised Beef (page 246) or Beef and Chestnut Casserole (page 247) with baked potatoes or Garlic Bread (page 221). Pumpkin Cheesecake (page 204) makes a seasonal ending.

Maggot Soup
(opposite)

Creepy Cake (above)

CREEPY CAKE

CAKE
lard for greasing
125 g (4 oz) cocoa powder, sifted
275 g (10 oz) light soft brown sugar
300 ml (½ pint) milk
125 g (4 oz) butter, softened
5 ml (1 tsp) vanilla flavouring
3 eggs
225 g (8 oz) plain flour
15 ml (1 level tbsp) baking powder
GREEN SLIME ICING
175 g (6 oz) icing sugar
30 ml (2 tbsp) water
2.5 ml (½ level tsp) cream of tartar
good pinch of salt
2 egg whites
few drops almond flavouring
edible green food colouring
CREEPY-CRAWLIES
450–700 g (1–1½ lb) ready-to-roll fondant icing or white marzipan, assorted edible food colourings including black, brown, yellow and non-toxic silver
a little royal icing
liquorice bootlaces, jelly snakes etc

1 Melt the lard and brush inside a 1.4 litre (2½ pint) ring mould. Leave to set and dust with flour. To make the cake, put the cocoa and 150 g (5 oz) sugar into a medium saucepan with the milk. Slowly bring to the boil, whisking all the time until the mixture thickens and starts to bubble. Cool.

2 Cream the butter with the remaining sugar and the vanilla flavouring, whisk in the eggs, add to the mixture and beat well. Sift the flour with the baking powder and fold into the mixture. Beat in the cocoa mixture. If necessary add a little more milk; it should *just* pour.

3 Pour into the prepared mould and bake in the oven at 180°C (350°F) mark 4 for about 40-45 minutes or until risen and firm. Cool in the tin for 5 minutes then turn out onto a wire rack to cool completely.

4 Using 125 g (4 oz) of fondant, knead in some brown food colouring and roll out to a thickness of 0.5 cm (¼ inch). Cut out a circle to generously cover the hole in the centre of the cake. Use a saucer as a guide. This is to be the trap door. With a blunt knife mark lines to resemble planks of wood. Place on a baking sheet lined with greaseproof paper and leave in a warm place to dry overnight.

5 Next day, paint the grooves with black or brown food colouring and shape a ring for a handle and attach with a little royal icing.

6 Using the remaining fondant or marzipan like modelling clay, decide what creatures to make, and colour the fondant accordingly. A selection of bats, spiders, worms, beetles, skulls and bones would be a start. Use the liquorice to make spiders' legs and the jelly snakes for further decoration. Pipe eyes onto the creatures with royal icing, allow to dry then paint on pupils with food colouring. Allow to dry overnight or longer.

7 When all the creatures have been made, make the icing. Beat the icing sugar, water, cream of tartar, salt, egg whites and almond flavouring together in a medium heatproof bowl. Stand the bowl over a pan of simmering water and, using an electric hand whisk, beat until stiff and shiny. Whisk in enough green food colouring to give the desired colour. Remove from the heat and beat until cooled and easy to spread.

8 Place the cake on a board or plate and cover with the icing. Secure the trap door over the hole in the middle of the cake and prop open with a cocktail stick. Arrange the creatures over the cake, crawling all over and onto the plate. Make trails in the icing. Make sure that some creepies are crawling out of the trap door. Spiders' webs can then be piped from the cake to the board with royal icing, left to dry then painted with non-toxic silver food colouring.

THANKSGIVING DINNER

Thanksgiving is celebrated in the United States on the fourth Thursday in November. It is also celebrated by expatriate Americans all over the world. Thanksgiving is a family time, children come home (with their own children) to be with their parents, and the generations enjoy together the holiday weekend that follows. Traditionally, turkey is eaten at Thanksgiving, because the Pilgrims who came to pioneer the new country ate wild turkeys.

This dinner starts with a delicious Egg Nog, accompanied by two sorts of pecan cookies. The golden roast turkey (wild or otherwise!) is stuffed with a chestnut and cornbread mixture, and garnished with pears filled with cranberry sauce. Sweet potatoes with pineapple, glazed onions with peas, and roast potatoes accompany the bird. To complete the feast comes a pumpkin cheesecake, with layers of orange and creamy white filling.

Egg Nog with Pecan Cookies (right)

DRINKS TO SERVE
A very good dry white wine with the turkey, Chablis would be ideal, or a Californian Chardonnay. For the dessert a Muscat Dessert Wine –Muscat De Baumes De Venise or Muscat De Rivesaltes.

MENU SUGGESTIONS
Celeriac Purée (page 261), Glazed Carrots with Turnips (page 261) or Wild Rice and Thyme Salad (page 260) would all complement roast turkey. For dessert, Brandy Snap Baskets filled with Ginger Ice Cream and served with Apricot and Ginger Sauce (page 264) makes a suitable alternative.

COOK'S HINT
Pecan nuts belong to the walnut family and are grown in North America where they are known as hickory nuts. They are available in their shells, which are smooth and reddish-brown, or shelled, looking rather like narrow, elongated walnuts.
   If pecans are unavailable, walnuts may be used in this recipe.

PECAN COOKIES

Traditionally pecan cookies are served at the end of the meal, but they can also be handed round with the pre-dinner drink.

PECAN COOKIES I
125 g (4 oz) plain flour
50 g (2 oz) cornflour
3.75 ml (¾ level tsp) baking powder
pinch of salt
10 ml (2 tsp) ground ginger
5 ml (1 tsp) ground mixed spice
5 ml (1 tsp) ground cinnamon
50 g (2 oz) pecan nuts, finely chopped
75 g (3 oz) butter
50 g (2 oz) light soft brown sugar
25 g (1 oz) dark muscovado sugar
40 g (1½ oz) golden syrup

30 pecan nut halves, to decorate
PECAN COOKIES II
1 egg white,
40 g (1½ oz) caster sugar
75 g (3 oz) pecan nuts, finely ground
small pieces of pecan nut, to decorate

1 To make Pecan Cookies I, lightly grease several baking sheets. Sift the flour, cornflour, baking powder, salt and the spices into a bowl. Stir in the chopped pecans.

2 Beat the butter with the sugars until very soft, light and fluffy. Beat in the golden syrup, then mix in the flour and nut mixture. Knead the dough very lightly on a floured surface until smooth.

3 Divide the dough into walnut-sized pieces. Roll each one into a ball and place on the greased baking sheets, spacing the balls well apart. Flatten each ball of dough with a fork, then press a pecan nut half into the centre of each one.

4 Bake at 180°C (350°F) mark 4 for 15–20

EGG NOG

You will need a very large punchbowl to make the egg nog in and to serve it. This smooth creamy libation that packs quite an alcoholic punch can be made several hours in advance. If it separates as it chills, just whisk it up before serving.

6 eggs, separated
125 g (4 oz) caster sugar
600 ml (1 pint) double cream
350 ml (12 fl oz) whisky
200 ml (7 fl oz) light rum
450 ml (¾ pint) ice-cold milk
finely grated rind of 1 orange
finely grated rind of 1 lemon
finely grated rind of 1 lime
freshly grated nutmeg
little freshly ground cinnamon

1 Put a large mixing bowl into the refrigerator to chill for about 1 hour. Alternatively, fill it with iced water about 10 minutes before it is needed, then empty and dry it.

2 Put the egg yolks and caster sugar into the chilled mixing bowl and whisk using an electric hand whisk until the mixture is very thick, and leaves a trail when the whisk is lifted out.

3 Whisk the egg whites until they form soft peaks. Whip the cream until it forms soft peaks. Fold the egg whites into the egg yolks mixture, then fold in the cream.

4 Pour the egg and cream mixture into a large punchbowl. Very, very slowly (using a balloon or wire whisk - not an electric whisk) whisk in the whisky, rum and milk. Cover the bowl and refrigerate for at least 2 hours before serving.

5 To serve, sprinkle the top of the egg nog with the grated orange, lemon and lime rind, freshly grated nutmeg and cinnamon. Serve immediately.

minutes, until just lightly browned around the edges. Allow to cool slightly on the bak ing sheets, then remove with a palette knife to cooling racks to cool completely.

5 To make Pecan Cookies II, line several baking sheets with rice paper.

6 Whisk the egg white until it is very stiff, then fold in the sugar and the ground pecans. Put the mixture into a piping bag fitted with a large star nozzle. Pipe stars of the mixture onto the rice paper, spacing them apart. Press a small piece of pecan nut into the centre of each star.

7 Bake the cookies at 180°C (350°F) mark 4 for 20 minutes, until firm. Allow to cool completely, then remove the cookies from the rice paper, tearing it away from the edges.

8 To serve, arrange both types of cookies together on a doily-lined plate or in a basket. Serve with the Egg Nog.

To Freeze Pack in a rigid container, interleaved with greaseproof paper, freeze for up to 3 months. Thaw at room temperature for 1–2 hours.

ROAST TURKEY WITH CHESTNUT AND CORNBREAD STUFFING

If at all possible, get a fresh turkey, not a frozen one. The texture and flavour of a fresh bird is incomparable. Make the cornbread for the stuffing a few days before and store it in an airtight tin. Or make it well ahead and freeze it.

5.9 kg (13 lb) oven ready turkey
75 g (3 oz) butter, softened
salt and freshly ground pepper
STUFFING
125 g (4 oz) butter
2 large onions, skinned and finely chopped
900g (2 lb) pork sausagemeat
450 g (1 lb) fresh or canned unsweetened chestnut purée
225 g (8 oz) cornbread (See page 203), crumbled (or fresh white breadcrumbs)
45 ml (3 tbsp) mixed dried herbs
60 ml (4 tbsp) chopped fresh parsley
finely grated rind of 1 lemon
1 egg, beaten
GRAVY
the giblets from the turkey
1 onion, skinned and roughly chopped
1 carrot, roughly chopped
1 bay leaf
fresh parsley sprig
fresh thyme sprig
1 garlic clove, unskinned
about 45 ml (3 level tbsp) plain flour
200 ml (7 fl oz) single cream
watercress, to garnish

1 Wipe the turkey inside and out, with absorbent kitchen paper. Using a very small sharp knife, carefully remove the wish bone from the neck cavity to make carving easier.

2 To make the stuffing, melt the butter in a frying pan. Pour off half into a small bowl and set aside. Add the onions to the frying pan and cook very gently for about 10–15 minutes, until soft but not brown. Cool.

3 Put all of the remaining ingredients for the stuffing into a large mixing bowl. Add the softened onions and the reserved butter, then season very well with salt and pepper. Knead the ingredients together until they are thoroughly blended. To test for seasoning, fry or microwave a little of the stuffing until cooked, then taste. Adjust the seasoning if necessary.

4 Stuff the neck end of the turkey with the stuffing, then truss the bird neatly. Place in a large roasting tin. Spread with softened butter, then season well with salt and pepper. Cover the turkey with foil. Any remaining stuffing can be placed in a roasting tin and cooked for the final hour with the turkey.

5 Roast the turkey in the centre of the oven at 180°C (350°F) mark 4 for 4-5 hours, removing the foil for the last hour to brown the skin. Baste frequently during cooking. Test to see if the turkey is done by piercing the thighs at their thickest parts; if the juices run clear, it is cooked (if the juices are pink, then continue cooking a little longer). Be sure to test both thighs, sometimes one side can be cooked before the other.

6 While the turkey is cooking, prepare the stock for the gravy. Put the giblets into a saucepan with the onion, carrot, herbs and garlic. Season well with salt and pepper. Bring slowly to the boil, then skim off any scum from the surface. Reduce the heat, partially cover the saucepan and simmer gently for about 2 hours. Strain the stock into a measuring jug, and make up to 600 ml (1 pint) with water, if necessary.

7 When the turkey is cooked, lift it onto a large serving dish. Loosely cover with foil and stand for 30 minutes before serving.

8 To make the gravy, tilt the roasting tin and very carefully skim off all of the fat from the surface of the juices in the tin. Stir the flour into the juices left in the tin, using a wire whisk, then whisk in the turkey stock. Bring the gravy to the boil, whisking all the time until the gravy thickens. By this time the residue from the roasting tin will have dissolved into the gravy, so the gravy can be strained into a saucepan, for easier handling. Simmer the gravy gently for 15 minutes, to cook off the raw flour taste. Season the gravy with salt and pepper, then stir in the cream. Allow to heat through, but not to boil. Pour the gravy into a hot serving boat.

9 To serve the turkey, remove the trussing string, then garnish with pear halves filled with cranberry sauce, and watercress.

CORNBREAD

225 g (8 oz) cornmeal (maize flour)
125 g (4 oz) plain flour
5 ml (1 tsp) salt
15 ml (1 level tbsp) baking powder
175 g (6 oz) butter
2 eggs, beaten
300 ml (½ pint) milk

1 Grease and flour a loaf tin, about 25 × 12.5 × 6 cm (9 × 5 × 2½ inches).
2 Sift the cornmeal, flour, salt and baking powder into a mixing bowl. Rub in the butter until the mixture resembles fine breadcrumbs. Add the beaten eggs and the milk, and mix to a soft consistency.
3 Pour the mixture into the prepared loaf tin. Bake in the centre of the oven at 200°C (400°F) mark 6 for 40–45 minutes, until well risen, golden brown and firm to the touch. Carefully remove the cornbread from the tin onto a cooling rack, and leave to cool.
To Freeze Cool, overwrap and freeze for up to 3 months. Thaw overnight at cool room temperature.

SWEET POTATOES WITH PINEAPPLE

The pineapple can be prepared and the sweet potatoes parboiled in the morning for dinner that evening.

1 medium-sized pineapple
1.4 kg (3 lb) sweet potatoes or yams
salt and freshly ground pepper
175 g (6 oz) butter
chopped fresh parsley, to garnish

1 Cut away the skin from the pineapple, removing all of the 'eyes'. Cut the pineapple into eight wedges lengthways, then cut away the hard centre core from each wedge. Cut the wedges into thick triangular-shaped pieces. Cover and set aside until needed.
2 Peel the sweet potatoes and cut them into thick slices, putting them into cold water in a large saucepan immediately they are sliced. Add 10 ml (2 tsp) of salt to the water and bring to the boil, then drain.
3 Melt the butter in a large ovenproof dish or roasting tin. Add the parboiled sweet potato slices to the dish and turn in the butter until well coated. Add seasoning.
4 Bake on the top shelf of the oven with the turkey for 1 hour. Add the pineapple pieces and baste well with butter. Continue cooking for about another 45 minutes, until the sweet potatoes are golden brown and tender.
5 Spoon the sweet potatoes and pineapple into a warmed serving dish and sprinkle with chopped parsley.

GLAZED ONIONS WITH PEAS

A quick way to skin tiny onions is to cover them with boiling water, leave for a minute and then drain them. Their skins will slip off easily, thereby saving you from flowing tears if you laboriously skin them! This preparation of the onions can be done in advance.

30 ml (2 tbsp) olive oil
25 g (1 oz) butter
45 ml (3 tbsp) granulated sugar
900 g (2 lb) baby onions, skinned
700 g (1½ lb) frozen peas
salt and freshly ground pepper

1 Heat the olive oil and the butter in a very large sauté pan or frying pan with a lid. Sprinkle the sugar into the pan and heat gently until the sugar dissolves and turns a golden caramel colour.
2 Add the onions to the pan and shake well until they are evenly coated with the caramel mixture. Cover the pan tightly, reduce the heat and cook very gently for 45 minutes to 1 hour, until the onions are tender yet still retain their shape. Shake the pan frequently to ensure even cooking.
3 Add the peas to the pan and cook for a further 10 minutes. Season well.

COOK'S HINTS
1 **Cornbread** is traditionally included in stuffing in the United States in the same way as white breadcrumbs are used in Britain. It's also delicious served with cheese or as an accompaniment to spicy stews; if you don't have time to make cornbread, use fresh white breadcrumbs for the stuffing instead.

2 **Roast potatoes** can be peeled in the morning, ready for cooking; keep them in cold water to prevent discoloration.
You will need about 1.8-2 kg (4-4½ lb) old floury potatoes, peeled, and about 50 g (2 oz) lard or dripping, or use vegetable oil. Cut the potatoes into even-sized pieces and place in boiling, salted water. Cook for 2-3 minutes, then drain. Heat the lard, dripping or oil in a roasting tin in the oven. Add the potatoes, baste with fat and cook with the turkey for about 2 hours, or at 220°C (425°F) mark 7 for 45 minutes or until golden brown.

MICROWAVE HINT

To cook the **cranberries** in the microwave, put the ingredients in a heatproof bowl, cover and cook on HIGH for about 10 minutes or until soft, stirring occasionally. Drain as above. Stir the dissolved arrowroot into the sauce and microwave on HIGH for 3–4 minutes, until boiling, thickened and smooth.

PEAR HALVES FILLED WITH CRANBERRY SAUCE

225 g (8 oz) granulated sugar
thinly pared rind and juice of 3 lemons
6 large ripe, but firm pears
225 g (8 oz) fresh cranberries
75 g (3 oz) caster sugar
20 ml (4 tsp) arrowroot
finely grated rind of 2 limes

1 Put 600 ml (1 pint) of cold water into a saucepan with the granulated sugar and lemon rind and juice. Heat slowly until the sugar dissolves, then bring to the boil. Boil gently for 10 minutes.

2 Peel the pears, leaving the stalk on. Very carefully cut each pear in half lengthways, cutting right through the stalk, so that each half retains a stalk. Using a teaspoon, scoop out the core from each pear half.

3 Put the pear halves into the hot lemon syrup and cook very gently for about 20 minutes, until they are only just tender. Pour the pears and the syrup into a large bowl and allow to cool, then cover and refrigerate.

4 Put the cranberries and caster sugar into a saucepan, with 600 ml (1 pint) cold water. Cover the saucepan with a tightly fitting lid and cook the cranberries gently for 15–20 minutes, until soft. Pour the cranberries into a nylon sieve place over the mixing bowl, to drain off the juice.

5 Return the cranberry juice to the saucepan. Dissolve the arrowroot in a little cold water to make a smooth paste, then stir it into the cranberry juice. Bring to the boil, stirring all the time until the sauce thickens and clears. Stir the cranberries and lime rind into the sauce. Pour the cranberry sauce into a bowl and cover the surface closely with greaseproof paper, to prevent a skin from forming. Cool, then refrigerate.

6 To serve, lift the pear halves from the syrup with a slotted spoon, and drain them well on absorbent kitchen paper. Fill each pear half with a little cranberry sauce. Put any remaining sauce into a serving bowl and serve separately. Arrange the pears around the cooked turkey. Or, if the serving dish is too small, arrange them on a separate dish.

PUMPKIN CHEESECAKE

The cheesecake can be prepared the day before Thanksgiving. Add the decoration shortly before serving.

700 g (1½ lb) peeled and seeded pumpkin, chopped
75 g (3 oz) granulated sugar
thinly pared rind and juice of 3 oranges
6 passion fruit
4½ sachets of powdered gelatine
125 g (4 oz) unsalted butter
45 ml (3 tbsp) golden syrup
350 g (12 oz) digestive biscuits, crushed
4 eggs, separated
175 g (6 oz) caster sugar
finely grated rind of 3 lemons
60 ml (4 tbsp) lemon juice
700 g (1½ lb) full fat soft cheese
450 ml (¾ pint) double cream
200 ml (7 fl oz) double cream, whipped and a few skinned pistachio nuts, to decorate

Pumpkin Cheesecake (left)

COUNTDOWN
The week before or earlier:
Make the cornbread, wrap and freeze. Remove from the freezer to thaw 2 days before the meal. Make the Pecan Cookies and freeze.
The day before:
Make the cornbread stuffing. Make the cranberry sauce. Cool, cover and refrigerate. Cook the pears, cool, cover and refrigerate. Make the cheesecake but do not decorate. Refrigerate. Make the giblet stock, cool, cover and refrigerate.
On the morning:
Remove the Pecan Cookies from the freezer to thaw. Pre-pare the pineapple and parboil the sweet potatoes for the Sweet Potatoes with Pineap-ple. Peel the potatoes for the Roast Potatoes. Keep them in a bowl covered with cold water to prevent dis-colouration. Skin the onions.
To serve at 8.00pm:
2.30pm: Stuff the turkey and roast in the oven at 180°C (350°F) mark 4 for 4-5 hours.
6.00pm: Decorate the cheesecake. Make the Egg Nog. Cook the Sweet Potatoes with Pineapple and the Roast Potatoes.
7.00pm: Cook the Glazed Onions with Peas.
7.30pm: Remove the turkey from the oven, cover and leave to rest.
8.00pm: Whisk the Egg Nog and serve with the Pecan Cookies.

◆

1 Put the pumpkin into a large saucepan with the granulated sugar and orange rind and juice. Cover the saucepan and cook the pumpkin gently for about 45 minutes, until it is very soft. Allow to cool slightly, then purée the pumpkin in a blender or food pro-cessor.

2 Cut each passion fruit in half and scoop out the seeds into a nylon sieve placed over a small bowl. Work the seeds in the sieve with the back of a spoon until all of the juice is extracted into the bowl. Stir the juices into the pumpkin purée. Set aside.

3 Put the butter and golden syrup into a large saucepan and heat gently until the but-ter melts. Stir in the crushed biscuits and mix well. Spread the biscuit mixture evenly over the base of a 30 cm (12 inch) spring-form tin, pressing gently to firm. Refrigerate whilst making the cheese mixture.

4 Whisk the egg yolks with the caster sugar and the lemon rind until the mixture is very thick, and will hold a ribbon trail for at least 5 seconds when the whisk is lifted out. Grad-ually whisk in the lemon juice.

5 Beat the cream cheese with a wooden spoon until it is very soft, then gradually beat in the lemon mixture.

6 Dissolve the 3 sachets of gelatine by sprin-kling over 90 ml (6 tbsp) cold water in a small bowl. Soak for a few minutes until the gelatine swells and turns opaque. Stand in a pan of hot water until the gelatine melts. Whip the cream until it will hold soft peaks. Whisk the egg whites until stiff.

7 Mix the dissolved gelatine into the cheese and lemon mixture, then quickly fold in the cream, followed by the egg whites. Pour the mixture into the biscuit-lined tin. Refriger-ate for at least 1 hour until set.

8 Dissolve the remaining gelatine in 45 ml (3 tbsp) water, as above. Stir the gelatine into the pumpkin purée, then put the purée aside to cool.

9 Remove the set cheesecake from the refrigerator, then very carefully pour the cold, but not yet set, pumpkin mixture on top. Smooth the surface. Refrigerate for at least 3 hours or preferably overnight, until well set.

10 To serve, carefully run a palette knife around the side of the cheesecake then gen-tly remove the side of the tin. Place the cake on a serving dish. Decorate with whipped cream and pistachios. Refrigerate until serving.

CHRISTMAS CELEBRATION

M	E	N	U

BLUE BRIE TOASTS

CHRISTMAS MULLED WINE

SPICED CASHEWS

BALLONTINE OF TURKEY

CHESTNUT AND SPROUT SAUTÉ

BABY CARROTS

FANTAIL ROAST POTATOES

BREAD SAUCE

SPICED RATATOUILLE SALAD

CHRISTMAS PUDDING WITH ORANGE WHISKY BUTTER

TRIFLE

SERVES 8

Extend a warming welcome to your guests on Christmas morning with our delicious mulled Christmas wine. Served with Blue Brie Toasts and Spiced Cashew Nuts it makes a festive start to the day.

For a change from the ubiquitous roast turkey, a boned stuffed Turkey Ballontine is ideal. It takes time to prepare (or you might prefer to ask your butcher to do it for you) but it drastically reduces last minute carving panic since it makes the job so much easier. It is served hot with the traditional accompaniments; any leftovers are equally delicious served cold with salads. Serve the Ballontine on a large platter surrounded with the accompaniments as well as baby carrots, and our spicy Ratatouille Salad.

For pudding there's a delightfully old-fashioned boiled, round Christmas pudding or a wickedly rich Trifle.

Christmas Mulled Wine
with Blue Brie Toasts
(above)

BLUE BRIE TOASTS

The toasts can be prepared ahead, covered and refrigerated until you're ready to bake them.

MAKES ABOUT 60
350 g (12 oz) blue brie cheese, rind removed
45 ml (3 tbsp) mayonnaise
salt and freshly ground pepper
10 thick slices of crustless bread
butter, for spreading

1 Beat together the cheese, mayonnaise and seasoning.
2 Spread one side of each slice of bread with butter, the other with the cheese and mayonnaise mixture, and cut into triangles.
3 Place buttered side down, on baking sheets and bake at 220°C (400°F) mark 6 for 12 minutes or until crisp and brown underneath. Serve hot.

CHRISTMAS MULLED WINE

3 small apples, studded with cloves
pared rind of 1 lemon
about 1.7 litres (3 pints) red wine
225 g (8 oz) brown sugar
3 cinnamon sticks
300 ml (½ pint) brandy

1 Put the clove studded apples in a saucepan with the pared lemon rind, red wine, brownsugar and cinnamon.
2 Bring to simmering point and simmer gently, covered, for 2–4 minutes to allow the flavours to develop.
3 Remove from the heat, add the brandy. Serve at once.

COOK'S HINT

It takes time (about 30 minutes) to bone the turkey, but, fortunately, it can be done a day or two before the Christmas rush. Given ample warning, most butchers will bone the turkey for you. Reserve all bones to make stock.

The most important thing is not to puncture the skin, and to completely enclose the stuffing before roasting the ballontine. We trimmed away some of the turkey flesh before cooking to make a more slender version; you need enough flesh to wrap right around the pork loin.

The ballontine can be pressed lightly after cooking and while cooling to make it easier to slice; we preferred not to press it to retain a well-rounded joint.

SPICED CASHEWS

275 g (10 oz) unsalted cashew nuts
25 g (1 oz) butter, melted
2.5 ml (½ tsp) salt
10 ml (2 tsp) soy sauce
few drops Tabasco

1 In a medium bowl, mix together all the ingredients. Spoon evenly onto edged baking sheets.
2 Bake at 150°C (300°F) mark 2 for 15–20 minutes, stirring halfway through. Cool. Store in an airtight container for up to two weeks.

BALLONTINE OF TURKEY

5.5 kg (12 lb) oven ready turkey
butter or margarine
225 g (8 oz) onion, skinned and roughly chopped
225 g (8 oz) button mushrooms, roughly chopped
2 large garlic cloves, skinned and crushed
700 g (1½ lb) pork sausagemeat
125 g (4 oz) fresh breadcrumbs
90 ml (6 tbsp) chopped fresh parsley
60 ml (4 tbsp) Dijon mustard
rind and juice of 2 lemons
1 egg, beaten
salt and freshly ground pepper
450 g (1 lb) smoked loin of pork
bacon rolls and chipolata sausages, to serve (optional)

1 First bone the turkey. Place the bird breast side down on a large chopping board. Using a small sharp knife, cut straight along the backbone. Gradually fillet the flesh away from the carcass, keeping the knife as close to the bones as possible. Take great care not to puncture the skin as it has to act as a 'case' for the turkey roast – if the skin is split, the stuffing will burst out as the joint roasts.
2 Loosen the leg and wing ball-and-socket joints with the point of the knife. Push these joints away from the carcass until they loosen and partially come away. Carefully split the leg flesh and ease out the bones and sinews. Ease out the large wing joint, reserving the small wing tips for the stock pot. Run your fingers all over the turkey flesh to ensure there are no bones or sinews remaining.
3 You should have a large oblong of skin covered with turkey meat. Remove the parson's nose. Fillet most of the leg and thigh meat from one side of the bird and trim any excessively fat portions of breast flesh – you should have about 900 g (2 lb) trimmed meat to freeze and use in casseroles. (It is not essential to trim this flesh, but without it the ballontine will have a better shape, with even distribution of both turkey meat and stuffing.) Cover and refrigerate the boned turkey while preparing the stuffing.
4 Heat 50 g (2 oz) butter in a sauté pan. Add the onion and fry until beginning to brown. Increase the heat, mix in the mushrooms and garlic and fry until all excess liquid has evaporated. Stir frequently. Turn into a large bowl and cool.
5 Stir the sausagemeat, breadcrumbs, parsley, mustard, grated lemon rind and 30 ml (2 tbsp) lemon juice, and plenty of seasoning into the mushroom mixture. Beat well to combine thoroughly.
6 Lay the boned turkey flat on a board, flesh side up, and spread the stuffing mixture over the flesh. Place the smoked loin (cut in half lengthways if necessary – see Cook's Hint) on top and then fold the turkey skin around to enclose the stuffing completely. Secure with fine skewers or cocktail sticks, or sew the skin together.
7 Spread the turkey generously with butter and season liberally with pepper. Wrap in foil and place in a roasting tin.
8 Bake at 180°C (350°F) mark 4 for 2½ hours. Fold back the foil and return to the oven for about 1 hour or until well browned. Test with a fine skewer; if it is cooked, the juices should run clear.
9 Lift the ballontine onto a serving plate. Cool for about 20 minutes before slicing thickly. Any leftovers can be eaten cold the next day. Serve with the bacon rolls and chipolata sausages.
To Freeze To serve cold only, cool, pack and freeze once completely cold. Thaw overnight at cool room temperature.

CHESTNUT AND SPROUT SAUTÉ

900 g (2 lb) fresh chestnuts or 879 g (1 lb 15 oz) can whole chestnuts
600 ml (1 pint) chicken stock
900 g (2 lb) Brussels sprouts
salt and freshly ground pepper
450 g (1 lb) medium onions, skinned
225 g (8 oz) celery, trimmed
125 g (4 oz) butter
finely grated rind of 1 lemon

1 If using fresh chestnuts, snip the brown outer skins, or nick with a sharp knife. Place in boiling water for 3–5 minutes.

2 Lift the chestnuts out a few at a time, then peel off both the brown and inner skins. Put the nuts in a saucepan, cover with the stock and simmer for 40–45 minutes until tender. Drain well.

3 Meanwhile, trim the sprouts and pull off any damaged or discoloured outer leaves. With a sharp knife, make a cross in the stalk end of each one.

4 Cook the sprouts in boiling salted water for 3–4 minutes only; drain well.

5 Quarter the onions and separate out the layers. Cut the celery into 2.5 cm (1 inch) pieces.

6 Melt the butter in a large sauté or frying pan. Add the onions and celery with the lemon rind and sauté for 2–3 minutes until softened. Add the cooked chestnuts, Brussels sprouts and salt and pepper to taste. Sauté for a further 1–2 minutes until heated through. Serve immediately.

FANTAIL ROAST POTATOES

These semi-sliced potatoes open out attractively as they cook.

about 1.8 kg (4 lb) old potatoes
salt and freshly ground pepper
vegetable oil
sesame seeds

1 Peel the potatoes and cut into large even-sized chunks. Cover with cold salted water and bring to the boil, bubble for 2 minutes. Drain and run under the cold tap to cool slightly.

2 Using a sharp knife, slice down each potato at 3–5 mm (⅛–¼ inch) intervals, cutting three-quarters of the way through.

3 Heat a good film of oil in a large roasting tin. Add the potatoes and turn over in the oil. Sprinkle with sesame seeds.

4 Roast at 180°C (350°F) mark 4 for about 2 hours, basting occasionally. If necessary, raise the oven temperature to 220°C (425°F) mark 7 for another 15–20 minutes to complete the browning. (At this stage the turkey should be out of the oven, firming up before carving.) Keep warm, uncovered.

BREAD SAUCE

4 whole cloves
1 medium onion, skinned
1 small bay leaf
568 ml (1 pint) milk
125 g (4 oz) fresh white breadcrumbs
salt and white pepper
15 g (½ oz) butter
45 ml (3 tbsp) single cream

1 Stick the cloves into the onion and place in a small heavy-based pan with the bay leaf and milk to cover.

2 Bring slowly to the boil, remove from the heat, cover and leave to infuse for 10 minutes.

3 Remove the onion and bay leaf, then add the breadcrumbs and salt and pepper to taste. Return to the heat and simmer gently for 10–15 minutes, stirring occasionally. Stir in the butter and cream.

To Freeze before adding butter and cream. Cool, pack into a rigid container and freeze for up to 3 months. Thaw at cool room temperature overnight. Reheat gently and complete step 3.

MENU SUGGESTIONS
For traditionalists there's a recipe for Roast Turkey (page 202) and Celeriac Purée (page 261). For those wanting something different, Marinated Salmon en Croûte (page 245) is delicious enough for Christmas lunch. Serve it with roast potatoes and Glazed Carrots with Turnips (page 261).

SPICED RATATOUILLE SALAD

For maximum flavour, cook the vegetables until soft and mushy.

450 g (1 lb) aubergines, roughly chopped
salt and freshly ground pepper
450 g (1 lb) fresh tomatoes, skinned
45 ml (3 tbsp) olive oil
2 medium onions, skinned and roughly chopped
1 green pepper, cored, seeded and chopped
1 red pepper, cored, seeded and chopped
450 g (1 lb) courgettes, sliced
2.5 ml (½ tsp) chilli powder
2 garlic cloves, skinned and crushed
397 g (14 oz) can chopped tomatoes
5 ml (1 tsp) dried oregano
2 bay leaves
15 ml (1 tbsp) vinegar

1 Place the aubergine in a colander, sprinkle with salt and leave to stand for about 20 minutes. Quarter and de-seed the tomatoes, reserving the juices; roughly chop the flesh.

2 Heat the oil in a large flameproof casserole. Add the onion, aubergines, peppers and chilli powder and stir fry over high heat for 2–3 minutes.

3 Mix in the garlic and all the remaining ingredients. Bring to the boil, cover and simmer for 30–40 minutes, or until all the vegetables are soft and the liquid is reduced. Taste and adjust the seasoning.

4 Cool and chill well before serving.

To Freeze Pack into rigid containers, and freeze for up to 2 months. Thaw overnight at cool room temperature and chill again before serving.

CHRISTMAS PUDDING

MAKES TWO 900 G (2 LB) PUDDINGS
225 g (8 oz) shredded suet
225 g (8 oz) fresh white breadcrumbs
50 g (2 oz) plain flour
450 g (1 lb) sultanas
225 g (8 oz) raisins
50 g (2 oz) chopped mixed peel
grated rind of 2 lemons
50 g (2 oz) glacé cherries, halved
1.25 ml (¼ tsp) salt
225 g (8 oz) dark muscovado sugar
5 ml (1 tsp) ground mixed spice
5 eggs, well beaten
50 ml (2 fl oz) brandy
50 ml (2 fl oz) rum

1 In a large bowl, mix together all the ingredients except the eggs, brandy and rum. Then add the eggs and liquor and beat vigorously.

Christmas Pudding with Orange Whisky Butter (left)

MICROWAVE HINT

To reheat **Christmas pudding**. Remove all the wrappings and put the pudding on an ovenproof serving plate. Cut into the required number of portions and pull apart so that there is a space in the centre.

Place a small tumbler of water in the centre. This introduces steam and helps to keep the pudding moist. Cover with a large upturned bowl.

Cook on HIGH for 2–3 minutes, depending on the size of the pudding, or until hot.

Remove the cover and glass and reshape the pudding with the hands. Decorate with a sprig of holly and serve.

To reheat an individual portion of Christmas pudding, put on a plate and cook, uncovered, for 1–1½ minutes until hot.

2 Divide the mixture between two 40.5 cm (16 inch) squares of foil inside a double thickness of butter muslin and gather up around the mixture. Shape the pudding into a firm round. Secure with string.

3 To keep the round shape, the pudding should be boiled suspended by a string so that it doesn't touch the bottom of the pan. Choose a large pan that will hold the pudding easily, leaving a good 2.5 cm (1 inch) space around, below and above when suspended. Tie the pudding to a long-handled wooden spoon or cooling rack laid across the top of the pan. Pour in enough boiling water to cover the pudding. Cover the pan with a lid of foil. Simmer for 5 hours. Top up the water to keep the pudding submerged.

4 Drain off the water and leave the pudding suspended until cold. Rewrap in clean, dry muslin then overwrap with foil. Store in the refrigerator for up to 6 weeks.

5 To serve, remove the foil. Suspend and boil the pudding as before. Boil for 4 hours. Lift out, unwrap and serve.

To Freeze Cool, overwrap in foil and a polythene bag. Freeze for up to 4 months. Thaw at cool room temperature, rewrap and complete step 5.

ORANGE WHISKY BUTTER

125 g (4 oz) unsalted butter, softened
125 g (4 oz) light muscovado sugar
grated rind of 1 small orange
1.25 ml (¼ tsp) mixed spice
pinch ground green cardamom
45 ml (3 tbsp) whisky
lemon juice

1 Cream the butter and sugar until pale and soft. Add the orange rind and spices.

2 Gradually beat in the whisky and 5 ml (1 tsp) lemon juice. Spoon into small, wide-necked pots. Cover and store in the fridge for up to one week.

To Freeze Pack into freezerproof pots, leaving headspace. Seal, label and freeze for up to 3 months. Thaw at cool room temperature overnight.

COOK'S HINT

This **pudding** mixture is boiled rather than steamed, which produces a rich, moist pudding. However, it must be stored in the refrigerator or frozen or it will go mouldy.

If you don't want to make round puddings, pack the mixture into two 1.1 litre (2 pint) pudding basins. Cover with greased greaseproof paper and foil. Secure with string. Boil for 5 hours, cool, then cover with fresh greaseproof paper and foil. Store and boil to reheat.

Trifle (above)

TRIFLE

The great British trifle, with its layers of sherry-soaked sponge sandwiched with jam, layered with fruit and egg custard, then topped with whipped cream, brings an air of celebration whatever the occasion.

10 trifle sponges or about 1½ Madeira cakes, 400 g (14 oz) total weight
225 g (8 oz) fruit jam or jelly such as raspberry, strawberry or blackberry
150 ml (¼ pint) sherry and brandy, mixed
450 g (1 lb) fresh or frozen berries, such as raspberries, blackberries, loganberries or tayberries
vanilla pod
568 ml (1 pint) creamy milk or single cream
8 eggs
175 g (6 oz) caster sugar
450 ml (¾ pint) double cream
a little icing sugar
glacé fruits or toasted nuts, to decorate

1 Split the trifle sponges in two and lay the bottom halves over the base of a deep glass bowl. Warm the jam or jelly until just melted, sieve and carefully pour over the trifle sponges. Top with the remaining sponges. If using Madeira cake, slice thinly before using.

2 Spoon the sherry and brandy evenly over the sponges, making sure they are saturated. Scatter over the fruit, halving some of the berries if wished. Cover and refrigerate for 1 hour or more.

3 Split open the vanilla pod to reveal the seeds. Add to the milk or cream and bring to the boil. Take off the heat; cover and infuse for about 20 minutes.

4 Preferably using an electric whisk, whisk the eggs and sugar until pale and foaming. Strain on the milk.

5 Stir the custard well and return to the pan. Over a low heat, stir the custard until it begins to thicken - this will take some time (15–20 minutes) as you must not allow the mixture to boil or it will curdle. Once lightly thickened, pour out into a bowl and leave to cool – it will thicken up quite considerably when chilled.

6 Lightly whisk, then pour the cool custard over the fruit. Cover and chill for several hours, preferably overnight.

7 Whip the double cream, with icing sugar to taste, until it just holds its shape. Carefully spread this over the custard and decorate with the fruits or nuts.

TURKEY TABLE

Thawing: Frozen turkeys must be thoroughly thawed before cooking. They should be left in their bags and thawed at cool room temperature, not in the fridge. Remove giblets as soon as they are loose – these can be used to make stock for the gravy. To check that the bird is thawed, make sure there are no ice crystals in the cavity and that the legs are quite flexible. Once it is thoroughly thawed, cover and store in the refrigerator. Cook as soon as possible.

Stuffing: Loosely stuff the neck end only of the bird to ensure heat penetrates the centre more quickly. Extra stuffing can be baked separately in a covered dish for about 1 hour. Allow about 225 g (8 oz) stuffing for each 2.3 kg (5 lb) dressed weight of turkey and stuff the bird just before cooking. Sew up the neck skin or use skewers: truss bird.

Cooking: Weigh the bird and calculate the cooking time, to be ready 30 minutes before carving. This allows the flesh to firm up, making it easier to slice. Spread the turkey with butter or margarine and grind over black pepper. Wrap the turkey loosely in foil or put it straight into a roasting tin. Preheat the oven to 180°C (350°F) mark 4 and put the turkey in. Fold back the foil about 45 minutes before the end of the calculated cooking time to brown. Baste regularly.

Testing: Insert a fine skewer into a turkey thigh. If the juices run clear, it is cooked. If it is not ready, return to the oven to cook a little longer.

Note:

Leftover turkey should be cooled quickly, then refrigerated. Do not leave it standing in a warm room.

Oven-ready weight	Approx. thawing time (at room temperature)	Cooking without foil	Cooking foil wrapped	Approx. no of servings
550 g–1.4 kg* (1¼ –3 lb)	4–10 hr	1½–1¾ hr	1¾ –2 hr	2–4
1.4–2.3kg (3–5 lb)	10–15 hr	1¾–2 hr	2–2½ hr	4–6
2.3–3.6kg (5–8 lb)	15–18 hr	2–2½ hr	2½–3½ hr	6–10
3.6–5 kg (8–11 lb)	18–20 hr	2½–3¼ hr	3½ –4 hr	10–15
5–6.8 kg (11–15 lb)	20–24 hr	3¼–3¾ hr	4–5 hr	15–20
6.8–9kg (15–20 lb)	24–30 hr	3¾–4¼ hr	5–5½ hr	20–30
9–11.3kg (20–25 lb)	30–36 hr	4¼ –4¾ hr	not recommended	30–40
11.3–13.5 kg (25–30 lb)	36–48 hr	4¾–5½hr	not recommended	40–50

*For smaller weights, use turkey roast or drumsticks and cook according to instructions.

COUNTDOWN

Freezing ahead: Prepare and freeze Bread Sauce, Orange Whisky Butter, and the stock for the gravy.

Early November: Make Christmas Pudding and freeze.

Beginning of December: Order your poultry.

One week before: If not already frozen, make and refrigerate the Orange Whisky Butter. Calculate the thawing time of the turkey and thaw on the appropriate day (see our chart above). Buy non-perishable goods now.

23 December: If frozen, thaw the Bread Sauce and Orange Whisky Butter. Refrigerate. Buy fresh ingredients and store in the fridge. If not already made, prepare breadcrumbs for the Bread Sauce; make dry stuffing mixtures for the turkey and refrigerate in polythene bags. If not already frozen, prepare the stock for the gravy; simmer the giblets with 1.1 litres (2 pints) water, seasoning, and a few vegetables for about 2 hours. Cool and then refrigerate. Thaw the Christmas Pudding.

Christmas Eve: Peel the potatoes for roasting. Keep covered in cold water. Trim the sprouts and prepare the chestnuts. Pare the carrots and store in polythene bags in the refrigerator. Make the stock thicker than required so that it is the right consistency when added to the turkey juices. Thread bacon rolls onto skewers. If not already made; make the Bread Sauce. Cool, cover and then refrigerate. Make the Spiced Ratatouille Salad and refrigerate. Prepare the Blue Brie Toasts. Make the Spiced Cashews and store in an airtight container. Make the trifle, chill overnight. Prepare the turkey. Cover and chill.

Christmas Day: Based on a 4.5–5.4 kg (10–12 lb) stuffed turkey in foil (see chart).

To serve at 1pm:
8.30am: Put the turkey in to roast.
9am: Reheat pudding as directed, see page 213 (check water regularly). Prepare the potatoes, as step 2.
10.30am: Lay table. Prepare the wines.
11.15am: Boil the potatoes, as step 1. Follow steps 2 and 3 and place in the oven. Unwrap the turkey, baste and continue cooking.
12.30pm: Place the chipolatas and bacon rolls alongside the turkey, or cook under a hot grill. When cooked, wrap in foil and keep warm. Test turkey thigh with a skewer. Turn the oven down to low and leave the bird to rest for about 20 minutes (or wrap in foil and keep warm beside the cooker). Complete the gravy by adding giblet stock to the defatted juices. Cook the Brussels Sprout and Chestnut Sauté and carrots. Drain, cover and keep warm. Reheat the Bread Sauce, adding a little milk to thin if necessary. Remove the Spiced Ratatouille Salad and the Trifle from the refrigerator.
12.50pm: Unwrap the Christmas Pudding: cover with foil until ready to serve. Cook the Blue Brie Toasts. Make the Mulled Wine.
1pm: Put turkey on a carving dish. If serving a large number, carve in the kitchen, transfer to a serving plate, cover and keep warm.

BUFFETS

Introduction

It is difficult to be a good host at a large party – even if there are two of you – if you are also involved in serving food and pouring drinks. There is little point in giving a party if you spend all your time carrying dishes in and out of the room or wrestling with a corkscrew, so think in advance about whether you might need help in the form of professional waitresses or local friends, neighbours or relations.

A buffet party is the ideal way to entertain a large number of people. Plan the menu well in advance to allow time to decide on the quantity of food you will need (using the charts as a guide). As a general rule, the more people you are catering for the less food per head you need to provide – however, it's better to have too much than too little.

It is easier to serve mostly cold dishes when entertaining a large number of people, but try to include one or two hot dishes. When planning the menu, choose dishes that can be cooked and/or frozen ahead of time, such as flans, pâtés, tarts, pastries, sandwich fillings, cakes and gâteaux, leaving time for preparing perishable ingredients like salads on the day of the party.

Take into consideration the amount of refrigerator space you have, otherwise you may find yourself with too many perishable items and no storage. Use space in a friend's or neighbour's refrigerator or store covered dishes in a cool place, such as a garage.

SALMON BUFFET

M	E	N	U

SUMMER HERB SAUCE

ROAST SPICED BEEF

DILL-GLAZED SALMON

SWEET ONION SALAD

CRISP VEGETABLE SALAD

WARM GARLIC BREAD

BAKED POTATOES

LEMON MOUSSE

SERVES 8

*F*or a cold buffet at any time of year a whole poached salmon looks impressive served with its head and tail left on. If this doesn't appeal or if you don't have a fish kettle or large enough roasting tin, the salmon will still make an excellent centrepiece with the head and tail removed. Serve the salmon with a bowl of lemon or lime mayonnaise, preferably homemade (see page 220, add lemon or lime rind to the basic recipe) or cheat and add freshly grated rind to a good shop bought mayonnaise.

The menu also features a perennial buffet favourite – roast beef. Ours is a wickedly extravagant fillet of beef, served rare with a spiced mustard crust. You'll need to serve one or two extras to complete your buffet, such as a simple tomato salad and baked potatoes. Bake medium sized potatoes weighing about 125 g (4 oz) each so that they aren't too large and bulky. Split them with a cross and top with a knob of butter.

For dessert, there's a refreshing, light as air lemon mousse. Serve it on its own or with crisp biscuits.

SUMMER HERB SAUCE

Choose whatever combination of herbs is fresh and plentiful. This selection partners the beef particularly well. It will keep, covered in the refrigerator, for up to three days, although the herbs will lose a little colour during that time.

350 ml (12 fl oz) olive oil
60 ml (4 tbsp) lemon juice
30 ml (2 tbsp) each chopped fresh parsley, thyme and basil
3 drops Tabasco sauce
any reserved pan juices from Roast Spiced Beef (see recipe)
salt and freshly ground pepper

1 Blend together the first 6 ingredients in a blender or food processor. Skim any fat from the reserved pan juices, then whisk into the dressing. Season to taste.

ROAST SPICED BEEF

The marinated beef can be cooked as in stage 3 the day before it's required, then kept, covered, overnight in the refrigerator.

1 fillet of beef, about 900 g (2 lb)
10 ml (2 tsp) black peppercorns
75 ml (3 fl oz) vegetable oil
1 clove garlic, skinned and crushed
2.5 ml (½ tsp) salt
10 ml (2 tsp) dry mustard
5 ml (1 tsp) ground ginger
30 ml (2 tbsp) wholegrain mustard
15 ml (1 tbsp) light soft brown sugar
oak-leaf lettuce, radicchio and fresh figs to garnish

1 Trim any excess fat or sinew from the beef. Tie with fine string at 2.5 cm (1 inch) intervals. Place in a small non-metallic dish.
2 Coarsely grind the peppercorns in a pestle and mortar or put in a strong polythene bag and crush with a rolling pin. Beat together with the next 7 ingredients. Spread all over the beef, cover; refrigerate overnight.
3 Preheat the oven to 240°C (475°F) mark

9. Transfer the beef and marinade to a small roasting tin. Roast the beef for 20 minutes, basting occasionally. Reduce the oven temperature to 220°C (425°F) mark 7 for a further 20 minutes for medium beef or 25 minutes for well done. Remove the meat from the oven, drain off and reserve any pan juices (see Summer Herb Sauce recipe). Allow to cool completely.
4 With a very sharp knife, remove the string and cut the beef into wafer-thin slices. Serve on a platter of oak-leaf lettuce, radicchio and quartered figs. Serve accompanied by Summer Herb Sauce.

DILL-GLAZED SALMON

This method of cooking salmon is by far the best way of producing a moist, perfectly cooked fish every time. It may sound strange but the larger the fish the more liquid required and therefore the longer it takes to boil and cool down again. It does work! The salmon can be prepared to the end of stage 6 the day before needed.

1.8 kg (4 lb) whole salmon or sea trout
dry white wine
onion and carrot slices, black peppercorns and bay leaf for flavouring
1 small bunch fresh dill
2.5 ml (½ level tsp) powdered gelatine
rocket or other green salad leaves and lemon and lime slices to garnish
lemon or lime mayonnaise to accompany

1 Rinse the salmon well under cold running water. Remove the head and tail if wished. Place the salmon in a fish kettle or large roasting tin. Pour over just enough water and a little dry white wine to cover. Add the flavouring ingredients and dill stalks. Divide the feathery dill tops into small sprigs, cover and refrigerate.
2 Cover the salmon with the kettle lid or foil. Bring the liquid slowly to the boil. Simmer for 2 minutes. Turn off the heat and leave the salmon (still covered) in the liquid until cold.
3 Carefully remove the salmon from the poaching liquid. Strain and reserve 150 ml (¼ pint) liquid. Carefully skin the salmon, gently scraping away any dark brown flesh to

DRINKS TO SERVE
Serve simple aperitifs such as gin and tonic or a dry sherry and then offer a choice of full flavoured Californian wines to serve throughout the meal. A Sauvignon Blanc partnered by a Cabernet Sauvignon will suit most palates.

COOK'S HINTS
1 **Fillet of beef** is expensive. A cheaper alternative is a 900 g (2 lb) piece of boned and rolled sirloin (trim the fat and re-tie if necessary) but cook at 200°C (400°F) mark 6 for about 1 hour and 20 minutes.

2 To make a simple **tomato salad**, thinly slice really ripe tomatoes. Arrange in a large shallow dish, sprinkle with olive oil and a little raspberry or white wine vinegar, salt and pepper and chopped basil, chervil or tarragon.

Dill - Glazed Salmon with Lemon Mayonnaise and Crisp Vegetable Salad (opposite)

Roast Spiced Beef,
Summer Herb Sauce and
Sweet Onion Salad (right)

COOK'S HINT
To make about 400 ml (12 fl oz) **mayonnaise,** put 3 egg yolks in a bowl with 7.5 ml (1½ tsp) each dry mustard and salt and 2.5 ml (½ tsp) freshly ground pepper. Add 7.5 ml (1½ tsp) sugar, if liked, and beat with a whisk. Continue beating and add 150 ml (¼ pint) of sunflower oil (or a mixture of ½ olive oil and ½ vegetable oil) a drop at a time. Once the mixture starts to thicken, gradually add 45 ml (3 tbsp) white wine vinegar or lemon juice, beating constantly. Add 300 ml (½ pint) more oil 15 ml (1 tbsp) at a time or in a thin stream, beating continually until completely absorbed.
Variations:
To make **lemon or lime mayonnaise** using fruit juice in place of vinegar, add the finely grated rind of 1 lemon or 2 limes, or to taste, to the prepared mayonnaise.

For **tomato mayonnaise,** add 2 tomatoes, skinned, seeded and diced; 3 small spring onions, trimmed and chopped; 3.75 ml (¾ tsp) sugar and 15 ml (1 tbsp) vinegar or lemon juice to the prepared mayonnaise.

For **garlic mayonnaise,** add 2 garlic cloves, skinned and crushed, to the finished mayonnaise.

---

reveal the pink underneath.

4 Place the salmon on a flat serving platter. If the head and tail are still on, cut a 'v' shape into the tail to neaten it. Cover the salmon with greaseproof paper and refrigerate for at least 30 minutes.

5 Place the reserved poaching liquid in a small bowl. Sprinkle over the powdered gelatine and leave to soak for 3–4 minutes. Place the bowl in a saucepan of simmering water and heat gently until the gelatine has completely dissolved. Cool the liquid until just beginning to thicken.

6 Brush a little of the poaching liquid over the salmon. Press the reserved dill sprigs onto the exposed salmon flesh. Brush all over with more liquid. Return to the refrigerator to set.

7 To serve the salmon, garnish with a little rocket or other green salad leaves, and lemon and lime slices. Accompany with lemon or lime mayonnaise.

To Freeze Pack and freeze the salmon at the end of step 3. Thaw in the refrigerator and finish as above.

SWEET ONION SALAD

To make sure button onions stay whole when cooked, simply trim the root end when peeling – don't remove it completely.

900 g (2 lb) button onions
300 ml (½ pint) red wine
150 ml (¼ pint) olive oil
120 ml (8 tbsp) tomato purée
1 bay leaf
60 ml (4 tbsp) light soft brown sugar
salt and freshly ground pepper

1 Put the button onions in a large bowl and pour over enough boiling water to cover. Leave to soak for 3–4 minutes then drain and peel.

2 Place the onions in a saucepan with all the remaining ingredients. Cover and simmer for 20 minutes or until the onions are tender but still retain their shape. Stir occasionally to prevent the sugar burning onto the pan.

3 Spoon the mixture into a medium bowl. Cool, cover and refrigerate for 10–15 minutes before serving, or for up to 2 days.

CRISP VEGETABLE SALAD

The French beans, cucumber and fennel can be prepared ahead as in stage 1, then kept in the refrigerator.

900 g (2 lb) French beans, topped and tailed
salt and freshly ground pepper
2 small heads Florence fennel
1 large cucumber
300 ml (½ pint) olive oil
125 ml (4 fl oz) white wine vinegar
15 ml (1 tbsp) Dijon mustard
2 avocados
about 20 black olives

1 Halve the French beans and cook in boiling, salted water until just tender. Drain; refresh under cold water. Remove the feathery fennel tops, finely chop and reserve. Thinly slice the fennel; blanch in boiling water for 1 minute. Drain and refresh. Peel, halve and thickly slice the cucumber.

2 Whisk together the oil, vinegar, mustard and reserved fennel tops. Season to taste. Peel, halve and stone the avocado. Thickly slice into the dressing.

3 Toss together all the prepared vegetables, olives, avocado and dressing. Serve immediately.

WARM GARLIC BREAD

225 g (8 oz) butter, softened
2 -3 garlic cloves, skinned and crushed
45 ml (3 tbsp) lemon juice
2 long French or round crusty loaves

1 Beat the butter and garlic together until blended. Work in the lemon juice – the mixture won't be completely smooth.

2 Slice the bread into 1 cm (½ inch) slices or chunks and sandwich together again with the butter, spreading a little over the top of the bread. Wrap the loaves tightly in foil.

3 Place the loaves on a baking sheet. Cook at 200°C (400°F) mark 6 for about 20 minutes. If you like the bread really crisp, open up the foil and return to the oven for about 5 minutes.

LEMON MOUSSE

grated rind and juice of 4 lemons
9 eggs, separated
175 g (6 oz) caster sugar
45 ml (3 level tbsp) powdered gelatine
600 ml (1 pint) double cream
pinch of salt

1 Put the lemon rind, egg yolks and the sugar into a medium-sized bowl and whisk until pale and creamy.

2 In a small bowl, sprinkle the gelatine over 150 ml (5 fl oz) lemon juice and allow to soak for about 10 minutes. Place in a saucepan of gently simmering water until dissolved, about 3–4 minutes. Stir into the egg yolk mixture.

3 Light whip the cream until it just begins to hold its shape and set aside. (Do not refrigerate or it will become too cold.) Place the gelatine mixture over a bowl of iced water and stir until the mixture is just beginning to thicken. Remove the bowl from the ice immediately and fold in the cream.

4 Whisk the egg whites in a large bowl with a pinch of salt (to strengthen the whites) until stiff but not dry. Stir a spoonful of egg whites into the yolk mixture to loosen it. Then, with a large metal spoon, quickly and carefully fold in the rest of the whites until evenly mixed.

5 Gently pour the mixture into a serving dish and level the top. Chill in the refrigerator for at least 4 hours or until set. Serve decorated with whipped cream and pistachio caramel (see Cook's Hint).

To Freeze Overwrap loosely and freeze without the decoration. Thaw overnight in the refrigerator and finish as above.

COOK'S HINT
To make **pistachio caramel**, melt 175 g (6 oz) granulated sugar slowly in a small heavy-based saucepan until it bubbles and turns golden brown. Stir in 125 g (4 oz) chopped pistachio nuts. Immediately pour the mixture onto an oiled baking sheet and leave to cool and set. Put the set mixture in a polythene bag and crush with a rolling pin. Store in an airtight container for several weeks.

MENU SUGGESTIONS
Chicken Breasts in Muscat Wine with Apricots or Glazed Gammon with Mustard Sauce (both on page 269) are good alternatives to the beef. Cucumber and Fennel Salad (page 260) makes an exellent accompaniment.

COUNTDOWN
2 days before:
Make the Summer Herb Sauce, the Sweet Onion Salad, the Crisp Vegetable Salad to the end of step 1, and the Garlic Bread and store in the refrigerator.
1 day before:
Marinate the beef.
The day before:
Make the Lemon Soufflé and refrigerate. Roast the beef, cool quickly and refrigerate. Prepare the salmon to the end of step 6 and refrigerate.
In the morning:
Prepare the salads.
1 ½ hours before serving:
Bake the potatoes. Remove everything from the refrigerator about ½ hour before serving and bake the Garlic Bread.

AT-HOME WEDDING RECEPTION

M	E	N	U

SAVOURIES

FIVE-SPICE PORK AND MANGO DIP

SMOKED TROUT CANAPÉS

CRAB AND GINGER SCONES

QUICK MEATBALLS WITH MUSTARD AND CHIVE CREAM

COLD BUFFET

GLAZED LAMB CUTLETS WITH REDCURRANTS

COCONUT, RICE AND LENTIL SALAD

FRAGRANT SAFFRON CHICKEN

CHERRY TOMATO, BEAN AND MOZZARELLA SALAD

CUCUMBER RIBBON AND ASPARAGUS SALAD

MIXED LEAF SALAD

PEACH AND PASSIONFRUIT SOUFFLÉ

ALMOND CREAM GÂTEAU

FRUITS IN FRAMBOISE

CHEESEBOARD

WHITE CHOCOLATE WEDDING CAKE

SERVES 25-150

For an at-home wedding reception, a cold buffet is ideal for a large number. You can offer a sumptuous display of food and yet serve it simply. The recipes are all easy to make in bulk, making this menu suitable for numbers from 25-150 (see the chart on page 233 before starting).Our reception begins with a colourful selection of finger savouries, followed by a delicious buffet. You will find the recipe for Crab and Ginger Scones on page 274; Cucumber Ribbon and Asparagus Salad on page 261; and suggestions for Mixed Leaf Salad on page 75. The cake is a light sponge filled with a rich chocolate and brandy cream, all covered in a mass of white chocolate curls. For something more traditional, see the Wedding Cake recipe on page 267. Most of the food can be made well ahead and frozen. Ask your neighbours early if you can book space in their freezers and refrigerators and enlist and brief willing kitchen helpers.

Unless this is a formal affair, provide as many tables and chairs as possible for the elderly, but remember that people will be happy to stand or mingle while they eat. Arrange the food and drink in separate areas to avoid congestion. It's a good idea to set up one buffet table for every 50 guests to cut queuing. Finding cutlery, crockery and glass may be difficult. Glasses can usually be obtained from a local off-licence – free if it provides the drink. Order glasses for at least one and a half times the number of guests.

Lay the tables so that guests can first pick up a plate, cutlery and napkin, then move on to the food. Offer several small serving platters of each dish, rather than just one or two larger ones, and keep some food and garnishes in reserve so that dishes can be replenished. Provide hot bread rolls for each table (bought or homemade), allowing about 1½ rolls per person.

MENU SUGGESTIONS
See the recipes on pages 269-273 for alternative buffet dishes.

COOK'S HINTS

1 **Tahini** is a thick creamy paste made from ground sesame seeds and sesame oil, which has long been popular in the Middle East. Light and dark varieties are available, the dark being made with unhusked sesame seeds and having a stronger, slightly bitter flavour. Some brands are thicker than others. Always stir the contents of the jar thoroughly before using, as the oil tends to separate. If yours is very thick, thin it with a little vegetable oil before using in this recipe.

2 We decorated the **Smoked Trout Canapés** with tiny hearts cut from thin strips of red pepper using an aspic cutter. If you don't own any aspic cutters, cut the pepper into small diamonds using a sharp knife. Alternatively decorate each canapé with black or red lumpfish roe or small sprigs of fresh herbs.

FIVE-SPICE PORK AND MANGO DIP

Five-spice powder is commonly used in Chinese cooking and lends a very fragrant aniseed flavour. If it is not available, you could easily use a mild curry powder instead.

MAKES ABOUT 25
900 g (2 lb) pork tenderloins
5 ml (1 tsp) five-spice powder
120 ml (8 tbsp) runny tahini
60 ml (4 tbsp) tomato ketchup
vegetable oil
2 large garlic cloves , skinned and crushed
lemon juice
1 ripe mango, peeled and sliced
30 ml (2 tbsp) mango chutney
150 ml (5 fl oz) natural yogurt
mango slices, to garnish

1 Cut the pork into bite-sized pieces. Mix together the five-spice powder, tahini, tomato ketchup, a little oil and the garlic. Stir into the pork pieces, with a little lemon juice, cover and marinate overnight in the refrigerator.

2 Heat some oil in a large sauté pan. Fry the pork, about half at a time until golden brown and tender, about 3 minutes.

3 Return all the pork to the pan with any remaining marinade. Stir over a high heat for 2–3 minutes. Spoon the pork and pan juices into a shallow dish and put to one side to cool. When the pork is cold thread it onto wooden cocktail sticks or small satay sticks.

4 Purée the mango with the chutney and natural yogurt until quite smooth. Serve the pork kebabs on a platter with the mango dip, garnished with mango slices.

To Freeze Cool, pack and freeze the kebabs at the end of step 3. Thaw overnight at cool room temperature. Serve with the mango dip, as above.

SMOKED TROUT CANAPÉS

You could also use thinly sliced smoked salmon or turkey for this recipe.

MAKES ABOUT 50
125 g (4 oz) butter
15 ml (1 tbsp) grated Parmesan cheese
225 g (8 oz) plain flour
1 egg, beaten
225 g (8 oz) thinly sliced smoked trout
50 g (2 oz) full fat soft cheese
30 ml (2 tbsp) mayonnaise
10 ml (2 tsp) chopped fresh dill or 2.5 ml (½ tsp) dried dill weed
small hearts cut from strips of red pepper to garnish

1 Rub the butter and Parmesan cheese into the flour. Add the egg and about 30 ml (2 tbsp) cold water, enough to bind to a smooth dough.

2 Turn out the dough onto a lightly floured surface and roll out to about 5 mm (¼ inch) thick. With a 3.5 cm (1½ inch) plain round, square, or heart-shaped cutter, stamp out as many shapes as possible, re-using the trimmings.

3 Place on baking sheets. Prick with a fork and bake at 200°C (400°F) mark 6 for about 15 minutes or until golden brown and cooked through. Cool.

4 Lay the smoked trout slices out flat and, using the same cutter, stamp out the same number of rounds as before. Place each one on top of a pastry round. Cover lightly with greaseproof paper.

5 Place about 50 g (2 oz) of the smoked trout trimmings in a food processor or blender with the cheese, mayonnaise and dill. Blend until smooth. Place in a piping bag fitted with a 1 cm (½ inch) star nozzle. Pipe a round of pâté mixture onto each shape. Garnish with red pepper hearts (see Cook's Hints).

To Freeze Open freeze without the garnish at the end of step 5. Pack into rigid containers.Place on trays, loosely cover and thaw overnight in the refrigerator. Garnish as above to serve.

QUICK MEATBALLS WITH MUSTARD AND CHIVE CREAM

MAKES ABOUT 32

450 g (1 lb) large pork sausages
15 ml (1 tbsp) oil
grated rind and juice of 1 lemon
30 ml (2 tbsp) wholegrain mustard
150 ml (¼ pint) double cream
15 ml (1 tbsp) snipped chives
vine leaves, lemon slices and chives, to serve

1 Skin the sausages and cut into quarters. With wet hands roll into small balls.

2 Heat the oil in a large sauté pan and brown the sausage balls on all sides.

3 Stir in the grated lemon rind, 15 ml (1 tbsp) lemon juice and 15 ml (1 tbsp) lemon juice and 15 ml (1 tbsp) mustard. Sauté, stirring, for 2–3 minutes until the meatballs are cooked through. Drain and cool.

4 Whip the cream until it holds its shape, stir in the remaining mustard and the chives.

5 Arrange the meatballs on a platter lined with vine leaves. Serve with the mustard and chive cream garnish.

To Freeze Cool, pack and freeze the meatballs at the end of step 3. Pack and freeze the Mustard & Chive Cream. Thaw overnight in the refrigerator. Re-whisk the Mustard and Chive Cream before serving.

GLAZED LAMB CUTLETS WITH REDCURRANTS

12 French-trimmed lamb cutlets
150 g (5 oz) redcurrant jelly
90 ml (6 tbsp) dry sherry
30 ml (2 tbsp) orange juice
30 ml (2 tbsp) green peppercorns (in brine), finely chopped
150 ml (¼ pint) olive oil
nasturtium leaves and redcurrants, to garnish

1 Trim the cutlets of any excess fat. Place in a large, non-metallic dish. In a small saucepan, melt the redcurrant jelly with the sherry, orange juice and green peppercorns. Whisk in the olive oil. Cool. Pour over the lamb. Cover and marinate overnight in the refrigerator. Turn once.

2 Place the cutlets and marinade in a grill pan. Cook under a hot grill, basting frequently, for about 5 minutes on each side.

3 Drain the cutlets from the cooking juices. Pat dry with absorbent kitchen paper to remove any excess fat. Cool the cutlets. Cool and refrigerate the cooking juices. Skim off the fat. Spoon the juices over the chops and garnish with nasturtium leaves and a few redcurrants.

To Freeze Pack and freeze the cutlets and juices without garnish at end of stage 3. Thaw overnight at cool room temperature. Finish as above.

COCONUT, RICE AND LENTIL SALAD

60 ml (4 tbsp) vegetable oil
225 g (8 oz) onion, skinned and finely chopped
2 bay leaves
1 cinnamon stick
4 whole green cardamom pods, split open
175 g (6 oz) moong dal (dehusked split green lentils)
175 g (6 oz) red lentils
50 g (2 oz) creamed coconut, chopped
175 g (6 oz) long grain white rice
salt and freshly ground pepper
45 ml (3 tbsp) chopped fresh parsley and 25 g (1 oz) toasted flaked almonds or cashew nuts, to serve

1 Heat the oil in a large saucepan and sauté the onion with the bay leaves, cinnamon and cardamoms until golden brown.

2 Stir in the moong dal, red lentils, coconut and rice. Add about 1.7 litre (3 pints) cold water and 2.5 ml (½ tsp) salt. Bring to the boil. Boil gently for about 10 minutes or until the rice and lentils are just cooked but still retain some 'bite'.

3 Drain well and rinse under the cold tap. Leave to drain. Stir and season.

4 To serve, add parsley and nuts.

> **COOK'S HINT**
> French-trimmed **lamb cutlets** are now widely on sale ready prepared in butcher's shops and supermarkets. If you buy the lamb as a roasting joint (called best end of neck, or rack of lamb) you will have to separate it into cutlets first. There are usually 6-7 rib bones on each joint, so you will need two joints for this recipe. Ask the butcher to remove the chine bone (backbone). Trim off most of the outer covering of fat, then separate the cutlets by cutting down between each bone.
>
> Trim each cutlet to remove the meat and fat from the bone to within 2.5 cm (1 inch) of the 'eye' of the meat. Scrape the bone absolutely clean.

FRAGRANT SAFFRON CHICKEN

Freshly poached chickens are very moist and tender.

two 1.6 kg (3½ lb) chickens
few slices of onion, carrot and celery, 6 black peppercorns and 1 bay leaf for flavouring
50 g (2 oz) butter
225 g (8 oz) onion, skinned and finely chopped
5 ml (1 tsp) saffron strands
4 no-soak dried apricots
grated rind of 1 lemon
300 ml (½ pint) dry white wine
45 ml (3 tbsp) clear honey
5 ml (1 tsp) mild curry paste
1 bay leaf
300 ml (½ pint) mayonnaise
300 ml (½ pint) double cream
salt and freshly ground pepper

1 Place the chickens in large saucepans. Cover with cold water and add the flavouring ingredients. Bring slowly to the boil, cover and simmer very gently for about 1 hour. Pierce the thigh joint with a skewer to test if cooked. The juices should run clear. Leave the chickens to cool in their liquid.

2 Drain the chickens (skim the stock and use in soups or stews). Remove and discard the skin. Take off all the flesh and discard the bones. Cut the flesh into bite-sized pieces. Cool, cover and refrigerate until required.

3 Melt the butter in a medium saucepan and sauté the onion until soft. Grind the saffron strands to a powder with a pestle and mortar. Stir into the onions with the apricots, lemon rind, white wine, honey, curry paste and bay leaf. Bring to the boil. Simmer uncovered until well reduced and the consistency of chutney, about 10 minutes – longer for larger quantities. Cool. Purée in a blender or food processor. There should be about 225 ml (8 fl oz). Sieve.

4 Fold the cold saffron mixture into the mayonnaise. Whip the cream until it just holds its shape. Fold it in. Season.

5 Mix together the chicken and mayonnaise mixture. Serve on a bed of Coconut, Rice and Lentil Salad.

To Freeze Cool, pack and freeze the chicken pieces with a little of the cold cooking liquor at the end of stage 2. Pack and freeze the completed sauce separately. Thaw the chicken and the sauce overnight at cool room temperature. Drain off any excess liquid from the chicken. Whisk sauce. Finish as above.

CHERRY TOMATO, BEAN AND MOZZARELLA SALAD

Broad beans are more appealing if skinned. You could use frozen broad beans or a 440 g (14 oz) can of lima beans, if preferred.

225 g (8 oz) broad beans (podded weight)
salt and freshly ground pepper
225 g (8 oz) French beans, topped and tailed
150 ml (¼ pint) olive oil
1 garlic clove , skinned and crushed
30 ml (2 tbsp) lemon juice
45 ml (3 tbsp) chopped fresh basil
125 g (4 oz) mozzarella cheese, diced
700 g (1½ lb) cherry tomatoes, halved
basil leaves, to garnish

1 Cook the broad beans in boiling, salted water for about 3 minutes. Drain, skin, if wished. Cook the French beans in boiling water for 7-10 minutes. Drain.

2 Place the oil, garlic, wine and lemon juice in a food processor and blend. Stir in the chopped basil and seasoning.

3 Mix together the beans, mozzarella and tomatoes. Pour over the dressing and stir to coat completely. Cover and marinate for at least 1 hour. Garnish with basil leaves, to serve.

Almond Cream Gâteau,
Fruits in Framboise and
Peach and Passionfruit
Soufflé (left to right)

COOK'S HINT
Passion fruit (also known as granadilla and grenadilla) is a tropical vine fruit that usually looks like a large wrinkled purple plum. Passion fruit originated in South America but are grown in the West Indies, Africa, Australia and Malaysia.

The inedible skin of the passion fruit is deeply wrinkled when ripe and the flesh is sweet and juicy and pitted with small edible black seeds. To eat raw, cut in half and scoop out the pulp with a spoon. Sieve the pulp to obtain the juice, and use to make drinks or flavour ice cream.

PEACH AND PASSION FRUIT SOUFFLÉ

If you don't have a straight-sided soufflé dish, use a large 2.8 litre (5 pint) glass serving bowl instead, omitting the greaseproof collar.

450 g (1 lb) small ripe peaches
1 large ripe mango
3 large passion fruit
50 ml (2 fl oz) fresh orange juice
powdered gelatine
4 eggs, separated
125 g (4 oz) caster sugar
300 ml (½ pint) double cream
nasturtium leaves and blooms, optional

1 Tie a double band of greaseproof paper round a 1.7 litre (3 pint) straight-sided soufflé dish to stand about 5 cm (2 inches) above the rim.

2 Wash, halve and stone all but one of the peaches. Roughly chop the flesh. Peel the mangoes and remove the flesh. Place the peach and mango flesh in a large saucepan with the pulp of 1 passion fruit and the orange juice. Heat gently, stirring continuously for 3–4 minutes or until soft and pulpy. Purée and rub through a nylon sieve, cool slightly. There should be 450–600 ml (¾–1 pint) purée.

3 In a small bowl, sprinkle 30 ml (2 tbsp) powdered gelatine over 90 ml (6 tbsp) water and leave to soak for 5 minutes.

4 Whisk together the egg yolks and sugar until very thick and pale. Gradually whisk in the fruit purée.

5 Place the bowl of gelatine over a pan of gently simmering water until dissolved, about 2–3 minutes. Whisk into the fruit mixture.

6 Whip the double cream until it just begins to hold its shape. Fold into the mixture. Whisk the egg whites until stiff but not dry and fold in. (The cream and egg whites should be of similar consistency to the fruit mixture.)

7 Pour the mixture into the prepared soufflé dish. Refrigerate to set, for about 5 hours.

8 Place the pulp of the 2 remaining passion fruit in a small bowl with 125 ml (5 fl oz) water. Sprinkle over 7.5 ml (1½ tsp) powdered gelatine. Leave to soak for about 5 minutes and heat gently to dissolve, as in stage 5. Cool the passionfruit gelatine mixture until beginning to set.

9 Thinly slice the remaining peach. Arrange at random over the surface of the soufflé. Spoon the passion fruit gelatine mixture over the peach slices. Refrigerate to set, about 1 hour. Carefully peel away the greaseproof-paper collar. Serve on a plate lined with nasturtium leaves and blooms, if wished.

To Freeze Open freeze at the end of step 7. Thaw for 24 hours in the refrigerator. Complete.

ALMOND CREAM GÂTEAU

Although not difficult, this dessert does take some time to make. The whole dessert, however, can be frozen complete, ready to thaw and decorate when required.

plain flour
75 g (3 oz) ground almonds
butter, softened
caster sugar
5 eggs, 1 egg yolk
few drops vanilla flavouring
few drops almond flavouring
25 g (1 oz) cornflour
450 ml (¾ pint) milk
300 ml (10 fl oz) double cream
125 g (4 oz) granulated sugar
icing sugar, strawberries and strawberry leaves, to decorate

1 To make almond pastry, sift 175 g (6 oz) flour onto a surface, make a small well in the centre and sprinkle the almonds on the flour. Place 75 g (3 oz) butter, 75 g (3 oz) caster sugar, 1 egg, 1 egg yolk and the vanilla flavouring in the centre. Blend the ingredients well with the fingertips.

2 Draw the flour and almonds into the butter mixture and knead together lightly until smooth. Wrap and chill for about 30 minutes.

3 To make choux pastry, place 75 g (3 oz) butter in a saucepan with 200 ml (7 fl oz) water. Melt the butter over a low heat, then bring the water to the boil. Off the heat, tip in 90 g (3½ oz) flour. Beat until smooth. Cool before gradually beating in 3 eggs.

4 Using a 1 cm ½ inch plain nozzle, pipe 24 rounds of choux pastry onto a greased and dampened baking sheet. Bake at 200°C (400°F) mark 6 for 20–25 mintues until well risen and golden. Split each round with a knife and return to the oven for 5–10 minutes until dried out. Cool on a wire rack.

5 On a lightly floured surface, roll out the almond pastry into a circle about 28 cm (11 inch) diameter. Use to line the base and sides of a 23 cm (9 inch) deep fluted flan ring. Freeze for 15 minutes. Bake blind at 200°C (400°F) mark 6 for 20 minutes. Remove the baking beans and continue to cook for 5–10 minutes or until the pastry is golden brown and cooked through. Cool.

6 To make the custard, whisk 50 g (2 oz) caster sugar with 25 g (1 oz) flour, the remaining egg, almond flavouring and cornflour. Put the milk in a saucepan and bring to the boil. Pour onto the flour mixture, whisking all the time. Return the mixture to the pan and simmer gently for 2–3 minutes, stirring all the time until smooth and thick. Spoon into a heat-proof bowl and cover with damp greaseproof paper. Cool.

7 Lightly whisk the double cream until it just begins to hold its shape. Fold into the cold custard mixture, whisking lightly together if necessary. Fill the choux rounds with about half the mixture. Spoon the remainder into the cold flan case. Pile the choux rounds into the flan on top of the custard. Chill.

8 To make the caramel sauce, melt the granulated sugar slowly over a gentle heat in a heavy saucepan. When it is dissolved and golden brown, remove it from the heat and drizzle over the choux buns. Decorate with icing sugar, strawberries and leaves.

To Freeze Open freeze at the end of step 7, then overwrap.Unwrap, place on a flat serving dish and thaw at cool room temperature for about 3½ hours. Decorate.

FRUITS IN FRAMBOISE

Framboise is deliciously sharp and fruity and not as sweet and cloying as similar liqueurs can be.

900 g (2 lb) strawberries, washed
450 g (1 lb) raspberries, washed
90 ml (6 tbsp) framboise (raspberry liqueur)
60 ml (4 tbsp) lemon juice
25 g (1 oz) icing sugar
450 ml (¾ pint) single cream, to accompany

1 Halve any large strawberries and mix together with 225 g (8 oz) raspberries..

2 Purée the remaining raspberries in a blender or food processor with the framboise liqueur, lemon juice and icing sugar. Sieve over the fruit mixture. Stir lightly to mix without breaking up the fruit.

3 Cover and macerate overnight in the refrigerator. Serve with single cream.

White Chocolate Wedding Cake (opposite)

WHITE CHOCOLATE CURLS

1.1 kg (2½ lb) white chocolate

Break the chocolate into a bowl. Stand over a pan of simmering water and stir until the chocolate melts. Spread half of the chocolate thinly on a marble slab or clean, smooth work surface. When the chocolate is just set, push a clean stripping knife (a decorators' tool used for scraping off wallpaper. We suggest that you buy one and keep it specifically for this purpose. A large very sharp knife can be used instead but does not make such large, fat curls.) across the surface at an angle of about 25° to roll off large fat curls. Re-melt the remaining chocolate and repeat as above to make more curls. The curls can be made in advance and kept in the refrigerator, in an airtight container, interleaved with greaseproof paper, for at least 2 weeks.

WHITE CHOCOLATE WEDDING CAKE

A spectacular three tiered concoction of light sponges with a rich gooey chocolate mousse filling covered in cream and masses of white chocolate curls. You will need three large round cake tins measuring 35.5 cm (14 inches), 28 cm (11 inches), 20.5 cm (8 inches). To assemble the cake you will need two pieces of thick cardboard the same diameter as the middle and top cakes and about 16 wooden chopsticks. Decorate the cake with fresh flowers to complement the bride's bouquet. The undecorated cake freezes well and will thaw out overnight at room temperature. It can be decorated the night before the wedding and stored in a cool place (it doesn't have to be the fridge) overnight. It is easiest and safest to make and bake one sponge at a time. Do not attempt this recipe if you don't own an electric whisk (your arm will not be strong enough to whisk the mixture sufficiently by hand!). A very large bowl is also necessary, especially for the largest cake. To make a smaller version, omit the bottom cake and make just the middle and top layers as below. Freeze the sponges as soon as they are cool.

white vegetable fat, for greasing
BOTTOM CAKE 35.5 CM (14 INCHES)
200 g (7 oz) butter
14 eggs
400 g (14 oz) caster sugar
275 g (12 oz) plain flour
125 g (4 oz) cornflour
MIDDLE CAKE 28 CM (11 INCHES)
125 g (4 oz) butter
8 eggs
225 g (8 oz) caster sugar
200 g (7 oz) plain flour
25 g (1 oz) cornflour
TOP CAKE 20.5 CM (8 INCHES)
75 g (3 oz) butter
6 eggs
175 g (6 oz) caster sugar
150 g (5 oz) plain flour
25 g (1 oz) cornflour

1 Grease tins thoroughly and line with greaseproof paper, using white vegetable fat.
2 Make one cake at a time. Put the butter into a saucepan and heat gently until melted, then remove from the heat and leave to stand for a few minutes to cool slightly.

3 Put the eggs and sugar in a large bowl, place over a pan of hot water and whisk with an electric whisk until very pale and creamy and thick enough to leave a trail on the surface when the whisk is lifted. As an approximate guide the large cake should be whisked for about 25–30 minutes, the medium for 15 minutes and the small for about 10 minutes. Remove the mixture from the heat and whisk until cool.

4 Sift the flours together in a bowl. Fold half of the flour into the egg mixture with a metal spoon. Pour half the cooled butter around the edge of the mixture and fold in *very* lightly and carefully or the butter will sink and result in a heavy cake. Gradually fold in the remaining flour and butter as before.

5 Pour into the prepared tin. Bake in the oven at 180°C (350°F) mark 4 for 1–1¼ hours for the largest cake, 40–45 minutes for the middle cake and 30–35 minutes for the smallest cake. When cooked the cake should be well risen, firm to the touch and just shrinking away from the sides of the tin. Turn out and cool on a wire rack. Wrap and store in the freezer until ready to assemble.

MOUSSE FILLING
700 g (1½ lb) plain chocolate
120 ml (8 tbsp) brandy
8 eggs, separated
1.1 litres (2 pints) double cream
2 sachets of gelatine (20 ml (4 tsp))
DECORATION
1.1 litres (2 pints) double cream
white chocolate curls, (see box)
icing sugar
fresh flowers

1 To make the mousse. Break the chocolate into small pieces. Put into a bowl and stand over a saucepan of simmering water, until the chocolate melts. Remove from the heat and stir in the brandy and egg yolks. Whip the cream until it just stands in soft peaks, then fold into the chocolate mixture.

2 In a small bowl, sprinkle the gelatine onto 60 ml (4 tbsp) water. Stand over a pan of simmering water and stir until dissolved. Cool, then stir into the chocolate mixture. Whisk the egg whites until stiff then fold in.

3 Cut each cake in half. Put the bottom half of each cake into the base of each tin. Pour the mousse on top, dividing it proportionally between each tin. Chill until set. Put the second half of sponge back into its tin on top of the mousse, and press together. Carefully turn the cakes out.

4 Whip the cream until it just holds its shape. Put the largest cake onto the cake board and cover with a thin layer of cream. Place the middle cake on a round of stiff cardboard (see the introduction).

5 Push a wooden chopstick through the middle of the bottom layer. With a pen mark it about 2.5 cm (1 inch) above the top of the cake. Pull it out and cut it off using the mark as a guide. Cut seven more chopsticks to the same height.

6 Insert the chopsticks in a circle into the bottom cake. Stand the middle cake on top to check that it stands level. Remove the cake, then repeat the procedure with the middle and top sponges, cutting eight more chopsticks to the required height.

7 Cover the middle and top cakes with whipped cream (do this on a board, not with the cakes in position). Cover all the cakes completely with chocolate curls and dredge with icing sugar.

8 Assemble the cake where it is to be served (Do not attempt to move the cake once the tiers are in position!) Stack the cakes one on top of another, and decorate with fresh flowers as desired.

CATERING QUANTITIES

	25	50	75	100	150
SAVOURIES					
5-Spice Pork and Mango Dip	× 1	× 1	× 2	× 2	× 3
Smoked Trout Canapés	× 1	× 1	× 1½	× 2	× 3
Quick Meat Balls	× 1	× 1	× 2	× 2	× 3
Crab and Ginger Scones	× 1	× 1	× 1	× 2	× 3
MAIN COURSE					
Fragrant Saffron Chicken	6 chickens	12 chickens	17 chickens	24 chickens	36 chickens
sauce	plus 2½ sauce	plus 5 sauce	plus 7 sauce	plus 10 sauce	plus 15
Glazed Lamb Cutlets	36 cutlets	72 cutlets	108 cutlets	144 cutlets	216 cutlets
with Redcurrants	plus 3 glaze	plus 5 glaze	plus 7 glaze	plus 10 glaze	plus 14 glaze

Salad quantities are difficult to judge so we suggest that you keep additional prepared ingredients and separate dressings available in case they are needed.

	25	50	75	100	150
SALADS					
Coconut, Rice and Lentil salad	× 2	× 3	× 5	× 7	× 10
Cherry Tomato, Bean and Mozzarella Salad	× 2	× 3	× 4	× 6	× 8
Cucumber Ribbon and Asparagus Salad	× 1	× 2	× 3	× 5	× 7
DESSERTS					
Fruits in Framboise	× 2	× 4	× 6	× 8	× 12
Peach and Passionfruit Soufflé	× 2	× 4	× 6	× 7	× 10
Almond Cream Gâteau	× 2	× 5	× 7	× 9	× 12
Single cream to accompany	900 ml	1.4 litres	2.3 litres	2.8 litres	4.3 litres
	(1½ pints)	(2½ pints)	(4 pints)	(5 pints)	(7½ pints)

GENERAL

Cheese: allow 40–50g (1½ –2 oz) per person and 2 biscuits

Coffee (ground): allow 700 g (1½ lb) per 50 × 180 ml (6½ fl oz) cups

Coffee (instant): allow 225 g (8 oz) per 50 × 180 ml (6½ fl oz) cups

Tea: allow 16 teabags per 50 × 180 ml (6½ fl oz) cups

Milk: allow 568 ml (1 pint) per 20 cups.

Sugar: allow 225 g (8 oz) per 50 cups

COUNTDOWN

Up to four weeks ahead:

Make and freeze all the savouries. Make a list of all the garnishes that need to be bought the day before. Cook and freeze the chicken and the mayonnaise sauce for Fragrant Saffron Chicken. Cook and freeze the lamb cutlets and juices for Glazed Lamb Cutlets with Redcurrants. Make and freeze the Peach and Passion-fruit Soufflés and the Almond Cream Gâteaux.

One week before:

Look out any dishes, crockery, cutlery, vases, decorations and so on you want to use. There'll still be time to hire some extra.Confirm any orders for wine, ice and waitresses. (See Page 216 for our advice on the above). Make the dressings for Cherry Tomato, Bean and Mozzarella Salad, Cucumber Ribbon and Asparagus Salad (without the chives). Store in airtight containers at cool room temperature until you are ready to serve the salads.

Four days before:

Make the Mango Dip for Five-spice Pork. Cover and refrigerate. Make the purée for Fruits in Framboise. Cover and refrigerate. Make the caramel sauce for the Almond Cream Gâteaux. Store in an airtight container at cool room temperature until needed.

Two days before:

Make the Coconut, Rice and Lentil Salad. Chop the parsley and toast the nuts, but don't add them at this stage. Cool, cover and refrigerate the salad. Store the parsley and nuts separately in polythene bags. Take the Peach and Passion fruit Soufflés from the freezer to thaw. Buy cheese, biscuits and grapes or celery for the cheeseboard.

The day before

Prepare all the garnishes for the savouries and main dishes. Store in polythene bags or airtight containers in the refrigerator. Complete the Cherry Tomato, Bean and Mozzarella Salad. Cover and refrigerate. Cook the asparagus for Cucumber Ribbon and Asparagus Salad. Cool, cover and refrigerate.

Finish the Peach and Passionfruit Soufflés; keep in the refrigerator. Finish the Fruits in Framboise. Cover and refrigerate. As late as possible, wash the salad leaves for Mixed Leaf Salad. Drain well. Refrigerate separately in polythene bags. Slice, bag and refrigerate the cucumber. Remove the frozen savouries, the cooked chicken and sauce and lamb cutlets with juices from the freezer.Make a list of things to do for the next day. Don't forget extra rubbish sacks.

On the day:

About 2 hours before the guests are due to arrive at the reception:

Set out and garnish the savouries. Finish the Fragrant Saffron Chicken and Coconut, Rice and Lentil Salad. Assemble dishes and garnish. Finish the Glazed Lamb Cutlets with Redcurrants. Assemble the Cucumber Ribbon and Asparagus Salad and Mixed Leaf Salad but don't dress these yet.

Decorate the Almond Cream Gâteaux with caramel sauce and icing sugar. Stir the Fruits in Framboise. Keep the desserts refrigerated for a while. Set out the cheeseboard. Chill the wines.

Dress the Cucumber Ribbon and Asparagus Salad and the Mixed Leaf Salad.

VEGETARIAN BUFFET

| M | E | N | U |

BRIE WITH MUSHROOM FORCEMEAT WRAPPED IN FILO PASTRY

VEGETABLE SALAMAGUNDY

SPINACH AND GARLIC TARTS

GREEN SALAD

NEW POTATOES

STRAWBERRY MOUSSE GÂTEAUX

SERVES 20

This exciting, colourful buffet will please vegetarians and meat eaters alike. The striking centrepiece is a whole Brie topped with a coarse mushroom forcemeat and the entire thing is encased in filo pastry. It's served while warm, so that the cheese is soft and creamy. It's unlikely that you'll have a plate large enough for the finished dish, so we suggest that you hire or borrow one, or serve it on a pretty tray lined completely with edible leaves and herbs. It is very rich, so plain accompaniments are best – a bowl of new potatoes and a simple green salad are most suitable along with our delicious Vegetable Salamagundy. As well as the whole cheese, there are Spinach and Garlic Tarts. For the pudding, luxurious Strawberry Mousse Gâteau is irresistible.

Brie with Mushroom Forcemeat Wrapped in Filo (right)

DRINKS TO SERVE
This hearty meal needs a full red wine as an accompaniment, so choose a Beaujolais and make it a 'nouveau' if you can find some. A light elegant dessert wine such as a Juraçon would be perfect with the Strawberry Mousse Gâteaux.

MICROWAVE HINT
Cook the **mushroom forcemeat** in a large, wide bowl on HIGH for 15-20 minutes, or until all of the liquid has evaporated.

COOK'S HINT
Strict vegetarians could substitute a Pencarreg cheese for the Brie. It's a soft creamy cheese rather like a Brie, but is organic and made without animal rennet. Look for it in larger supermarkets on the cheese counter.

Whichever cheese you're using it's a good idea to place your order for a whole cheese a week in advance of the party because supermarkets tend to cut them in half for display.

Pencarreg cheese is smaller than Brie, so you will only need half of the mushroom forcemeat and, because it's denser than Brie, cook it at 180° C (350° F) mark 4 for 40-45 minutes, covering with foil if it browns too quickly.

BRIE WITH MUSHROOM FORCEMEAT WRAPPED IN FILO

A sublime concoction of melting cheese surrounded by a coarse mushroom forcemeat, the whole thing held together by a crisp pastry crust. The success of this depends on two things, firstly patience when making the forcemeat; it must be cooked until all the liquid has gone and secondly, the whole cheese and forcemeat must be completely and carefully enclosed within the pastry; any gaps or tears should be patched over with extra pastry or the filling will leak out.

vegetable oil
2 garlic cloves, skinned and crushed
3 juniper berries, crushed
1.4 kg (3 lb) flat black mushrooms, roughly chopped
175 g (6 oz) fresh brown breadcrumbs
120 ml (8 tbsp) chopped fresh mixed herbs such as thyme, sage, parsley, chervil
lemon juice
salt and freshly ground pepper
400 g packet filo pastry (see page 82)
1 whole Somerset Brie, firm but ripe
paprika

1 To make the mushroom forcemeat, heat 60 ml (4 tbsp) of the oil in a large saucepan. Add the garlic and juniper berries and cook for a couple of minutes, stirring. Do not allow the garlic to brown.

2 Add the mushrooms to the oil and cook over a high heat for about 10–15 minutes or until the mushrooms are cooked and most of the liquid has evaporated, stirring frequently.

3 Add the breadcrumbs and herbs and season generously with salt and pepper and lemon juice. Cool.

4 When the forcemeat is cold, lightly grease a large baking sheet. Cut two lengths of foil, long enough to cover the baking sheet, cover the edges and fold in half. Lay over the baking sheet to make a cross. (This helps remove the cooked pie from the baking sheet). Lay one sheet of filo pastry on the baking sheet and brush with oil, lay a second sheet of pastry on top so that one corner just overlaps the first sheet. Brush with more oil.

5 Repeat with all but one sheet of the remaining pastry (the pastry will hang over the edges of the baking sheet; don't worry at this stage).

6 Lay the cheese in the centre of the pastry. Spoon the forcemeat on top. Bring the pastry up and over the cheese and forcemeat to enclose it completely. Use the reserved sheet to patch up any holes, or cracks.

7 Brush with oil. Bake in the oven at 200°C (400°F) mark 6 for 30–35 minutes until just golden brown. Sprinkle with paprika. Then carefully remove from the baking sheet using the foil to help you (enlist the help of a friend too!). Leave to cool for 5 minutes before cutting. Serve garnished with fresh herbs.

VEGETABLE SALAMAGUNDY

Salamagundy is an old English supper dish which dates back to the eighteenth century. It originally contained a varied mixture of meats. Here we make the most of fresh colourful vegetables. Use others in season if you prefer. Add hard-boiled quail's eggs, or nuts, if liked.

125 g (4 oz) green lentils
1 bay leaf
salt and freshly ground pepper
450 g (1 lb) French beans, trimmed
450 g (1 lb) mange tout, trimmed
450 g (1 lb) beef tomatoes, sliced
450 g (1 lb) cherry tomatoes
2 yellow peppers, seeded and cut into strips
1 small head of celery, trimmed and sliced
225 g (8 oz) lamb's lettuce, trimmed
2 small onions, skinned and thinly sliced
4 Cox's apples, sliced
black olives
300 ml (½ pint) vinaigrette dressing
fresh herbs, to garnish

1 Cook the lentils in boiling salted water with the bay leaf, until just tender. Drain and leave to cool. Blanch the beans and mange tout in boiling salted water for 2 minutes. Drain and rinse under cold running water. Drain again.

2 Arrange all the ingredients on one or two large platters in a symmetrical pattern. Sprinkle with the dressing and garnish with the fresh herbs.

Vegetable Salamagundy (above)

SPINACH AND GARLIC TARTS

Look out for bags of ready-prepared spinach in your supermarket. You will need a very large pan to cook it in. If yours is not large enough, cook it in two batches.

500 g (1 lb 2 oz) plain flour
salt and freshly ground pepper
250 g (9 oz) butter or margarine
15 ml (1 tbsp) olive oil
3 medium onions, skinned and chopped
2–3 garlic cloves, skinned and crushed
900 g (2 lb) prepared fresh spinach
50 g (2 oz) freshly grated Parmesan cheese
300 ml (½ pint) double cream
90 ml (6 tbsp) ground almonds
2 egg yolks
freshly grated nutmeg
25 g (1 oz) pine kernels
25 g (1 oz) piece Parmesan cheese

1 To make the pastry put the flour and salt in a bowl, rub in the fat until the mixture resembles fine breadcrumbs. Stir in enough water to bind the mixture together. Knead lightly, then roll out on a floured surface and use to line two shallow, loose bottomed 28 cm (11 inch) round, fluted flan tins. Cover and chill in the refrigerator for at

COOK'S HINT
Beef tomatoes are also known as beefsteak or marmande tomatoes. They are very large, weighing anything up to 450 g (1 lb) each. Underripe tomatoes ripen quickly if placed in a paper bag with one ripe tomato amongst them.

MENU SUGGESTIONS
For a hot buffet a Mushroom Lasagne (page 272) is a good choice. It can be made in advance, frozen and reheated just before the party. Serve with Vegetable Salamagundy or any of the salads on pages 260-261. All the puddings on pages 262–263 are suitable for vegetarians.

COUNTDOWN
About 1 week before:
Bake the pastry cases
for the Spinach and
Garlic Tarts, cool, wrap
and freeze.Make the
sponges for the gâteaux.
The day before:
Thaw the pastry cases
and sponges.Make the
mushroom forcemeat,
cool and refrigerate.
Prepare and cook the
vegetables for the
Salamagundy, cool,
refrigerate. Wash and
scrub the new
potatoes. Complete the
Gâteaux to the end of
step 9, leave to set
overnight.
On the day:
Arrange the vegetables
for the Salamagundy on
a platter, cover and
refrigerate. Make the
dressing and
chill.Complete the Brie
with Mushroom
Forcemeat to the
end of step 6.
Refrigerate. Prepare the
filling for the tarts and
refrigerate. Complete
the decoration for the
Strawberry Mousse
Gâteaux.
To serve at 1.00pm:
12.15pm: Prepare the
Green Salad, cover and
refrigerate.
12.20pm: Bake the filo
wrapped cheese.
12.25pm: Boil the
potatoes until tender,
drain and keep warm.
12.40pm: Complete
the spinach tarts and
bake.
12.55pm: Pour the
dressing over the
Salamagundy. Garnish
the food and serve.

COOK'S HINT
Agar agar is derived
from seaweed, has
useful gelling properties
that can be used as a
vegetarian substitute for
gelatine. Available in
powder, flakes or
sheets, agar agar will
only dissolve in boiling
water. Follow the
manufacturer's
instructions carefully
when using.To set the
mousse with gelatine
you will need 60 ml (4
level tbsp) dissolved in
90 ml (6 tbsp) water.

least 30 minutes.

2 Meanwhile heat the oil in a very large, heavy-based saucepan. Add the onions and garlic and cook, stirring for a couple of minutes. Reduce the heat, cover the pan with a tightly fitting lid and sweat the onion until very soft.

3 Add the spinach and stir to mix with the onion mixture. Re-cover the pan and cook for 4–5 minutes until the spinach is just cooked. Remove from the heat. Stir in the grated Parmesan, cream, almonds and egg yolks. Season generously with nutmeg, salt and pepper.

4 Bake the pastry cases blind in the oven at 190°C (375°F) mark 5 for 15-20 minutes. Remove the baking beans and greaseproof paper and cook for a further 10 minutes or until the base is cooked through.

5 Divide the filling between the pastry cases and sprinkle with the pine kernals. Stand each tart on a baking sheet and cook at 200°C (400°F) mark 6 for 10 minutes until the filling is lightly set. While still warm coarsely grate over the Parmesan cheese. Serve warm or cold.

STRAWBERRY MOUSSE GÂTEAUX

This recipe will make two cakes. Each cake will serve at least ten people. The undecorated sponges can be frozen.

SPONGE
8 eggs
225 g (8 oz) caster sugar
225 g (8 oz) plain flour
MOUSSE
700 g (1½ lb) ripe strawberries, hulled
6 eggs, separated
225 g (8 oz) caster sugar
120 ml (8 tbsp) agar agar flakes or powder
300 ml (½ pint) double cream
DECORATION
600 ml (1 pint) double cream
150 g (5 oz) flaked almonds, toasted
about 900 g (2 lb) small ripe strawberries
120 ml (8 tbsp) redcurrant jelly

1 Grease two 23 cm (9 inch) spring release cake tins and line the bases with greased greaseproof paper.

2 To make the sponge, put the eggs and sugar in a very large heatproof bowl, standing over a pan of simmering water. Using an electric hand whisk, whisk until doubled in volume and thick enough to leave a trail when the whisk is lifted. This will take about 10 minutes.

3 Remove from the heat and continue whisking until the mixture is cool.

4 Sift in half of the flour and fold in very lightly with a large metal spoon. Repeat with the remaining flour. Divide the mixture evenly between the two tins and bake in the oven at 190°C (375°F) mark 5 for 20–25 minutes until well risen, and firm to the touch. Turn out and cool on wire racks.

5 Meanwhile, clean the tins and re-line with non-stick paper.

6 To make the mousse, purée the strawberries in a blender or food processor. Put into a medium saucepan with the agar agar. Bring to the boil, reduce the heat and simmer for 5 minutes. Cool slightly.

7 Meanwhile in a large bowl, whisk together the egg yolks and the sugar until thick and mousse like.

8 Whip the cream until it just holds its shape, then fold into the mousse. Whisk the egg whites until stiff, then fold into the mousse.

9 Cut the sponges in half and place one half in the base of each prepared tin. Carefully pour over the mousse. Cover and chill for 30 minutes or until lightly set. Carefully place the second layer of sponge on top. Chill until completely set.

10 To serve, carefully remove from the tin and peel off the paper. Whip the cream until just firm. Then spread around the top and sides of the gâteaux. Coat the sides with the toasted nuts. Arrange the strawberries on top of the gâteaux.

11 Warm the redcurrant jelly with 30 ml (2 tbsp) water until just melted then brush over the strawberries to glaze. Chill until ready to serve.

To Freeze Over wrap and freeze the unfilled cakes, store for up to 3 months. To use, unwrap and thaw at cool room temperature. Complete as above.

BUFFET QUANTITY CHART

Below are the approximate quantities to serve 12 people. For 25 people, multiply the quantities by two. For 50 people multiply by four. For 75 people multiply by five and a half. For 100 people multiply by seven.

Cocktails Eats
Allow about 80 small eats for 12 people to serve before a meal.
Allow about 120 small eats for 12 people to serve alone.

Starters
Soups	allow 2.6 litre (4½ pints) for 12
Pâtés	allow 1.1 kg (2½ lb) for 12
Smoked Salmon	allow 900 g (2 lb) for 12
Prawns	900 g (2 lb) for 12

Main Dishes
Boneless chicken or turkey	allow 1.8 kg (1 lb) for 12
Whole chicken	allow three 1.4 kg (3 lb) for oven ready birds for 12
Turkey	allow one 5.5 kg (12 lb) oven ready bird for 12

Lamb/beef/pork
boneless	allow 2–2.3 kg (4½–5 lb) for 12
on the bone	allow 3.2–3.6 kg (7–8 lb) for 12
mince	allow 2 kg (4½ lb) for 12

Fish
Whole with head	allow 2.3 kg (5 lb) for 12
Steaks	allow twelve 175 g (6 oz) steaks for 12
Fillets	allow 2 kg (4½ lb) for 12
Prawns	allow 1.4 kg (3 lb) for 12 (main course)

Accompaniments
Potatoes	
Roast and mashed	allow 2 kg (4½ lb) for 12
new	allow 1.8 kg (4 lb) for 12
Rice and pasta	allow 700 g (1½ lb) for 12
Green vegetables	allow 1.4 kg (3 lb) for 12

(for fresh spinach allow about 3.6 kg (8 lb) for 12)

Salads
Tomato	allow 700 g (1½ lb) for 12
Salad leaves	allow 2 medium heads for 12
Cucumber	allow 1 large for 12

French dressing – allow 175 ml (6 fl oz) for 12
Mayonnaise	allow 300 ml (10 fl oz) for 12

Bread
Fresh bread	allow 1 large loaf for 12
Medium sliced bread	allow 1 large loaf for 12 (approx 24 slices)

Cheeses
For a wine and cheese party	allow 1.4 kg (3 lb) for 12
To serve at the end of a meal	allow 700 g (1½ lb) for 12

Butter
To serve with bread or biscuits and cheese	allow 225 g (8 oz) for 12
To serve with bread and biscuits and cheese	allow 350 g (12 oz) for 12
For sandwiches	allow 175 g (6 oz) softened butter for 12 rounds

Cream
For pudding or dessert	allow 569 ml (20 fl oz) single cream for 12
For coffee	allow 300 ml (10 fl oz) single cream for 12

Milk
Allow 450 ml (15 fl oz) for 12 cups tea

Coffee and Tea
Ground coffee	allow about 125 g (4 oz) for 12 medium cups
Instant	allow about 75 g (3 oz) for 12 large cups
Tea	allow ab out 25 g (1 oz) for 12 medium cups

BASIC RECIPES

This collection of over 150 recipes is a mixture of traditional favourites, such as Beef Wellington and Chocolate Profiteroles, and exciting new recipes, such as Turkey and Watercress Roulades and Asparagus Risotto. These recipes can be used to compile your own menus if you wish. Alternatively, all the menus in the first section of this book contain suggestions for menu variations using the following recipes. This means you can ring the changes, but still prepare a menu that provides a balanced meal. All recipes serve eight unless otherwise stated.

TARRAGON CONSOMMÉ

1.7 litres (3 pints) chicken stock

350 g (12 oz) chicken meat, minced

2 leeks, trimmed and thinly sliced

2 celery sticks, trimmed and fairly thinly sliced

2 carrots, fairly thinly sliced

2 shallots, skinned and diced

2 egg whites, lightly whisked

2 egg shells, crushed

45 ml (3 tbsp) finely chopped fresh tarragon

shapes cut from lemon rind, to garnish

1 Bring the stock to the boil.

2 Mix the chicken and vegetables together in a large saucepan, then mix in the egg whites and shells. Gradually pour in the stock, whisking all the time, then bring to the boil, still whisking.

3 Immediately boiling point is reached, stop whisking, lower the heat and simmer very gently for 1 hour.

4 Carefully make a small hole in the scum on the surface of the liquid. Without disturbing the scum, ladle the liquid out into a sieve lined with muslin or cheesecloth and strain into a large bowl.

5 Leave the liquid until cold, then carefully lift the fat from the surface.

6 Put the tarragon into a mortar. Bring 200 ml (7 fl oz) of the consommé to the boil, then gradually pour it on to the tarragon, pounding it well with the pestle. Cover and leave to infuse for 10 minutes.

7 Mix the tarragon liquid and tarragon with the remaining consommé. Heat gently to boiling point. Ladle into warmed soup bowls and float shapes cut from lemon rind on top.

VICHYSSOISE

50 g (2 oz) butter or margarine

4 medium leeks, trimmed and sliced

2 small onions, skinned and finely chopped

700 g (1½ lb) potatoes, peeled and finely sliced

1.1 litres (2 pints) chicken stock

salt and freshly ground pepper

1 blade of mace

300 ml (½ pint) single cream

snipped fresh chives, to garnish

1 Melt the butter in a saucepan, add the leeks and onion and cook gently without browning for 10–12 minutes. Add the potatoes, stock, seasoning and mace.

2 Bring to the boil, cover and simmer very gently for 30–35 minutes, until the vegetables are tender.

3 Allow to cool slightly, then sieve or purée in a blender or food processor until smooth. Chill thoroughly.

4 To serve, stir in the cream, adjust the seasoning and sprinkle with snipped fresh chives.

MINTED MELON AND CUCUMBER SOUP

4 medium-sized, ripe cantaloupe or rock melons

1 cucumber, about 350 g (12 oz)

thinly pared rind and juice of 2 lemons

50 g (2 oz) caster sugar

6 large stems of fresh mint, crushed

salt and freshly ground pepper

sprigs of fresh mint, to garnish

1 Halve and de-seed the melons. Scoop out and roughly chop the flesh. Peel, halve lengthways, de-seed and roughly chop the cucumber. Place the melon flesh and the chopped cucumber in a large saucepan. Add the lemon rind to the pan with the sugar and 300 ml (½ pint) water. Stir well.

2 Heat gently, stirring all the time, until the sugar has dissolved, then simmer for about 10 minutes. Add the mint stems and allow to cool.

3 Remove the mint and transfer the soup to a blender or food processor. Purée until smooth, then push through a nylon sieve into a bowl. Cover and chill for at least 2 hours, preferably overnight.

4 Add a little strained lemon juice to taste, if wished. Adjust the seasoning and serve in chilled bowls, garnished with fresh mint sprigs.

FENNEL AND ORANGE SOUP

1½ large oranges

salt and freshly ground pepper

1.4 kg (3 lb) Florence fennel

75 g (3 oz) butter or margarine

25 ml (1½ tbsp) plain flour

2.1 litres (3¾ pints) chicken stock

1 Pare a few strips from the rind of one orange and blanch in boiling salted water for 1 minute. Drain, cool, cover and refrigerate.

2 Thinly slice the fennel, discarding the cores and reserving the feathery tops.

3 Melt the butter in a large saucepan. Add the fennel, cover tightly and cook gently until beginning to soften but not brown.

4 Stir in the flour and cook for 1–2 minutes.

5 Finely grate the remaining orange rind and add to the fennel with the stock and seasoning. Bring to the boil, cover and simmer for 20–30 minutes.

6 Cool the soup a little, then purée in a blender or food processor until quite smooth. Stir in about 180 ml (12 tbsp) orange juice, then reheat gently. Adjust the seasoning and garnish with fennel tops and pared orange rind.

ASPARAGUS WITH CORIANDER HOLLANDAISE SAUCE

800 g (1¾ lb) asparagus, stalks trimmed and scraped

salt

15 ml (1 tbsp) lemon juice

SAUCE

225 g (8 oz) unsalted butter, diced

45 ml (3 tbsp) coriander seeds, crushed and lightly toasted

45 ml (3 tbsp) lemon juice

25 ml (1½ tbsp) white wine vinegar

4 egg yolks

pinch of sugar

pinch of salt

long fine strips of orange and lemon rind, blanched and knotted, and sprigs of fresh chervil, to garnish

1 To make the sauce, melt the butter, add the coriander seeds and warm gently until the butter just begins to bubble. Remove from the heat, cover and leave to infuse for 20 minutes.

2 Tie the asparagus in four equal bundles. Stand them in a large saucepan of boiling salted water, to which the lemon juice has been added, packing foil around them if necessary so that they stand upright. The tips should be out of the water.

3 Cover with a lid or dome of foil and cook gently for about 10 minutes or until tender, depending on the size of the spears.

4 For the sauce, put the lemon juice and vinegar in a saucepan and bring to the boil. Gently reheat the coriander butter until just beginning to foam.

5 Put the egg yolks, sugar and salt in a blender and blend briefly, then, with the motor running, slowly pour in the lemon juice and vinegar mixture. When it has all been absorbed, slowly pour in the coriander butter, with the motor still running.

6 Drain the asparagus well and arrange on warmed serving plates. Place a small pool of sauce on each plate. Garnish with fine strips of orange and lemon rind and sprigs of chervil.

7 Alternatively, the asparagus can be piled on to one large, warmed plate and the sauce served in a warmed bowl for the guests to help themselves. Garnish as above.

DEVILLED WHITEBAIT WITH DEEP FRIED PARSLEY

120 ml (8 tbsp) plain flour
2.5 ml (½ tsp) curry powder
2.5 ml (½ tsp) ground ginger
2.5 ml (½ tsp) cayenne
salt
1.1 kg (2½ lb) whitebait, fresh or frozen
oil, for deep frying
25 g (1 oz) parsley sprigs
sea salt
4 lemons, cut into wedges

1 Sift the flour, curry powder, ginger, cayenne and salt together into a large plastic bag. Put a quarter of the whitebait into the bag and shake well to coat in the flour mixture. Lift the fish out and shake in a sieve to remove excess flour. Repeat with the remaining whitebait.

2 Heat the oil in a deep-fat fryer to 190°C (375°F). Put a single layer of whitebait into the frying basket and lower it into the oil. Fry for 2–3 minutes, shaking the basket occasionally, until the whitebait make a rustling sound as they are shaken. Tip out on to a warmed plate lined with absorbent kitchen paper. Fry the remaining whitebait in the same way.

3 Allow the oil temperature to reduce to about 186°C (365°F). Deep fry the parsley for a few seconds until it stops sizzling. Drain on absorbent kitchen paper, then sprinkle with sea salt.

4 Divide the whitebait between eight individual warmed serving plates. Scatter over the parsley sprigs and garnish with lemon wedges.

SEAFOOD ROULADE

butter or margarine
350 g (12 oz) cooked prawns in shells
200 ml (7 fl oz) dry white wine
onion slices and a bay leaf, for flavouring
225 g (8 oz) fresh scallops
225 g (8 oz) fresh haddock fillet
200 ml (7 fl oz) milk
salt and freshly ground pepper
plain flour
4 eggs, separated
30 ml (2 tbsp) single cream
fresh herbs, to garnish

1 First prepare the paper case. Cut two sheets of foil (to use as a double layer) or one sheet of strong non-stick baking parchment into a rectangle measuring 40.5×30.5 cm (16×12 inches). Fold up 2.5 cm (1 inch) around the edges, then snip in at the corners and secure with paper clips or staples. Brush the case generously with melted butter.

2 To prepare the fish stock, remove the heads and shells from the prawns, reserving the flesh, and place in a small saucepan with the wine, 200 ml (7 fl oz) water and the flavouring ingredients. Bring to the boil and simmer for 10 minutes. Strain the stock into a food processor, add the scallop roes and blend until smooth. Strain into a jug and reserve. Cut the white scallop flesh into small pieces and reserve.

3 Place the haddock in a small saucepan with the milk and seasoning. Bring to the boil, cover and simmer for about 8 minutes or until the fish is tender. Strain and reserve the liquor – there should be about 200 ml (7 fl oz). Flake the fish, discarding skin and bone.

4 Melt 50 g (2 oz) butter in a saucepan. Stir in 50 g (2 oz) flour followed by the reserved milk, then bring to the boil and cook for 1 minute, stirring all the time to make a very thick sauce. Take off the heat, allow to cool slightly, then mix in the flaked haddock and the egg yolks. Adjust the seasoning.

5 Whisk the egg whites until stiff but not dry. Stir one large spoonful into the fish sauce, then lightly fold in the remaining egg whites and pour gently into the paper case. Push the mixture out carefully to fill the case to the edges. Bake at 200°C (400°F) mark 6 for about 12 minutes or until lightly browned and just firm to the touch.

6 Meanwhile, add the scallops to the fish stock and simmer for 1–2 minutes. Take off the heat. Melt 25 g (1 oz) butter in a saucepan and stir in 30 ml (2 tbsp) flour, followed by the stock mixture. Bring to the boil, stirring all the time, and cook for 1 minute. Take off the heat and mix in the prawns and cream. Adjust the seasoning and keep warm in a bain-marie.

7 Have ready a large sheet of damp greaseproof paper. Snip the edges of the paper case, then flip the cooked roulade on to the sheet of paper.

8 Carefully ease off the paper case. Make a shallow cut along one short edge – this helps to start the roulade rolling up. Spread thinly with the sauce and fish mixture and roll up from the short edge. Lift carefully on to a serving platter and garnish with fresh herbs. Serve immediately, accompanied by the remaining sauce.

PÂTÉ DE FOIE DE VOLAILLE

225 g (8 oz) butter, softened
2 garlic cloves, skinned and crushed
1 bay leaf
5 ml (1 tsp) chopped fresh herbs or a pinch of dried mixed herbs
450 g (1 lb) chicken livers, trimmed
30 ml (2 tbsp) brandy
30 ml (2 tbsp) Madeira
salt and freshly ground pepper
extra butter and chopped parsley, to seal (optional)

1 Melt half the butter in a large sauté pan and add the garlic, bay leaf, herbs and chicken livers. Cook over a high heat for 5 minutes, stirring. Leave to cool.

2 Remove the bay leaf, then transfer the contents of the pan to a blender or food processor and blend until smooth. (Push the mixture through a sieve for an extra fine texture, if wished.)

3 Add the brandy and Madeira to the sauté pan. Bring to the boil, scraping any sediment from the base, then strain into the liver mixture. Beat in the remaining butter and season to taste.

4 Pour the pâté mixture into an earthenware dish, cover and refrigerate overnight. Leave at room temperature for 15–20 minutes before serving. If the pâté is to be kept for 3–4 days, pour melted butter and chopped parsley over the surface to form a seal.

AVOCADO WITH FENNEL AND PRAWNS

45 ml (3 tbsp) light salad oil
15 ml (1 tbsp) lemon juice
salt and freshly ground pepper
1 head of fennel, trimmed
2 ripe avocados, halved, stoned and peeled
225 g (8 oz) cooked peeled prawns or 16 large cooked peeled prawns
30 ml (2 tbsp) chopped fresh dill
brown bread and butter, to accompany

1 Whisk together the oil, lemon juice and seasoning.
2 Cut the fennel and avocado into neat strips and arrange on serving plates with the prawns.
3 Spoon over the dressing, sprinkle with dill and serve immediately, accompanied by brown bread and butter.

TOMATOES WITH GOAT'S CHEESE AND BASIL

200 ml (7 fl oz) olive oil
2 small garlic cloves, skinned and crushed
75 ml (5 tbsp) white wine vinegar
25 ml (1½ tbsp) Dijon mustard
salt and freshly ground pepper
8 medium-sized tomatoes
150 g (5 oz) mozzarella cheese
fresh basil
225 g (8 oz) rindless goat's cheese
8 thick slices of white bread
butter or margarine
salad leaves, to garnish

1 To make the vinaigrette dressing, whisk together the first five ingredients.
2 Cut a thin slice from the bottom (opposite the stalk end) of each tomato and discard. Using a small, sharp knife or a teaspoon, carefully scoop out all the flesh and seeds, keeping the tomato shells whole. Strain the scooped-out tomato pulp and reserve the juices.
3 Coarsely grate or finely chop the mozzarella cheese. Finely chop 45 ml (3 tbsp) fresh basil. Mix both together with the goat's cheese and enough reserved tomato juice to form a thick, creamy mixture. Season to taste, then spoon into the prepared tomato shells.

4 Using a plain, round 9 cm (3½ inch) pastry cutter, stamp out eight rounds from the bread slices. Toast the rounds on both sides and lay in a lightly buttered ovenproof dish. Place each tomato on top of a toasted bread round.
5 Cook, uncovered, in the oven at 180°C (350°F) mark 4 for about 25 minutes or until the cheese mixture looks melted and golden and the tomatoes are lightly cooked but not too soft. Remove from the oven and finish by browning under a hot grill.
6 Garnish the tomatoes with salad leaves and serve the dressing separately.

ARTICHOKE AND HAM SALAD

three 312 g (11 oz) cans artichoke hearts, drained
75 g (3 oz) pine nuts, toasted
135 ml (9 tbsp) olive oil
45 ml (3 tbsp) red wine vinegar
25 ml (1½ tbsp) snipped fresh chives (optional)
18 black olives, pitted and roughly chopped
freshly ground black pepper
350 g (12 oz) prosciutto crudo, very thinly sliced
Warm Lemon Bread, to accompany

1 Cut the artichokes into quarters and place in a medium mixing bowl. Stir in the toasted pine nuts.
2 Whisk together the olive oil, red wine vinegar and chives, if using. Stir in the olives. Pour the dressing over the artichoke mixture and stir well. Season with pepper only, as the ham and olives will add enough salt.
3 Arrange the ham on individual dishes. Spoon over the artichoke mixture and the dressing. Serve accompanied by Warm Lemon Bread (below).

WARM LEMON BREAD

1 large crusty loaf
olive oil
juice of 1 large lemon
freshly ground black pepper

1 Cut the loaf into large chunks and place on a large sheet of foil. Drizzle over 90–120 ml (6–8 tbsp) olive oil and about 45 ml (3 tbsp) lemon juice. Season generously with black pepper, then wrap tightly in foil.
2 Heat at 200°C (400°F) mark 6 for about 25 minutes. Serve immediately.

CHICKEN LIVER AND WALNUT PÂTÉ

30 ml (2 tbsp) oil
550 g (1¼ lb) chicken livers, trimmed
1 small onion, skinned and finely chopped
7.5 ml (1½ tsp) dried tarragon
2 garlic cloves, skinned and crushed
275–350 g (10–12 oz) unsalted butter
25 ml (1½ tbsp) brandy or sherry
150 g (5 oz) walnut pieces, toasted
75 ml (5 tbsp) double cream
salt and freshly ground pepper

1 Heat the oil in a large sauté pan and sauté the livers, onion, tarragon and garlic for 3–4 minutes or until well browned. The livers should still be slightly pink in the centre. Stir in 225 g (8 oz) butter, the brandy or sherry and 125 g (4 oz) walnuts. Mix until evenly blended, then leave to cool slightly.
2 Put the liver mixture in a blender or food processor and process with the double cream until smooth. Season to taste. Push the mixture through a fine sieve, then spoon into a serving dish. Refrigerate for at least 1 hour to set.
3 Melt the remaining butter. Roughly chop the remaining walnuts and sprinkle over the surface of the pâté. Spoon over the melted butter to cover the pâté completely. Refrigerate again to set. The pâté will keep in the refrigerator for about a week.

TAPENADE

two 50 g (2 oz) cans anchovy fillets
milk
175 g (6 oz) pitted black olives – about 72
120 ml (8 tbsp) capers
two 100 g (3½ oz) cans tuna fish in oil, drained
125 ml (4 fl oz) olive oil
30 ml (2 tbsp) lemon juice
about 30 ml (2 tbsp) brandy
freshly ground black pepper
hot bread or toast, to accompany

1 Soak the anchovies for 30 minutes in a little milk. Drain well.
2 Place the anchovies, olives, capers and tuna fish in a blender or food processor and blend to a thick paste.
3 Add the olive oil and lemon juice, drop by drop, as if making mayonnaise, to form a smooth paste. Add the brandy and black pepper to taste.

BEEF WELLINGTON

1.8 kg (4 lb) beef fillet, in one piece
20 ml (4 tsp) brandy
salt and freshly ground pepper
125 g (4 oz) butter
2 onions, skinned and finely chopped
350 g (12 oz) mushrooms, wiped and finely chopped
450 g (1 lb) puff pastry
175 g (6 oz) smooth pâté (chicken, duck or goose liver)
2 eggs, lightly beaten
S A U C E
50 g (2 oz) butter
1 small onion, finely chopped
125 g (4 oz) mushrooms, wiped and finely chopped
30 ml (2 level tbsp) plain flour
600 ml (1 pint) beef stock
300 ml (½ pint) red wine
salt and freshly ground pepper

1 Trim the fat from the beef, brush with brandy and season with pepper. Melt the butter in a frying pan, add the beef and fry for 2 minutes, turning to seal all over. Remove from the pan and roast in the oven at 200°C (400°F) mark 6 for 15 minutes.

2 Meanwhile, add the onion to the pan and fry for 10 minutes. Add the mushrooms and fry for 4–5 minutes or until most of the moisture has evaporated. Season and leave to cool. Remove the meat from the oven and cool completely.

3 Roll out the pastry to a large rectangle. Mix the pâté with 60 ml (4 tbsp) of the onion and mushroom mixture and spread it over the top of the beef. Place the meat, pâté side down, in the centre of the pastry and cover the meat with the remaining mushroom mixture. Brush the edges of the pastry with beaten egg and wrap the fillet in the pastry. Press the edges to seal and place, join side down, on a baking sheet.

4 Re-roll the pastry trimmings and use to decorate. Brush with beaten egg. Bake in the oven at 200°C (400°F) mark 6 for 20 minutes or until the pastry is golden brown. Transfer to a warmed serving dish.

5 Meanwhile, make the sauce. Melt the butter in a saucepan and fry the onion for 5 minutes, then add the mushrooms and cook for a further 3 minutes. Stir in the flour and cook for 1 minute. Gradually stir in the stock and red wine, bring to the boil, then simmer for 10 minutes. Season, strain and serve with the beef.

BOEUF BOURGUIGNON

50 g (2 oz) butter
60 ml (4 tbsp) vegetable oil
225 g (8 oz) bacon in a piece, rinded and diced
1.8 kg (4 lb) braising steak or topside, cubed
2 garlic cloves, skinned and crushed
60 ml (4 level tbsp) plain flour
salt and freshly ground pepper
bouquet garni
300 ml (½ pint) beef stock
600 ml (1 pint) red Burgundy
24 small onions, skinned
350 g (12 oz) button mushrooms, wiped
chopped fresh parsley, to garnish

1 Heat half the butter and oil in a flameproof casserole and fry the bacon for 5 minutes. Drain. Fry the meat in batches for about 8 minutes or until browned.

2 Return the bacon to the casserole with the garlic. Sprinkle with the flour and stir in. Add seasoning, the bouquet garni, stock and wine, then bring to the boil, stirring. Cover and cook in the oven at 170°C (325°F) mark 3 for 1½ hours.

3 Meanwhile, heat the remaining butter and oil and sauté the whole onions for 10 minutes or until golden brown. Remove from the pan. Add the mushrooms to the pan and fry for 5 minutes.

4 Add the mushrooms and onions to the casserole and cook for a further 30 minutes or until the meat is tender. Skim and serve garnished with parsley.

STEAK AND STILTON PARCELS

4 quick-fry steaks, about 700–900 g (1½–2 lb) total weight
oil
175 g (6 oz) blue Stilton cheese
30 ml (2 tbsp) chopped fresh tarragon or 5 ml (1 tsp) dried
120 ml (8 tbsp) single cream
freshly ground black pepper
125 g (4 oz) butter
10 large sheets of filo pastry, measuring about 45.5 × 25.5cm (18 × 10 inches) each
lemon juice, to serve

1 Halve each steak. Heat some oil in a frying pan and seal the meat quickly in the hot oil. Leave to cool.

2 Grate the cheese or soften with a fork. Mix with the tarragon, cream and black pepper (the Stilton should add sufficient salt) and spread the mixture over the cold steaks.

3 Melt the butter. Brush one sheet of filo pastry with butter and wrap around one steak to enclose it completely like a parcel. Place on a baking sheet and brush with more butter. Repeat to wrap all the steaks in the same way.

4 Brush the last two sheets of filo with butter and fold over and over to form strips about 2.5 cm (1 inch) wide. Cut into diamond shapes and use to decorate the parcels. Brush with melted butter. Chill for about 20 minutes.

5 Bake the steak parcels at 220°C (425°F) mark 7 for 15–20 minutes or until well browned. Squeeze lemon juice over the parcels before serving.

ITALIAN BRAISED BEEF

1.4 kg (3 lb) braising steak
450 g (1 lb) onions, skinned and roughly chopped
3 large garlic cloves, skinned and crushed
1 litre (1¾ pints) Chianti
olive oil
45 ml (3 tbsp) tomato purée
25 ml (1½ tbsp) wine vinegar
salt and freshly ground pepper
large bunch of fresh thyme or 15 ml (1 tbsp) dried thyme
75 g (3 oz) plain flour
450 ml (¾ pint) stock
225 g (8 oz) brown cap or button mushrooms, halved or quartered
397 g (14 oz) can artichoke hearts, drained and halved or quartered
about 24 pitted black olives

1 Cut the beef into large cubes, discarding any excess fat. Place the beef, onion and garlic in a glass bowl with the wine, 60 ml (4 tbsp) olive oil, the tomato purée, vinegar and seasoning. Add the fresh thyme, tied in a bundle, or sprinkle in the dried thyme. Stir thoroughly to mix, then cover and leave to marinate in the refrigerator for at least 24 hours.

2 Strain off the marinade and reserve. Heat about 90 ml (6 tbsp) olive oil in a large flameproof casserole. Brown the meat, in batches, adding a little more oil if necessary. Remove all the meat from the casserole using a slotted spoon.

3 Stir the flour into the remaining oil and cook for about 1 minute. Pour in the marinade and stock and bring to the boil.

Replace the meat, cover tightly, then bake at 170°C (325°F) mark 3 for about 2 hours or until the meat is tender.

4 About 15 minutes before serving, stir the mushrooms and artichokes into the casserole with the olives. Adjust the seasoning and serve.

STEAK DIANE

8 pieces of fillet steak, 0.5 cm (¼ inch) thick, trimmed of excess fat
50 g (2 oz) butter or margarine
60 ml (4 tbsp) vegetable oil
60 ml (4 tbsp) Worcestershire sauce
30 ml (2 tbsp) lemon juice
2 small onions, skinned and grated
15 ml (1 tbsp) chopped fresh parsley

1 Fry the steaks in the butter or margarine and oil for 1–2 minutes on each side. Remove with a slotted spoon and keep warm. Stir the Worcestershire sauce and lemon juice into the pan juices.

2 Warm through, then add the onion and parsley and cook gently for 1 minute. Serve the sauce spooned over the steaks.

STEAK AU POIVRE

8 sirloin, rump or fillet steaks, trimmed of excess fat
60 ml (4 tbsp) black or green peppercorns, coarsely crushed
8 sirloin, rump or fillet steaks, trimmed of excess fat
50 g (2 oz) butter or margarine
30 ml (2 tbsp) vegetable oil
salt
60 ml (4 tbsp) brandy
300 ml (½ pint) double cream

1 Place the steaks on the crushed peppercorns and press hard to encrust the surface of the meat. Turn to encrust the other side of each steak.

2 Heat the butter or margarine and oil in a frying pan and fry the steaks for 2 minutes on each side. Reduce the heat and continue cooking until cooked to taste. Season with salt.

3 Remove the steaks from the pan and keep warm. Add the brandy to the pan, remove from the heat and set it alight. Keep off the heat until the flames have died down, then stir in the cream. Season and reheat gently. Pour over the steaks.

BEEF AND CHESTNUT CASSEROLE

450 g (1 lb) fresh, unpeeled chestnuts
700 g (1½ lb) stewing beef, in a piece
225 g (8 oz) haunch of venison
oil
1 garlic clove, skinned and crushed
450 g (1 lb) onions, skinned and roughly chopped
225 g (8 oz) carrots, thickly sliced
225 g (8 oz) celery, trimmed and thickly sliced
15 ml (1 level tbsp) plain flour
15 ml (1 tbsp) tomato purée
450 ml (¾ pint) beef stock
150 g (5 oz) no-soak dried apricots
2 bay leaves
pared rind and juice of 1 orange
300 ml (½ pint) Madeira
salt and freshly ground pepper
chopped fresh parsley, to garnish

1 Make a small slit in the skin of each chestnut. Drop into boiling water, cover and cook for 1 minute, then drain and peel off the outer and inner skins. Trim the meats and cut into 4 cm (1½ inch) pieces.

2 Heat 45 ml (3 tbsp) oil in a large, flameproof casserole. Brown the meat well in batches, adding more oil if necessary. Remove the meat and drain.

3 Add the garlic, onion, carrots and celery to the casserole and sauté, stirring, until golden. Add the flour and tomato purée. Cook for a further 1 minute before stirring in the stock, chestnuts, apricots, bay leaves, orange rind, 45 ml (3 tbsp) orange juice and all but 50 ml (2 fl oz) of the Madeira. Season and stir in the meat.

4 Bring to the boil, cover tightly and cook at 170°C (325°F) mark 3 for 2–2½ hours or until the meat is very tender. Adjust the seasoning, stir in the remaining Madeira and garnish with parsley.

VEAL AND ROSEMARY GRATIN

175 ml (6 fl oz) olive oil
1 large onion, skinned and finely chopped
175 g (6 oz) carrot, finely chopped
3 celery sticks, trimmed and finely chopped
225 g (8 oz) red pepper, cored, seeded and finely chopped
350 g (12 oz) each of minced beef and minced veal, or all beef
plain flour
450 ml (¾ pint) beef stock
200 ml (7 fl oz) red wine
175 g (6 oz) Parma ham, snipped into pieces (optional)
45 ml (3 tbsp) chopped fresh rosemary or 15 ml (1 tbsp) dried
1 bay leaf
salt and freshly ground black pepper
200 g (7 oz) conchiglie rigate (about 36) or cannelloni (about 24)
75 g (3 oz) butter or margarine
750 ml (1¼ pints) milk
75 g (3 oz) pecorino or Parmesan cheese, grated

1 Heat the oil in a large sauté pan, add the onion, carrot, celery and red pepper and cook until the vegetables soften and begin to colour.

2 Add the beef and veal and cook over a high heat, stirring frequently until the meat begins to brown. Stir in 10 ml (2 tsp) flour and cook for a further minute. Pour in the stock and red wine with the ham, rosemary and bay leaf and season to taste. Slowly bring to the boil, cover and simmer gently for about 1 hour. (If necessary, uncover the pan, increase the heat and cook until the mixture has reduced to a thick sauce.)

3 Cook the pasta in plenty of boiling salted water until just tender. Drain well.

4 Fill the shells or tubes with the mince mixture and place in a single layer in one or two ovenproof dishes.

5 Melt the butter or margarine in a saucepan. Add 75 g (3 oz) flour and cook, stirring, for 1–2 minutes before gradually adding the milk. Bring to the boil, then simmer, stirring occasionally, for 2–3 minutes. Remove the pan from the heat and beat in half the grated cheese, adding black pepper to taste. Spoon over the pasta and sprinkle with the remaining cheese.

6 Bake at 180°C (350°F) mark 4 for about 40 minutes or until golden and bubbling.

THYME ROASTED LOIN OF LAMB

125 g (4 oz) butter or margarine
275 g (10 oz) button mushrooms, wiped and finely chopped
2 garlic cloves, skinned and crushed
175 g (6 oz) fresh spinach, trimmed
salt and freshly ground pepper
2 boned and rolled loins of lamb, about 900 g (2 lb) each
grated nutmeg
25 ml (1½ tbsp) chopped fresh thyme or 15 ml (1 tbsp) dried
grated rind and juice of 1 large lemon
thyme sprigs, to garnish

1 Melt 25 g (1 oz) butter or margarine in a sauté pan and add the mushrooms and garlic. Cook, stirring, over a high heat for 4-5 minutes or until the mushrooms are well reduced and all the excess liquid has evaporated. Leave to cool.

2 Wash the spinach well in several changes of cold water. Blanch in boiling salted water for 10–15 seconds or until just beginning to wilt. Drain well. Separate the leaves out on to absorbent kitchen paper, then leave to cool.

3 Unroll the loins of lamb and line the insides with cold spinach. Spoon the mushroom mixture along the middle of each joint. Season with salt, pepper and nutmeg, then re-roll the joints and tie securely with fine string. Beat the remaining butter or margarine with the thyme, lemon rind and 30 ml (2 tbsp) lemon juice. Spread all over the lamb.

4 Place the lamb joints in a roasting tin and cook at 220°C (425°F) mark 7 for 20 minutes. Reduce the oven temperature to 180°C (350°F) mark 4 for a further 30 minutes. Serve the lamb carved into thin slices garnished with fresh thyme sprigs.

CROWN ROAST OF LAMB

2 best end necks of lamb, chined, each with 8 cutlets
40 g (1½ oz) butter or margarine
1 large onion, skinned and chopped
4 celery sticks, trimmed and chopped
1 large eating apple, peeled, cored and chopped
50 g (2 oz) dried apricots, soaked overnight
150 g (5 oz) fresh breadcrumbs
30 ml (2 tbsp) chopped fresh parsley
finely grated rind of ½ a large lemon
25 ml (1½ tbsp) lemon juice
1 egg, beaten
salt and freshly ground pepper
75 g (3 oz) lard or 45 ml (3 tbsp) vegetable oil
45 ml (3 level tbsp) plain flour
600 ml (1 pint) stock

1 Trim each cutlet bone to a depth of 2.5 cm (1 inch). Bend the joints around, fat side inwards, and sew together using strong cotton or fine string to form a crown. Cover the exposed bones with foil.

2 Melt the butter or margarine in a saucepan and cook the onion, celery and apple until brown. Drain, dry and chop the apricots and stir into the pan with the breadcrumbs, parsley, lemon rind and juice, egg and seasoning. Allow to cool, then fill the centre of the joint with the stuffing and weigh.

3 Place the joint in a small roasting tin with the lard or oil. Roast at 180°C (350°F) mark 4 for 25 minutes per 450 g (1 lb) plus 25 minutes. Baste occasionally and cover with foil if necessary.

4 Transfer the crown roast to a warmed serving dish and keep warm. Drain off all but 45 ml (3 tbsp) of the fat in the roasting tin, add the flour and blend well. Cook for 2–3 minutes, stirring all the time. Add the stock and boil for 2–3 minutes. Season and serve hot with the joint.

Variation:

GUARD OF HONOUR

This is also prepared from two best ends of neck. Trim as above but interlace the bones, fat side outwards, to form an arch. Fill the cavity with the stuffing (as above) and fasten together with strong thread or fine string. Cook as above.

ROAST LAMB FILLETS WITH GARLIC

900 g (2 lb) lamb neck fillet, trimmed
4 large garlic cloves, skinned and thinly sliced
30 ml (2 tbsp) chopped fresh rosemary or 10 ml (2 tsp) dried
salt and freshly ground pepper
16 rashers of streaky bacon, rinded
oil
15 ml (1 level tbsp) plain flour
600 ml (1 pint) stock
20 ml (4 tsp) Dijon mustard
a dash of gravy browning (optional)

1 Divide the fillet into eight pieces. Split each piece lengthways and open out like a book. Sprinkle the garlic and rosemary inside the fillets and season with pepper. Close the fillets.

2 Stretch the bacon rashers with the back of a knife and wrap around the fillets, securing with cocktail sticks.

3 Heat a little oil in a roasting tin. Add the lamb and bake at 200°C (400°F) mark 6 for 30–35 minutes until tender.

4 Slice the lamb into 5 mm (¼ inch) thick pieces, discarding the cocktail sticks. Cover and keep warm.

5 Pour all but 60 ml (4 tbsp) juice out of the tin. Stir in the flour and brown lightly. Add the stock, mustard, gravy browning, if using, and seasoning and bubble for a few minutes.

LAMB NOISETTES WITH MUSHROOMS AND ONIONS

16–24 noisettes of lamb
plain flour, for coating
25 g (1 oz) butter
60 ml (4 tbsp) vegetable oil
450 g (1 lb) button onions, skinned
2 garlic cloves, skinned and finely chopped
900 g (2 lb) small button mushrooms, wiped
600 ml (1 pint) dry white wine
sprigs of fresh rosemary or 5 ml (1 tsp) dried
salt and freshly ground pepper
sprigs of fresh rosemary, to garnish

1 Coat the lamb noisettes in flour. Heat the butter and oil in a large frying pan and brown the noisettes quickly on both sides. Remove from the pan.

2 Add the onions and garlic to the fat remaining in the pan and fry for about 5 minutes or until lightly browned. Add the mushrooms and fry for 2–3 minutes.

3 Stir in the wine, rosemary and salt and pepper to taste. Replace the noisettes in the pan, bring to the boil, then cover and simmer for 30–40 minutes or until tender, turning once.

4 Remove the string from the noisettes and arrange on a warmed serving dish. Add the vegetables and keep warm.

5 Bring the remaining liquid to the boil and boil rapidly until reduced by half. Pour the wine sauce over the noisettes and serve garnished with sprigs of rosemary.

LOIN OF PORK WITH FRUIT STUFFING

2.7 kg (6 lb) loin of pork, boned
15 ml (1 tbsp) ground allspice
salt and freshly ground pepper
6 garlic cloves, skinned and sliced
350 g (12 oz) mixed dried fruit (pears, prunes, apricots, figs), finely chopped
175 g (6 oz) fresh cranberries or frozen cranberries, thawed
450 ml (¾ pint) full-bodied red wine
3–4 bay leaves
45 ml (3 tbsp) bottled cranberry sauce
fresh bay leaves, to garnish

1 Cut the rind off the pork, together with all but a very thin layer of fat next to the meat.

2 Lay the meat flat, fat side down. Slice lengthways, two thirds of the way through the thick side of the 'eye' of the meat. Open up the joint like a book. Rub the allspice into the flesh, with salt and pepper to taste.

3 Sprinkle the garlic along the length of the meat. Mix the dried fruit with the cranberries, then place on top of the garlic.

4 Form the joint into a roll and tie at close intervals. Weigh the joint and calculate the cooking time, allowing 35 minutes per 450 g (1 lb) plus 35 minutes. Put the joint in a large flameproof casserole or roasting tin and place over moderate heat. Fry the joint in its own fat until browned on all sides, then pour in the wine. Add the bay leaves and seasoning.

5 Bring to the boil, then cover and cook in the oven at 150°C (300°F) mark 2 for the calculated cooking time. Baste frequently and turn the joint round in the liquid every 30 minutes.

6 Place the joint on a warmed serving dish and leave to stand in a warm place for 15 minutes before carving. Transfer the casserole or tin to the top of the cooker. Discard the bay leaves, then boil the cooking liquid to reduce slightly. Stir in the cranberry sauce and heat through, then pour into a gravy boat or jug. Slice the pork, garnish with fresh bay leaves and serve with the sauce.

BAKED HAM GLAZED WITH HONEY, ORANGE AND GINGER

1.8 kg (4 lb) smoked middle cut gammon
1 onion stuck with 3 cloves
1 bay leaf
6 peppercorns
300 ml (½ pint) dry white wine
40 g (1½ oz) dark brown sugar
125 ml (4 fl oz) orange juice
15 ml (1 tbsp) clear honey
2.5 ml (½ tsp) ground ginger
15 ml (1 tbsp) Dijon mustard
whole cloves

1 Soak the ham in sufficient cold water to cover for 3 hours, then discard the water.

2 Place the ham, onion stuck with cloves, bay leaf, peppercorns and 225 ml (8 fl oz) of the white wine in a saucepan. Add cold water to cover. Bring to the boil, cover the pan and boil gently for 1 hour.

3 Meanwhile, make the glaze. Place the brown sugar, 30 ml (2 tbsp) of the orange juice, the honey, ginger and mustard in a bowl and mix well.

4 Drain the ham and discard the onion and spices. (Reserve the stock for soup if it is not too salty.) Remove the skin from the ham, score the fat into a diamond pattern, and stud with cloves. Place the ham in a baking dish and pour the remaining wine and orange juice into the pan.

5 Cover the ham with one third of the glaze. Bake at 200°C (400°F) mark 6 for 45 minutes. Baste the ham with the pan juices, and glaze 3–4 times during cooking. Discard the pan juices and serve the ham hot or cold.

ITALIAN-STYLE BRAISED PORK

25 ml (1½ tbsp) vegetable oil
40 g (1½ oz) butter
2.7 kg (6 lb) loin of pork, boned, rinded and tied into a neat joint
3 garlic cloves, skinned
2 small onions, skinned and chopped
900 ml (1½ pints) milk
7 juniper berries
3 rosemary sprigs, plus extra for garnish
salt and freshly ground pepper
150 ml (¼ pint) double cream

1 Heat the oil and the butter in a large saucepan or flameproof casserole into which the meat will just fit and fry the pork, garlic and onion for about 15 minutes or until the pork is browned on all sides. Add the milk, juniper berries, rosemary and seasoning.

2 Bring to the boil, cover, turn the heat down and cook for about 1½ hours or until the pork is tender, turning and basting from time to time.

3 Transfer the pork to a warmed serving dish and carve into thick slices. Keep warm. The milky cooking juices will look curdled, so rub the sauce through a sieve. Return the sauce to the saucepan, skim off any fat, then stir in the cream. Bring to the boil and simmer for about 5 minutes until slightly reduced. Taste and adjust the seasoning. Pour a little of the sauce over the pork and serve the remaining sauce separately. Garnish with sprigs of rosemary.

COQ AU VIN

1 large chicken, jointed, or 8 chicken joints
30 ml (2 level tbsp) plain flour
salt and freshly ground pepper
125 g (4 oz) butter
125 g (4 oz) lean bacon, diced
1 medium onion, skinned and quartered
1 medium carrot, quartered
60 ml (4 tbsp) brandy
600 ml (1 pint) red wine
1 garlic clove, skinned and crushed
bouquet garni
1 sugar lump
30 ml (2 tbsp) vegetable oil
450 g (1 lb) button onions, skinned
pinch of sugar
5 ml (1 tsp) wine vinegar
225 g (8 oz) button mushrooms, wiped
6 slices of white bread, crusts removed

1 Coat the chicken pieces with 15 ml (1 tbsp) of the flour, liberally seasoned with salt and pepper.

2 Melt 25 g (1 oz) of the butter in a flameproof casserole, add the chicken pieces and fry gently until they are golden brown on all sides. Add the bacon, onion and carrot and fry until softened.

3 Heat the brandy in a small saucepan, pour over the chicken and ignite, shaking the pan so that all the chicken pieces are covered in flames. Pour on the wine and stir to loosen any sediment from the bottom of the casserole. Add the garlic, bouquet garni and sugar lump. Bring to the boil, cover and simmer for 1–1½ hours or until tender.

4 Meanwhile, melt another 25 g (1 oz) of the butter with 10 ml (2 tsp) of the oil in a frying pan. Add the button onions and fry until they begin to brown. Add the sugar and the vinegar, together with 15 ml (1 tbsp) water. Cover and simmer for 10–15 minutes or until just tender. Keep warm.

5 Melt 25 g (1 oz) of the butter with 10 ml (2 tsp) oil in a pan and add the mushrooms. Cook for a few minutes. Keep warm. Remove the chicken from the casserole and place in a serving dish. Surround with onions and mushrooms and keep hot.

6 Discard the bouquet garni. Skim the excess fat off the cooking liquid and boil the liquid in the casserole briskly for 3–5 minutes to reduce it.

7 Add the remaining oil to the fat in the frying pan and fry the pieces of bread until golden brown on both sides. Cut each slice into triangles.

8 Work the remaining flour and butter together to make a *beurre manié*. Take the casserole off the heat and add the *beurre manié* in small pieces to the cooking liquid. Stir until smooth, then bring just to the boil. The sauce should now be thick and shiny. Adjust the seasoning and pour over the chicken. Garnish with fried bread.

CHICKEN IN WHITE WINE

175 g (6 oz) lean bacon, rinded and diced
700 g (1½ lb) button onions, skinned
350 g (12 oz) button mushrooms, wiped
8 chicken quarters, halved
75 g (3 oz) plain flour
salt and freshly ground pepper
40 g (1½ oz) butter
45 ml (3 tbsp) vegetable oil
450 ml (¾ pint) dry white wine
450 ml (¾ pint) chicken stock
1 large garlic clove, skinned and crushed
sprigs of fresh thyme or 5 ml (1 tsp) dried
3 bay leaves
chopped fresh parsley, to garnish

1 Fry the bacon in its own fat in a large frying pan until beginning to brown. Add the onions and fry until browned, then add the mushrooms and fry for 2 minutes. Transfer the bacon and vegetables to a flameproof casserole with a slotted spoon.

2 Coat the chicken joints with the flour, seasoned with salt and pepper. Heat the butter and oil in the frying pan, add the chicken and fry until browned all over. Transfer the chicken to the casserole.

3 Gradually stir the white wine into the frying pan. Bring to the boil, scraping any sediment from the bottom of the pan, then pour over the chicken joints in the casserole.

4 Add the chicken stock, garlic, herbs and seasoning to taste to the frying pan. Bring to the boil, then pour over the chicken.

5 Cover and cook in the oven at 170°C (325°F) mark 3 for 1 hour or until the chicken is tender. Skim any fat from the cooking liquid. Garnish with chopped parsley.

CHICKEN WITH ORANGE AND OLIVES

5 red peppers
45 ml (3 tbsp) olive oil
40 g (1½ oz) butter or margarine
8 chicken breast fillets, skinned
2 medium onions, skinned and roughly chopped
1 large garlic clove, skinned and crushed
5 tomatoes, skinned, seeded and finely chopped
45 ml (3 tbsp) brandy
200 ml (7 fl oz) dry white wine
200 ml (7 fl oz) chicken stock
1 bay leaf
salt and freshly ground pepper
2 large oranges, peeled and segmented
8–10 green or black olives, halved and pitted

1 Core, seed and finely chop three of the red peppers.

2 Heat the oil and butter or margarine in a large flameproof casserole. Brown the chicken pieces, half at a time. Remove with a slotted spoon and drain on absorbent kitchen paper.

3 Lower the heat and add the onion and garlic. Sauté for 2–3 minutes or until beginning to soften but not colour. Stir in the chopped peppers and tomatoes and continue to cook, stirring occasionally, until the mixture gradually begins to soften and becomes pulpy.

4 Return the chicken to the casserole. Heat the brandy in a small pan, set alight and pour over the chicken. When the flames have subsided, add the wine, stock, bay leaf and seasoning. Bring to the boil, cover and cook at 170°C (325°F) mark 3 for about 45 minutes or until the chicken is tender.

5 Meanwhile, place the remaining two peppers under a hot grill and cook, turning occasionally, until the skins blacken. Peel away the skins with a small knife, running cold water over them at the same time. Cut the flesh into neat strips, discarding the seeds.

6 Remove the chicken from the casserole with a slotted spoon. Discard the bay leaf and purée the tomato and pepper juices in a blender or food processor. Return the chicken to the casserole and sieve in the puréed juices. Stir in the pepper strips with the orange segments and the olives. Simmer gently for 5–10 minutes and adjust the seasoning before serving.

CHICKEN AND SPICED APRICOT CASSEROLE

1.1 kg (2 ½ lb) chicken breast fillets, skinned
15 ml (1 tbsp) chopped fresh thyme or 5 ml (1 tsp) dried
pinch of ground cloves
2 garlic cloves, skinned and crushed
15 g (4 oz) no-soak dried apricots
15 ml (1 tbsp) clear honey
30 ml (2 tbsp) white wine vinegar
300 ml (½ pint) dry cider
2 whole cloves
50 g (2 oz) back bacon rashers, rinded
40 ml (2 ½ tbsp) vegetable oil
1 large onion, skinned and chopped
grated rind and juice of 1 orange
150 ml (¼ pint) Marsala
175 g (6 oz) fresh spinach, washed
about 15 ml (1 level tbsp) cornflour
salt and freshly ground pepper

1 Cut the chicken into chunks and place in a bowl with the thyme, ground cloves and garlic. Mix well and leave to marinate overnight in the refrigerator. Put the apricots, honey, vinegar, cider and cloves in a small saucepan and heat gently. Leave overnight, then discard the cloves.

2 Cut the bacon rashers in half and form into small rolls. In a large flameproof casserole, sauté the chicken in the oil until browned, then remove from the pan. Add the onion, bacon and orange rind and sauté for 2–3 minutes.

3 Return the chicken to the pan and stir in 45 ml (3 tbsp) orange juice, the Marsala, apricots and the liquid. Cover and simmer for 20–25 minutes or until the chicken is tender. Meanwhile, cook the spinach in the water clinging to its leaves. Drain well, finely chop then stir into the casserole.

4 Mix the cornflour with a little cold water and stir into the casserole to thicken the juices. Adjust the seasoning and serve.

LEMON AND LIME STIR FRIED CHICKEN

30 ml (2 tbsp) walnut oil
30 ml (2 tbsp) olive oil
90 ml (6 tbsp) each fresh lime and lemon juice
2 garlic cloves, skinned and crushed
salt and freshly ground pepper
1.1 kg (2 ½ lb) chicken breast fillets, skinned
2 bunches of spring onions, trimmed and sliced
350 g (12 oz) mange tout, trimmed
60 ml (4 tbsp) vegetable oil
125 g (4 oz) shelled pecan nuts or walnuts

1 Whisk together the oils, lime and lemon juice, garlic and seasoning in a medium bowl. Cut the chicken into fine strips. Add the chicken and spring onions to the marinade, cover and leave to marinate in the refrigerator for at least 4 hours.

2 Blanch the mange tout in boiling salted water for 1 minute only. Drain and rinse in cold water.

3 Heat the vegetable oil in a large wok or frying pan. Drain the chicken from the marinade, reserving the juices. Add the chicken and nuts to the pan and stir fry over a high heat for a few minutes or until the chicken is golden brown and tender.

4 Add the mange tout with the reserved marinade juices and bubble for 1–2 minutes or until piping hot. Adjust the seasoning and serve immediately.

TURKEY AND WATERCRESS ROULADES

125 g (4 oz) butter or margarine
125 g (4 oz) Brazil nuts, roughly chopped
15 ml (1 tbsp) ground cumin
2 garlic cloves, skinned and crushed
2 bunches of watercress, trimmed and finely chopped
350 g (12 oz) full fat soft cheese, such as Philadelphia
finely grated rind and juice of 2 lemons
salt and freshly ground pepper
1.4 kg (3 lb) turkey breast steaks (escalopes)
60 ml (4 level tbsp) plain flour
30 ml (2 tbsp) vegetable oil
600 ml (1 pint) turkey or chicken stock
225 ml (8 fl oz) dry vermouth
60 ml (4 tbsp) single cream
watercress sprigs or chopped watercress, to garnish

1 Heat half of the butter or margarine in a frying pan. Add the nuts, cumin and garlic and stir fry until beginning to brown. Mix in the watercress and stir fry until all excess moisture has been driven off. Turn into a bowl and leave to cool.

2 Beat the watercress mixture together with the cheese and lemon rind. Season, cover and chill.

3 Meanwhile, place the turkey breast steaks between sheets of film and bat out until very thin. Cut them up into 20–24 even-sized pieces.

4 Divide the stuffing mixture among the turkey steaks. Roll up and secure with wooden cocktail sticks. Sprinkle the rolls with seasoned flour, reserving any excess.

5 Heat the oil with the remaining butter or margarine in a shallow flameproof casserole. Brown the turkey rolls in two batches. Remove from the casserole.

6 Stir any remaining flour into the pan juices. Pour in the stock and vermouth and bring to the boil. Season and stir in 30 ml (2 tbsp) lemon juice. Return the turkey rolls to the pan.

7 Cover the casserole and bake at 180°C (350°F) mark 4 for about 35 minutes or until the meat is tender. Lift the rolls out of the casserole and remove the cocktail sticks. Cover and keep warm.

8 Strain the cooking juices and boil to reduce slightly. Take off the heat, stir in the cream and adjust the seasoning. Halve the turkey rolls and spoon over a little of the sauce. Serve the remainder separately. Garnish with watercress.

BONED TURKEY WITH CHICKEN LIVER MOUSSE

125 g (4 oz) unsalted butter
450 g (1 lb) chicken livers, trimmed
1 eating apple, peeled, cored and roughly chopped
75 g (3 oz) rindless streaky bacon, roughly chopped
1 small onion, skinned and roughly chopped
45 ml (3 tbsp) chopped fresh tarragon or 2.5 ml (½ tsp) dried
60 ml (4 tbsp) dry sherry
salt and freshly ground pepper
two 700 g (1½ lb) boneless turkey breasts, not previously frozen
45 ml (3 tbsp) chopped fresh parsley
24 pistachio nuts, shelled and skinned
mixed salad leaves, radicchio, lamb's lettuce, frisée, endive etc, and fresh poached and cooled cranberries, to serve

1 Melt half of the butter in a large sauté pan and brown the chicken livers well on all sides, adding half at a time.

2 Return all the livers to the pan with the apple, bacon, onion and tarragon. Stir together over a high heat for about 5 minutes. Remove from the heat and stir in the sherry, then leave to cool.

3 Blend the mixture in a blender or food processor with the remaining butter. Press it all through a fine sieve into a bowl and season to taste. Cover the dish with film and chill well for 30 minutes.

4 Skin the turkey breasts and remove the false fillets (the loose piece of flesh underneath) from each one. Place all the turkey pieces between two sheets of damp greaseproof paper and bat out the flesh as much as possible with a rolling pin to make thinner, flatter pieces.

5 Place one of the larger turkey pieces on a sheet of buttered foil. Sprinkle with 15 ml (1 tbsp) chopped fresh parsley. Spread one third of the chicken liver mousse over the parsley and dot over the top with one third of the pistachio nuts.

6 Place one of the false fillets on top and repeat the parsley, mousse and pistachio layers. Add the remaining false fillet and repeat the layers as before. Finish with the remaining large piece of turkey. Tie the whole turkey together securely at 2.5 cm (1 inch) intervals with fine string. Wrap tightly in a double layer of foil and place in a baking tin.

7 Cook at 190°C (375°F) mark 5 for about 1½ hours or until the juices run clear. Carefully pour off any excess fat. Place the wrapped turkey joint in a 900 g

(2 lb) loaf tin. Cover with foil and weight down. When cool enough, place in the refrigerator and leave overnight.

8 To serve, turn out of the tin, unwrap, slice thickly and serve with mixed salad leaves and fresh poached and cooled cranberries.

MUSTARD ROASTED TURKEY

1 quantity Apricot and Pecan Stuffing (see opposite)
oven ready turkey (about 4.5 kg/10 lb)
45 ml (3 tbsp) Dijon mustard
butter or margarine
salt and freshly ground black pepper
about 450 ml (¾ pint) turkey or chicken stock
60 ml (4 tbsp) Madeira (optional)
grated rind and juice of 1 orange
about 60 ml (4 level tbsp) cornflour
watercress, to garnish

1 Spoon the Apricot and Pecan Stuffing into the neck end of the turkey only. Secure the flap of skin with a fine skewer or wooden cocktail sticks. Truss or tie the turkey and weigh the bird. Calculate the cooking time, allowing about 20 minutes per 450 g (1 lb).

2 Place the turkey on a large, strong sheet of foil, then lift into a large roasting tin. Spread the breast and legs thinly with the Dijon mustard. Dot generously with butter or margarine and grind over some black pepper. Fold the sheet of foil loosely around the turkey to enclose completely.

3 Cook in the oven at 180°C (350°F) mark 4 for about 3 hours. Fold the foil back, baste well and return to the oven for a further 45 minutes–1 hour. The turkey will be a rich golden brown. Test the thickest part of the leg with a fine skewer, the juices should run clear if the bird is cooked. Return to the oven for a little longer if necessary, laying a sheet of foil loosely over the bird once well browned.

4 Lift the turkey on to a serving dish, cover and keep warm. Pour the cooking liquor into a saucepan and skim well. Add the stock, Madeira, if using, orange rind and juice. Boil for 4–5 minutes to reduce slightly.

5 Mix the cornflour to a smooth paste with a little water. Stir into the pan juices and bring to the boil. Simmer for 1–2 minutes or until slightly thickened. Adjust the seasoning. Garnish the turkey with sprigs of watercress and serve with the gravy.

DUCKLING WITH MUSHROOM STUFFING

50 g (2 oz) butter or margarine
1 medium onion, skinned and finely chopped
1 large garlic clove, skinned and crushed
125 g (4 oz) button mushrooms, wiped and finely chopped
175 g (6 oz) ham, in one piece, diced
1 large bunch of watercress, trimmed and finely chopped
225 g (8 oz) minced pork
125 g (4 oz) fresh white breadcrumbs
grated rind and juice of 3 lemons
2 eggs, 1 egg yolk
salt and freshly ground pepper
2.7 kg (6 lb) oven ready duckling, boned
watercress and celery tops, to garnish
Apple and Celery Glaze, to serve (see opposite)

1 Melt the butter or margarine in a medium pan and sauté the onion, garlic and mushrooms, stirring, for 4–5 minutes or until the mixture softens and most of the liquid has evaporated. Leave to cool.

2 In a medium bowl, mix together the ham, watercress, pork, breadcrumbs, lemon rind and 45 ml (3 tbsp) strained lemon juice. Stir in the onion and mushroom mixture, then beat in the whole eggs, egg yolk and seasoning.

3 Lay the duckling, skin side down, on a worksurface.

4 Pile the stuffing down the centre of the duckling and pat into a thick sausage shape. Fold the flesh over the stuffing to enclose completely and sew up neatly with needle and cotton. Weigh the duckling.

5 Put the duckling on a wire rack over a roasting tin. Prick lightly with a skewer and sprinkle with a little salt. Cook at 180°C (350°F) mark 4 for 25 minutes per 450 g (1 lb) or until the juices run clear. Garnish with sprigs of watercress and leafy celery tops. Serve thickly sliced with Apple and Celery Glaze

POT ROASTED POUSSINS WITH TOASTED OATMEAL AND TARRAGON STUFFING

75 g (3 oz) butter or margarine
2 medium onions, skinned and roughly chopped
50 g (2 oz) pine nuts
225 g (8 oz) eating apple, cored and roughly chopped
30 ml (2 tbsp) chopped fresh tarragon or 5 ml (1 tsp) dried
grated rind of 2 oranges and juice of 3–4 oranges
225 g (8 oz) medium oatmeal, toasted
4 poussins (about 550 g /1¼ lb each)
175 g (6 oz) mixed chopped onion, carrot, turnip and celery
125 ml (4 fl oz) white wine vinegar
150 ml (¼ pint) chicken stock
salt and freshly ground pepper
2 egg yolks

1 Melt 50 g (2 oz) of the butter or margarine in a saucepan and sauté the onion with the pine nuts until golden brown. Stir in the apple. Cook for 1–2 minutes before adding half the tarragon, the orange rind, 60 ml (4 tbsp) orange juice and the oatmeal. Leave to cool.
2 With the thumb and forefinger, loosen the skin away from the breast flesh of the poussins to make pockets. Divide the stuffing mixture between the poussins, spooning as much as possible into each pocket and any remaining into the cavity of the bird.
3 Melt the remaining butter or margarine in a large flameproof casserole. Brown the poussins, until golden on all sides. Add more butter if necessary. Drain on absorbent kitchen paper. Stir the vegetables into the casserole and sauté, stirring, until golden brown. Place the poussins on top of the vegetables. Pour on the vinegar, stock and 60 ml (4 tbsp) orange juice. Season to taste.
4 Bring to the boil, cover and simmer for 35–40 minutes or until just tender. Test with a skewer. The juices should run clear, not pink.
5 Remove the poussins and cut in half. Place on a warmed serving dish, cover and keep warm in a low oven. Strain the contents of the casserole into a small saucepan. Discard the vegetables. Whisk in the egg yolks and remaining tarragon. Cook over a low heat until slightly thickened and smooth. Do not boil. Adjust the seasoning. Spoon a little sauce over the poussins and serve the remainder separately.

APPLE AND CELERY GLAZE

1 large crisp red apple, halved, cored and thickly sliced
lemon juice
125 g (4 oz) granulated sugar
60 ml (4 tbsp) distilled white vinegar
600 ml (1 pint) chicken stock
45 ml (3 tbsp) brandy
coarsely grated rind of 3 oranges
75 g (3 oz) celery, trimmed and thickly sliced

1 Put the apple in a bowl and cover with water with a few drops of lemon juice added. Put the sugar and vinegar in a medium saucepan and warm over a very low heat until the sugar completely dissolves. Bring to the boil and bubble until the mixture is golden.
2 Add the chicken stock (take care, it will splutter), brandy and orange rind.
3 Bring to the boil, stirring, then simmer for 4–5 minutes. Cool, then stir in the celery and drained apple slices. Serve with Duckling with Mushroom Stuffing (opposite).

APRICOT AND PECAN STUFFING

50 g (2 oz) butter or margarine
225 g (8 oz) leeks, trimmed, washed and roughly chopped
75 g (3 oz) no-soak dried apricots, roughly chopped
175 g (6 oz) crisp dessert apples, peeled, cored and chopped
125 g (4 oz) pecan nuts or walnut pieces, roughly chopped
1.25 ml (¼ tsp) grated nutmeg
175 g (6 oz) fresh brown breadcrumbs
30 ml (2 tbsp) mixed chopped fresh herbs or 5 ml (1 tsp) dried
45 ml (3 tbsp) single cream
1 small egg
salt and freshly ground pepper

1 Melt the butter or margarine in a medium saucepan and sauté the leeks until they are beginning to soften. Stir in the apricots, apple, nuts and nutmeg. Continue to sauté, stirring, for 3–4 minutes or until the apple begins to soften.
2 Place all the remaining ingredients in a large bowl and stir in the leek mixture. Adjust the seasoning, bind together lightly and leave to cool. Use to stuff Mustard Roasted Turkey (opposite).

HONEYED PIGEON WITH KUMQUATS

8 small wood pigeons (about 240 g/8½ oz each)
16 rashers of rindless streaky bacon (about 275 g/10 oz total weight)
25 ml (1½ tbsp) oil
40 g (1½ oz) butter or margarine
275 g (10 oz) button onions, skinned, and halved if large
1 cinnamon stick
1 bay leaf
750 ml (1¼ pints) chicken stock
300 ml (½ pint) dry cider
salt and freshly ground pepper
45 ml (3 tbsp) clear honey
350 g (12 oz) kumquats, halved
45 ml (3 level tbsp) cornflour

1 Using strong scissors, halve the pigeons, discarding the backbones. Rinse, drain and dry on absorbent kitchen paper. Stretch the bacon with the back of a knife, then wrap around the pigeon halves. Secure with wooden cocktail sticks.
2 Heat the oil and butter in a large flameproof casserole. Add about four pigeon halves at a time and cook until browned. Remove with a slotted spoon and allow to drain on absorbent kitchen paper.
3 Lower the heat, add the onions and sauté, stirring, until golden brown. Add the cinnamon, bay leaf, stock, cider and seasoning. Return the pigeons to the casserole, bring to the boil, cover and cook in the oven at 170°C (325°F) mark 3 for 1½ hours.
4 Stir in the honey and kumquats. Cook for a further 30 minutes or until the pigeon is very tender.
5 Using draining spoons, lift the pigeons out of the casserole. Remove the cocktail sticks, cover the birds and keep warm. Remove the bay leaf and cinnamon stick. Blend the cornflour to a smooth paste with a little cold water. Add to the casserole and bring to the boil, stirring all the time, until the juices are lightly thickened. Adjust the seasoning before spooning over the pigeons to serve.

GUINEA FOWL WITH GRAPES AND MADEIRA

*3 small guinea fowl
(about 1.1–1.4 kg/2½–3 lb each)*

25 ml (1½ tbsp) oil

75 g (3 oz) butter or margarine

3 shallots, skinned and finely chopped

grated rind and juice of 3 oranges

200 ml (7 fl oz) dry white wine

75 ml (3 fl oz) Madeira

900 ml (1½ pints) chicken stock

175 g (6 oz) walnut halves, toasted

salt and freshly ground pepper

450 g (1 lb) seedless white grapes

60 ml (4 level tbsp) cornflour

60 ml (4 tbsp) chopped fresh parsley

1 Using sharp scissors, halve, then quarter the guinea fowl (discarding the backbones). Heat the oil and butter in a flameproof casserole. Brown the guinea fowl and drain on kitchen paper.

2 Lower the heat and add the shallots to the pan. Sauté, stirring, until soft. Add the orange rind and juice, the wine, Madeira, stock, walnuts and seasoning.

3 Return the guinea fowl to the casserole, bring to the boil, cover and cook at 170°C (325°F) mark 3 for 1 hour. Stir in the grapes, cover and cook for a further 30 minutes or until the guinea fowl are tender. Trim the joints and keep warm.

4 Blend the cornflour to a smooth paste with a little water. Add to the casserole and bring to the boil, stirring, until the juices are lightly thickened. Stir in the parsley. Season to taste.

VENISON FILLET WITH POMEGRANATE

2 pomegranates

700 g (1½ lb) venison fillet or loin steaks

salt and freshly ground pepper

30 ml (2 level tbsp) plain flour

90 ml (6 tbsp) vegetable oil

125 g (4 oz) mushrooms, wiped and thickly sliced

400 ml (14 fl oz) stock

1 Using a sharp knife, halve the pomegranates. Scoop out and reserve the seeds and juices. Discard the membrane.

2 Slice the venison fillet into 5 mm (¼inch) thick pieces, or divide each steak into two or three pieces. Place between sheets of damp greaseproof paper and bat out until quite thin. Season the flour and use to coat the meat pieces, shaking off and reserving any excess.

3 Heat the oil in a large sauté or frying pan and brown the venison, a quarter at a time. Return all the meat to the pan with any remaining flour. Add the mushrooms and stock with the pomegranate seeds and juices.

4 Bring to the boil and simmer for 2–3 minutes or until thoroughly hot. Adjust the seasoning before serving.

CASSEROLE OF GROUSE WITH RED WINE

4 brace of grouse

vegetable oil

900 g (2 lb) shallots or button onions, skinned

8 large celery sticks, trimmed and sliced

400 ml (14 fl oz) red wine

4 bay leaves

salt and freshly ground pepper

400 ml (14 fl oz) stock

30 ml (2 level tbsp) arrowroot

30 ml (2 tbsp) lemon juice

chopped fresh parsley, to garnish

1 Wipe the grouse, trim the feet and remove any feather ends. Heat 90 ml (6 tbsp) oil in a flameproof casserole and brown the birds well, in batches if necessary. Lift out of the pan.

2 Add the shallots and celery to the casserole with a little extra oil, if necessary, and brown lightly.

3 Pour in the wine and bring to the boil. Add the bay leaves and seasoning and return the grouse to the pan.

4 Cover tightly and bake at 170°C (325°F) mark 3 for about 50 minutes or until the grouse are just tender. Lift the birds out of the juice, cover and keep warm.

5 Add the stock to the casserole and warm slightly. Mix the arrowroot to a smooth paste with a little water and add to the pan ingredients. Bring to the boil, stirring, and cook until slightly thickened. Stir in the lemon juice, adjust the seasoning and spoon over the birds. Garnish with parsley.

PHEASANT BREASTS WITH VERMOUTH

2 brace of pheasants

60 ml (4 level tbsp) plain flour

salt and freshly ground pepper

60 ml (4 tbsp) vegetable oil

1 medium onion, skinned and chopped

300 ml (½ pint) dry vermouth

300 ml (½ pint) light stock

60 ml (4 tbsp) chopped fresh sage or 10 ml (2 tsp) dried

60 ml (4 tbsp) single cream

350 g (12 oz) white grapes, halved and seeded, if necessary

fresh sage leaves, to garnish

1 Using a sharp knife, cut all the breast flesh off the bones of each pheasant, keeping the fillets in one piece. You will end up with eight breast fillets, two from each bird. Ease off the skin and trim away any fat.

2 Dip the fillets in seasoned flour, shaking off and reserving any excess. Heat the oil in a large sauté pan, add the breast fillets, in batches if necessary, and cook until well browned.

3 Add the onion with any remaining flour to the pan and cook, stirring, for 1–2 minutes. Blend in the vermouth, stock, sage and seasoning. Bring to the boil, stirring, then return the pheasants to the pan.

4 Cover tightly and simmer for about 30 minutes, turning once. Lift the pheasant out of the juices and place on a warmed serving dish. Cover and keep warm.

5 Stir the cream and grapes into the juices and simmer for 1 minute. Adjust the seasoning. Spoon over the pheasant and garnish with fresh sage leaves.

HADDOCK AND PRAWN PAELLA

700 g (1½ lb) fresh haddock fillet, skinned
450 g (1 lb) tomatoes, skinned
good pinch of saffron strands
90 ml (6 tbsp) olive oil
350 g (12 oz) onion, skinned and chopped
450 g (1 lb) long grain white rice
about 600 ml (1 pint) light stock
300 ml (½ pint) white wine
1 yellow pepper, cored, seeded and cut into bite-sized pieces
1 green pepper, cored, seeded and cut into bite-sized pieces
30 ml (2 tbsp) chopped fresh thyme
1 garlic clove, skinned and crushed
salt and freshly ground pepper
225 g (8 oz) cooked shelled mussels, canned or frozen
225 g (8 oz) cooked peeled prawns
whole prawns in shells and sprigs of fresh thyme, to garnish

1 Cut the fish into large bitesize chunks. Quarter and de-seed the tomatoes. Sieve the pulp, reserving the juices.
2 Place the saffron in a heatproof jug, pour on 150 ml (¼ pint) boiling water and leave to soak for about 10 minutes, then strain, reserving the liquid.
3 Heat the oil in one large or two medium flameproof casseroles. Add the onion and fry until just brown. Stir in the rice, then the stock, wine and saffron liquid. Bring to the boil, stirring occasionally.
4 Gently mix in the haddock pieces, peppers, tomato and reserved tomato juices, thyme, garlic and seasoning to taste. Cover the casserole(s) tightly.
5 Bake in the oven at 180°C (350°F) mark 4 for 20 minutes. Carefully stir in the mussels and prawns, recover and bake for 10 minutes or until the rice is quite tender and all the liquid is absorbed.
6 Adjust the seasoning and serve the paella immediately, garnished with whole prawns and thyme sprigs.

ROLLED PLAICE WITH PESTO

16 small plaice fillets, about 1.1 kg (2½ lb) total weight, skinned
6 spring onions, trimmed
225 g (8 oz) fine asparagus or fine French beans, trimmed
225 g (8 oz) mange tout
225 g (8 oz) carrots, trimmed
225 g (8 oz) whole baby sweetcorn
30 ml (2 tbsp) pesto sauce
60 ml (4 tbsp) lemon juice
250 ml (8 fl oz) light stock
salt and freshly ground pepper
175 g (6 oz) oyster mushrooms, trimmed
60 ml (4 tbsp) vegetable oil

1 Divide each plaice fillet along the natural centre line into two fillets. Roll up loosely (keeping the skin side inside).
2 Cut the spring onions and asparagus into 6.5 cm (2½ inch) lengths. Top and tail the mange tout and French beans, if using. Cut the carrots into thick 6.5 cm (2½ inch) long sticks. Halve the sweetcorn lengthways.
3 Place the fish, pesto sauce, lemon juice, stock and seasoning in a medium saucepan. Bring to the boil, then cover tightly with damp greaseproof paper and a lid. Simmer for 10 minutes or until the fish is cooked.
4 Meanwhile, steam the prepared vegetables until just tender or heat the oil in a sauté pan and stir fry the vegetables for 3–4 minutes.
5 To serve, spoon the vegetables on to individual serving plates and top with the fish fillets and pan juices.

STUFFED TROUT IN A WINE SAUCE

175 g (6 oz) fresh white breadcrumbs
30 ml (2 tbsp) chopped fresh mixed herbs, such as parsley, thyme, rosemary
finely grated rind and juice of ½ large lemon
pinch of freshly grated nutmeg
salt and freshly ground pepper
1 egg, beaten
8 trout, each weighing about 275 g (10 oz), cleaned
50 g (2 oz) butter or margarine
60 ml (4 level tbsp) plain flour
300 ml (½ pint) dry white wine
300 ml (½ pint) fish or vegetable stock
150 ml (¼ pint) single cream

1 Put the breadcrumbs, herbs, grated lemon rind and juice and nutmeg in a bowl. Season, add the egg and mix well.
2 Fill the cavities of the trout with the stuffing. Wrap the fish in greased foil. Place the parcels on two baking sheets and bake at 180°C (350°F) mark 4 for 30–35 minutes or until tender.
3 Meanwhile, put the butter, flour, wine and stock in a saucepan and heat, whisking continuously, until the sauce thickens, boils and is smooth. Simmer for 3–4 minutes. Stir in the cream and season.
4 Pour a litte sauce over the trout and serve the remaining sauce in a warmed sauceboat or jug.

FILLETS OF TROUT WITH PRAWNS AND DILL

75 g (3 oz) long grain white rice
salt and freshly ground pepper
125 g (4 oz) oyster or button mushrooms, wiped and roughly chopped
50 g (2 oz) butter or margarine
60 ml (4 tbsp) chopped fresh dill or 1.25 ml (¼ tsp) dried dill weed
225 g (8 oz) cooked peeled prawns, chopped
1 egg
15 ml (1 tbsp) lemon juice
8 small trout, filleted and skinned
200 ml (7 fl oz) dry vermouth
3 egg yolks
45 ml (3 tbsp) double or single cream
sprigs of fresh dill, to garnish

1 Cook the rice in boiling salted water until just tender. Drain well and leave to cool. Sauté the mushrooms in the butter until tender. Stir into the rice. Add the dill, prawns, egg and lemon juice. Season.
2 Rinse the fish and pat dry with absorbent kitchen paper. Divide the stuffing between the fillets, roll up and secure with wooden cocktail sticks. Arrange in one or two shallow ovenproof dishes in a single layer. Pour over the vermouth with 200 ml (7 fl oz) water and season to taste. Cover tightly and bake at 190°C (375°F) mark 5 for 25 minutes.
3 Using draining spoons, transfer the fish to a warmed serving dish. Cover and keep warm. Strain the cooking juices into a saucepan. Whisk together the egg yolks and cream and stir into the pan juices. Heat gently, without boiling, stirring all the time until the liquor thickens slightly. Season and spoon a little sauce over the fish. Garnish with dill and serve the remaining sauce separately.

SWEET AND SOUR MONKFISH KEBABS

900 g (2 lb) monkfish fillet
450 g (1 lb) streaky bacon (about 22 rashers)
1 large aubergine, about 450 g (1 lb), thinly sliced
4 small red onions, skinned
4 lemons or limes, sliced
30 ml (2 tbsp) lemon juice
60 ml (4 tbsp) clear honey
30 ml (2 tbsp) soy sauce
30 ml (2 tbsp) tomato purée
salt and freshly ground pepper
frisée lettuce, to garnish

1 Cut the fish into 2.5 cm (1 inch) cubes. Stretch the bacon rashers with the back of a knife and cut into three. Wrap a piece of bacon around each fish cube.
2 Blanch the aubergines, drain and dry on absorbent kitchen paper. Quarter the onions, then separate each quarter into two, to give thinner pieces.
3 Thread the fish, onions, aubergines and lemon or lime slices on to wooden skewers. Place the kebabs side by side in a non-metallic dish.
4 Whisk together the lemon juice, honey, soy sauce, tomato purée and seasoning. Spoon over the kebabs, then cover and leave to marinate in the refrigerator for at least 12 hours, turning once.
5 Place the kebabs in a grill pan. Brush with a little of the marinade and grill for 10–12 minutes, turning occasionally, until all the ingredients are tender. Serve garnished with frisée lettuce.

SALMON AND THYME BUTTER PARCELS

8 salmon cutlets
60 ml (4 tbsp) oil
125 g (4 oz) butter
2 garlic cloves, skinned and crushed
15 ml (1 tbsp) mustard seeds
30 ml (2 tbsp) chopped fresh thyme or 10 ml (2 tsp) dried
salt and freshly ground pepper
8 tomatoes, skinned, seeded and chopped
fresh thyme, to garnish

1 Carefully remove the centre bone from each cutlet. Curl each half cutlet around to form a medallion and tie with string.

2 Heat the oil in a sauté pan and brown the salmon on both sides, cooking in batches, if necessary. Drain on absorbent kitchen paper and leave to cool.
3 Blend together the butter, garlic, mustard seeds, thyme and seasoning.
4 Cut 16 pieces of greaseproof paper, each about 25.5 cm (10 inches) square. Place a salmon medallion in the centre of each and top with some herb butter and tomato. Tie the paper with string to form bundles.
5 Bake at 200°C (400°F) mark 6 for 10–15 minutes or until the salmon is cooked through. Garnish with thyme.

MARINATED SALMON EN CROÛTE

1.6–1.8 kg (3½–4 lb) salmon or sea trout, cleaned, skinned and filleted (about 900 g/2 lb filleted weight)
coarsely grated rind and juice of 1 orange
5 ml (1 tsp) coarsely ground black pepper
15 ml (1 tbsp) chopped fresh dill or 10 ml (2 tsp) dried dill weed
700 g (1½ lb) ready-made puff pastry
350 g (12 oz) frozen chopped spinach, thawed
125 g (4 oz) low fat soft cheese
salt and freshly ground pepper
25 g (1 oz) butter or margarine
125 g (4 oz) spring onions, trimmed and chopped
125 g (4 oz) cooked peeled prawns
125 g (4 oz) small scallops
1 egg, beaten
fresh dill and orange slices, to garnish

1 Sandwich the two salmon fillets together and place in a non-metallic dish. Mix 45 ml (3 tbsp) orange juice with the coarsely ground pepper and the chopped dill. Rub the mixture into the salmon flesh. Cover and leave to marinate for at least 1 hour.
2 On a lightly floured surface, roll out half the pastry thinly to a rectangle measuring 38×20.5 cm (15×8 inches). Place on a large baking sheet and prick all over with a fork. Bake at 200°C (400°F) mark 6 for about 15 minutes or until golden brown and cooked through. Cool on a wire rack.
3 Squeeze all the excess liquid from the thawed spinach. Mix with the soft cheese and season to taste. Melt the butter in a small saucepan and sauté the spring onions for 3–4 minutes or until just beginning to soften. Cool, then stir in the prawns, scallops and orange rind. Season to taste.

4 Return the cooked pastry to a baking sheet and place one fish fillet on top, skin side down. Trim the pastry, allowing a border of 1 cm (½ inch) all round. Spread the spinach mixture over the fish, then spoon the prawn mixture on top and finish with the remaining fillet of salmon, skin side up.
5 Brush the cooked pastry edge with beaten egg, roll out the remaining pastry thinly and place over the fish to enclose completely. Trim off most of the excess pastry and reserve, leaving about 2.5 cm (1 inch) to tuck under all round. Decorate with a fine lattice of pastry cut from the trimmings. Brush all over with beaten egg to glaze. Make two small holes in the pastry to allow steam to escape and bake at 200°C (400°F) mark 6 for about 40–45 minutes or until the pastry is well risen and golden brown. Serve warm garnished with dill and orange.

BAKED SALMON WITH HOLLANDAISE SAUCE

butter
8 salmon steaks
salt and freshly ground pepper
lemon juice
SAUCE
45 ml (3 tbsp) wine or tarragon vinegar
15–30 ml (1–2 tbsp) water
3 egg yolks
350 g (12 oz) unsalted butter, softened
salt and white pepper

1 Line two baking sheets with foil and butter the surface. Place the salmon on the foil, dot each steak with butter and season with salt, pepper and lemon juice.
2 Wrap loosely and bake in the oven at 170°C (325°F) mark 3 for 20–40 minutes, according to the thickness of the fish.
3 Meanwhile, to make the sauce, put the vinegar and water in a saucepan. Boil gently until reduced by half, then cool.
4 Put the egg yolks and reduced vinegar liquid in a double saucepan or bowl over a pan of gently simmering water and whisk until thick and fluffy.
5 Gradually add the butter, a tiny piece at a time. Whisk briskly until each piece has been absorbed by the sauce and the sauce itself is the consistency of mayonnaise. Season to taste. If the sauce is too sharp, add a little more butter.
6 Serve the salmon warm or cold, accompanied by the warm sauce.

GOLDEN TOPPED FISH PIE

1.8 kg (4 lb) old potatoes, peeled
salt and freshly ground pepper
450 g (1 lb) Florence fennel
lemon juice
900 g (2 lb) fresh haddock fillet
300 ml (½ pint) dry white wine
450 g (1 lb) medium-sized scallops
350 g (12 oz) cooked peeled prawns
175 g (6 oz) butter
75 g (3 oz) plain flour
150 ml (¼ pint) single cream
30 ml (2 tbsp) chopped fresh dill or 5 ml (1 tsp) dried dill weed
about 200 ml (7 fl oz) hot milk
60 ml (4 tbsp) fresh white breadcrumbs
sprigs of fresh dill, to garnish

1 Cut the potatoes into large chunks then cook in boiling, salted water until just tender; drain well.
2 Thinly slice the fennel, discarding any coarse core or stems (use these in the cooking liquor of the fish). Blanch the fennel in boiling, salted water with a dash of lemon juice for 5 minutes or until just tender. Drain well.
3 Place the haddock in a large sauté or saucepan and pour over the wine together with 600 ml (1 pint) water; season and add the fennel core and stems. Bring slowly to the boil; cover and simmer until just tender – about 10 minutes. Add the scallops for the last minute of cooking time.
4 Lift the haddock out of the pan and flake the flesh, discarding any skin and bone. Slice each scallop into two or three pieces, discarding any membrane. Divide the haddock and scallop between two 2.3 litre (4 pint) shallow ovenproof dishes with the fennel and prawns.
5 Melt 125 g (4 oz) butter in a saucepan. Add the flour and cook for 1 minute before stirring in the strained cooking liquor. Bring to the boil, stirring all the time, and cook for a minute or two. Off the heat mix in the cream and dill; adjust seasoning and pour over the fish.
6 Mash the potatoes. Beat in the hot milk, with the remaining butter and plenty of seasoning. Cover the fish mixture with spoonfuls of potato. Sprinkle with breadcrumbs. Brush with a little melted butter.
7 Bake at 190°C (375°F) mark 5 for about 40–45 minutes or until lightly browned and bubbling hot. Garnish with sprigs of dill.

FRITTO MISTO DI MARE

700 g (1½ lb) squid, cleaned
350 g (12 oz) whitebait
6 small red mullet, cleaned and heads and tails removed, sliced
350 g (12 oz) firm, white fish fillets (cod, haddock or sole), skinned, and cut into long thin strips
12–18 large raw prawns, peeled
90 ml (6 level tbsp) seasoned flour
vegetable oil, for deep frying
sprigs of fresh parsley and lemon wedges, to garnish

1 Slice the body of the squid into rings 5 mm (¼ inch) thick and the tentacles into 1 cm (½ inch) pieces. Toss all the fish in seasoned flour.
2 Heat the oil in a deep fat fryer to 190°C (375°F). Add the fish pieces a few at a time and fry until crisp and golden brown. Drain on absorbent kitchen paper and keep each batch warm while frying the remainder.
3 Divide the fish between eight warmed plates. Garnish with parsley and lemon.

SPINACH AND SEAFOOD PASTRIES

8 cod steaks, about 125 g (4 oz) each
6 eggs
25 g (1 oz) butter or margarine
25 g (1 oz) plain flour
300 ml (½ pint) milk
salt and freshly ground pepper
700 g (1½ lb) frozen leaf spinach, thawed and thoroughly drained
225 g (8 oz) cooked peeled prawns
60 ml (4 tbsp) chopped fresh parsley
60 ml (4 tbsp) lemon juice
nutmeg
two 370 g (13 oz) packets puff pastry, thawed
watercress, to garnish

1 Skin the cod and carefully remove the central bone. Cook four of the eggs in boiling water for 8–10 minutes, then cool, shell and roughly chop. Beat the remaining eggs.
2 Melt the butter or margarine in a saucepan, stir in the flour and cook for 1 minute. Remove from the heat, add the milk, then bring to the boil, season and simmer for 1–2 minutes. Mix in the spinach, chopped egg, prawns and parsley, stir in the lemon juice and nutmeg. Leave to cool slightly.
3 Divide the pastry into eight. Roll each piece out to a large square measuring about 23 cm (9 inches). Place a piece of cod on one half of each pastry square and top with spinach and prawn sauce.
4 Brush the pastry edges with beaten egg and fold the pastry over the fish to enclose totally, tucking the edges under the parcels to neaten. With a sharp knife, carefully score the pastry in one direction only. Place on a baking sheet and glaze with the remaining egg.
5 Bake at 220°C (425°F) mark 7 for 25 minutes or until the pastry is crisp.

ITALIAN FISH STEW

good pinch of saffron strands
about 1.8 kg (4 lb) mixed fish fillets (red mullet, bream, brill, monkfish, plaice or cod), skinned
20-24 whole prawns, cooked
120 ml (8 tbsp) olive oil
2 large onions, skinned and finely chopped
4 garlic cloves, skinned and crushed
4 slices of drained canned pimiento, sliced
900 g (2 lb) tomatoes, skinned, seeded and chopped
4 anchovy fillets, drained
300 ml (½ pint) dry white wine
300 ml (½ pint) water
4 bay leaves
90 ml (6 tbsp) chopped fresh basil
salt and freshly ground pepper
20–24 mussels, in their shells

1 Soak the saffron strands in a little boiling water for 30 minutes.
2 Meanwhile, cut the fish into chunky bite-sized pieces. Peel the prawns.
3 Heat the oil in a large heavy-based saucepan, add the onion, garlic and pimiento and fry gently for 5 minutes.
4 Add the tomatoes and anchovies and stir to break them up. Add the wine and water, bring to the boil, then lower the heat and add the bay leaves and half the basil. Simmer, uncovered, for 20 minutes.
5 Add the firm fish to the tomato mixture, then strain in the saffron water and season to taste. Cook for 10 minutes, then add the delicate-textured fish and cook for a further 5 minutes.
6 Add the prawns and mussels, cover and cook for 5 minutes or until the mussels open. Remove the bay leaves and discard.
7 Put one slice of toast in each of eight soup bowls and spoon over the stew.

STIR FRY SALAD WITH PANEER

60–75 ml (4–5 tbsp) vegetable oil
450 g (1 lb) courgettes, trimmed and thinly sliced
350 g (12 oz) mange tout, trimmed
1 yellow pepper, cored, seeded and cut into strips
1 red pepper, cored, seeded and cut into strips
450 g (1 lb) paneer, cut into 1 cm (½ inch) cubes
50 g (2 oz) salted cashew nuts
75 ml (5 tbsp) lemon juice
60 ml (4 tbsp) clear honey
2.5 cm (1 inch) piece of fresh root ginger, peeled and finely chopped (optional)
salt and freshly ground pepper

1 Heat 30 ml (2 tbsp) oil in a large, non-stick sauté pan. Add the courgettes for 2–3 minutes, stirring occasionally, until they soften but retain some bite. Remove with a slotted spoon to a large bowl. Add the mange tout and peppers to the pan and sauté for 2–3 minutes, stirring occasionally. Add to the courgettes.

2 Heat the remaining oil in the pan and add the paneer. Sauté for 1–2 minutes. Stir in the cashew nuts, lemon juice, honey and ginger, if using, and cook, stirring, for a further 1–2 minutes. Spoon the contents of the pan on to the vegetables and stir well. Stir well and adjust the seasoning before serving with rice or noodles.

Note: Paneer is a mild cheese used in Indian vegetarian cookery. It is available from delicatessens and supermarkets.

FETTUCCINI WITH GORGONZOLA SAUCE

50 g (2 oz) butter
350 g (12 oz) Gorgonzola cheese
300 ml (½ pint) double cream
60 ml (4 tbsp) dry white wine
30 ml (2 tbsp) chopped fresh basil
salt and freshly ground pepper
900 g (2 lb) fettuccini

1 Melt the butter in a saucepan. Crumble in the Gorgonzola cheese, then stir over gentle heat for 2–3 minutes or until melted. Pour in the cream and wine, whisking vigorously. Mix in the basil, salt and pepper and cook, stirring, until the sauce thickens. Remove from the heat.

2 Cook the fettuccini in a large pan of boiling, salted water until al dente. Drain.

3 Gently reheat the Gorgonzola sauce, whisking vigorously all the time. Taste and adjust the seasoning. Turn the pasta into eight warmed serving bowls and pour over the sauce. Serve at once.

SPAGHETTI WITH TOASTED GARLIC CRUMBS

50 ml (2 fl oz) olive oil
4 garlic cloves, skinned and crushed
175 g (6 oz) fine fresh white breadcrumbs
salt and freshly ground pepper
90 ml (6 tbsp) chopped fresh chives or parsley
700 g (1½ lb) mixed egg and spinach spaghetti or linguini

1 Heat the oil in a large sauté pan. Add the garlic and breadcrumbs and stir over a medium heat for 3–4 minutes until golden brown. Add a little more oil if necessary. Season and stir in the herbs.

2 Cook the pasta in boiling, salted water until just tender. Drain and toss with the breadcrumb mixture.

PASTA GRATIN

125 g (4 oz) butter or margarine
350 g (12 oz) salted cashew nuts, roughly chopped
350 g (12 oz) button mushrooms, wiped and roughly chopped
175 g (6 oz) onions, skinned and roughly chopped
125 g (4 oz) celery, trimmed and roughly chopped
450 g (1 lb) fresh spinach, trimmed
salt and freshly ground pepper
48 large pasta shells (about 275 g/10 oz)
65 g (2½ oz) plain flour
1.4 litres (2½ pints) milk
1 bay leaf
550 g (1¼ lb) Lancashire cheese, coarsely grated
90 ml (6 tbsp) chopped fresh parsley
2 eggs

1 Melt half the butter in a large sauté pan. Add all the chopped nuts and vegetables and fry until golden.

2 Wash the spinach and cook in a covered saucepan over a low heat until just wilted. Drain well, then roughly chop. Stir into the nut and vegetable mixture, season and leave to cool.

3 Cook the pasta shells in plenty of boiling salted water until just tender. Drain well. Fill the shells with the nut mixture and place in a single layer in two large, shallow ovenproof dishes.

4 Melt the remaining butter in a small saucepan. Add the flour and cook, stirring, for 1–2 minutes before adding the milk and bay leaf. Bring to the boil and simmer, stirring, for 2–3 minutes. Discard the bay leaf. Off the heat, beat in the cheese, parsley, eggs and seasoning. Spoon evenly over the pasta.

5 Bake at 180°C (350°F) mark 4 for about 40 minutes.

SPRING VEGETABLE PASTA

225 g (8 oz) fresh asparagus or French beans, trimmed and cut into 5 cm (2 inch) lengths
450 g (1 lb) leeks, trimmed, washed and cut into thin diagonal slices
salt and freshly ground pepper
275 g (10 oz) creamy chèvre or full fat soft cheese with garlic and herbs
350 g (12 oz) mascarpone cheese or 300 ml (½ pint) extra-thick double cream
50 g (2 oz) butter or margarine
60 ml (4 tbsp) olive oil
2 medium onions, skinned and finely chopped
225 g (8 oz) carrots, cut into thin diagonal slices
450 g (1 lb) brown cap mushrooms, wiped and thinly sliced
225 ml (8 fl oz) dry white wine
700 g (1½ lb) crème fraîche
75 ml (5 tbsp) chopped fresh herbs, such as parsley, thyme, sage
225 g (8 oz) petits pois
penne, to serve

1 Briefly blanch the sliced asparagus or beans and the prepared leeks in boiling salted water for 3–4 minutes. Drain thoroughly. Mix together the chèvre and mascarpone.

2 In a large sauté pan, heat together the butter and oil. Stir in the onion and cook, stirring, for 3–4 minutes. Add the carrots and mushrooms and continue to cook for 2–3 minutes or until beginning to soften.

3 Stir in all the remaining ingredients except the cheese mixture. Simmer very gently until thickened to a good coating consistency. Remove the pan from the heat and gently stir in the cheese mixture until thoroughly mixed. Season to taste. Spoon on to hot, cooked penne and serve immediately.

MIXED LENTIL CASSEROLE

7.5 ml (1½ tsp) cumin seeds
25 ml (1½ tbsp) coriander seeds
7.5 ml (1½ tsp) mustard seeds
60 ml (4 tbsp) olive oil
450 g (1 lb) onions, skinned and sliced
550 g (1¼ lb) carrots, sliced
450 g (1 lb) trimmed leeks, sliced
450 g (1 lb) mooli (white radish), peeled and roughly chopped
450 g (1 lb) button mushrooms, wiped and halved if large
3 garlic cloves, skinned and crushed
40 g (1½ oz) piece of fresh root ginger, peeled and finely chopped or grated
2.5 ml (½ tsp) ground turmeric
225 g (8 oz) split red lentils
75 g (3 oz) brown or green lentils
salt and freshly ground pepper
75 ml (5 tbsp) chopped fresh coriander

1 Crush the cumin, coriander and mustard seeds in a mortar with a pestle or in a bowl with the end of a rolling pin.
2 Heat the oil in a large flameproof casserole. Add the onions, carrots, leeks and mooli and sauté, stirring, for 2–3 minutes before adding the mushrooms, garlic, ginger, turmeric and crushed spices. Sauté for a further 2–3 minutes.
3 Stir the lentils into the casserole with 1 litre (1¾ pints) boiling water. Season and return to the boil. Cover and cook in the oven at 180°C (350°F) mark 4 for about 45 minutes or until the vegetables and lentils are tender. Stir in the coriander and adjust the seasoning before serving.

ASPARAGUS RISOTTO

2 litres (3½ pints) vegetable stock
300 ml (½ pint) dry white wine
900 g (2 lb) thin green asparagus
175 g (6 oz) butter
1 medium onion, skinned and finely chopped
700 g (1½ lb) arborio rice
pinch of saffron strands
salt and freshly ground pepper
125 g (4 oz) freshly grated Parmesan cheese

1 Bring the stock and the wine to the boil in a large saucepan and keep at barely simmering point.

2 Meanwhile, cut off the tips of the asparagus. Peel the remaining asparagus and cut into 5 cm (2 inch) lengths.
3 In a large, heavy-based saucepan, melt 50 g (2 oz) butter, add the onion and fry gently for 5 minutes or until soft.
4 Add the asparagus stems and the arborio rice to the pan and stir well for 2–3 minutes until the rice is well coated with the butter.
5 Add a ladleful of stock to the pan, cook gently, stirring occasionally until the stock is absorbed. Stir in more stock as soon as each ladleful is absorbed.
6 When the rice becomes creamy, sprinkle in the saffron with salt and pepper to taste. Continue adding stock and stirring until the risotto is thick and creamy, tender but not sticky. This process should take 20–25 minutes. It must not be hurried.
7 Meanwhile, steam or microwave the asparagus tips.
8 Just before serving, stir in the asparagus tips with the remaining butter and the Parmesan cheese.

WINTER VEGETABLE CASSEROLE

450 g (1 lb) celeriac
lemon juice
40 g (1½ oz) butter or margarine
450 g (1 lb) onions, skinned and sliced
3 garlic cloves, skinned and crushed
700 g (1½ lb) carrots, thinly sliced
700 g (1½ lb) parsnips, peeled and thinly sliced
450 g (1 lb) button mushrooms, wiped
600 ml (1 pint) vegetable stock
salt and freshly ground pepper
90 ml (6 tbsp) single cream
45 ml (3 tbsp) chopped fresh parsley

1 Peel and chop the celeriac into large chunks and cover immediately with cold water lightly acidulated with lemon juice.
2 Melt the butter in a large flameproof casserole. Add the onions and garlic and sauté for 2–3 minutes or until beginning to soften. Stir in the carrots, parsnips and mushrooms and sauté for a further 4–5 minutes before adding the stock and seasoning. Bring to the boil, cover and cook at 170°C (325°F) mark 3 for 50 minutes or until the vegetables are tender.
3 Meanwhile, cook the celeriac in boiling, salted water for about 35 minutes or until very tender. Drain and purée in a blender or food processor with a little of the casserole juices.

4 Stir into the casserole, return to the boil and adjust the seasoning. Stir in the cream and parsley just before serving.

MIXED VEGETABLE CURRY

125 ml (4 fl oz) ghee or vegetable oil
2 large onions, skinned and finely chopped
3–4 green chillies, seeded and finely chopped
10 ml (2 tsp) chilli powder
2.5 ml (½ tsp) turmeric
120 ml (8 tbsp) tomato purée
300 ml (½ pint) natural yogurt
450 g (1 lb) young turnips, peeled and sliced
450 g (1 lb) small carrots, diced
450 g (1 lb) cauliflower florets
1.1 litres (2 pints) coconut milk (see page 120)
salt
450 g (1 lb) frozen peas
16 whole cloves
16 black peppercorns
seeds of 16 green cardamoms
20 ml (4 tsp) fennel seeds
2.5 ml (½ tsp) grated nutmeg

1 Heat the ghee in a heavy-based saucepan or flameproof casserole, add the onion and fry gently for about 5 minutes or until soft and lightly coloured.
2 Add the chillies and stir to mix with the onion, then add the chilli powder and turmeric and fry, stirring, for 2 minutes.
3 Add the tomato purée and stir for a further 2 minutes, then add the yogurt, 15 ml (1 tbsp) at a time. Cook each addition over high heat, stirring constantly, until the yogurt is absorbed.
4 Add the turnips and carrots and fry, stirring frequently, for 5 minutes, then add the cauliflower and fry for 5 minutes.
5 Gradually stir in the coconut milk and 600 ml (1 pint) water. Add salt to taste and bring to the boil. Lower the heat, cover and simmer for about 40 minutes or until the vegetables are very tender, adding the peas for the last 10 minutes.
6 Meanwhile, dry fry the whole spices in a heavy-based frying pan for a few minutes, then grind to a fine powder with a pestle and mortar.
7 Remove the pan from the heat, sprinkle the ground spices and nutmeg over the vegetables and fold to mix. Cover the pan tightly with a lid, and remove from the heat. Leave to stand for 5 minutes, for the flavours to develop. Taste and adjust the seasoning, then turn into a warmed serving dish.

CUCUMBER AND FENNEL SALAD

2 large cucumbers
salt and freshly ground pepper
1 head of fennel, trimmed and shredded
1 bunch of spring onions, trimmed and finely chopped
450 ml (¾ pint) natural yogurt

1 Thinly peel the cucumbers, cut them in half lengthways and scoop out the seeds. Cut the cucumber halves crossways into slices about 5 mm (¼ inch) thick. Put the slices into a large mixing bowl and sprinkle lightly with salt. Cover and leave to stand for at least 1 hour. (The salt extracts the excess water, and crisps the cucumber.)
2 Rinse the cucumber and drain well in a colander or pat dry with absorbent kitchen paper.
3 Put the cucumber, fennel and onions in a large salad bowl. Add the yogurt and seasoning. Mix together until well mixed. Cover the salad and refrigerate until ready to serve.

CURRIED NEW POTATO SALAD

1.4 kg (3 lb) small new potatoes
12.5 ml (2½ tsp) white wine vinegar
2.5 ml (½ tsp) dry mustard
1–2 garlic cloves, skinned and crushed
salt and freshly ground pepper
45 ml (3 tbsp) olive oil
450 ml (¾ pint) mayonnaise
25 ml (1½ level tbsp) mild curry powder
chopped fresh parsley, to garnish

1 Cook the potatoes in boiling salted water until they are just tender. Drain well and allow to cool. Cut larger potatoes into thick slices.
2 Put the vinegar into a large mixing bowl with the mustard, garlic and seasoning and stir until the salt dissolves. Whisk in the olive oil. Add the cooled potatoes to the dressing and mix together gently until the potatoes are well coated.
3 Mix the mayonnaise and curry powder together. Pour over the potatoes and carefully fold together.
4 Spoon the salad into a large serving bowl and sprinkle with parsley. Cover and refrigerate until ready to serve.

SPINACH AND CORN SALAD

350 g (12 oz) fresh young spinach
175 g (6 oz) whole baby sweetcorn
salt and freshly ground pepper
50 ml (2 fl oz) olive oil
1 garlic clove, skinned and crushed
15 ml (1 tbsp) white wine vinegar
10 ml (2 tsp) Dijon mustard
5 ml (1 tsp) caster sugar
125 g (4 oz) alfalfa sprouts
1 head of chicory, trimmed and shredded

1 Wash the spinach well in several changes of cold water. Remove any coarse stalks. Drain well and pat dry on absorbent kitchen paper. Refrigerate in a polythene bag until required.
2 Halve the sweetcorn lengthways. Cook in boiling salted water for about 10 minutes or until just tender. Drain and refresh under cold running water. Cover and refrigerate.
3 Whisk together the olive oil, garlic, vinegar, mustard and sugar. Season to taste.
4 Mix the spinach, sweetcorn, alfalfa sprouts and chicory, toss in the dressing and serve immediately.

WILD RICE AND THYME SALAD

175 g (6 oz) French beans, trimmed and halved
salt and freshly ground pepper
175 g (6 oz) broad beans, shelled
50 g (2 oz) wild rice
175 g (6 oz) long grain white rice
50 ml (2 fl oz) grapeseed oil
50 g (2 oz) chanterelle, trompets des morts or small button mushrooms, wiped and roughly sliced
30 ml (2 tbsp) chopped fresh thyme
25 ml (1 fl oz) walnut oil
30 ml (2 tbsp) white wine vinegar
15 ml (1 tbsp) Dijon mustard

1 Cook the French beans in boiling, salted water until just tender. Drain and refresh under cold water and set aside to cool completely.
2 Cook the broad beans in boiling, salted water until just tender. Drain and refresh under cold running water, slipping off their outer skins if wished. Set aside to cool completely.

3 Place the wild rice in a large pan of boiling salted water. Boil for 25 minutes before adding the long grain white rice. Boil together for a further 10 minutes, or until both are just tender. Drain and refresh the rice under cold running water. Stir together the French beans, broad beans and rice in a large bowl.
4 Heat the grapeseed oil in a small saucepan, add the mushrooms and thyme and sauté for 2–3 minutes. Off the heat, stir in the walnut oil, vinegar, mustard and seasoning. Spoon into the rice mixture and stir well. Adjust the seasoning. Cool, cover and chill until required.

SPINACH AND BACON SALAD

450 g (1 lb) fresh young spinach
225 g (8 oz) streaky bacon, rinded
60 ml (4 tbsp) olive oil
30 ml (2 tbsp) wine vinegar
7.5 ml (1½ tsp) Dijon mustard
salt and freshly ground pepper

1 Pull any coarse stalks off the spinach and discard. Rinse the spinach in several changes of cold water. Drain well, pat dry with absorbent kitchen paper and tear into bite-sized pieces. Place in a salad bowl.
2 Meanwhile, grill the bacon until crisp. Drain on absorbent kitchen paper to remove excess fat, then snip into small pieces.
3 Whisk together the oil, vinegar, mustard and seasoning, toss with the spinach then scatter over the bacon.

CUCUMBER RIBBON AND ASPARAGUS SALAD

700 g (1½ lb) fresh asparagus spears
salt and freshly ground pepper
2 large cucumbers
150 ml (¼ pint) oil
60 ml (4 tbsp) lemon juice
15 ml (1 tbsp) caster sugar
½ bunch chives
alfalfa sprouts, to garnish

1 With a sharp knife or vegetable peeler, scrape each asparagus stalk from tip to base, then trim off any woody parts at the stem base. Tie the stalks in bundles of about 10 and stand upright in a saucepan

of boiling, salted water. Cover the tips with a tent of foil. Simmer for 10–15 minutes, or until just tender. Drain and cool.

2 Peel the cucumbers. With a swivel peeler, 'shave' off ribbons of cucumber into a bowl until all the cucumber is used, discarding the central core. Toss in the asparagus. Cover and refrigerate.

3 Whisk together the oil, lemon juice and sugar. Season. Snip the chives into 2.5 cm (1 inch) lengths and stir into the dressing. Spoon over the cucumber and asparagus mixture. Garnish with alfalfa.

CARROTS WITH GINGER AND HONEY

50 g (2 oz) butter
900 g (2 lb) carrots, cut into thick diagonal slices
450 g (1 lb) button onions or shallots, skinned
coarsely grated rind and juice of 1 lemon
1 cm (½ inch) piece of fresh root ginger, peeled and finely chopped
15 ml (1 tbsp) clear honey
30 ml (2 tbsp) chopped fresh parsley

1 Melt the butter in a large saucepan and sauté the carrots and onions, stirring, for 2–3 minutes. Add the lemon rind, strained lemon juice, ginger, if using, honey and 200 ml (7 fl oz) water.

2 Bring to the boil, cover tightly and cook gently for 15 minutes or until just tender. Uncover and bubble down the juices until the carrots are lightly glazed, shaking the pan occasionally to prevent the carrots sticking. Stir in the parsley before serving.

CELERIAC PURÉE

1 . 6 kg (3 lb) celeriac, peeled and chopped
salt and white pepper
600 ml (1 pint) milk
50 g (2 oz) unsalted butter
45 ml (3 tbsp) double cream

1 Cook the celeriac in simmering salted milk until tender. Drain, reserving the milk, then purée in a blender or food processor.

2 Heat the butter in a non-stick saucepan and stir in the celeriac purée, then heat, stirring constantly to drive off excess moisture. Beat in the cream and enough of the reserved milk to give a creamy consistency. Season to taste.

GLAZED CARROTS WITH TURNIPS

900 g (2 lb) carrots, cut into thick sticks
900 g (2 lb) turnips, peeled and cut into thick sticks
50 g (2 oz) butter or margarine
30 ml (2 tbsp) lemon juice
60 ml (4 tbsp) granulated sugar
salt and freshly ground black pepper

1 Place the vegetables in a medium saucepan and *just* cover with cold water. Add the butter, lemon juice, sugar and seasoning to taste.

2 Bring to the boil and boil rapidly over a high heat for about 15 minutes or until all the liquid has evaporated and the vegetables are tender and lightly glazed. Shake the pan occasionally to prevent the vegetables sticking.

3 Cover and keep warm until required. Season with black pepper just before serving, adding an extra knob of butter, if wished.

LEMON SESAME POTATOES

1.8 kg (4 lb) small new potatoes
salt
60 ml (4 tbsp) soy sauce
60 ml (4 tbsp) vegetable oil
60 ml (4 tbsp) lemon juice
25 g (1 oz) sesame seeds

1 Wash the potatoes well but do not peel. Halve any large ones. Cook in boiling salted water for 5 minutes only, then drain.

2 Put the potatoes in one or two shallow roasting tins. Drizzle over the soy sauce, oil and lemon juice. Sprinkle over the sesame seeds.

3 Bake in the oven at 200°C (400°F) mark 6 for about 45 minutes.

SWEDE AND ORANGE PURÉE

1.8 kg (4 lb) swedes, peeled and thinly sliced
salt and freshly ground pepper
50 g (2 oz) butter or margarine
finely grated rind and juice of 2 oranges
90 ml (6 tbsp) soured cream

1 Put the swede in a saucepan, cover with cold salted water, bring to the boil and cook for about 20 minutes or until quite tender.

2 Mash the swede, then add the butter, seasoning and orange rind. Stir over a moderate heat for several minutes or until thoroughly hot and all excess moisture has been driven off.

3 Stir in 60 ml (4 tbsp) orange juice and the soured cream. Reheat gently, stirring all the time to prevent the purée sticking to the pan. Adjust the seasoning just before serving.

RICH CHOCOLATE MOUSSE

350 g (12 oz) plain chocolate, broken into pieces
30 ml (2 tbsp) rum
175 g (6 oz) butter
175 g (6 oz) caster sugar
2 eggs, separated
300 ml (½ pint) double cream
chocolate curls, to decorate

1 Put the chocolate in a bowl over simmering water, with 30 ml (2 tbsp) water and the rum. Stir until melted. Cool slightly.
2 Whisk together the butter and sugar until pale and fluffy, then beat in the egg yolks one at a time.
3 Add the chocolate to the butter mixture and beat for 5 minutes until light.
4 Whisk the whites until stiff but not dry and fold into the chocolate. Pour into a serving dish or individual glasses and chill until set. Whip the fresh cream until stiff. Decorate the mousse with the cream and chocolate curls.

STICKY UPSIDE DOWN PUDDING

175 g (6 oz) butter or margarine
275 g (10 oz) soft light brown sugar
two 415 g (14½ oz) cans pear halves in natural juices
225 g (8 oz) plain flour
5 ml (1 tsp) bicarbonate of soda
pinch of salt
10 ml (2 tsp) ground ginger
2.5 ml (½ tsp) grated nutmeg
15 ml (1 tbsp) ground cinnamon
finely grated rind and juice of 1 large lemon
175 g (6 oz) black treacle
200 ml (7 fl oz) milk
2 eggs, beaten

1 Warm together half of the butter and 125 g (4 oz) of the sugar until the sugar has dissolved. Spoon into a 2.3–2.6 litre (4–4½ pint) shallow, ovenproof dish. Drain the pears and arrange, cut side down, around the base of the dish.
2 In a large bowl, mix together the flour, the remaining sugar, the bicarbonate of soda, salt and spices. Add the lemon rind, then make a well in the centre of the dry ingredients.

3 Warm together the treacle and remaining butter. When evenly blended, pour into the well with the milk and 45 ml (3 tbsp) lemon juice. Add the eggs, then beat well until evenly mixed.
4 Spoon the ginger mixture over the pears. Stand the dish on an edged baking sheet.
5 Bake at 200°C (400°F) mark 6 for about 25 minutes. Reduce the temperature to 190°C (375°F) mark 5 and continue to cook for about a further 50 minutes, covering lightly, if necessary. When cooked, the pudding should be firm to the touch and a skewer inserted into the centre should come out clean.
6 Leave the pudding to stand for about 5 minutes. Run a blunt-edged knife around the edge of the dish and invert the pudding on to an edged platter. Serve warm with yogurt or cream.

CHOCOLATE PROFITEROLES

CHOUX PASTRY
150 g (5 oz) plain flour
pinch of salt
125 g (4 oz) butter, diced
4 eggs (size 4), beaten
CHOCOLATE SAUCE
450 g (1 lb) plain chocolate
600 ml (1 pint) double cream
45 ml (3 tbsp) brandy, rum or liqueur of your choice
45 ml (3 tbsp) very strong black coffee
FILLING
450 ml (¾ pint) double cream
icing sugar, to taste (optional)

1 Sift the flour with the salt twice on to a sheet of greaseproof paper. Put the butter in a heavy-based saucepan with 300 ml (½ pint) water. Slowly heat until the butter melts, then bring to a rolling boil.
2 Take off the heat and immediately add the flour, all at once. Beat well until all the lumps are gone and the mixture is smooth and shiny and beginning to leave the sides of the pan. Do not overbeat at this point as this will make the butter run out of the mixture and prevent the pastry from rising. Leave the mixture to cool for 5–10 minutes.
3 Add the eggs, a little at a time, beating well between each addition until the mixture becomes thick and shiny. The more you beat, the better the pastry will be – you can use an electric or hand mixer. If it becomes slightly runny and won't

thicken again, don't add any more egg.
4 Wet one or two baking sheets. Using two teaspoons, place small mounds of choux on the sheets, positioned well apart to allow for swelling. Alternatively, pipe the choux mixture on to the baking sheets using a 1 cm (½ inch) plain nozzle.
5 Bake at 200°C (400°F) mark 6 for 20–25 minutes or until well risen and golden brown. Remove from the oven and split in two. Replace on the baking sheets and return to the oven for a further 5 minutes or until well dried out. Cool on a wire rack.
6 Meanwhile, break up the chocolate and put in a saucepan with the remaining sauce ingredients. Heat gently, stirring occasionally, until the chocolate has melted. Do not boil. Reheat when required.
7 Whip the cream with icing sugar, to taste, until it just holds its shape. Separate the profiterole halves and fill them with the whipped cream. Replace the tops and pile into one large or eight individual serving dishes. Cover and refrigerate for up to 1 hour before serving with the warm chocolate sauce.

CRÈME CARAMEL

350 g (12 oz) granulated sugar
1 vanilla pod (or a few drops of vanilla flavouring)
1 litre (1¾ pints) milk
8 whole eggs, 8 egg yolks
120 ml (8 tbsp) caster sugar (or more to taste)

1 To make the caramel, slightly warm eight 150 ml (¼ pint) ramekin dishes. Put the granulated sugar in a heavy-based saucepan with enough water just to moisten. Place over a low heat and heat without boiling until the sugar has dissolved, stirring occasionally.
2 Bring to the boil and boil rapidly for a few minutes or until the sugar begins to turn pale brown. Do not leave the sugar. At this stage it will go brown very quickly and could easily burn. Gently swirl the caramel to ensure even browning.
3 Once the caramel has reached the desired colour, dip the base of the pan in cool water to prevent further cooking. Pour a little caramel into each of the warm ramekins and rotate each one to coat the bottom and part way up the sides.
4 To make the custard, split the vanilla pod to expose the seeds. Place in a pan with the milk and heat gently. (If using vanilla flavouring, add after heating the milk first.) Meanwhile, beat the whole eggs, yolks and caster sugar until well mixed. Strain on to the milk. Stir well

and strain again into the ramekins.

5 Place the ramekins in a roasting tin and fill the tin with hot water to come two thirds of the way up the sides of the dishes.

6 Bake in the oven at 170°C (325°F) mark 3 for 20–30 minutes or until just set. To test, insert the tip of a small sharp knife into the centre of a custard – if done, it should come out clean. Remove from the bain-marie, cool, then refrigerate overnight.

7 To turn out, allow the custards to come to room temperature for 15 minutes. Free the edge of each custard by pressing with the fingertips, then loosen the sides with a thin-bladed, blunt-edged knife. Place a serving dish over the top and invert. Lift off the ramekin.

HAZELNUT BRÛLÉE

75 g (3 oz) hazelnuts, toasted and skinned
40 g (1½ oz) granulated sugar
oil
6 egg yolks
caster sugar
450 ml (¾ pint) each double and single cream
1 vanilla pod or a few drops of vanilla flavouring

1 Place the nuts and granulated sugar in a small saucepan and heat gently to caramelise the sugar. Do not stir, but tilt the saucepan carefully to coat the nuts in caramel. Transfer to a lightly oiled baking sheet to harden. When cold, break up roughly, then place in a blender or food processor and process to a fine powder.

2 Beat the egg yolks with 25 ml (1½ tbsp) caster sugar until slightly thickened and pale. Heat the single cream and the double cream with the vanilla pod until almost boiling, then pour on to the egg yolks, stirring all the time. Remove the vanilla pod. Add a few drops of vanilla flavouring, if using.

3 Return the mixture to the saucepan and heat gently, stirring, until slightly thickened – about the consistency of single cream. Do not boil or the mixture will curdle. Stir in the nut powder, then pour the mixture into eight 150 ml (¼ pint) ramekins.

4 Bake at 150°C (300°F) mark 2 for 20–25 minutes or until just beginning to set. Cool and refrigerate for 2–3 hours, preferably overnight.

5 Heat the grill. Dust the tops of the custards with caster sugar to cover completely. Place under the grill. Allow the sugar to melt and turn a light golden caramel. Remove from the heat, cool and refrigerate for about 2 hours before serving.

GINGER MERINGUES WITH RHUBARB SAUCE

4 egg whites
225 g (8 oz) caster sugar
60 ml (4 tbsp) Advocaat liqueur
30 ml (2 tbsp) finely chopped preserved stem ginger
10 ml (2 tsp) preserved stem ginger syrup
300 ml (½ pint) double cream
450 g (1 lb) rhubarb
50 g (2 oz) granulated sugar
5 ml (1 level tsp) arrowroot
icing sugar, to decorate

1 Line two baking sheets with non-stick baking parchment. Whisk the egg whites until stiff but not dry. Add 30 ml (2 tbsp) caster sugar and whisk again until very stiff and shiny. Fold in the remaining caster sugar.

2 Spoon or pipe the meringue mixture into 48 walnut-sized rounds, well spaced on the baking sheets.

3 Bake at 130°C (250°F) mark ½ for 2 hours or until completely dried out. Cool on a wire rack and store in an airtight container until required.

4 Mix together the Advocaat, chopped preserved stem ginger and syrup. Whip the cream until it just begins to hold its shape and fold in the ginger mixture. Whip again for 1 minute. Cover and refrigerate.

5 Cut the rhubarb into 4 cm (1½ inch) lengths. Place in a medium saucepan with the granulated sugar and 300 ml (½ pint) water. Cover and cook over a very gentle heat for about 20 minutes or until tender. Cool slightly then purée. Sieve the purée back into the rinsed out pan.

6 Blend the arrowroot with 15 ml (1 tbsp) water. Stir into the rhubarb purée and bring to the boil, stirring all the time. Boil for 1–2 minutes or until thickened. Leave to cool.

7 To serve the meringues, sandwich the rounds together with a little of the ginger cream. Refrigerate for about 30 minutes to soften slightly. Dust with icing sugar and serve with the rhubarb sauce.

CHOCOLATE MILLES FEUILLES

350 g (12 oz) plain chocolate, broken into small pieces
225 g (8 oz) white chocolate, broken into small pieces
600 ml (1 pint) double cream
cocoa powder, to dust
12 oranges, preferably blood variety
20 ml (4 level tsp) cornflour
50 g (2 oz) caster sugar

1 Put the plain chocolate in a small bowl and melt slowly over a saucepan of gently simmering water.

2 Draw eight 15×10 cm (6×4 inch) rectangles on sheets of foil or non-stick baking parchment. Place on large flat baking sheets. With a small palette knife, spread the chocolate thinly and evenly into the rectangles. Refrigerate for about 1 hour.

3 Melt the white chocolate as before.

4 Whip the cream until it begins to hold its shape. Stir about 60 ml (4 tbsp) into the melted white chocolate to loosen. Fold in the remaining cream.

5 To assemble, carefully peel away the foil or baking parchment from the set chocolate rectangles. Place two on a sheet of foil, on a chilled, flat baking sheet. Spread with a little of the white chocolate cream. Continue layering the rectangles with the cream, ending with a chocolate rectangle, to make two milles feuilles. Press down lightly. Dust heavily with cocoa powder. Chill for at least 2 hours or until set.

6 With a potato peeler, pare and set aside the rind from two oranges. Squeeze the juice from all the oranges into a measuring jug and make up to 600 ml (1 pint) with water if necessary. Strain into a saucepan. Blend the cornflour to a smooth paste with 60 ml (4 tbsp) water. Stir into the orange juice with the sugar.

7 Bring slowly to the boil, stirring continuously. Simmer until slightly thickened and clear. Pour into a bowl then cool.

8 Cut the reserved orange rind into needle-thin shreds. Drop into a saucepan of boiling water, then simmer for 3–4 minutes or until tender. Drain, cool in cold water, then add to the sauce.

9 To serve, dust the milles feuilles with more cocoa powder. Heat a serrated knife in boiling water for 4–5 seconds, dry, then use to cut each mille feuille into four. Pour a little of the orange sauce on to eight plates and place a portion of the mille feuille on top. Serve immediately, accompanied by the remaining sauce.

PINEAPPLE TARTE TATIN

50 g (2 oz) caster sugar
175 g (6 oz) butter or margarine
2 egg yolks
125 g (4 oz) self-raising flour
125 g (4 oz) granulated sugar
60 ml (4 tbsp) double cream
900 g (2 lb) pineapple, peeled, cored and thinly sliced
Kirsch (optional)
fresh mint sprigs, to decorate

1 In a medium bowl, beat together the caster sugar and 50 g (2 oz) of the butter until pale and light. Beat in the egg yolks, then fold in the flour and knead lightly together to form a smooth dough. Wrap and chill for 30 minutes.

2 In a small saucepan, slowly heat the remaining butter with the granulated sugar until both have melted. Bring to the boil, then simmer for 3–4 minutes, beating continuously until the mixture is smooth, dark and fudge-like. (It will probably separate at this stage, but don't worry as it will come back together again.) Take off the heat, cool for 1 minute and stir in the cream, beating until smooth. If necessary, warm gently, stirring, until completely smooth. Spoon into a shallow 21.5 cm (8½ inch) round non-stick sandwich tin.

3 Arrange the pineapple neatly in overlapping circles on the fudge mixture. Drizzle over 15 ml (1 tbsp) Kirsch, if wished.

4 Roll out the prepared pastry to a 25.5 cm (10 inch) round. Place over the pineapple, tucking and pushing the edges down the side of the tin. Trim off any excess pastry. Stand the tin on a baking sheet.

5 Bake at 200°C (400°F) mark 6 for about 20 minutes or until the pastry is a deep golden brown. Run the blade of a knife around the edge of the tin to loosen the pastry. Leave to cool for 2–3 minutes. Turn out on to a heatproof serving dish and place under a hot grill for 2–3 minutes to caramelise the top. Decorate with fresh mint sprigs.

BRANDY SNAP BASKETS

ICE CREAM
1 litre (1¾ pints) real dairy vanilla ice cream
75 g (3 oz) stem ginger, chopped
SAUCE
175 g (6 oz) no-soak dried apricots
75 g (3 oz) caster sugar
45 ml (3 tbsp) apricot brandy or brandy (optional)
40 g (1½ oz) crystallised or stem ginger, chopped
BASKETS
75 g (3 oz) caster sugar
75 g (3 oz) butter or margarine
45 ml (3 tbsp) golden syrup
75 g (3 oz) plain flour
20 ml (4 tsp) lemon juice
pinch of ground ginger
Cape gooseberries (physalis), to decorate (optional)

1 First, make the ginger ice cream. Allow the ice cream to soften slightly, then beat in the stem ginger and place in the freezer for at least 3 hours or until hard.

2 Next prepare the sauce. Finely shred two or three apricots and set aside. Place the remaining apricots in a medium saucepan with the sugar and 500 ml (18 fl oz) water. Bring to the boil, cover, then simmer for 25 minutes or until tender. Purée in a blender or food processor before stirring in the shredded apricots, apricot brandy and ginger. Reheat or chill to serve, as preferred.

3 Now make the brandy snap baskets. Put the sugar, butter and syrup in a small saucepan and heat gently until evenly blended. Stir in the flour, lemon juice and ginger. Line a heavy baking sheet with non-stick baking parchment.

4 Place a good teaspoonful of the mixture on the middle of the sheet. Bake at 180°C (350°F) mark 4 for 10–12 minutes or until an even golden brown.

5 Remove from the oven and allow to cool slightly for about 1 minute. With a palette knife or fish slice, carefully ease the brandy snap off the baking sheet, taking care not to tear it. If the brandy snap has already become too brittle, pop it back in the oven for a few seconds to soften again. Working quickly, drape the biscuit over the base of an upturned oiled ramekin or jam jar, and then shape it gently but quickly with your hands to form a basket shape.

6 Allow to cool and harden before storing in an airtight container for not more than 2 days. Use the remaining mixture to make more baskets – you should eventually have 8–10 baskets. The non-stick baking parchment can be re-used.

7 To serve, place the brandy snap baskets on individual plates, fill with scoops of ginger ice cream and pour over the hot or chilled apricot and ginger sauce. Decorate with Cape gooseberries, if wished.

AUTUMN FRUIT PIE

65 g (2½ oz) butter or margarine
65 g (2½ oz) white vegetable fat
275 g (10 oz) plain flour
pinch of salt
450 g (1 lb) cooking apples, peeled, cored and diced
225 g (8 oz) pears, peeled, cored and diced
50 g (2 oz) seedless raisins, chopped
50 g (2 oz) fresh dates, stoned and chopped
grated rind and juice of 1 lemon
45–60 ml (3–4 tbsp) caster sugar
5 ml (1 tsp) ground cinnamon
pinch of grated nutmeg
beaten egg and caster sugar, to glaze

1 Rub the fats into the flour and salt until the mixture resembles fine breadcrumbs. Bind to a firm dough with 75–90 ml (5–6 tbsp) water. Wrap and chill for 15 minutes.

2 Roll out about two thirds of the pastry thinly and use to line a 23 cm (9 inch) loose-bottomed fluted flan tin. Bake blind at 200°C (400°F) mark 6 for about 10 minutes, then remove the paper and baking beans and cook for a further 5–10 minutes or until set and light brown. (Leave the baking sheet in the oven to give 'bottom heat' to the pie later.)

3 Meanwhile, place the apples and pears in a large bowl with the raisins and dates. Add the lemon rind and juice, caster sugar to taste and the spices. Mix well.

4 Place the fruit in the baked flan case. Moisten the edges of the pastry case with a little water. Roll out the remaining pastry and use to cover the fruit. Seal the edges well. Make two or three holes in the top with the point of a sharp knife. Glaze with beaten egg and dust with caster sugar.

5 Place the pie on the hot baking sheet and bake at 180°C (350°F) mark 4 for 45 minutes – 1 hour or until set and golden brown. Serve hot or cold.

MINCEMEAT AND COINTREAU FLAN

175 g (6 oz) plain flour
75 g (3 oz) butter, softened
1 whole egg, 2 yolks
75 g (3 oz) caster sugar
2–3 drops of vanilla flavouring
450 g (1 lb) mincemeat
50 g (2 oz) ground almonds
30 ml (2 tbsp) Cointreau
2 lemons
2 oranges
175 g (6 oz) seedless white grapes, halved
1 medium banana, peeled and sliced
300 ml (½ pint) double cream

1 To make the pastry, sift the flour on to a clean surface. Make a large well in the centre, and add the butter, cut into small pieces, the three egg yolks, the sugar, vanilla flavouring and 15 ml (1 tbsp) water.
2 Using the fingertips of one hand, mix the central ingredients together. When they are well mixed, begin to draw in the flour, first using a palette knife to cut through the mixture.
3 With one hand, draw the mixture together and knead gently until smooth. Wrap and chill for 1 hour.
4 Meanwhile, mix together the mincemeat, ground almonds, Cointreau, grated rind of one lemon and one orange, the grapes and banana.
5 Roll out the pastry on a lightly floured surface to a thickness of about 3 mm (⅛ inch). Use to line a 19 cm (7½ inch) deep, fluted, loose-bottomed flan tin. Bake blind at 200°C (400°F) mark 6 for 10 minutes, then remove the paper and baking beans and cook for a further 5–10 minutes or until the pastry is light brown. Allow to cool slightly.
6 Not more than 2 hours before serving, spoon the mincemeat filling into the pastry case. Bake at 180°C (350°F) mark 4 for 10–15 minutes or until lightly set. Leave to cool. Meanwhile, pare the rind from half of the remaining orange and lemon. Blanch, drain and reserve. Finely grate the remaining rind and add to the cream.
7 Just before serving, whip the cream until it just holds its shape. Whisk the egg white until stiff but not dry and fold into the cream. Spoon on to the mincemeat and decorate with the reserved rind. The flan is best served immediately, but can be kept, chilled, for up to 1 hour.

ALMOND FUDGE CAKE

125 g (4 oz) blanched almonds
125 g (4 oz) white almond paste
225 g (8 oz) softened butter or margarine
175 g (6 oz) caster sugar
5 ml (1 tsp) vanilla flavouring
3 eggs, size 2, beaten
225 g (8 oz) self-raising flour
5 ml (1 tsp) ground cinnamon
2.5 ml (½ tsp) ground cloves
15–30 ml (1–2 tbsp) milk
125 g (4 oz) light muscovado sugar
15 ml (1 tbsp) double cream

1 Grease and base line an 18 cm (7 inch) deep round cake tin.
2 Neatly shred the nuts and grill until golden. Roll out the almond paste to an 18 cm (7 inch) circle, cover loosely with greaseproof paper and set aside.
3 Beat together 175 g (6 oz) of the softened butter, the caster sugar and the vanilla flavouring until pale and fluffy. Add the eggs, a little at a time, to the mixture, beating thoroughly after each addition.
4 With a large metal spoon, fold in the flour, spices and 75 g (3 oz) of the almonds. Add enough milk to give a dropping consistency.
5 Spoon half of the cake mixture into the tin and place the circle of almond paste on top. Add the remaining cake mixture and level the surface. Bake at 180°C (350°F) mark 4 for 1–1¼ hours or until well risen, golden and firm to the touch. Cool for 5 minutes before turning out on to a wire rack to cool. Stand the wire rack on a baking tray.
6 For the topping, heat the remaining butter, the muscovado sugar and cream until blended. Bring to the boil, remove from the heat and stir in the remaining almonds. Pour over the cake. Allow to cool for 5–10 minutes or until set. Store for up to 1 week in an airtight container.

HAZELNUT AND LEMON CRISPS

MAKES ABOUT 52
125 g (4 oz) hazelnuts, toasted and skinned
125 g (4 oz) butter
50 g (2 oz) soft light brown sugar
25 g (1 oz) icing sugar
1 egg yolk
175 g (6 oz) plain flour
lemon curd (preferably home made)
icing sugar, to dust

1 Process or grind the nuts, preferably through a nut mouli, to a fine powder.
2 Beat the butter until soft, then add the sugars a little at a time and beat until very soft, pale and fluffy. Add the egg yolk with 15 ml (1 tbsp) water. Gradually work in the flour and nuts until the mixture forms a smooth, pliable dough. Knead well then wrap and chill for 15–20 minutes.
3 Roll out the dough to 3 mm (⅛ inch) thick. Stamp out rounds using a 5 cm (2 inch) plain cutter. Prick lightly with a fork and place on greased baking trays. Bake at 180°C (350°F) mark 4 for 7–10 minutes or until golden brown.
4 Cool slightly before transferring to a wire rack to cool. Serve plain or sandwich with lemon curd. Dust with icing sugar.

DEVONSHIRE FRUIT SCONES

MAKES ABOUT 12
225 g (8 oz) self-raising flour
25 g (1 oz) caster sugar
75 g (3 oz) butter or margarine
50 g (2 oz) dried mixed fruit
1 egg, beaten
milk, to mix and glaze

1 Mix together the flour and sugar. Rub in the butter until the mixture resembles fine breadcrumbs. Stir in the dried fruit. Add the beaten egg and 45–60 ml (3–4 tbsp) milk to make a soft, but not sticky, dough. Knead lightly.
2 On a lightly floured surface, roll out the dough to a thickness of about 2 cm (¾ inch). Use a 5 cm (2 inch) fluted cutter to stamp into rounds. Place on a greased baking sheet, brush with milk and bake at 220°C (425°F) mark 7 for about 8 minutes or until well risen and golden. Serve warm or cold.

CARDAMOM FINGERS

MAKES ABOUT 30

8–10 fresh green cardamom pods

50 g (2 oz) butter

50 g (2 oz) caster sugar

2 egg whites

50 g (2 oz) plain flour, sifted

1 Split open the cardamom pods and crush the black seeds to a fine powder in a small mortar and pestle.

2 Beat the butter until soft, then add the sugar and cardamom and mix well. Gradually add the egg whites to the mixture, beating thoroughly after each addition. Lightly fold in the flour.

3 Spoon the mixture into a piping bag fitted with a 5 mm (¼ inch) plain nozzle. Pipe the mixture into 7.5 cm (3 inch) lengths on to greased baking sheets, dusted with flour. Bake at 220°C (425°F) mark 7 for about 5 minutes or until golden and tinged with brown at the edges. Cool on a wire rack.

BLUEBERRY SHORTBREAD TARTLETS

MAKES ABOUT 16

125 g (4 oz) butter

50 g (2 oz) caster sugar

50 g (2 oz) semolina

125 g (4 oz) plain flour

120 ml (8 tbsp) low fat soft cheese

a little single cream

fresh blueberries and/or raspberries

redcurrant jelly (optional)

1 Beat the butter until soft. Add the sugar, semolina and flour and work together to form a smooth, pliable dough. Cover and chill for 20 minutes.

2 Roll out the shortbread to just under 5 mm (¼ inch) thick. Use a 7.5 cm (3 inch) plain cutter to stamp out rounds. Ease the rounds into small brioche tins. Prick the bases well. Bake at 150°C (300°F) mark 2 on the centre shelf for 25–35 minutes or until firm and golden. Ease out of the tins and cool on a wire rack.

3 Mix the cheese with about 20 ml (4 tsp) cream to lighten the consistency. Spoon a little into the base of each tartlet. Arrange the fruit on top.

4 If wished, glaze the fruit. Melt redcurrant jelly in a small pan, adding a little water if necessary. Allow to cool a little before brushing ove the fruit.

STRAWBERRY AND PASSION FRUIT CREAM CAKE

125 g (4 oz) plain flour

4 eggs

125 g (4 oz) caster sugar

grated rind and juice of 1 orange

25 g (1 oz) icing sugar

450 g (1 lb) strawberries, hulled

2 passion fruit

600 ml (1 pint) double cream

1 Grease and base line a 23 cm (9 inch) cake tin, then dust with flour and sugar. Sift the flour twice and leave on one side.

2 Place the eggs, caster sugar and the orange rind in a large mixing bowl. Use an electric whisk to whisk the ingredients together until the mixture is very pale and thick enough to leave a trail for about 5 seconds. Sift the flour again over the egg mixture. Fold in carefully using a metal spoon or spatula. Pour into the prepared tin.

3 Bake at 190°C (375°F) mark 5 just above the centre of the oven for 40–50 minutes or until pale brown and springy to the touch. Carefully loosen the cake from the edges of the tin using a palette knife. Turn out and cool on a wire rack.

4 Meanwhile, mix together the orange juice and icing sugar. Reserve about eight small strawberries for decoration. Quarter the remainder and toss lightly into the orange mixture. Cut the passion fruit in half, scoop out the pips and pulp and add to the strawberries. Leave for about 20–30 minutes in the refrigerator to allow the flavours to develop.

5 Carefully split the cake in three horizontally. Whip the cream until it just holds its shape. Use to fill the cake with the drained strawberries and passion fruit.

6 Cover the top with cream, smooth over lightly and decorate with reserved strawberries. Keep in the refrigerator until required.

MINIATURE FLORENTINES

MAKES ABOUT 35

125 g (4 oz) butter

75 g (3 oz) caster sugar

15 ml (1 tbsp) double cream

125 g (4 oz) flaked almonds

50 g (2 oz) chopped candied peel

50 g (2 oz) glacé cherries, halved

175 g (6 oz) plain chocolate, melted

1 Melt the butter in a saucepan, add the sugar and stir to dissolve. Add the cream and let the mixture bubble for 1 minute. Stir in the nuts, peel and cherries.

2 Drop neat 1 cm (½ inch) rounds of the mixture on to baking sheets lined with non-stick baking parchment, spacing well apart. Bake at 180°C (350°F) mark 4 for about 8 minutes or until golden.

3 Leave for 30 seconds then, with a spatula, push each florentine into a neat round. Transfer to a wire rack to cool.

4 When hard, coat the base of each biscuit with melted chocolate.

CHOCOLATE ALMOND TRUFFLES

MAKES ABOUT 30

125 g (4 oz) blanched almonds, toasted

125 g (4 oz) plain chocolate, broken into small pieces

75 g (3 oz) butter, flaked

150 g (5 oz) Madeira cake, crumbled

30 ml (2 level tbsp) icing sugar

30 ml (2 tbsp) Amaretto liqueur or brandy

TOPPING

175 g (6 oz) plain chocolate, melted and cooled

30 whole almonds

1 Coarsely grind or chop the almonds.

2 Melt the chocolate in a bowl over a pan of simmering water. Cool slightly, then add the butter and stir until melted. Stir in the nuts, cake crumbs, icing sugar and liqueur or brandy.

3 Chill the mixture until it is firm enough to handle, then roll into about 30 balls. Chill again until the truffles are firm.

4 Coat with melted chocolate and top each truffle with an almond. Leave on a wire rack until set, then place in paper cases to serve.

CELEBRATION CAKES

To give the cake time to mature, make it at least 1 month ahead, longer if possible.

CAKES:

CHRISTENING CAKE

550 g (1¼ lb) sultanas
450 g (1 lb) currants
450 g (1 lb) raisins
350 g (12 oz) glacé cherries, halved
125 g (4 oz) chopped mixed peel
finely grated rind of 1 orange
finely grated rind of 1 lemon
45 ml (3 tbsp) Grand Marnier
250 g (9 oz) butter
125 g (4 oz) soft light brown sugar
150 g (5 oz) muscovado sugar
7 eggs, size 2
125 g (4 oz) ground almonds
275 g (10 oz) plain flour

WEDDING CAKE

900 g (2 lb) sultanas
700 g (1½ lb) currants
700 g (1½ lb) raisins
550 g (1¼ lb) glacé cherries, halved
175 g (6 oz) chopped mixed peel
finely grated rind of 2 oranges
finely grated rind of 2 lemons
90 ml (6 tbsp) Grand Marnier
425 g (15 oz) butter
200 g (7 oz) soft light brown sugar
225 g (8 oz) muscovado sugar
12 eggs, size 2
175 g (6 oz) ground almonds
450 g (1 lb) plain flour

EXTRA SPIRIT FOR SOAKING BAKED CAKE

60 ml (4 tbsp) brandy, whisky or rum

ALMOND PASTE:

CHRISTENING CAKE

450 g (1 lb) ground almonds
225 g (8 oz) caster sugar
225 g (8 oz) icing sugar, sifted
2.5 ml (½ tsp) almond flavouring
8 egg yolks, size 2
1 egg white

ALMOND PASTE:

WEDDING CAKE

700 g (1½ lb) ground almonds
350 g (12 oz) caster sugar
350 g (12 oz) icing sugar, sifted
5 ml (1 tsp) almond flavouring
12 egg yolks, size 2
1 egg white

ROYAL ICING:

CHRISTENING CAKE

6 egg whites, size 2
1.4 kg (3 lb) icing sugar, sifted
25 ml (1½ tbsp) glycerine

WEDDING CAKE

8 egg whites, size 2
1.8 kg (4 lb) icing sugar, sifted
25 ml (1½ tbsp) glycerine

DECORATIONS:

CHRISTENING CAKE

450 g (1 lb) icing sugar
2 egg whites
few drops acetic acid
ribbon in a colour of your choice

WEDDING CAKE

33 cm (13 inch) round cake board
23 cm (9 inch) round cake board
1¾ metres (1¾ yards) of 5 cm (2 inch) wide lace
about 20 silver leaves
silver balls
4 cake pillars
flowers to match the bride's bouquet or 2 orchids

1 To make the cake, put the sultanas, currants, raisins, cherries, peel and orange and lemon rinds into a large mixing bowl. Add the Grand Marnier and mix well. Cover and leave to stand for 2–3 hours.

2 For the Christening cake, line a 25 cm (10 inch) cake tin with a double thickness of greaseproof paper. Cut a strip of thick brown paper, double thickness, long enough to fit around the tin, and as deep as the tin. For the wedding cake, use a 25 cm (10 inch) round tin and an 18 cm (7 inch) round tin.

3 Beat the butter with the sugars until very light, soft and fluffy. Beat in the eggs, one at a time, beating well between each addition. Fold in the ground almonds and flour. Add the soaked fruit, and mix thoroughly together.

4 Spoon the cake mixture into the prepared tin(s) and spread evenly. When filling the tins for the wedding cake, to ensure that each tier is exactly the same

in depth, insert a clean ruler in the centre of each cake – they should measure about 6 cm (2½ inches) deep. Wrap the brown paper strips(s) around the tin(s) and secure with string.

5 Bake at 150°C (300°F) mark 2. For the 25 cm (10 inch) round cakes allow 4–4½ hours; for the 18 cm (7 inch) round cake allow 3–3½ hours. Bake until a skewer inserted in the centre of the cake comes out clean. Allow the cake(s) to cool in the tin(s) for 1 hour, then turn out onto a wire rack to cool completely.

6 To store, wrap the cold cake(s) in greaseproof paper and then in foil. Store in a cool, dry, airy cupboard. Start to apply the almond paste and ice the cake(s) 2 weeks before the celebration date.

7 To make the almond paste, mix the almonds and sugars together in a large mixing bowl. Add the almond flavouring and egg yolks and mix together to make a stiff paste. Knead only just enough to smooth the paste. Do not overwork it as this will cause the oil in the almonds to seep out, spoiling the icing.

8 To make the royal icing, lightly whisk the egg whites, then gradually beat in the icing sugar, beating until the icing is very white. Beat in the glycerine.

9 To cover the cakes with almond paste, remove the cake(s) from their wrapping and place upside-down on a cake board. Prick the cake(s) all over with a fine skewer, then carefully pour the chosen spirit over the top, a little at a time, and allow it to soak in.

10 Cut off one third of the almond paste and set it aside. For a round cake, roll out the remaining almond paste to a long strip, long enough and wide enough to fit around the side of the cake. Brush the strip with a little beaten egg white, then fit it around the cake (egg white side to the cake) and press firmly into position. Roll a clean jam jar gently around the side of the cake until the almond paste is smooth, and the ends are well joined together. Trim the almond paste level with the top of the cake, if necessary.

11 For a square cake, divide the remaining almond paste into four equal pieces. Take one piece and roll it out until it is the same length and depth as one side of the cake. Brush with a little beaten egg white, and place firmly in position against the side of the cake. Repeat with the remaining pieces, shaping the corners well.

12 Roll the reserved almond paste out to a round or square, large enough to fit the top of the cake. Brush the top of the cake with egg white, then place the almond paste on top, and roll gently into position with a rolling pin. Smooth the joins with a small palette knife. Leave in a cool place for 24 hours before icing.

13 To flat ice the cakes with royal icing, spread a good layer of the icing over the top of the cake with a palette knife, working the knife backwards and forwards to expel air bubbles. Pull a ruler, preferably a metal one, across the top of the cake to smooth the icing.

14 Spread the sides of the cake with icing (one side at a time for a square cake), spreading it as smoothly as possible. Pull a cake scraper around the side, or along the side, to smooth the icing – put a round cake on a turntable, if possible. Leave overnight, in a cool place, to dry.

15 Put the remaining icing into a clean mixing bowl and cover the surface closely with greaseproof paper. Cover the bowl and refrigerate until the next day. Beat the icing well before using again. Store the icing in this way after each application.

16 Next day, scrape away the rough icing from the top edge of the cake, and from the board, with a small sharp knife. Brush off loose icing from the cake with a clean dry pastry brush. Give the cake three more coats of icing, allowing each coat to dry overnight before applying the next. Reserve the remaining icing for decoration.

17 To decorate the wedding cake, put the lace around the side of each cake, securing it neatly with pins.

18 Put some of the remaining icing into a paper piping bag fitted with a small star nozzle. Decorate the top of each cake with a shell border, piping one shell on the top of the cake at a slight angle, then piping the next shell on the side of the cake, so that it very slightly overlaps the end of the shell piped on the top of the cake. Continue all around the edges. Decorate with silver balls.

19 To complete the larger cake, pipe the same shell pattern around the bottom of the cake, then decorate with silver leaves. To complete the smaller cake, pipe a single row of shells around the bottom edge of the cake, then decorate with silver balls. Allow the decoration to dry for 24 hours before assembling the cake.

20 To assemble the cake, place the four pillars in the centre of the cake, spacing them evenly apart. Carefully place the small cake on the top, then decorate with flowers.

21 The Christening cake is decorated with swans, made from royal icing. If you feel unable to make the swans, you can decorate the top of the cake with flowers, or a bought decoration of your choice.

22 You only need three swans, but it is advisable to make a few extra to allow for breakages. Make up royal icing as above but add a few drops of acetic acid to harden the icing. Cut several squares of

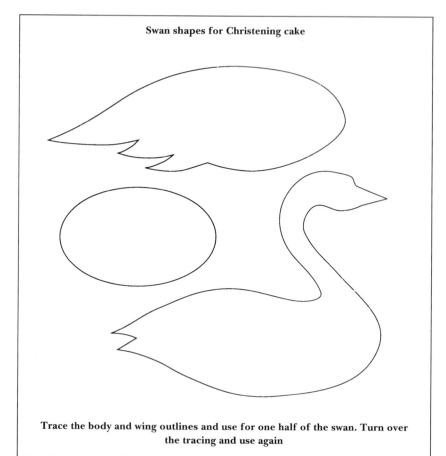

Swan shapes for Christening cake

Trace the body and wing outlines and use for one half of the swan. Turn over the tracing and use again

non-stick baking parchment, just large enough to cover the swan diagram – see above. Put a little icing into a small icing bag, and cut a small hole in the bottom of the bag.

23 Place a piece of the paper over a right-hand swan body. Trace the outline of the body, just as if you were drawing with a pencil. Fill the outline in completely with icing. Then, to smooth the icing out, gently rub a small palette knife from side to side under the paper, holding the paper firmly on the work surface. Make 4–5 more right-hand body pieces. Make an equal number of left-hand body pieces. Lay on a large flat tray to dry.

24 To make the wings, put a little more icing into a new paper piping bag and cut a small hole in the bottom. Making one wing at a time, place a piece of the paper over a wing diagram, then start to pipe from the tip of the wing in a continuous line from side to side across the wing, each line touching the other.

25 Make a pair of wings for each swan. Place on the tray with the swan bodies. Make a base for each swan in the same way as making the bodies. Dry in a cool place for at least 24 hours.

26 To assemble the swans, put the body pieces into pairs, then join them together with a little icing. Pipe a small 'blob' of

icing on one of the base pieces, then place a swan body on top. Pipe a good 'blob' of icing at either side of the body, then place the wings in position – angling the wings out slightly.

27 To support the swan until the icing has set hard, stand it on a flat tray and place an egg cup or a ball of aluminium foil at each side, just behind each wing – this will take the weight and prevent the swan falling over. Repeat with the other swans.

28 To decorate the cake, mark a row of evenly spaced scallops around the side of the cake so that they end just about halfway down the side of the cake. Put a little icing into a small paper piping bag and cut a small hole in the bottom of the bag. Pipe continuous squiggly lines to give a filigree effect. Put some more icing into a paper piping bag fitted with a small star nozzle, then pipe a star edge to each scallop. Tie ribbon around the side of the cake, just under the scallops, ending with a neat bow. Secure the ribbon around the edge of the cake board.

29 Decorate the top edge of the cake with three rows of stars, then pipe a row of stars around the bottom edge. To complete the cake, make three pretty bows with thin ribbon and tie one around each swan neck. Place the swans on top of the cake.

CHICKEN BREASTS IN MUSCAT WINE WITH APRICOTS

SERVES 20 AS PART OF A BUFFET

2 bottles of dry muscat wine

3 large shallots, skinned and finely chopped

about 8 sprigs of fresh thyme

2 bay leaves, torn in half

15 ml (1 tbsp) finely chopped lemon rind

salt and freshly ground pepper

20 chicken breasts (on the bone)

150 g (5 oz) sugar

2 cinnamon sticks

1.8 kg (4 lb) ripe apricots, halved and stoned

fresh chervil sprigs, to garnish

1 Boil 900 ml (1½ pints) of the wine in a large flameproof casserole until reduced to 75 ml (3 fl oz). Pour in the remaining wine and add the shallots, herbs, lemon rind and seasoning.

2 Add the chicken breasts, skin side down. Bring just to boiling point, then cover tightly and transfer to the oven. (Use 2 or 3 casserole dishes if you don't have one large enough.) Cook at 175°C (325°F) mark 3 for 45–50 minutes, turning the chicken over every 20 minutes. Leave to cool in the liquor.

3 Drain the chicken, reserving the liquor. Discard the skin and remove the breasts from the bones in one piece. Remove any fat from the surface of the liquor. Return the breasts to the liquor, cover and refrigerate overnight.

4 The next day, the liquor should have gelled slightly. Remove any remaining fat from the surface. Lift out the chicken breasts and set aside. Warm the liquor slightly, then pour it through a sieve lined with muslin or cheesecloth.

5 Reserve about 150 ml (¼ pint) of the liquor and put the remainder in a saucepan. Add the sugar. Heat, stirring, until the sugar has dissolved, then add the cinnamon sticks and bring to the boil. Lower the heat and add about one third of the apricots. They should be covered by the liquor. Poach the fruit for about 5 minutes. Transfer to a bowl using a slotted spoon. Poach the remaining apricots and add to the bowl.

6 Pour the liquor over the apricots and leave to cool, stirring from time to time. Cover and chill.

7 Carve the chicken breasts into thin slices. Arrange the slices in fan shapes on one or two large, cold platters. Brush the slices lightly with the reserved liquor.

8 Remove the apricots from their liquor, using a slotted spoon, and arrange them on and around the chicken, cutting some of the apricot halves in half again. Garnish the platter with sprigs of chervil.

GLAZED GAMMON WITH MUSTARD SAUCE

SERVES 16–20 AS PART OF A BUFFET

5.4 kg (12 lb) cooked whole gammon, on the bone

425 g (15 oz) can of pineapple rings

75–125 g (3–4 oz) glacé cherries, halved

whole cloves

225 g (8 oz) clear honey

225 g (8 oz) demerara sugar

MUSTARD SAUCE

60 ml (4 tbsp) mustard powder

200 ml (7 fl oz) mayonnaise

150 ml (¼ pint) soured cream

1 Carefully remove the skin from the gammon. Score the fat deeply with an attractive diamond pattern.

2 Drain the pineapple rings, reserving the juice. Cut each pineapple ring equally into six. Decorate the gammon attractively with the pineapple pieces and the cherries, securing them to the fat with cloves.

3 Place the decorated gammon in a large roasting tin and carefully spoon the honey evenly all over it. Sprinkle the sugar evenly all over the honey, reserving about 45 ml (3 tbsp). Spoon about 60 ml (4 tbsp) of the pineapple juice over the sugar and honey.

4 Bake the gammon at 220°C (425°F) mark 7 for about 45 minutes, basting it frequently with the sugar and honey mixture, until it is nicely glazed but not over-browned. Remove the gammon from the oven and sprinkle evenly with the reserved sugar. Allow to cool, then cover loosely with foil and refrigerate until ready to serve.

5 To make the mustard sauce, blend the mustard powder with 60 ml (4 tbsp) cold water until smooth. Cover and allow to stand for about 15 minutes. Mix the mustard, mayonnaise and soured cream together until smooth. Pour into a serving bowl, cover and refrigerate until required.

6 To serve, place the gammon on a ham stand, or a board, and decorate the end of the bone with a ham frill. Serve in slices with the sauce.

CHICKEN AND CORIANDER NUT CRUMBLE

two 1.1 kg (2½ lb) oven-ready chickens

slices of onion and 2 bay leaves, for flavouring

pared rind and juice of 1 lemon

salt and freshly ground pepper

2 bunches of spring onions, trimmed

200 g (7 oz) butter or margarine

350 g (12 oz) small button mushrooms, wiped

60 ml (4 tbsp) wholegrain mustard

165 g (5½ oz) plain flour

150 ml (¼ pint) single cream

about 75 ml (5 tbsp) chopped fresh coriander

75 g (3 oz) plain wholemeal flour

30 ml (2 tbsp) ground coriander

125 g (4 oz) unsalted shelled peanuts, roughly chopped

1 Place the chickens in saucepans, cover well with water, add the flavouring ingredients with the pared rind of the lemon and seasoning. Bring to the boil, cover and simmer for about 50 minutes or until the chickens are tender and cooked through. Test the thickest part of the leg with a skewer – when cooked the juices should run clear.

2 Lift the chickens out of the stock. Cool slightly, then strip all the flesh off the chickens, discarding the skin but returning the bones to the stock. Boil the stock for about 30 minutes or until reduced by about half. Strain into a measuring jug. Meanwhile, cut the chicken into bite-sized pieces and place in a single layer in one or two shallow ovenproof dishes.

3 Cut the spring onions into 2.5 cm (1 inch) lengths. Heat 75 g (3 oz) of the butter in a large saucepan. Add the mushrooms, onions and mustard and stir over a moderate heat until soft.

4 Stir in 65 g (2½ oz) plain flour followed by 1 litre (1¾ pints) of the chicken stock. Bring to the boil, stirring all the time, then bubble for a couple of minutes – the sauce will be quite thin at this point. Take off the heat, stir in the cream, 30 ml (2 tbsp) lemon juice, the fresh coriander and seasoning. Pour over the chicken, stirring gently to mix.

5 Mix together the remaining flours with the coriander. Rub in the remaining butter and then stir in the peanuts. Sprinkle this topping over the chicken mixture.

6 Bake at 200°C (400°F) mark 6 for about 45–50 minutes or until piping hot and golden brown. If using two dishes, swap them around halfway through.

SPICED CHICKEN TERRINES

SERVES 12 AS PART OF A BUFFET

175 g (6 oz) brown rice

salt and freshly ground pepper

150 g (5 oz) dried apricots, soaked and drained

two 300 g (11 oz) packets frozen leaf spinach

125 g (4 oz) walnut pieces, roughly chopped

15 ml (1 tbsp) ground cumin

10 ml (2 tsp) ground coriander

1 egg, size 2, beaten

10–12 chicken breast fillets (about 125 g/4 oz each)

vegetable oil

24 g (0.85 oz) packet aspic jelly

watercress, to garnish

300 ml (½ pint) thick home-made mayonnaise

1 Cook the brown rice in boiling salted water for about 30 minutes or until tender. Drain well.

2 Cut the apricots into slivers. Thaw the spinach and drain well, pressing out excess moisture. Mix together the rice, apricots, spinach, walnuts, spices, seasoning and egg.

3 Trim the chicken of any fat or sinew and sear 3–4 pieces at a time in a very hot, lightly oiled frying pan. Remove the pieces and set aside while cooking the rest. Cool.

4 Cut through each chicken breast (slightly on the diagonal) making three or four fairly thick slices. Arrange half the chicken in the base of two 11 × 23 cm (4½ × 9 inch) non-stick loaf tins. Spoon over the rice mixture. Cover with the rest of the chicken, and put a piece of foil over the top.

5 Stand the tins in a dish half filled with warm water and bake at 180°C (350°F) mark 4 for about 1 hour 20 minutes or until the chicken feels firm when pressed. Leave to cool in the tins.

6 When cold, refrigerate for 2–3 hours only. Turn out of the tins, wash the tins and replace the terrines.

7 Make up the packet of aspic following manufacturer's instructions. Cool, then pour over the two terrines. Return to the refrigerator for about 2 hours or until set. Turn out and slice. Garnish with watercress and serve with mayonnaise flavoured with fresh herbs.

QUICK CHICKEN AND GRUYÈRE SALAD

SERVES 8 AS PART OF A BUFFET

1.1 kg (2½ lb) cooked, boned chicken

4 celery sticks, trimmed and thickly sliced

125 g (4 oz) Gruyère or Emmenthal cheese, coarsely grated

2 firm, red apples, cored and roughly chopped

175 g (6 oz) seedless black grapes, halved

200 ml (7 fl oz) oil

30 ml (2 tbsp) white wine vinegar

60 ml (4 tbsp) soured cream

60 ml (4 tbsp) mayonnaise

60 ml (4 tbsp) chopped fresh parsley

75 g (3 oz) toasted pecan nuts or walnuts

salt and freshly ground pepper

1 Skin the chicken if necessary. Cut the flesh into large bite-sized pieces.

2 Place the chicken, celery, cheese, apple and grapes in a large bowl. Add all the other ingredients and toss well. Adjust the seasoning, cover and refrigerate for at least 10–15 minutes before serving.

BACON AND PISTACHIO TERRINE

SERVES 10 AS PART OF A BUFFET

25 g (1 oz) shelled pistachio nuts

125 g (4 oz) hazelnuts

1 large onion, skinned and roughly chopped

15 g (½ oz) butter or margarine

4 eggs

18 rashers rindless streaky bacon, about 450 g (1 lb)

450 g (1 lb) minced pork

175 g (6 oz) fresh white breadcrumbs

5 ml (1 tsp) dried thyme

90 ml (6 tbsp) single cream

salt and freshly ground pepper

1 Cover the pistachio nuts with boiling water. Leave for about 1 minute, then drain, skin and reserve. Toast the hazelnuts, then remove the skins by rubbing the nuts in a tea towel. Cook the onion in the butter or margarine until soft, then cool. Hard-boil two of the eggs, then leave to cool.

2 Stretch six rashers of bacon with the back of a round-bladed knife and use to line a 1.1 litre (2 pint) loaf tin. Place another six rashers of bacon, the pork, onions, breadcrumbs, thyme, hazelnuts, the hard-boiled and remaining raw eggs in a blender or food processor and blend until thoroughly combined. Work in batches, if necessary. Beat in the cream and season to taste.

3 Spoon a third of the mixture into the prepared tin and cover with a layer of half the remaining bacon and half the pistachio nuts. Spoon on half the remaining minced mixture, top with the remaining bacon and pistachio nuts and finish with a layer of the minced mixture.

4 Cover with foil and place in a roasting tin half-filled with water. Bake at 180°C (350°F) mark 4 for about 2 hours or until firm to the touch and the juices run clear when the terrine is pierced with a fine skewer. Remove from the oven and weigh down for at least 2 hours, preferably overnight, in the refrigerator.

5 Turn out and serve, thickly sliced. Covered, the terrine will keep in the refrigerator for 7–10 days.

WING RIB OF BEEF WITH MANGO AND HORSERADISH SAUCE

SERVES 16–20 AS PART OF A BUFFET

5.4 kg (12 lb) wing rib of beef, chined

30 ml (2 tbsp) olive oil

salt and freshly ground pepper

finely chopped fresh parsley, to garnish

SAUCE

1 ripe mango, peeled, stoned and chopped

175 g (6 oz) horseradish sauce

30 ml (2 tbsp) double cream

30 ml (2 tbsp) finely chopped fresh parsley

1 Stand the beef joint in a large roasting tin, fat side uppermost. Rub all over with the olive oil, then season well.

2 Roast the beef at 220°C (425°F) mark 7 for 1 hour, then reduce the oven temperature to 190°C (375°F) mark 5, and continue roasting for a further 1½ hours, basting the beef frequently during cooking with its dripping. Remove from the oven and allow to cool, then cover loosely with foil and refrigerate overnight.

3 Mix the mango, horseradish sauce, cream and parsley together, then spoon into a serving bowl. Cover and refrigerate until ready to serve.

4 To serve the beef, carefully cut away the feather bones from the meat with a sharp knife. Leave the rib bones still attached. Trim off as much fat as possible from the meat, leaving behind just a thin layer. Cover the fat with a thin layer of finely chopped parsley – this gives a very attractive appearance. Place the beef on a board, rib bones down. Carve into thin slices down to the bones, freeing the meat from the bones with the knife held horizontally against the bones. Serve with the sauce.

ROUGH GAME PÂTÉ

SERVES 12 AS PART OF A BUFFET
450 g (1 lb) streaky bacon, rinded
225 g (8 oz) pig's liver, skinned and roughly chopped
225 g (8 oz) onions, skinned and roughly chopped
700 g (1½ lb) hare joints or venison
225 g (8 oz) pork sausagemeat
1 small orange
45 ml (3 tbsp) brandy
45 ml (3 tbsp) chopped fresh coriander or parsley
1 egg
salt and freshly ground pepper
orange slices and fresh coriander, to garnish

1 Stretch half the bacon rashers with the back of a blunt-edged knife. Coarsely mince the remaining bacon with the liver and onion, then place the mixture in a large bowl.
2 Cut all the hare meat off the bone and divide into small pieces (not larger than 5 mm/¼ inch). If using venison, cut it into pieces of a similar size. Add to the bowl with the sausagemeat, grated rind of half the orange and 45 ml (3 tbsp) orange juice, the brandy, coriander, egg and plenty of seasoning. Stir well until evenly mixed. Cover tightly and refrigerate for about 8 hours or overnight.
3 Line a 1.4-1.7 litre (2½-3 pint) terrine with the prepared bacon rashers. Stir the pâté mixture, then spoon into the lined terrine. Cover tightly with foil and stand the dish in a roasting tin. Pour in enough water to come halfway up the sides of the terrine.
4 Bake at 170°C (325°F) mark 3 for 2½-3 hours or until the juices run clear when the pâté is pierced with a fine skewer. Leave to cool slightly.
5 Place a few heavy weights on top of the pâté and complete cooling. Cover and refrigerate overnight.
6 Turn out the pâté, reserving any juices to add to gravies or stocks. Slice and serve garnished with orange and coriander.

GLAZED STUFFED TURKEY

SERVES 15 AS PART OF A BUFFET
45 ml (3 tbsp) oil
butter or margarine
350 g (12 oz) onions, skinned and roughly chopped
6 celery sticks, trimmed and roughly chopped
2 eating apples, cored and roughly chopped
175 g (6 oz) fresh breadcrumbs
125 g (4 oz) coarse oatmeal
50 g (2 oz) suet
45 ml (3 tbsp) chopped fresh sage or 5 ml (1 tsp) dried rubbed sage
finely grated rind and juice of 2 oranges
salt and freshly ground black pepper
1 egg, beaten
about 5 kg (11 lb) oven-ready turkey
45 ml (3 tbsp) thick honey
45 ml (3 tbsp) dry sherry
about 450 ml (¾ pint) turkey or chicken stock
about 60 ml (4 level tbsp) cornflour
fresh herbs or watercress, to garnish

1 Heat the oil in a frying pan. Add 50 g (2 oz) butter and fry the onions and celery until beginning to brown. Stir the apples into the pan and fry for a minute or two. Turn out into a large bowl to cool.
2 Stir in the breadcrumbs, oatmeal, suet and sage. Add the orange rind with 45 ml (3 tbsp) orange juice (reserving the remaining juice for the gravy). Season well, add the egg and mix thoroughly.
3 Spoon the stuffing into the neck end of the turkey only. Secure the flap of skin with a fine skewer. Place the remaining stuffing in a greased ovenproof dish to bake later (see step 5).
4 Place the turkey on a large strong sheet of foil, then lift into a large roasting tin. Spread the breast and legs thinly with the honey. Dot generously with butter and grind over some black pepper. Carefully spoon over the sherry and fold the foil loosely around the turkey.
5 Bake at 180°C (350°F) mark 4 for about 4 hours. Fold the foil back, baste well and return to the oven for about a further 1 hour. (Put the dish of stuffing in the oven to bake for about 1 hour.) The turkey should be a rich dark brown. Test the thickest part of the leg with a fine skewer. The juices should run clear when the bird is cooked. Return to the oven for a little longer, if necessary, laying a sheet of foil over the bird, once well browned.

6 Lift the turkey on to a serving dish, cover and keep warm.
7 Pour the cooking liquor into a saucepan and skim well. Add the stock with the remaining orange juice and bubble for 4–5 minutes to reduce slightly and strengthen the flavour.
8 Mix the cornflour to a smooth paste with a little water. Stir into the pan juices and bring to the boil. Cook for a minute or two. If necessary, thicken further before adjusting the seasoning. Garnish the turkey with fresh herbs or watercress.

SMOKED SALMON QUICHES

MAKES ABOUT 16-20 SLICES
175 g (6 oz) butter or margarine
350 g (12 oz) plain flour
90 ml (6 tbsp) finely chopped black olives
2 large onions, peeled and finely chopped
45 ml (3 tbsp) vegetable oil
225 g (8 oz) smoked salmon trimmings
4 eggs
350 g (12 oz) low fat soft cheese
50 g (2 oz) soft fresh goat's cheese
600 ml (1 pint) single cream
30 ml (2 tbsp) chopped fresh thyme or dill
salt and freshly ground pepper

1 Rub the butter into the flour. Stir in the olives, then bind to a firm dough with about 75-90 ml (5-6 tbsp) water. Knead lightly until just smooth. Wrap and chill for about 30 minutes.
2 On a lightly floured surface, thinly roll out half the pastry at a time and use each piece to line a 23 cm (9 inch) fluted flan ring, about 4 cm (1½ inches) deep, placed on a baking sheet. Chill well, then bake blind until golden brown and well dried out.
3 Meanwhile, cook the onion in the oil until soft and golden. Cool slightly. Roughly chop the smoked salmon trimmings. Whisk the eggs and cheeses together until almost smooth then whisk in the cream, herbs and seasoning. Add salt sparingly. Divide the onion and smoked salmon between the flans and pour over the egg custard.
4 Bake at 170°C (325°F) mark 3 for 50-60 minutes or until lightly set. Serve warm or cold.

SOLE AND SMOKED SALMON TERRINE

SERVES 8–10 AS PART OF A BUFFET

550 g (1¼ lb) Dover sole fillets, skinned
15 ml (1 tbsp) lemon juice
salt and white pepper
2 egg whites
150 ml (¼ pint) double cream
175 g (6 oz) young spinach leaves, shredded
SMOKED SALMON CREAM
175 g (6 oz) smoked salmon
lemon juice
1 egg white, size 6
75 ml (3 fl oz) crème fraîche or double cream
cayenne pepper
red and green peppers, cucumber skin, lemon rind and very small watercress sprigs, to garnish

1 Purée the sole in a blender or food processor. Add the lemon juice and salt and then the egg whites. For a really smooth terrine, pass the mixture through a fine sieve.

2 Return the mixture to the blender or food processor bowl. With the motor running, very gradually pour in the cream. Season with pepper. Chill for 1 hour.

3 To make the salmon cream, purée the smoked salmon in a blender or food processor. Add a squeeze of lemon juice and then the egg white. Pass through a fine sieve as for the sole, then return to the blender or food processor. With the motor running, gradually pour in the crème fraîche or cream. Season with cayenne pepper. Chill for about 1 hour.

4 Cook the spinach with 15 ml (1 tbsp) water until wilted. Drain well, then rinse in cold running water. Drain again well, pressing down on the spinach to extract all the water. Purée and season.

5 For the garnish, grill the peppers until they are soft and the skins are charred all over. Allow to cool, then peel the peppers. Remove the core and seeds. Cut the peppers into decorative shapes. Arrange the pepper shapes, cucumber skin and lemon rind on the bottom of a lightly oiled 25 × 10 cm (10 × 4 inch) terrine.

6 Carefully cover the bottom and sides of the terrine with about two thirds of the sole mixture. Leave an open channel in the centre. Place about half of the smoked salmon mixture in the channel, then cover the salmon with the spinach purée. Cover with the remaining salmon mixture and cover this with the remaining sole mixture. Cover the terrine with greased greaseproof paper.

7 Put the terrine into a roasting tin. Surround with boiling water and bake at 170°C (325°F) mark 3 for about 50 minutes or until just set in the centre. Remove the terrine from the oven and leave to cool. Drain off any excess cooking liquid.

8 Carefully unmould the terrine on to a cold plate. Garnish with watercress.

CHICKEN AND MUSHROOM LASAGNE

SERVES 8–10

225 g (8 oz) frozen leaf spinach, thawed
1.8 kg (4 lb) oven-ready chicken
slices of carrot and onion and a bay leaf, for flavouring
salt and freshly ground pepper
oil
275 g (10 oz) lasagne
450 g (1 lb) mushrooms, wiped
175 g (6 oz) butter or margarine
30 ml (2 tbsp) lemon juice
125 g (4 oz) plain flour
1 litre (1¾ pints) milk
150 g (5 oz) full fat soft cheese with garlic and herbs
45 ml (3 tbsp) chopped fresh tarragon or 10 ml (2 tsp) dried
2 large garlic cloves, skinned and crushed
75 g (3 oz) thinly sliced Parma ham or roast ham, shredded
175 g (6 oz) Gruyère cheese, grated
175 g (6 oz) fresh white breadcrumbs

1 Drain the spinach well, then finely chop.

2 In a large saucepan, cover the chicken with cold water. Add the carrot, onion and bay leaf together with the seasoning and bring to the boil. Cover and simmer for about 1 hour or until the chicken is thoroughly cooked. Test by inserting a skewer into the thigh; the juices should run clear if the chicken is cooked.

3 Lift the chicken on to a plate and leave to cool slightly. Divide the flesh into bite-sized pieces and set aside. Return the skin and bones to the saucepan of stock. Bubble down the stock until you are left with about 1 litre (1¾ pints). Strain, skim away the fat and reserve the stock.

4 Meanwhile, bring a large saucepan of salted water to the boil (use two if necessary). Add a dash of oil to each, followed by the lasagne. Cook according to packet instructions, stirring occasionally. (If using no-cook lasagne, but still boiling it

as we recommend for this recipe, it will probably take about 7 minutes.) When tender, drain in a colander and immediately run cold water over the pasta. This will stop it from cooking further and rinses off some of the starch. Spread the pasta out on clean tea towels and cover with a damp tea towel until required.

5 Leave the mushrooms whole or quarter and slice, depending on their size. Melt 50 g (2 oz) of the butter in a large saucepan. Add the mushrooms with the lemon juice and seasoning. Cover and cook over a fairly high heat for 3–4 minutes or until the mushrooms are tender. Remove from the pan with a slotted spoon, bubble the juices to evaporate any excess moisture until there is only butter left in the saucepan.

6 Melt the remaining butter in the same saucepan. Carefully stir in the flour and cook for 1 minute before slowly blending in the milk and the reserved chicken stock. Gradually bring to the boil, making sure that you keep stirring all the time, and cook for 1–2 minutes. Mix in the soft cheese with the tarragon, garlic and spinach. Adjust the seasoning to taste.

7 Spoon a little of the sauce into the base of a 4.5 litre (8 pint) ovenproof dish or two smaller dishes. Top with a layer of pasta followed by the chicken, mushrooms and ham. Spoon over more of the sauce, then continue layering the ingredients, finishing with the sauce, making sure that it completely covers the ingredients underneath. Sprinkle over the Gruyère cheese and fresh breadcrumbs.

8 Stand the dish on a baking tray, then cook at 200°C (400°F) mark 6 for 1–1¼ hours, depending on the size of dish. The lasagne should be piping hot and well browned.

VARIATION

MUSHROOM LASAGNE

Substitute an extra 450 g (1 lb) of mixed mushrooms for the chicken and Parma ham. Prepare the recipe as directed above, cooking the mushrooms in all the butter and using milk to replace the chicken stock (2 litres/3½ pints milk in all). Stir half the grated Gruyère cheese into the cool sauce and sprinkle the remainder liberally over the lasagne with the fresh breadcrumbs.

GOLDEN VEGETABLE BAKE

SERVES 10

1.8 kg (4 lb) aubergines, roughly chopped
90 ml (6 tbsp) vegetable oil
450 g (1 lb) onions, skinned and roughly chopped
225 g (8 oz) celery, trimmed and roughly chopped
2 bay leaves
120 ml (8 tbsp) chopped fresh basil
90 ml (6 tbsp) tomato purée
300 ml (½ pint) white wine
300 ml (½ pint) vegetable stock
225 g (8 oz) pitted black olives
900 g (2 lb) tomatoes, skinned, quartered and seeded
two 400 g (14 oz) cans artichoke hearts, drained and quartered
salt and freshly ground black pepper
125 g (4 oz) butter or margarine
125 g (4 oz) plain flour
1.1 litres (2 pints) milk
225 g (8 oz) feta cheese, crumbled
4 eggs, separated
30 ml (2 tbsp) chopped fresh parsley

1 Place the aubergines in a large saucepan and cover with cold water. Bring to the boil and simmer for 3–4 minutes. Drain well and pat dry.

2 Transfer the aubergines to a baking sheet. Drizzle over 30 ml (2 tbsp) oil. Brown under a hot grill, turning.

3 Heat the remaining oil in two large saucepans. Sauté the onion, celery and aubergines with the bay leaves for 2–3 minutes. Add 90 ml (6 tbsp) basil, the tomato purée, wine and stock. Bring to the boil, cover and simmer for 10–15 minutes or until the aubergines are tender. Off the heat, stir in the olives, tomatoes and artichokes. Discard the bay leaves. Season to taste. Transfer the mixture to two large ovenproof dishes.

4 Melt the butter in a large saucepan. Stir in the flour. Cook, stirring, for 1–2 minutes before adding the milk. Bring to the boil, stirring, then simmer for 2–3 minutes. Off the heat, beat in 175 g (6 oz) of the feta cheese, the remaining basil and the egg yolks. Season with pepper. Whisk the egg whites and fold in.

5 Spoon the feta sauce evenly over the vegetables. Sprinkle with the remaining cheese and the parsley. Bake at 180°C (350°F) mark 4 for about 45 minutes. Brown under a hot grill before serving.

SPICED COCONUT CREAM CHICKEN

SERVES 8

60 ml (4 tbsp) oil
1.4 kg (3 lb) chicken breast fillets, skinned
1 medium onion, skinned and finely chopped
4 garlic cloves, skinned and crushed
7.5 ml (1½ level tsp) salt
12.5 ml (2½ tsp) ground cumin
10 ml (2 tsp) ground coriander
2.5 ml (½ tsp) ground turmeric
5 ml (1 tsp) each ground paprika, garam masala or mild curry powder and poppy seeds
50 g (2 oz) creamed coconut, coarsely grated
1 green chilli, seeded and chopped
175 g (6 oz) tomatoes, skinned, seeded and chopped
90 ml (6 tbsp) double cream
fresh coriander, to garnish

1 Heat the oil in a large sauté pan and brown the chicken, a few pieces at a time, until golden brown. Remove with a slotted spoon and drain on absorbent kitchen paper.

2 Lower the heat, add the onion and garlic and cook, stirring occasionally, until beginning to brown. Stir in the salt, spices and poppy seeds with the coconut and chilli. Cook, stirring, for 1 minute.

3 Add the tomatoes and continue to cook for a further 3–4 minutes.

4 Return the chicken to the pan with 225 ml (8 fl oz) water. (The sauce is very thick at this stage, but don't be tempted to add more water. More juices are produced on cooking.) Bring to the boil, cover and simmer gently for 20–30 minutes or until the chicken is tender. Stir halfway through cooking time.

5 Stir in the cream and simmer for 1–2 minutes. Adjust the seasoning. Serve garnished with coriander.

SEAFOOD FILO BUNDLES

MAKES ABOUT 36

200 g (7 oz) filo pastry
125 g (4 oz) butter, melted
400 g (14 oz) salmon fillet, skinned
175 g (6 oz) fresh peeled prawns
78 g (2¼ oz) packet full fat soft cheese with garlic and herbs
freshly ground black pepper

1 Cut the filo pastry into 15 cm (6 inch) squares, reserving any trimmings. Stack the squares together in a pile and cover with a clean damp tea towel.

2 Take one square and lightly brush both sides with the butter. Put a small piece of pastry trimming into the centre of the square to reinforce the base of the pastry.

3 Cut the salmon into 1 cm (½ inch) cubes and arrange two or three cubes of fish in the middle of the pastry. Top with two or three prawns and dot with a small spoonful of cheese. Season with black pepper.

4 Gather the pastry into a bundle, pressing firmly together. Transfer to a greased baking tray.

5 Repeat the buttering, filling and shaping process until all the fish is used. Bake the bundles at 180°C (350°F) mark 4 for 15–20 minutes or until the pastry is crisp and golden. Serve warm or cold.

SWEETCORN AND CHIVE QUICHE

MAKES ABOUT 8–10 SLICES

75 g (3 oz) butter or margarine
175 g (6 oz) plain flour
340 g (12 oz) can sweetcorn niblets
150 ml (¼ pint) single cream or milk
1 egg
30 ml (2 tbsp) grated Parmesan cheese
salt and freshly ground pepper
few fresh chives
75 g (3 oz) Cheddar cheese

1 Rub the fat into the flour until the mixture resembles fine breadcrumbs. Bind to a dough with 30–45 ml (2–3 tbsp) water. Knead lightly then roll out thinly and use to line a 23 cm (9 inch) round loose-based fluted flan tin. Bake blind until golden brown and well dried out.

2 Meanwhile, place the drained sweetcorn, cream, egg, Parmesan cheese, seasoning and a few chives in a blender or food processor. Blend for a few seconds only until just beginning to break up the corn and chop the chives, but not to a fine purée.

3 Pour into the prepared flan case. Sprinkle over a thick layer of grated cheese to cover.

4 Bake at 180°C (350°F) mark 4 for 30–45 minutes or until just set and beginning to brown. Serve warm or cold.

CRAB AND GINGER SCONES

MAKES ABOUT 60
225 g (8 oz) self-raising flour
5 ml (1 level tsp) baking powder
salt
50 g (2 oz) butter or margarine
1 cm (½ inch) fresh root ginger, peeled and grated
milk
175 g (6 oz) fresh white crabmeat
10 ml (2 tsp) lemon juice
freshly ground black pepper
150 ml (5 fl oz) soured cream
sprigs of dill and prawns, to garnish

1 Rub together the flour, baking powder, a pinch of salt, butter and ginger. Add about 100–125 ml (4–5 fl oz) milk and stir quickly with a roundbladed knife until *just* combined into a soft dough.
2 Turn out the dough onto a lightly floured surface and press lightly with fingertips into a round 1 cm (½ inch) thick. With a 4 cm (1½ inch) plain round cutter, stamp out as many rounds as possible. Re-use the trimmings.
3 Place the scone rounds on a heated baking sheet and cook at 200°C (400°F) mark 6 for about 8–10 minutes or until well risen and golden. Cool on a wire rack.
4 Mix together the crabmeat and lemon juice. Season with black pepper. Split the scones in half. Place a little soured cream on each scone and top with crabmeat. Serve garnished with dill and prawns.

STRAWBERRY FLANS WITH PRALINE CREAM

MAKES 2 FLANS EACH SERVING 8–10
900 g (2 lb) fresh strawberries, hulled
choux pastry, made with 65 g (2½ oz) plain flour (see page 141)
SWEET PASTRY
275 g (10 oz) plain flour
pinch of salt
50 g (2 oz) caster sugar
175 g (6 oz) butter
4 egg yolks
PRALINE CREAM
125 g (4 oz) blanched almonds
125 g (4 oz) caster sugar
600 ml (1 pint) double cream
SPUN SUGAR
225 g (8 oz) granulated sugar
90 ml (6 tbsp) water
15 ml (1 tbsp) liquid glucose

1 For the sweet pastry, sift the flour and salt into a mixing bowl. Stir in the sugar, then rub in the butter until the mixture looks like fine breadcrumbs. Mix to a dough with the egg yolks. Wrap the pastry and chill for 30 minutes.
2 Divide the pastry into two equal pieces, and roll out each one on an upturned baking sheet to a 28 cm (11 inch) round. Prick the pastry rounds well with a fork. Chill.
3 Put the choux pastry into a piping bag fitted with a 1 cm (½ inch) plain nozzle. Pipe a single ring of choux pastry round the edge of each pastry base, piping it 5 mm (¼ inch) in from the edge. Bake at 200°C (400°F) mark 6 for 25–30 minutes or until the choux pastry is well risen and golden brown. Remove from the oven and pierce the choux pastry at intervals, to allow the steam to escape. Return to the oven for 2–3 minutes to dry. Carefully transfer the pastry cases from the baking sheets to wire racks to cool.
4 For the praline cream, put the almonds and sugar into a small, heavy-based saucepan and heat gently until the sugar dissolves and turns a rich caramel colour. Immediately pour on to an oiled baking sheet and allow to cool and set hard. Grind in an electric grinder, or crush finely with a rolling pin. Whisk the cream until it just holds soft peaks, then gently fold in the praline.

5 Place the pastry cases on two large flat serving plates and fill them with the praline cream. Cut the strawberries into halves or slices, and arrange them neatly on top of the cream.
6 For the spun sugar, lightly oil a rolling pin. Cover the work surface with newspaper, and also cover the floor immediately below. Cover the newspaper on the work surface with greaseproof paper.
7 Put the sugar, water and liquid glucose into a saucepan and heat gently until every granule of sugar dissolves, brushing down the sides of the pan with a little hot water. Boil the sugar syrup to a temperature of 160°C (320°F). Immediately plunge the base of the pan into cold water to prevent further cooking. Dip two forks held together, into the syrup then hold them up high until a fine thread starts to fall. Gently throw, or spin, the sugar threads around the rolling pin until a good quantity of threads accumulate. Remove from the rolling pin and set aside. Repeat until all the syrup has been used.
8 Pile the sugar nests on top of the strawberry flans and keep until required.

CHOCOLATE AND GRAND MARNIER MERINGUES

SERVES 8–10
150 g (5 oz) sultanas, roughly chopped
45 ml (3 tbsp) Grand Marnier or Cointreau
4 egg whites
225 g (8 oz) caster sugar
300 ml (½ pint) double cream
200 g (7 oz) plain chocolate
icing sugar, to decorate

1 Place the sultanas in a small bowl with the Grand Marnier or Cointreau. Stir well to mix, then cover and leave the sultanas to soak up the liqueur for at least 4 hours.
2 Meanwhile, line two baking sheets with non-stick baking parchment. Whisk the egg whites until stiff. Whisk in 25 g (1 oz) sugar, keeping the mixture stiff, then fold in the remaining sugar.
3 Using a 1 cm (½ inch) plain nozzle, pipe the mixture on to the prepared baking sheets, making about 32 meringues.
4 Bake at 100°C (200°F) mark Low, for about 2 hours or until the meringues are well dried out. Switch the baking trays around halfway through the cooking time. Cool on wire racks. When they are cold, store in an airtight container until required.
5 About 2 hours before serving, pour

45 ml (3 tbsp) cream into a small saucepan. Whip the remainder until it holds its shape, then fold in the soaked sultanas and any remaining Grand Marnier or Cointreau. Sandwich the meringues together with the cream mixture and pile into a glass serving dish. Grate over a little chocolate and dust with icing sugar. Cover and keep in the refrigerator until required.

6 Meanwhile, make the chocolate sauce. Break up the remaining chocolate and add to the cream in the saucepan. Pour in 150 ml (¼ pint) water and warm gently until the chocolate melts, stirring occasionally. Simmer gently for about 3 minutes, stirring frequently until the sauce thickens slightly. Pour into a jug to serve.

BAKED CHEESECAKE

BASE

50 g (2 oz) ginger-snap biscuits, finely crushed
50 g (2 oz) digestive biscuits, finely crushed
50 g (2 oz) butter or margarine, melted
pinch of cinnamon (optional)

FILLING

4 eggs, size 4, separated
125 g (4 oz) caster sugar
275 g (10 oz) curd cheese or full fat soft cheese
150 g (5 oz) low fat natural yogurt
finely grated rind and juice of 1 lemon
a few drops of vanilla flavouring
45 ml (3 level tbsp) plain flour
75 g (3 oz) sultanas (optional)

SAUCE

400 g (14 oz) can each pear and apricot halves in natural juice

TOPPING

300 ml (½ pint) soured cream
225 g (8 oz) mixed fresh fruit of your choice

1 Lightly grease a deep 20.5 cm (8 inch) loose-bottomed or spring-released tin and line the base with foil or non-stick baking parchment.

2 To prepare the base, mix the biscuit crumbs with the butter and cinnamon, if using. Press evenly into the bottom of the prepared tin using the back of a spoon. Chill in the refrigerator until firm.

3 Whisk the egg yolks with the sugar and cheese until light and creamy, then gradually whisk in the yogurt, the finely grated lemon rind and 45 ml (3 tbsp) strained lemon juice, the vanilla flavouring, flour and sultanas.

4 In a separate bowl, whisk the egg whites until stiff but not dry. Carefully fold a large spoonful of egg white into the cheese mixture to loosen it, then gently fold in the rest of the whites. Turn into the prepared baking tin and level the surface.

5 Bake at 170°C (325°F) mark 3 for about 1 hour 10 minutes–1 hour 20 minutes or until set. Remove from the oven and leave until completely cold. The cheesecake will have sunk a little – this is normal.

6 Loosen around the edges of the cheesecake with a thin-bladed knife and remove from the tin. Chill for several hours before serving.

7 Meanwhile make the sauce. Drain the tinned fruits, reserving the juices. Purée the fruits with sufficient juice to give a thin pouring consistency. Rub through a nylon sieve, then cover and chill.

8 To serve, top the cheesecake with swirls of soured cream and decorate with fresh fruit of your choice. Accompany with the fruit sauce.

FRESH PEAR MOUSSE

SERVES 8-10

25 ml (5 level tsp) powdered gelatine
300 ml (½ pint) milk
a vanilla pod
3 egg yolks
45 ml (3 tbsp) light muscovado sugar
900 g (2 lb) ripe dessert pears, peeled, cored and quartered
30 ml (2 tbsp) Poire Williams liqueur or Kirsch
300 ml (½ pint) double cream
Caramelised Clementines (see right)

1 Lightly oil a 1.4 litre (2½ pint) ring mould. Turn upside down and drain on absorbent kitchen paper. Sprinkle the gelatine over 75 ml (5 tbsp) water and leave to soak for 5 minutes.

2 Bring the milk and vanilla pod to the boil. Off the heat, add the soaked gelatine and stir until dissolved. Cover and leave to infuse for 5 minutes. Remove the vanilla pod.

3 Whisk together the egg yolks and sugar until pale and thick. Strain over the hot milk, stirring until well blended.

4 Purée the pears with the egg custard and liqueur until smooth. Chill until just starting to set.

5 Whip the cream until it just begins to hold its shape and fold gently into the pear mixture. Pour into the prepared mould and chill overnight.

6 To serve, dip the mould quickly into hot water and then invert on to a flat serving plate. Serve with Caramelised Clementines (see below).

CARAMELISED CLEMENTINES

SERVES 8-10

75 g (3 oz) granulated sugar
45 ml (3 tbsp) lemon juice
50 g (2 oz) shelled pistachio nuts
900 g (2 lb) clementines – or other easy peelers

1 In a large saucepan, dissolve the sugar over a low heat until it is a rich golden brown. Off the heat, add 600 ml (1 pint) water and the lemon juice. Bring to the boil, stirring. Simmer for 2–3 minutes, then cool.

2 Blanch the nuts in boiling water, then drain and remove the skins.

3 Peel the clementines and remove the pith. Stir the fruit into the cold caramel syrup with the nuts. Cover and chill overnight.

PEARS IN CIDER

SERVES 8-10

1.4 kg (3 lb) pears, peeled, cored and thickly sliced
225 g (8 oz) mixed black and white seedless grapes
125 g (4 oz) light muscovado sugar
600 ml (1 pint) medium-dry cider
pared rind of 2 lemons
1 cinnamon stick

1 Place the pears in a deep ovenproof dish with the grapes, sugar, cider, pared lemon rind, cinnamon and 600 ml (1 pint) water. Mix the ingredients well.

2 Cover tightly with foil. Bake at 150°C (300°F) mark 2 for about 1 hour or until the pears are tender and translucent. Serve warm or chilled.

TOASTED SEED AND NUT MIX

SERVES ABOUT 10

75 g (3 oz) pumpkin seeds
75 g (3 oz) sunflower seeds
75 g (3 oz) pine nuts
225 g (8 oz) salted peanuts
ground mild paprika

1 Place the seeds and nuts in a large roasting tin. Grill under a moderate heat until tinged with colour, stirring and turning occasionally.
2 While still warm, sprinkle the nuts and seeds liberally with the ground paprika, mixing well. Serve warm or cold.

SMOKED SALMON SAVOURIES

MAKES ABOUT 100

125 g (4 oz) butter, softened
225 g (8 oz) low fat soft cheese
125 g (4 oz) plain flour
50 g (2 oz) smoked salmon
5 ml (1 tsp) chopped fresh dill
freshly ground black pepper
1 egg, beaten

1 Place the butter, half of the soft cheese and the flour in a food processor and blend until the mixture forms a dough. Wrap and chill for about 30 minutes.
2 Snip the salmon into small pieces and mix with the remaining cheese, the dill and pepper.
3 Turn the dough on to a lightly floured surface and roll out thinly. Cut into 4 cm (1½ inch) wide strips. Cover half of the strips loosely with kitchen paper.
4 Place 1.25 ml (¼ tsp) of the salmon mixture at intervals down the strips. Brush around the edges and between the filling with beaten egg. Use the remaining pastry strips to cover the filling. Press in between the filling with the side of the hand to seal. Neaten the edges with a sharp knife, then cut at an angle to form diamonds. Brush with the remaining egg.
5 Place the diamonds on a baking sheet and bake at 200°C (400°F) mark 6 for 10 minutes or until crisp and golden. Cool on a wire rack. Serve warm.
Variations:
1 Omit the smoked salmon and use 350 g (12 oz) full fat soft cheese with herbs. Add more fresh herbs as wished.

2 Omit the salmon and use 125 g (4 oz) chopped cooked peeled prawns.
3 Use a creamy goat's cheese for the filling with 15 ml (1 level tbsp) finely chopped spring onions. Top with a few poppy seeds at the end of stage 4.

STILTON ALMOND CRISPS

MAKES ABOUT 60

125 g (4 oz) unsalted butter, softened
125 g (4 oz) rindless Stilton cheese, crumbled
50 g (2 oz) blanched almonds, roughly chopped
125 g (4 oz) plain flour
a few drops of Tabasco sauce
beaten egg and poppy seeds, to glaze

1 Beat together the butter and cheese until soft and creamy. Add the almonds, flour and Tabasco and beat until thoroughly combined.
2 With floured hands, shape the mixture into a 5 mm (¼ inch) diameter log. Wrap and chill for 1 hour.
3 Cut thin slices from the log with a sharp knife. Lay on greased baking sheets, brush lightly with beaten egg and sprinkle with poppy seeds.
4 Bake at 180°C (350°F) mark 4 for about 15 minutes or until crisp and golden. Cool on a wire rack. The crisps may be stored in an airtight container for up to 1 week.

SMALL CRAB CAKES

MAKES ABOUT 30

125 g (4 oz) self-raising flour
2.5 ml (½ level tsp) baking powder
pinch of salt
50 g (2 oz) butter or margarine
125 g (4 oz) white crab meat, flaked
1 egg
milk
5 ml (1 tsp) chopped fresh dill or large pinch of dried dill weed
white vegetable fat, melted
15 ml (1 tbsp) grated Parmesan cheese

1 Sift together the flour, baking powder and salt. Rub in the butter until the mixture resembles breadcrumbs. Stir in the crab meat.
2 Whisk the egg with 30 ml (2 tbsp) milk and the dill. Add to the flour mixture and stir to form a smooth, thick batter, adding a little more milk if necessary.

3 Brush a biscuit tin or mini mince pie tins with white vegetable fat and spoon in the batter mixture until almost full. Sprinkle lightly with Parmesan cheese.
4 Bake at 200°C (400°F) mark 6 for 10–12 minutes or until well risen and golden. Remove from the tins and allow to cool slightly. Serve warm. Store in the refrigerator for up to 2 days. Refresh in a warm oven before serving.

BABY PIZZAS

MAKES 36

283 g (10 oz) packet white bread and pizza base mix

TOPPINGS

half a 170 g (6 oz) jar Pizza topping
125 g (4 oz) black olives
15 ml (1 tbsp) capers
50 g (2 oz) salami, cut into slivers
8–10 thin asparagus spears, blanched and cut into 5 cm (2 inch) lengths
175 g (6 oz) mozzarella cheese, grated
olive oil

1 Make up the bread dough following the packet instructions. Divide into 36 pieces and roll each into a circle about 5 cm (2 inches) in diameter.
2 Spread some pizza topping on each round, then add toppings of your choice. Sprinkle with mozzarella and olive oil.
3 Leave in a warm place to rise for 15–20 minutes, then bake at 200°C (400°F) mark 6 for 10–15 minutes.

CHEESY BREAD TWISTS

MAKES ABOUT 40

125 g (4 oz) butter or margarine
150 ml (¼ pint) milk
2 eggs
350 g (12 oz) strong white flour
5 ml (1 tsp) fast-acting dried yeast
5 ml (1 tsp) salt
oil
125 g (4 oz) Gruyère cheese, finely grated
paprika
poppy seeds and/or sesame seeds

1 Melt the butter, allow to cool a little, then beat together with the milk and one of the eggs.

2 Place the flour, yeast and salt in a bowl. Make a well in the centre, add the milk mixture and beat steadily to form a dough. Turn out on to a lightly floured surface and knead for 4–5 minutes or until smooth.

3 Place the dough in a lightly oiled bowl, cover and leave to rise in a warm place for about 1 hour or until doubled in size.

4 Turn the dough on to a lightly floured surface, knead gently, then roll out into a rectangle about 5 mm (¼ inch) thick.

5 Beat the remaining egg and brush over half of the dough. Sprinkle with the cheese. Fold the dough over to cover the filling completely. Roll out again to a thickness of 5 mm (¼ inch).

6 Cut the dough into strips 1 cm (½ inch) wide and about 15 cm (6 inches) long. Twist each strip several times and place on greased baking sheets. Brush lightly with egg, then sprinkle with paprika and poppy or sesame seeds.

7 Bake at 220°C (425°F) mark 7 for 10 minutes or until golden. Serve warm or cold. The twists may be stored in an airtight container for up to 2 days; refresh in a warm oven before serving.

CRISP CARAWAY BISCUITS

MAKES ABOUT 40
350 g (12 oz) plain flour
7.5 ml (1½ tsp) salt
7.5. ml (1½ tsp) dry mustard powder
175 g (6 oz) butter or margarine
350 g (12 oz) mature Gouda or Cheddar cheese, finely grated
3 eggs, beaten
caraway seeds

1 Sift the flour, salt and mustard powder into a medium bowl. Rub in the butter until the mixture resembles breadcrumbs, then stir in the cheese.

2 Reserve a little beaten egg for glazing and stir the remainder into the flour mixture. Bring the mixture together to form a soft dough. Wrap the pastry and chill for about 15 minutes.

3 Roll the pastry out to a thickness of about 5 mm (¼ inch). Cut out squares, triangles, circles or ovals – about 4 cm (1½ inches) in size.

4 Place the biscuits on baking sheets, brush with the remaining egg, then sprinkle with caraway seeds. Knead the pastry trimmings and re-roll once only. Repeat the cutting and glazing process.

5 Bake the biscuits at 200°C (400°F) mark 6 for about 10 minutes or until crisp and golden. Transfer the biscuits to a wire rack to cool. Store in an airtight container for up to 1 week.

FILO SAUSAGE ROLLS

MAKES 36–45 DEPENDING ON SIZE
9 sheets of filo pastry (45.5 × 28 cm/18 × 11 inches in size)
butter or margarine, melted
450 g (1 lb) pork and herb sausages, skinned
wholegrain mustard
lightly beaten egg and poppy seeds, to finish

1 Brush three sheets of filo pastry with melted butter, stacking them as you go. Keep the remaining pastry covered with a clean, damp tea towel.

2 Place a sausage along the shorter side of the filo and spread the sausage meat out to make it fit the width of the pastry. Spread over a little mustard to taste.

3 Roll the pastry to enclose the sausage then continue rolling three or four more times to use up one third of the length of pastry. Cut the pastry to release the sausage. Brush the sausage roll with melted butter, cut into four or six pieces and place on a baking sheet.

4 Repeat with two more sausages until the first stack of pastry is used. Butter and stack three more sheets of filo and repeat steps 2 and 3. Repeat the process for the final three sheets of filo.

5 Brush the sausage rolls with lightly beaten egg and sprinkle with poppy seeds. Bake at 200°C (400°F) mark 6 for about 20 minutes or until crisp and golden. The sausage rolls may be stored, covered, in the refrigerator for 2 days.

GRUYÈRE AND PEANUT SABLÉS

MAKES ABOUT 72
454 g (1 lb) packet shortcrust pastry
1 egg, beaten
75 g (3 oz) Gruyère cheese, grated
cayenne pepper
75 g (3 oz) salted peanuts, roughly chopped

1 Divide the pastry in half and roll each piece out to a 23 cm (9 inch) square. Place on a baking sheet and brush each square with beaten egg.

2 Sprinkle the cheese over one of the squares. Press down firmly and sprinkle with cayenne pepper. Cut the pastry into six strips and separate slightly.

3 Sprinkle a little cayenne over the second piece of pastry. Scatter with the peanuts and press down firmly. Cut into strips and separate as above.

4 Bake at 200°C (400°F) mark 6 for about 20 minutes or until crisp and golden brown.

5 Cool slightly on the baking sheet, then cut into squares or triangles.

MARINATED CHICKEN KEBABS

MAKES ABOUT 65
900 g (2 lb) chicken-breast fillet, skinned
150 g (5 oz) natural yogurt
1.25 ml (¼ tsp) chilli powder
2.5 ml (½ tsp) ground turmeric
15 ml (1 tbsp) lemon juice
salt and freshly ground black pepper
1 small ripe melon, peeled and seeded

1 Cut the chicken into small, bite-sized pieces. Mix with the yogurt, chilli powder, turmeric, lemon juice and seasoning. Cover and leave to marinate in the refrigerator overnight.

2 Meanwhile, cut the melon into cubes.

3 Place the chicken and marinade in a non-stick roasting tin. Bake at 220°C (425°F) mark 7, turning occasionally, for about 40 minutes or until cooked through and brown.

4 Serve warm or cold, speared on to cocktail sticks with the melon.

ASPARAGUS ROLLS

MAKES ABOUT 50
25 slices of fresh brown bread, crusts removed
50 g (2 oz) butter or margarine, softened
salt and freshly ground black pepper
350 g (12.3 oz) can of asparagus tips, drained

1 Spread each slice of bread with butter and sprinkle with salt and pepper. Place an asparagus tip on each slice and roll up with the asparagus inside.

2 Wrap in foil and store until required, but preferably serve the day they are made. Halve to serve. *Note* The bread slices can be lightly rolled with a rolling pin before buttering; this gives a thinner roll and prevents the bread cracking.

SMOKED SALMON PINWHEELS

MAKES ABOUT 96

1 large brown sliced loaf, crusts removed
125 g (4 oz) butter or margarine, softened
350 g (12 oz) smoked salmon, thinly sliced
lemon juice
freshly ground black pepper

1 Spread each slice of bread with butter and cover with salmon. Sprinkle with lemon juice and season with pepper.
2 Roll up the slices, then wrap in foil and chill for up to 1 hour before slicing into pinwheels.

BOUCHÉES

MAKES 25

225 g (8 oz) puff pastry or one 368 g (13 oz) packet frozen puff pastry, thawed
beaten egg, to glaze
fillings (see below)

1 Roll out the pastry until it is about 0.5 cm (¼ inch) thick. Cut out twenty-five 5 cm (2 inch) rounds, using a plain cutter. Place the rounds on dampened baking sheets.
2 Using a 4 cm (1½ inch) plain cutter, cut partway through the centre of each round. Glaze the tops with beaten egg. Bake at 230°C (450°F) mark 8 for 10 minutes or until well risen and golden brown.
3 Remove the lids and soft pastry centres, and either use the cases hot with a hot filling or cool them on a wire rack and use cold with a cold filling.
Note: When making bouchées for a party, it is better to fill cold cases with a cold filling and reheat in the oven at 180°C (350°F) mark 4 for about 15 minutes.
FILLINGS
(Each enough to fill 25 bouchée cases).
Mushroom Melt a knob of butter in a small saucepan and fry 100 g (4 oz) chopped button mushrooms with 1 skinned and crushed clove of garlic. Put on one side, wipe the pan and melt a further 25 g (1 oz) butter. Stir in 45 ml (3 tbsp) flour and cook for 2 minutes. Remove from the heat and gradually add 150 ml (¼ pint) milk. Bring to the boil and cook for about 2 minutes, stirring continuously. Fold in the mushrooms and about 45 ml (3 tbsp) single cream. Season to taste with salt, pepper and a dash of Worcestershire sauce.

Prawn Fry 125 g (4 oz) peeled prawns to replace the mushrooms (see above) and add 15 ml (1 tbsp) chopped fresh parsley and a little lemon juice instead of the Worcestershire sauce.
Chicken Fry 1 small skinned and finely chopped onion with 10 ml (2 level tsp) mild curry powder to replace the mushrooms (see above). Replace the Worcestershire sauce with Tabasco, and add 125 g (4 oz) diced cooked chicken meat before reheating.

DRY MARTINI

SERVES 1

1 part French vermouth
2 parts dry gin, chilled
crushed ice (optional)
1 stuffed olive or lemon rind curl

1 Shake the vermouth and gin together with some crushed ice if using.
2 Pour into a glass and float a stuffed olive or a curl of lemon rind on top.
Note: The proportions of a martini are a matter of personal taste; some people prefer equal parts of gin and vermouth; others prefer just a splash of vermouth.
VARIATION
Sweet Martini Cocktail
Follow the recipe above, but use sweet vermouth and decorate with a cocktail cherry.

MULLED WINE

MAKES ABOUT 1.1 LITRES (2 PINTS)

300 ml (½ pint) water
125 g (4 oz) sugar
4 cloves
5 cm (2 inches) cinnamon stick
2 lemons, thinly sliced
1 bottle burgundy or claret
1 orange or lemon, thinly sliced, to decorate

1 Boil the water, sugar and spices together. Add the lemon slices, stir and leave to stand for 10 minutes.
2 Add the red wine, return to the heat and heat gently but do not boil. Strain the wine into a bowl and serve hot, decorated with orange or lemon slices.

BLACK RUSSIAN

SERVES 1

2–3 ice cubes
2 parts vodka
1 part coffee-flavoured liqueur

1 Put the ice cubes in a tumbler and pour over the vodka and coffee-flavoured liqueur.
VARIATION
For a White Russian, float a measure of cream on top.

TOM COLLINS

SERVES 1

2–3 ice cubes
juice of 1 lemon
15 ml (1 tbsp) sugar
1 measure whisky
1 orange slice
soda water

1 Mix the ice cubes, lemon juice, sugar and whisky until a frost forms. Pour into a glass and add a slice of orange.
2 Top with soda water and stir before serving.

MARGARITA

SERVES 1

lemon juice
salt
4 parts tequila
1 part curaçao
1 part lemon or lime juice

1 Dip the edges of a chilled glass into lemon juice and then salt.
2 Mix the tequila, curacao and lemon or lime juice. Strain into the chilled glass and serve.

BUCKS FIZZ

SERVES 1

1 part fresh orange juice, chilled
2 parts champagne, chilled

1 Fill a champagne glass about one-third full with orange juice and top up with champagne.

SPECIAL INDEX

This unique index lists recipes suitable for those with specific dietary requirements. When faced with the prospect of entertaining someone who is following a regime that you are unfamiliar with, or perhaps you or one of your family are watching your weight, this index is invaluable.

LOW CALORIE

Low calorie dishes are usually low in fat and sugar. To lose weight an average woman should reduce her calorific intake to about 1000 calories a day and an average man should reduce his intake to about 1500 calories a day.

NO NEED TO COOK

Delicious meals without cooking, perfect for times when you're in a mad rush, or when the weather is hot and you don't relish the idea of cooking over a hot stove.

COOK AHEAD

These are all recipes that can be made in advance and frozen, stored in the refrigerator or in an airtight container.

STORE-CUPBOARD

The recipes below all use basic ingredients from
the store-cupboard and refrigerator.

VEGETARIAN

A vegetarian will not eat meat of any kind but
may eat eggs and dairy produce. Some will eat
fish. Check with your guests.

VEGAN

A vegan will not eat any food of animal origin. This includes all meats and poultry as well as dairy produce, eggs, gelatine, fish and shellfish.

QUICK AND EASY

These are all simple recipes that can be cooked in about 35 minutes.

INDEX

ACKNOWLEDGEMENTS

The publishers would like to thank the following companies for lending props for the photographs:

The Conran Shop (china for the Chinese Dinner Party)

Kate Innes of The General Trading Company (furniture for the Mediterranean Dinner Party and the dresser for the American Brunch)

Neal Street East (screen, matting and vase for the Chinese Dinner Party)

The Shaker Shop (chairs, little table, brooms, apron and napkins for the Thanksgiving Dinner)

Linda Wrigglesworth (silk hanging for the Chinese Dinner Party)

Special thanks, also, to Helen Casey for all her help.